Nineteenth-Century

British Novelists on the Novel

GOLDENTREE BIBLIOGRAPHIES

In Language and Literature

under the series editorship of

O.B. Hardison, Jr.

Edited by

George L. Barnett
Indiana University

Nineteenth-Century
British Novelists on the Novel

APPLETON-CENTURY-CROFTS
EDUCATIONAL DIVISION
New York MEREDITH CORPORATION

ACKNOWLEDGMENTS

AUSTEN   from *The Works of Jane Austen*, ed. R. W. Chapman (London: Oxford University Press, 1923–1954), VI, 428–30. By permission of The Pierpont Morgan Library.

BRONTË   from *The Brontë Letters*, ed. Muriel Spark (London: Macmillan, 1954; also published under title, *The Letters of the Brontës: A Selection*. Norman: University of Oklahoma Press, 1954),

DICKENS   from *The Letters of Charles Dickens*, ed. Walter Dexter (London: Nonesuch, 1938), III, 461–62.

EDGEWORTH   from *The Life and Letters of Maria Edgeworth*, ed. A. J. C. Hare (Boston: Houghton Mifflin, 1894), II, 248–55.

FERRIER   from *Memoir and Correspondence of Susan Ferrier*, 1782–1854, ed. John A. Doyle (London: John Murray, 1898), IV, 75–76; 86–87.

KINGSLEY   from *Charles Kingsley: His Letters and Memories of his Life*, ed. by his wife (London: Macmillan, 1901), III, 40–41.

MEREDITH   from *The Works of George Meredith* (New York: Scribner's, 1909–1912), XXIX, 398–99. By permission of Charles Scribner's Sons and of Constable & Company Limited.

THACKERAY   from *Thackeray's Contributions to the Morning Chronicle*, ed. Gordon N. Ray (Urbana: University of Illinois Press, 1955), pp. 70–77.

To
Mary and Glen

PREFACE

The purpose of this collection is to make available in convenient form authorial commentary on the British novel. A valuable supplement to reading the novels themselves as well as professional criticism, these selections provide a base for fuller understanding of problems concerning the growth and development of the novel as a literary form. The edition may recommend itself also to students of literary criticism and of advanced creative writing.

Three features distinguish this book from others having a superficial resemblance. First, the selections pertain only to the novel—using the word in its broadest sense—not to literature in general nor to other genres in particular. Second, the collection is limited to the British novel; Continental and American novelists and novels remain outside its scope. Third, the selections were written by novelists—even if their claim to the title depends on only one book. Commentary by critics who were not also novelists is thus excluded.

Novelists themselves are valid critics who develop ideas and attitudes about fiction and sometimes formulate, and frequently publish, theories—even though they have not always been successful in regulating their practice thereby. "No creative writer lacks—can afford to lack—the critical faculty," wrote Elizabeth Bowen.[1] The fallacy of relying exclusively, or too heavily, on critics who were not also practitioners was pointed up by Somerset Maugham: ". . . the critic who is not himself a creator is likely to know little about the technique of the novel, and so in his criticism he gives you either his personal impressions, which may well be of no great value . . . or else he proffers a judgment founded on hard and fast rules which must be followed to gain his approbation."[2] Earlier, H. G. Wells had also warned of the dangers attendant on professional criticism:

. . . and if the novel is to be recognized as something more than a relaxation, it has also, I think, to be kept free from the restrictions imposed upon it by the fierce pedantries of those who would define a general form for it. Every art nowadays

[1] "Forward," *Collected Impressions* (London, New York, and Toronto, 1950), p. v.
[2] "The Art of Fiction," *Ten Novels and their Authors* (Melbourne, London, and Toronto, 1954), pp. 18–19.

must steer its way between the rocks of trivial and degrading standards and the whirlpool of arbitrary and irrational criticism. Whenever criticism of any art becomes specialized and professional, whenever a class of adjucators is brought into existence . . . they begin to emulate the classifications and exact measurements of a science, and to set up ideals and rules as data for such classifications and measurements. . . . The novel has been treated as though its form was as well-defined as the sonnet.[3]

The guidelines distinguishing this collection make it possible to present passages of substantial length, usually complete prefaces or essays—thereby avoiding the fragmentary quality characteristic of some compilations wherein brief statements must be read out of context. No minimum length has been prescribed, however, and some short selections are included when they are believed to be significant. Omissions of nonrelevant portions are always indicated; this feature, as well as complete references to originals, enables this work to be used in a reliable manner by scholars quoting from it or desiring to go to the originals.

The order of the selections is basically chronological; however, where an author is represented by two or more passages of different date or where particular relevance to a preceding passage exists, this order may be transcended. Since college courses in the British novel ordinarily follow a chronological pattern, this arrangement should prove more useful than some conceptualized framework under such rubrics as "plot," "character," "story." With this book a student may observe the historical development of novelistic theories by British novelists as well as compare those of an individual author with his own performances.

The fact that several of the selections will be familiar to advanced students and are available in other places was not thought to constitute sufficient grounds for excluding them. They will not be familiar to the average undergraduate in a novel course, and the convenience of bringing them together is important for all students.

Many of the authors represented have been consigned by the judgment of time to a mediocre, or even low, order of excellence as novelists. Their inclusion is warranted in some cases by a contemporary popularity that gave force to their opinions; their comments point up the continuity of the issues under discussion and serve to amplify and sometimes substantiate ideas expressed by better known authors. In many cases, these selections have never before been reprinted from their original appearance in books now rare and difficult of access.

Novelists have expressed their theories on the novel in various forms. Prefaces and essays are frequent in this collection. Reviews written by novelists occasionally go beyond the consideration of a particular book to express or imply opinion on general principles; so also do some essays on individual authors and occasional chapters of self-appraisal. Novelists have

[3] "The Contemporary Novel," *An Englishman Looks at the World* (London, 1914), pp. 150–151.

frequently supplemented their more considered, published comments with epistolary statements; in some cases their correspondence contains their only recorded judgment. Journals and autobiographies have sometimes served the novelist-turned-critic. Less noticed by casual readers, but still valid indexes of opinion, are paragraphs, colloquies, and entire chapters in the novels themselves. The steadily increasing volume of authorial commentary throughout the history of the novel is, as might be expected, confirmed by this edition. The variety and nature of the aspects discussed, the persistence of some, changes in an author's attitude, and disagreements among novelists —these subjects are less obvious to a novel reader until he becomes acquainted with authorial opinion.

The headnotes do not pretend to completeness either in biographical or bibliographical data. Titles of the better known, more important, or more popular works may guide a potential reader. Indications of a novelist's particular forte or category and of his contemporary and present-day reputation may aid in evaluating the importance of his comments. References to additional commentary and citation of primary sources may be of interest to the more serious scholar. Dates of publication of the texts will enable a reader to place them in their author's career as well as their author in the history of the novel.

G.L.B.

CONTENTS

INTRODUCTION

Throughout the nineteenth century the volume of authorial commentary on fiction steadily mounted as both the number of author-critics and the frequency and length of their expressions increased. Articles and reviews written for the growing number of periodicals provided new media that supplemented the traditional prefaces. Many of these discussions were unsigned and their authors not identified until recently; many appeared in publications now rare. In consequence, some have not been reprinted, and most have not been sufficiently regarded in surveys of the century's criticism. Hence, with the exception of the period from 1880 to 1900, nineteenth-century authorial commentary has been seriously discounted and undervalued.[1] Yet, Thackeray, Eliot, Bulwer-Lytton, Collins, Trollope, and Meredith—all notable novelists—wrote thoughtful criticism in numerous prefaces, articles, and reviews.

As in the preceding century, no relationship exists between the volume of an author's creative work and that of his theorizing. Many of the most prolific novelists, like Catherine Gore, seem more concerned with promulgating doctrine or, like Mrs. Trollope, with making money than with contributing to a theory of fiction. Others, as prolific or more so, such as Bulwer-Lytton, filled innumerable prefaces with theory. Nor is success invariably associated with expression of theory: Scott was a voluminous critic, but Dickens produced very little commentary.

The trend, begun in the eighteenth century, away from a mere defense of the novel to a discussion of its aspects continued. Yet the century was never without an undercurrent of hostility: Jane Austen castigated the novel's detractors and lavished praise on the genre; years later, Bulwer-Lytton

---

[1] Writing of the "critical innocence" of "the mid-nineteenth century," Bradford Booth states that "we learn little or nothing about the problems of the craft from those who knew them best—the novelists themselves. The major writers produced not even a minor paper of critical importance" ("Trollope on the Novel," *Essays Critical and Historical*, Berkeley and Los Angeles, 1950, p. 219). Robert Davis is equally dogmatic in his generalization: "Between the first two and last two decades of the nineteenth century, there was amazingly little extended or serious discussion of the novel as a literary form, either by English critics or by the English novelists themselves" ("Forum on Realism," *Comparative Literature*, 1951, III, 214).

deplored the popular denigration of the novel. Not until about 1880 was the novel accorded a position of respect, and novelists a measure of status in society. Even after that, protests by Dinah Mulock and James Payn that writing novels was hard work seem designed as a defense against the detractors. As late as the sixties and seventies it was frequently alleged that amusement was the novel's only function. In reply, writers such as Trollope emphasized fiction's moral function; Kingsley termed the novel the highest organ of moral teaching next to the drama. Other authors based their defense on the value of fiction in inculcating ideas and aesthetic principles. Earlier, Lady Morgan and Mrs. Gore considered fiction the best form of history.

During the 1860's competition among the periodicals for serialized fiction resulted in higher financial rewards as well as a higher rate of productivity and a trend away from publication of novels in separate monthly parts. Scott, Maturin, Marryat, Mrs. Trollope, Thackeray, and others throughout the century expressed personal interest in fiction as a money-making profession, and although Besant warned against confusing financial success with literary excellence, the new prosperity helped to raise the novelist, and the novel, in popular esteem. At the same time, as the novel attained intellectual maturity about 1860, professed devotion to fiction in terms of *ars gratia artis* became more vocal.

The prodigious creative productivity from 1860 to 1890 was attended by a demand for theory and an attempt to codify the laws of fiction. Authors turned from their successful defense of the novel to a discussion of its techniques—although the form resisted restrictions that might hinder further growth, and exact prescriptions were rejected. A new awareness of the novel as art culminated in the 1880's with an epidemic of essays by novelists, motivated, in part, by the superficial criticism of the professional critics. Besant urged a recognition of the novel as one of the fine arts; stimulated by his observations, James produced his pivotal demand for realism; in reply, Robert Louis Stevenson argued the claims for romance. Moore delivered the death blow to the three-volume format that had imposed its requirements on authors since the days of Scott; less successfully, he rebelled against a prudish, restrictive censorship. Hardy argued for candor and examined the values of fiction.

From the beginning of the century, discussion continued on subjects inherited from the preceding period. One such subject was the comparison of the novel with the drama; it interested Robert Ward, Bulwer-Lytton, and Collins. Concern with categorizing novels into genres continued: at the beginning of the century, Scott's theory distinguished between the novel and the romance; the distinction was still being argued in the 1870's, and when the virtues of romance were urged by Stevenson and Haggard in the 1880's, the term *romance* was employed with a new emphasis. At the end of the century, James regarded such distinctions as ridiculous, while J. M. Barrie poked fun at the preoccupation with theorizing as well as classification.

Also carried over from the eighteenth century was the subject of the relationship of author to novel. Scott early anticipated James's later objection to authorial intrusion; yet Thackeray, Eliot, and Trollope— among a host of lesser writers—practiced and advocated it to the degree that it became a Victorian convention. However, condemnation of the practice by Reade—whose own work was inconsistent with his theory—and by Meredith—who bestowed unmerited praise on Trollope for absenting his authorial self—indicates the controversial nature of the matter. At the end of the century the practice of authorial intrusion was dated; yet it was discussed by Moore, objected to by Payn, and advocated by Wells in an 1896 review of Gissing. By that time the topic had assumed a subtlety that is apparent in the complaint that James lacked emotional involvement.

In a century of causes, it is not surprising that Harriet Martineau turned to fiction to illustrate political economy, that Mrs. Ward employed a religious theme, or that Disraeli, Dickens, Kingsley, Besant, and Gissing promoted political and social reform in their novels. "It was not originally the intention of the writer," Disraeli states in his Preface to *Conningsby* (1849), "to adopt the form of fiction as the instrument to scatter his suggestions, but, after reflection, he resolved to avail himself of a method which, in the temper of the times, offered the best chance of influencing opinion." Defendants of didacticism in fiction, such as Bulwer-Lytton—who regarded instruction as a legitimate function of the novelist, considered it as further justification of the novel and as evidence of its stature. Conceding that a novelist must teach, Trollope opposed employing fiction for purposes of philosophy or reform. Most opposition to the practice is based on an objection to methods or to the unnatural result.

The moral, like the philosophical, function of fiction was a perennial subject for discussion. Originally one of the attributes urged in defense of the novel, it became, in course of time, an essential if reviewers were to give their approbation. In this atmosphere the social code continued to shackle novelists right up to the end of the century in spite of pleas for an end to the prudery that Thackeray lamented as early as 1850. In 1887, Haggard deplored social restraints on novelists and felt that critical concern with moral qualities obscured a book's literary qualities. In supporting the moral function of fiction, Besant recognized (1890), but accepted, the self-assumed power of censorship exerted by the circulating libraries. Seeking emancipation for the novel, Moore attacked (1885) those institutions and was seconded by Hardy, who added to his protest (1890) the censorship exerted by periodicals. Characteristically aphoristic, Wilde opined (1890): "There is no such thing as a moral or an immoral book. Books are well written, or badly written. That is all."

The relative importance of character and plot—assumed to be separate entities until about 1880, when such analysis began to be unfashionable— served for lengthy and voluminous controversy, just as it had for the drama.

Some distinction is made between "story," which Lever regarded as unimportant, and "plot," to which Trollope, who felt that a novelist must have a story to tell, professed indifference. Story is important in the theory of Collins, Bulwer-Lytton, Stevenson, Moore, and Payn; Collins had a high regard for plot.

Associated with the discussion of plot and character is the larger one on realism, becoming prominent after 1860. Plot, unnatural and therefore inferior to character, was criticized as detracting from the naturalness or life-like quality of character—and truth to nature was an inviolate principle. The eighteenth-century passion for authenticity is reflected in the defense of dialect by Maria Edgeworth, Bulwer-Lytton, and Hardy. George Eliot expressed her objection to the unreal in her famous plea for simple veracity. Truth to life was advocated by Trollope and Gissing; for James, realism was the principal goal of the novelist. The propriety of modeling characters on real-life prototypes in an effort to attain reality in character is debated. Trollope argued that character traits must be known from observation but that the characters must be created. Caine later advocated altering details so that the prototypes would be unrecognizable. Verisimilitude in events and settings also had its day. Reade wrote novels based on facts; Collins insisted on extreme accuracy of detail; Besant ruled that "everything in Fiction which is invented and is not the result of personal experience and observation is worthless" (1884). Payn disagreed. Stevenson summarized such debates with a masterly distinction between fiction and life.

With the passing in the 1880's of the passion for the analytic approach, realism underwent modifications—in part, at least, because of the revival of romance and the reactions of its proponents to the extremes of realism. Total realism became less vital than a pleasant, or consolatory, effect; thus, ugly and disagreeable aspects of life should, so thought Payn and Dinah Mulock, give way to agreeable characters and happy endings. Contrasted to this "habit of mind," was Gissing's interpretation of realism as "nothing more than artistic sincerity in the portrayal of contemporary life" (1895). Naturalism was condemned by Haggard (1887), who pointed out that bad effects are not obviated by avowals of moral purpose.

Although contrary to the trend of fiction in the century, romance always appealed to those readers seeking escape or rejecting psychological realism. The romantic revival of the last part of the period forms a curious parallel with the emergence of the Gothic romance at the end of the preceding century. Stevenson, Haggard, and Caine carried the banner. Attacks on realism, a logical and frequent concomitant of promoting romance, complained, in addition to its extravagances, of the absence of imagination. Early in the century Scott had regarded this quality as absolutely indispensable; for Gissing it breathed life into otherwise "dead material"; at the end, Wilde writes: "The moment art surrenders its imaginative medium it surrenders everything. As a method Realism is a complete failure . . ." (1889).

Not all the commentary referred to here could be included in the following pages, but the selections provide the significant, as well as representative, criticism. In addition, pointing up the range of the topics, some discussions treat questions of lesser import. Of these, the indication of time-lapses posed for Reade and Payn a problem that the latter considered more difficult in fiction than in drama. Beginnings and endings bothered Reade, Eliot, and Lever. Stevenson and Moore evidence their time's increasing concern with style. The proponents of form evoked the opposing view that life's natural disorder should be reflected. James and Wells carried this last debate into the twentieth century, which, like the nineteenth, perpetuated, initiated—and sometimes resolved—the problems of fiction.

The texts in this volume are based on the best editions. In addition to silent corrections of obvious errors, obsolete practices in capitalization, punctuation, paragraphing, and use of italics have generally been modified in the direction of modern usage to facilitate reading. Original spellings and historically characteristic verb forms have been retained—even to the preservation of inconsistencies within a single selection—except where difficulty in comprehension would have resulted; in such cases the text is updated in conformity with modern British usage. Practical considerations were thought more important for readers of this book than a consistent retention of archaisms.

G.L.B.

1

MARIA EDGEWORTH

(1767–1849)

Maria Edgeworth has been honored—perhaps too narrowly—as a regional novelist, successfully depicting the life and character of the Irish peasantry. During the famine of 1846 a group of her admirers in Boston, Massachusetts, shipped 150 barrels of flour to "Miss Edgeworth for her poor."

The Great Maria, as one biographer titles her book, was born in Oxfordshire but lived in Edgeworthstown, Ireland, from the age of fifteen. On the proceeds of her writing, totaling by her accounts some £11,000, she took several tours and frequently visited London. Diminutive in stature, she suffered in her youth from vain attempts to increase her height by hanging by the neck. In later years, she is characterized as a sensible, amiable woman, possessing a vivacious intellect. She was admired and received at Abbotsford by Scott, to whom she referred in the highest terms.

One might generalize that Scott's *Waverley* (1814), the first historical novel, was inspired by Miss Edgeworth's *Castle Rackrent* (1800), the first regional novel in English. In a postscript to his novel Scott expressed his purpose "in some degree to emulate the admirable Irish portraits drawn by Miss Edgeworth." *Castle Rackrent*, to which the author's name was not put until the second edition, was her first real achievement, her most original, and an immediate success. Cast in the form of an autobiography "edited" by Miss Edgeworth, the novel establishes the narrator as a keen observer of Irish life and character; in its presentation of the latter it pioneers in its extensive use of dialect. In her preface she defends Thady's idiom as confirming the authenticity of her narrative; further, she recalls Fielding's identification of the function of the novelist with that of the biographer (*Joseph Andrews*, Book III, Chapter 1) in asserting his superiority over the historian.

The success of *Castle Rackrent* may be attributed in part to the fact that it was written without the knowledge—and the collaborating interference—of her father. The didactic morality that usually impairs her work is attributable to his influence. Maria was close to her father and constantly subjected to his theory of mutual activity. She kept his accounts and dealt with his tenants. She accepted a succession of three stepmothers and seventeen children, writing her novels in the common sitting room in spite of domestic disturbance, and placidly permitting her father to read everything and frequently to insert passages of his own. He wrote the prefaces—after *Castle Rackrent*—explaining the moral design; there was nothing for her to add. Chapter XII (entitled "Books") of *Practical Education*, a collaborative effort in three volumes published in 1798, the same year her father took his fourth wife, says nothing of fiction except that it must be moral. This passion of Richard Lovell Edgeworth for the moral utility of fiction influenced Miss Edgeworth's early and popular *Moral Tales* for children and her later fiction: *Belinda* (1801), *Leonora* (1806), *Tales of Fashionable Life* (1809 and 1812), *Patronage* (1814), and *Ormond* (1817).

After her father's death in 1817, Miss Edgeworth edited his *Memoirs* (1820), wrote a readable novel: *Helen* (1834), and discussed the problems of fiction in correspondence with friends and critics. One such letter is that of 6 September 1834, addressed to Mrs. Stark, who had sent her a critique of *Helen* by her cousin, Colonel Matthew Stewart.

PREFACE

CASTLE RACKRENT
(1800)

The prevailing taste of the public for anecdote has been censured and ridiculed by critics, who aspire to the character of superior wisdom; but if we consider it in a proper point of view, this taste is an incontestable proof of the good sense and profoundly philosophic temper of the present times. Of the numbers who study, or at least who read history, how few derive any advantage from their labours! The heroes of history are so decked out by the fine fancy of the professed historian, they talk in such measured prose, and act from such sublime or such diabolical motives, that few have sufficient taste, wickedness, or heroism to sympathize in their fate. Besides, there is much uncertainty even in the best authenticated ancient or modern histories; and that love of truth, which in some minds is innate and immutable, necessarily leads to a love of secret memoirs and private anecdotes. We cannot judge either of the feelings or of the characters of men with perfect accuracy from their actions or their appearance in public; it is from their careless conversations, their half-finished sentences, that we may hope with the greatest probability of success to discover their real characters. The life of a great or of a little man written by himself, the familiar letters, the diary of any individual published by his friends or by his enemies after his decease are esteemed important literary curiosities. We are surely justified in this eager desire to collect the most minute facts relative to the domestic lives, not only of the great and good but even of the worthless and insignificant, since it is only by a comparison of their actual happiness or misery in the privacy of domestic life that we can form a just estimate of the real reward of virtue or the real punishment of vice. That the great are not as happy as they seem, that the external circumstances of fortune and rank do not constitute felicity, is asserted by every moralist; the historian can seldom, consistently with his dignity, pause to illustrate this truth; it is therefore to the biographer we must have recourse. After we have beheld splendid characters playing their parts on the great theatre of the world, with all the advantages of stage effect and decoration, we anxiously beg to

3

be admitted behind the scenes that we may take a nearer view of the actors and actresses.

Some may perhaps imagine that the value of biography depends upon the judgment and taste of the biographer; but on the contrary it may be maintained that the merits of a biographer are inversely as the extent of his intellectual powers and of his literary talents. A plain unvarnished tale is preferable to the most highly ornamented narrative. Where we see that a man has the power, we may naturally suspect that he has the will to deceive us, and those who are used to literary manufacture know how much is often sacrificed to the rounding of a period or the pointing of an antithesis.

That the ignorant may have their prejudices as well as the learned cannot be disputed, but we see and despise vulgar errors; we never bow to the authority of him who has no great name to sanction his absurdities. The partiality which blinds a biographer to the defects of his hero, in proportion as it is gross, ceases to be dangerous; but if it be concealed by the appearance of candour, which men of great abilities best know how to assume, it endangers our judgment sometimes, and sometimes our morals. If her Grace the Duchess of Newcastle, instead of penning her lord's elaborate eulogium, had undertaken to write the life of Savage, we should not have been in any danger of mistaking an idle, ungrateful libertine for a man of genius and virtue. The talents of a biographer are often fatal to his reader. For these reasons the public often judiciously countenance those who, without sagacity to discriminate character, without elegance of style to relieve the tediousness of narrative, without enlargement of mind to draw any conclusions from the facts they relate, simply pour forth anecdotes, and retail conversations, with all the minute prolixity of a gossip in a country town.

The author of the following memoirs has upon these grounds fair claims to the public favour and attention; he was an illiterate old steward, whose partiality to *the family* in which he was bred and born must be obvious to the reader. He tells the history of the Rackrent family in his vernacular idiom, and in the full confidence that Sir Patrick, Sir Murtagh, Sir Kit, and Sir Condy Rackrent's affairs will be as interesting to all the world as they were to himself. Those who were acquainted with the manners of a certain class of the gentry of Ireland some years ago will want no evidence of the truth of honest Thady's narrative; to those who are totally unacquainted with Ireland, the following memoirs will perhaps be scarcely intelligible, or probably they may appear perfectly incredible. For the information of the *ignorant* English reader, a few notes have been subjoined by the editor, and he had it once in contemplation to translate the language of Thady into plain English; but Thady's idiom is incapable of translation, and, besides, the authenticity of his story would have been more exposed to doubt if it were not told in his own characteristic manner. Several years ago he related to the editor the history of the Rackrent family, and it was with some difficulty that he was persuaded to have it committed to writing; however, his feelings for "*the honour of the family*," as he expressed himself, prevailed over his habitual laziness, and he at length completed the narrative which is now laid before the public.

The editor hopes his readers will observe that these are "tales of other times"; that the manners depicted in the following pages are not those of the present age: the race of the Rackrents has long since been extinct in Ireland; and the drunken Sir Patrick, the litigious Sir Murtagh, the fighting Sir Kit, and the slovenly Sir Condy are characters which could no more be met with at present in Ireland than Squire Western or Parson Trulliber in England. There is a time when individuals can bear to be rallied for their past follies and absurdities, after they have acquired new habits and a new consciousness. Nations, as well as individuals, gradually lose attachment to their identity, and the present generation is amused, rather than offended, by the ridicule that is thrown upon its ancestors.

Probably we shall soon have it in our power, in a hundred instances, to verify the truth of these observations.

When Ireland loses her identity by an union with Great Britain, she will look back, with a smile of good-humoured complacency, on the Sir Kits and Sir Condys of her former existence.

LETTER TO MRS. STARK
(6 September 1834)

EDGEWORTHSTOWN, *Sept.* 6, 1834.

Some of my friends, knowing the timidity, not to say cowardice, of my nature, have feared that I should be *daunted* by Colonel Stewart's most just observations upon the defects and deficiencies of my past manner and principles of novel-writing; but, on the contrary, I, who know myself better, feel that, *in spite* of my timidity, I am, instead of being daunted, encouraged by such criticism. Such a writer and such a noble mind as Colonel Stewart's having bestowed so much thought and time upon me and my fictions, raises both them and myself in my own opinion far more than could the largest "draught of unqualified praise" from any common critic. From feeling that he does justice in many points to the past, I rely upon his prophecies as to the future, and I feel my ambition strongly excited by his belief that I CAN, and his prognostic that I shall do better hereafter. Boileau says, "Trust a critic who puts his finger at once upon what you know to be your infirm part." I had often thought and said to myself some of those things which Colonel Stewart has written, but never so strongly expressed, so fully brought home: my own rod of feathers did not do my business. I had often and often a suspicion that my manner was too Dutch, too minute; and very, very often, and warmly, admired the bold, grand style of the master hand and master genius. I *know* I feel how much *more is to be done, ought to be* done, by suggestion than by delineation, by creative fancy than by facsimile copying,—how much more by skilful selection and fresh and consistent combination—than can be effected by the most acute observation of individuals, or diligent accumulation of particulars.

But where I have erred or fallen short of what it is thought I might have done, it has not been from "drawing from the life, or from individuals, or from putting together actions or sayings noted in commonplace books from observation or hearsay in society." I have seldom or ever drawn any one character—certainly not any ridiculous or faulty character, from any individual. Wherever, in writing, a real character rose to my view, from memory or resemblance, it has always been hurtful to me, because, to avoid that resemblance, I was tempted by cowardice or compelled by conscience to throw in differences, which often ended in making my character inconsistent, unreal.

At the hazard of talking too much of myself, which people usually do when once they begin, I must tell my penetrating critic exactly the facts, as far as I know them, about my *habits of composition*. He will at least see, by my throwing open my mind thus, that he has not made me afraid of him, but has won my confidence, and made me look for his future sympathy and assistance. I have no "vast magazine of a commonplace book." In my whole life, since I began to write, which is now, I am concerned to state, upwards of forty years, I have had only about half a dozen little note-books, strangely and irregularly kept, sometimes with only words of reference to some book, or fact I could not bring accurately to mind. At first I was much urged by my father to note down remarkable traits of character or incidents, which he thought might be introduced in stories; and he often blamed that idleness or laziness, as he thought it in me, which resisted his urgency. But I was averse to noting down, because I was conscious that it did better for me to keep the things in my head, if they suited my purpose; and if they did not, they would only encumber me. I knew that, when I wrote down, I put the thing out of my care, out of my head; and that, though it might be put by very safe, I should not know where to look for it; that the labour of looking over a note-book would never do when I was in the warmth and pleasure of inventing; that I should never recollect the facts or ideas at the right time, if I did not put them up in my own way in my own head: that is, if I felt with hope or pleasure "that thought or that fact will be useful to me in such a character or story, of which I have now a first idea, the same fact or thought would recur, I knew, when I wanted it, in right order for invention." In short, as Colonel Stewart guessed, the process of combination, generalisation, invention, was carried on always in my head best. Wherever I brought in *bodily* unaltered, as I have sometimes done, facts from real life, or sayings, or recorded observations of my own, I have almost always found them objected to by good critics as unsuited to the character, or in some way *de trop*. Sometimes, when the first idea of a character was taken from life from some ORIGINAL, and the characteristic facts noted down, or even noted only in my head, I have found it necessary entirely to alter these, not only from propriety, to avoid individual resemblance, but from the sense that the character would be only an EXCEPTION to general feeling and experience, not a rule. In short, exactly what Colonel Stewart says about "the conical hills" being the worst subjects for painters. As an instance I may mention King Corny, who is, I believe, considered more of a fancy piece, more as a *romantic* character than my usual common-life Dutch figures: the *first idea* of him was taken from the facts I heard of an oddity, a man, I believe, like no other, who lived in a remote part of Ireland, an ingenious despot in his own family, who blasted out of the rock on which his house was built half a kitchen, while he and family and guests were living in the house; who was so passionate, that children, grown-up sons, servants and all, ran out of the house at once when he fell into a passion with his own tangled hair; a man who used, in his impatience and rages, to call at the head of the kitchen stairs to his servants, "Drop whatever you have in your hand, and come here and be d——d!" He was generous and kind-hearted, but despotic, and conceited to the most ludicrous degree: for instance, he thought he could work gobelin tapestry and play on the harp or mandolin better than any one living.

One after another, in working out King Corny, from the first wrong hint I was obliged to give up every fact, except that he propped up the roof of his house and built downwards, and to generalise all; to make him a man of expedients, of ingenious substitutes, such as any clever Irishman in middle life is used to. I was obliged to retain, but soften, the despotism, and exalt the generosity, to make it a character that would interest. Not one word I ever heard said by the living man, or had ever heard repeated of his saying, except "Drop what you have," etc., went into my King Corny's mouth—would not have suited him. I was obliged to make him according to the general standard of wit and acuteness, shrewd humour and sarcasm, of that class of *unread* natural geniuses, an overmatch for Sir Ulick, who is of a more cultivated class of acute and roguish Irish gentlemen. Colonel Stewart sees from this how far he has guessed rightly as to several points, but I think I have always aimed more at making my characters representatives of classes than he conceives. It is plain that I have not attained my aim.

I never could use notes in writing Dialogues; it would have been as impossible to me to get in the prepared good things at the right moment in the warmth of writing conversation, as it would be to lug them in in real conversation, perhaps more so—for I could not write dialogues at all without being at the time fully impressed with the characters, imagining myself each speaker, and that too fully engrosses the imagination to leave time for consulting note-books; the whole fairy vision would melt away, and the warmth and the pleasure of invention be gone. I might often, while writing, recollect from books or life what would suit, and often from note-book, but then I could not stop to look, and often quoted therefore inaccurately. I have a quick recollective memory and retentive for the sort of things I particularly want; they will recur to me at the moment I want them years and years after they have lain dormant, but alas! my memory is inaccurate, has hold of the object only by one side—the side or face that struck my imagination, and if I want more afterwards I do not know even where to look for it. I mention this because Dugald Stewart[1] once was curious to know what sort of memory I had, whether recollective or retentive.

I understand what Colonel Stewart so admirably says about parable, apologue, and fables being general truths and morals which cannot be conveyed or depended upon equally when we come to modern novels, where Lady B. or Lord D. are not universal characters like Fox or Goose. I acknowledge that even a perfectly true character absolutely taken as a fac-simile from real life would not be interesting in a fiction, might not be believed, and could not be useful. The value of these odd characters depends, I acknowledge, upon their being actually known to be true. In history, extraordinary characters always interest us with all their inconsistencies, feeling we thus add to our actual knowledge of human nature. In fiction we have not this *conviction*, and therefore not this sort or source of pleasure even if ever so well done; if it be quite a new inconsistency we feel doubtful and averse; but we submit when we know *it is* true: we say, "don't therefore tell me it is not in human nature."

I am not sure that I agree with Colonel Stewart about particular morals to stories, but this point might lead to long and intricate discussion.

I feel and admire all he says so eloquently, I am sure from his own heart, touching the advantage of raising the standard of our moral ambition; and the higher this standard can be raised by works of fiction the better. I feel and understand how many poets and novelists have raised in the mind that sort of enthusiasm which exalts and purifies the soul. Happy and gifted with heaven's best gift must be the poet, the inventor of any sort of fiction that can raise this enthusiasm. I recollect Mrs. Barbauld's lines describing—

> Generous youth that feeds
> On pictured tales of vast heroic deeds.[2]

---

[1] Dugald Stewart: Father of Colonel Stewart.
[2] Ye generous youth who love this studious shade,

.   .   .   .

And fond enthusiastic thought, that feeds
On pictured tales of vast heroic deeds;
   —Mrs. Anna L. Barbauld, "The Invitation."

How I wish I could furnish, as Scott has, some of those pictured tales coloured to the life; but I fear I have not that power, therefore it is perhaps that I strive to console myself for my deficiencies by flattering myself that there is much, though not such glorious use, in my own lesser manner and department. The great virtues, the great vices excite strong enthusiasm, vehement horror, but after all it is not so necessary to warn the generality of mankind against these, either by precept or example, as against the lesser faults; we are all sufficiently aware that we must not break the commandments, and the reasons against all vices all feel even to the force of demonstration, but demonstration does not need and cannot receive additional force from fiction. The Old Bailey trials, *Les Causes Célèbres*, come with more force, as with the force of actual truth, than can any of the finest fictions producing what Colonel Stewart calls "momentary belief in the reality of a fictitious character or event." Few readers do or can put themselves in the places of great criminals, or fear to yield to such and such temptations; they know that they cannot fall to the depth of evil at once, and they have no sympathy, no fear; their spirits are not "put in the act of falling." But show them the steep path, the little declivity at first, the step by step downwards, and they tremble. Show them the postern gates or little breaches in their citadel of virtue, and they fly to guard these; in short, show to them their own little faults which may lead on to the greatest, and they shudder; that is, if this be done with truth and brought home to their consciousness. This is all, which by reflection on my own mind and comparison with others and with records in books full as much as observations on living subjects, I feel or fancy I have sometimes done or can do.

But while I am thus *ladling* out praise to myself in this way, I do not flatter myself that I deserve the quantity of praise which Colonel Stewart gives me for laborious observation, or for steadiness and nicety of dissection. My father, to whose judgment I habitually refer to help out my own judgment of myself, and who certainly must from long acquaintance, to say no more, have known my character better than any other person can, always reproached me for trusting too much to my hasty glances, *aperçus*, as he called them, of character or truths; and often have I had, and have still (past my grand climacteric) to repent every day my mistaken conclusions and hasty jumps to conclusions. Perhaps you wish I should jump to conclusion now, and so I will.

2

CHARLES R. MATURIN

(1780–1824)

Born in Dublin to a family of French extraction, Charles Maturin gives the impression of being an unhappy man. Although an outstanding student at Trinity College, he seems neither to have excelled in, nor enjoyed, his work as a curate. His tastes and expenditures always exceeded his means, and his literary efforts were motivated by hope of financial reward rather than by any artistic impulse. In his Preface to a religious novel, *Women, or Pour et Contre* (1818), he expressed no surprise at the unpopularity of his former works: aside from lacking "*external* interest, (the strongest interest that books can have, even in this reading age,) they seem to want *reality*, vraisemblance; the characters, situations, and language are drawn merely from imagination; my limited acquaintance with life denied me any other resource."

Yet, by the standards of romance, Maturin's abilities were sufficient. *The Fatal Revenge, or the Family of Montorio* (1807) was favorably reviewed by Scott, who paid *The Milesian Chief* (1812) the compliment of imitating it in *The Bride of Lammermoor.* In a letter to Scott, Maturin wrote that "tales of superstition were always my favorites; I have in fact been always more conversant with the visions of another world than the realities of this, and in my Romance I have determined to display all by *diabolical* resources, out-Herod all the Herods of the German school, and get the possession of the Magic lamp with all its slaves from the Conjurer *Lewis* himself" (15 February 1813).

Although Maturin would have preferred to write of contemporary reality, his genius inclined toward the Gothic. *Women* did succeed in its presentation of Irish society, and *The Wild Irish Boy* (1808) is a caricature of life of the day. But there is no depth of characterization, no philosophy, in his fiction. "I have no power of affecting, no hope of instructing; no play or other production of mine will ever draw a tear from the eye, or teach a lesson to the Heart . . ." (Letter to Scott, 2 July 1816). To offset this self-pity somewhat is the successful

10

run of *Bertram*, a tragedy produced through the efforts of Byron; however other plays by Maturin were less successful.

Maturin's bitterness is apparent in his plans to print his sermons, six of which appeared in 1824: "I would indeed be glad to print them, if it was only to prove I can do something beside write Romances, and never did that voluntarily" (Letter to Scott, 17 July 1813). In his Preface to his masterpiece, *Melmoth the Wanderer* (1820), which demonstrates his total inability or unconcern with structural matters, he apologizes: "I cannot again appear before the public in so unseemly a character as that of a writer of romances without regretting the necessity that compels me to do it." And in his Preface to *The Wild Irish Boy* his attitude toward the contemporary novel is heavy with sarcasm.

PREFACE

THE WILD IRISH BOY
(1808)

Most authors have a vast deal to say of their writings; this is not the case with me. I have but a few observations to make, and then to "reading with what appetite you may." My first work was said to be too defective in female characters and female interest. I have tried to remedy both defects; I have introduced a sufficient number of females; and if they are not interesting, I cannot help them. Yet let me premise that of love, I have never in my life read (what I conceived to be) an adequate representation; it is therefore natural that I should despair of making one. Its folly, and fantasy, and fastidiousness—its high, remote, incommunicable modes of feeling and expression—its nice and subtle pleasures, its luxurious melancholy, its happiness that mocks mortality, and its despair that defies religion, seldom can, seldom ought to be represented.

This novel, from its title, purports to give some account of a country little known. I lament I have not had time to say more of it; my heart was full of it, but I was compelled by the laws of this mode of composition to consult the pleasure of my readers, not my own. The fashionable materials for novel-writing I know to be a lounge in Bond-street, a phaeton-tour in the Park, a masquerade with appropriate scenery, and a birthday or birthnight, with dresses and decorations, accurately copied from the newspapers.

He who writes with a hope of being read must write something like this. I say must, because this species of writing, not exacting a sacrifice of principles, but of taste, the public have reasonably a right to dictate in. He who would prostitute his morals is a monster—he who sacrifices his inclination and habits of writing is—an author.

At the same time, it is desirable to look forward to the time when independence, acquired without any sacrifice of integrity, will enable a man to consult only himself in the choice and mode of his subject. He who is capable of writing a good novel ought to feel that he was born for a higher purpose than writing novels.

3

SUSAN E. FERRIER

(1782–1854)

A modest nature and weakened eyesight combined to make Miss Ferrier's life a quiet one, her literary output small, and biographical records scant. Her father, James, was an estate manager for the Argyll family as well as for other notables, and when he became a principal clerk of sessions and a colleague of Sir Walter Scott, his connections with Edinburgh's literary society enabled Susan, youngest of his ten children, to make similar acquaintances. She visited Scott and dedicated *Destiny* (1831) to him. Her novels, favorably received, contained satirical sketches of characters from the upper classes of Scottish society. According to her Introduction to *The Inheritance* (1824), some characters therein were sketched from life.

At one time, Miss Ferrier hoped to collaborate with a niece of the Duke of Argyll on a work of fiction. Although the plan was abandoned, the former's letters to Miss Clavering discussing what she later published under the title *Marriage* (1818) reveal her opinion that "the taste of the times is undoubtedly for private memoirs and personal satire" (1810) and show her concept of fiction to be generally that of Miss Edgeworth.

FROM LETTER TO MISS CHARLOTTE CLAVERING
(undated)

Your proposals flatter and delight me, but how, in the name of postage, are we to transport our brains to and fro? I suppose we'd be pawning our flannel petticoats to bring about our heroine's marriage, and lying on straw to give her Christian burial. Part of your plot I like much, some not quite so well—for example, it wants a *moral*. Your principal characters are good and interesting, and they are tormented and persecuted, and punished from no fault of their own, and for no possible purpose. Now I don't think, like all penny-book manufacturers, that 'tis absolutely necessary that the good boys and girls should be rewarded, and the naughty ones punished. Yet, I think, where there is much tribulation, 'tis fitter it should be the *consequence*, rather than the *cause* of misconduct or frailty. You'll say that rule is absurd, inasmuch as it is not observed in human life; that I allow, but we know the inflictions of Providence are for wise purposes, therefore our reason willingly submits to them. But as the only good purpose of a book is to inculcate morality, and convey some lesson of instruction as well as delight, I do not see that what is called a *good moral* can be dispensed with in a work of fiction. Another fault is your making your hero attempt suicide, which is greatly too shocking, and destroys all the interest his misfortunes would otherwise excite—that, however, could be easily altered, and in other respects I think your plot has great merit. You'll perhaps be displeased at the freedom of my remarks; but in the first place freedom is absolutely necessary in the cause in which we are about to embark, and it must be understood to be one if not the chief article of our creed. In the second (though it should have been the first), know that I always say what I think, or say nothing. Now as to my own deeds—I shall make no apologies (since they must be banished from our code of laws) for sending you a hasty and imperfect sketch of what I think might be wrought up to a tolerable form. I do not recollect ever to have seen the sudden transition of a high-bred English beauty, who thinks she can sacrifice all for love, to an uncomfortable solitary Highland dwelling among tall red-haired sisters and grim-faced aunts. Don't you think this would make a good opening of the piece? Suppose each of us try our hands on it; the moral to be deduced from that is to warn all young ladies against runaway matches, and the character and fate of the two sisters would be *unexceptionable*. I expect it will be the first book every wise matron will put into the hand of

14

her daughter, and even the reviewers will relax of their severity in favour of the morality of this little work. Enchanting sight! already do I behold myself arrayed in an old mouldy covering, thumbed and creased, and filled with dog's-ears. I hear the enchanting sound of some sentimental miss, the shrill pipe of some antiquated spinster, or the hoarse grumbling of some incensed dowager as they severally inquire for me at the circulating library, and are assured by the master that 'tis in such demand, that though he has thirteen copies, they are insufficient to answer the calls upon it, but that each of them may depend upon having the very first that comes in!!! Child, child, you had need be sensible of the value of my correspondence. At this moment I'm squandering mines of wealth upon you, when I might be drawing treasures from the bags of time! But I shall not repine if you'll only repay me in kind—speedy and long is all that I require; for all things else I shall take my chance. Though I have been so impertinent to your book, I nevertheless hope and expect you'll send it to me. . . . One thing let me entreat of you: if we engage in this undertaking let it be kept a profound secret from every human being. If I was suspected of being accessory to such foul deeds my brothers and sisters would murder me, and my father bury me alive—and I have always observed that if a secret ever goes beyond those immediately concerned in its concealment it very soon ceases to be a secret.

FROM LETTER TO MISS CLAVERING
(February, 1810)

. . . You may laugh at the idea of its being at all necessary for the writer of a romance to be versed in the history, natural and political, the modes, manners, customs, &c. of the country where its wild and wanton freaks are to be played, but I consider it as most essentially so, as nothing disgusts an ordinary reader more than a discovery of the ignorance of the author, who is pretending to instruct and amuse him. If you'll wait a year perhaps I may have picked up a little lair[1] in that time, for, as you observe, I'm on the right road to it at present; but alas! I have but just entered upon it, and many a long day's journey lies before me! As to your other plans, I reject and spurn them all without hesitation. A Hottentot heroine and a wild man of the woods would be in truth a pair most "justly formed to meet by nature," but I should despair of doing justice to their wild paces and delicate endearments, though, by-the-bye, I do think something might be made of such a

[1] lair: dialectal variant of *lore*, learning.

couple. Then as to your men of the moon, I shall have nothing to say to them; this globe contains men enough for me. Better have one earthly man as a score of moonshine ones methinks; and as for their lives and conversation:

> What, I prithee, ist to us,
> If men o' the moon do thus or thus;
> How they eat their porridge, cut their corns,
> Or whether they have tails or horns.

In short, I don't think we'll come to any understanding upon paper, so we had best give up thoughts of the thing till we meet, which we'll surely do some day or another—at any rate, I'm determined not to engage with you till this of Lady Charlotte is at an end. And you likewise mention one with Miss Adair! Cæsar piqued himself, as I have been told, upon dictating three letters at a time. How must his great shade be racked with spite and envy if he sees a young lady composing three novels all in a breath!!! No, no; as the old saying says, always finish one thing before you begin another. I've the highest respect and admiration of your talents and genius, but I don't think there's a head in the world capable of containing and clearly arranging materials for three books, be they what they may; besides that, you can do nothing but write, and though I approve of it as an amusement I by no means commend it as the business of life—too much application is bad for the health and will spoil your eyes and complexion, and, to tell you a bit of my mind, I don't think you will ever write half so well as nature has written upon you . . . I've said nothing of my own obstacles, because I consider those on your side as sufficiently powerful; but I assure you I could no more accomplish such a letter as you propose every week than a poor wretch could promise to be witty and agreeable when writhing in the cholic. In the first place, I really have not much time I can absolutely command, for in a town, however privately or retired one may live, they're still liable to a thousand interruptions; in the next place, I have enough to do with my time in writing to my sisters three, sewing my seam, improving my mind, making tea, playing whist, with numberless other duties too tedious to mention; and, in the third and last place, there's sometimes for a week together that I can't bear the sight of a pen, and could no more invent a letter than I could have discovered the longitude. So for the present let us put our child to sleep and hope for better times to wake him. Only, once for all, let me promise to you that I *will not* enter into any of your raw head and bloody bone schemes. I would not even *read* a Book that had a spectre in it, and as for committing a mysterious and most foul murder, I declare I'd rather take a dose of asafœtida; so don't flatter yourself with the hope of associating me in your crimes and iniquities. . . .

4

SYDNEY OWENSON
LADY MORGAN

(? 1776–1859)

Although Lady Morgan left an autobiography, diaries, and letters for her biographers, she was inaccurate and unconcerned about dates, and even the year of her birth is uncertain. Born in Dublin, she served as a governess about 1798 to 1800, published a volume of sentimental verse in 1801, and may have acted on the stage. Her writings include an opera, "The First Attempt," which ran several nights at the Theatre Royal, Dublin, in March, 1807; a romance in four volumes, *Woman, or Ida of Athens* (1809); and two travel accounts: *France* (1817) and *Italy* (1821). Her first-hand observations of the political and social scene in France were so popular that she was commissioned to write the book on Italy and spent over a year in that country for the purpose. Byron was among those who praised it.

It was, however, her fictional depiction of Irish life and her ability to describe the lower class that brought Lady Morgan fame. The sentimental tone of *The Wild Irish Girl* (1806) appealed to readers who read through seven editions in less than two years. Characterized as witty and vivacious, Lady Morgan became known in literary circles as Glorvina—after the heroine of her novel. The liberal party championed her national sentiments. Becoming acquainted with fashionable society, she met and married (1812) Thomas Morgan, surgeon to her patron, the Marquis of Abercorn, through whose influence he was knighted by the Duke of Richmond. Ultimately (1839), the Morgans established residence in London.

Other novels followed—enlivened by humor but weakened by generally mediocre writing: *St. Clair: or, The Heiress of Desmond* (1803); *O'Donnel: A National Tale* (1814); *Florence Macarthy: An Irish Tale* (1818); and *The O'Briens and the O'Flaherties* (1827). The character Conway Crawley, an unscrupulous critic in *Florence Macarthy*, was recognized as a caricature of John Wilson

17

Croker, who had attacked her for years in the *Quarterly Review*. *O'Donnel*, considered her best novel, drew this criticism from Sit Walter Scott:

I have amused myself occasionally very pleasantly during the last few days, by reading over Lady Morgan's novel of *O'Donnel*, which has some striking and beautiful passages of situation and description, and in the comic part is very rich and entertaining. I do not remember being so much pleased with it at first. There is a want of story, always fatal to a book the first reading—and it is well if it gets a chance of a second. Alas! poor novel! (*Journal*, March, 1826)

The Preface to *O'Donnel* expresses Lady Morgan's theory that fiction forms the best history and that the novelist who would serve that function best must learn "to adopt, rather than create; to combine, rather than invent; and to take nature and manners for the grounds and groupings of works which are professedly addressed to popular feelings and ideas."

PREFACE

O'DONNEL: A NATIONAL TALE
(1814)

Literary fiction, whether directed to the purpose of transient amusement, or adopted as an indirect medium of instruction, has always in its most genuine form exhibited a mirror of the times in which it is composed; reflecting morals, customs, manners, peculiarity of character, and prevalence of opinion. Thus, perhaps, after all, it forms the best history of nations, the rest being but the dry chronicles of facts and events, which, in the same stages of society, occur under the operations of the same passions, and tend to the same consequences.

But, though such be the primary character of fictitious narrative, we find it, in its progress, producing arbitrary models, derived from conventional modes of thinking amongst writers, and influenced by the doctrines of the learned, and the opinions of the refined. Ideal beauties, and ideal perfection, take the place of nature, and approbation is sought rather by a description of *what is not*, than a faithful portraiture of *what is*. He, however, who soars beyond the line of general knowledge, and common feelings, must be content to remain within the exclusive pale of particular approbation. It is the interest, therefore, of the *novelist*, who is, *par état*,[1] the servant of the *many*, not the *minister* of the FEW, to abandon pure abstractions, and "thick coming fancies," to philosophers and to poets; to adopt, rather than create; to combine, rather than invent; and to take nature and manners for the grounds and groupings of works which are professedly addressed to popular feelings and ideas.

Influenced by this impression, I have for the first time ventured on that style of novel, which simply bears upon the "flat realities of life." Having determined upon taking Ireland as my theme, I sought in its records and chronicles for the groundwork of a story, and the character of a hero. The romantic adventures, and unsubdued valour of O'DONNEL *the Red*, Chief of Tirconnel,[2] in the reign of Elizabeth, promised, at the first glance, all

---

[1] *par état*: by profession.
[2] Tirconnel: "Modern Donegal, in the province of Ulster." [Morgan]

I wished, and seemed happily adapted to my purpose. I had already advanced as far as the second volume of my MS. and had expended much time and labour in arduous research and dry study, when I found it necessary to forego my original plan. The character of my sex, no less than my own feelings, urged me, in touching those parts of Irish history which were connected with my tale, to turn them to the purposes of conciliation, and to incorporate the leaven of favourable opinion with that heavy mass of bitter prejudice, which writers, both grave and trifling, have delighted to raise against my country. But when I fondly thought to send forth a dove bearing the olive of peace, I found I was on the point of flinging an arrow winged with discord. I *had* hoped, as far as *my feeble efforts could go*, to extenuate the errors attributed to Ireland, by an exposition of their causes, drawn from historic facts; but I found, that, like the spirit in *Macbeth*, I should at the same moment hold up a glass to my countrymen, reflecting but *too* many fearful images;

To "show their eyes and grieve their hearts:"[3]

for I discovered, far beyond my expectation, that I had fallen upon "evil men, and evil days;" and that in proceeding, I must raise a veil which ought never to be drawn, and renew the memory of events which the interests of humanity require to be forever buried in oblivion.

I abandoned, therefore, my original plan, took up a happier view of things, advanced my story to more modern and more liberal times, and exchanged the rude chief of the days of old, for his polished descendant in a more refined age: and I trust the various branches of the ancient house with whose name I have honoured him will not find reason to disown their newly-discovered kinsman.

SYDNEY MORGAN.

35, Kildare-street, Dublin,
    March 1, 1814.

[3] Show his eyes, and grieve his heart
        —Macbeth, 4. 1. 110.

5

JANE AUSTEN

(1775–1817)

Following Fanny Burney in the tradition of the novel of manners, Jane
Austen appealed to a relatively small but select number of readers in her day.
Her reputation has steadily increased, and she and Scott have emerged as the
two outstanding novelists of the Romantic period. Best known for *Pride and
Prejudice* (1813), *Mansfield Park* (1814), and *Emma* (1815; dated 1816), she
depicted the placid life of the upper middle class, to which her own experience
confined her. Her delineation of this social stratum is unsurpassed.

Jane Austen began her fictional career, however, with parodies of the
Gothic and sentimental romances, whose excesses were apparent to her earlier
than they were to the general public. In addition to the larger commentary on
the Gothic in *Northanger Abbey* (written in 1797, but not published until 1818)
and on the sentimental strain in *Sense and Sensibility* (begun about the same
time but not published until 1811), the former of these two early books includes
several passages—notably those ridiculing Mr. Thorpe's knowledge of fiction
and Catherine Morland's indiscriminate enthusiasm for Gothic romances—
that help to define Jane Austen's attitude.

Her protests against the popular denigration of the novel are expressed
in another place in *Northanger Abbey* as well as in one of her letters. These
defenses of fiction, written at the same time she was yielding to public opinion
by publishing anonymously, point up the hesitation of the early nineteenth
century to recognize the novel as a serious art form—and the consequent
prudence of concealing authorship.

Although her identity was not revealed until after her death, knowledge
of her authorship did spread and motivated advice from many quarters.
Forming their standards on the properties of romance or seeking the respect-
ability that would result from association with history, these well-meaning
advisors urged a wide variety of departures from her limited scope. Her firm
replies to such advice reveal her sound judgment of her limitations and her

determination to persevere with "the little bit (two inches wide) of Ivory on which I work with so fine a Brush." Her replies to the Rev. James S. Clarke, Chaplain-Secretary to the Prince Regent, one of her admirers, are notable.

Finally, her innate sense of comedy prompted her to ridicule the composite fiction that would result from indiscriminate acceptance of suggestions made by her many friends. In this "Plan of a Novel, According to Hints from Various Quarters," which she never published, she is careful to ascribe the hints to their authors in marginal notes.

NORTHANGER ABBEY
(1818)

from Chapter 5

The progress of the friendship between Catherine and Isabella was quick as its beginning had been warm, and they passed so rapidly through every gradation of increasing tenderness that there was shortly no fresh proof of it to be given to their friends or themselves. They called each other by their Christian name, were always arm in arm when they walked, pinned up each other's train for the dance, and were not to be divided in the set; and if a rainy morning deprived them of other enjoyments, they were still resolute in meeting in defiance of wet and dirt, and shut themselves up, to read novels together. Yes, novels;—for I will not adopt that ungenerous and impolitic custom so common with novel writers, of degrading by their contemptuous censure the very performances, to the number of which they are themselves adding—joining with their greatest enemies in bestowing the harshest epithets on such works, and scarcely ever permitting them to be read by their own heroine, who, if she accidentally take up a novel, is sure to turn over its insipid pages with disgust. Alas! if the heroine of one novel be not patronized by the heroine of another, from whom can she expect protection and regard? I cannot approve of it. Let us leave it to the Reviewers to abuse such effusions of fancy at their leisure, and over every new novel to talk in threadbare strains of the trash with which the press now groans. Let us not desert one another; we are an injured body. Although our productions have afforded more extensive and unaffected pleasure than those of any other literary corporation in the world, no species of composition has been so much decried. From pride, ignorance, or fashion, our foes are almost as many as our readers. And while the abilities of the nine-hundredth abridger of the History of England, or of the man who collects and publishes in a volume some dozen lines of Milton, Pope, and Prior, with a paper from the Spectator, and a chapter from Sterne, are eulogized by a thousand pens,—there seems almost a general wish of decrying the capacity and under-valuing the labour of the novelist, and of slighting the performances which have only genius, wit, and taste to recommend them. "I am no novel reader—I seldom look into novels—Do not imagine that *I* often read novels—It is really very well for a novel."—Such is the common cant.—"And what are you reading, Miss ——?" "Oh! it is only a novel!" replies the young lady, while she lays down her book with affected indifference, or momentary shame.—"It is only Cecilia, or Camilla, or Belinda;" or, in short, only some work in which the greatest powers of the mind are displayed, in which the most thorough knowledge of human nature, the happiest delineation of its varieties, the liveliest effusions of wit and humour are conveyed to the world in the best chosen language. Now, had the same young lady been engaged with a volume of the Spectator, instead of such a work, how proudly would she have produced the book, and told its name; though the chances must be against her being occupied by any part of that voluminous publication, of which either the matter or manner would not disgust a young person of taste: the substance of its papers so often consisting in the statement of improbable circumstances, unnatural characters, and topics of conversation which no longer concern anyone living; and their language, too, frequently so coarse as to give no very favourable idea of the age that could endure it.

from Chapter 7

This brought on a dialogue of civilities between the other two; but Catherine heard neither the particulars nor the result. Her companion's discourse now sunk from its hitherto animated pitch, to nothing more than a short decisive sentence of praise or condemnation on the face of every woman they met; and Catherine, after listening and agreeing as long as she could, with all the civility and deference of the youthful female mind, fearful of hazarding an opinion of its own in opposition to that of a self-assured man, especially where the beauty of her own sex is concerned, ventured at length to vary the subject by a question which had been long uppermost in her thoughts; it was, "Have you ever read Udolpho, Mr. Thorpe?"

"Udolpho! Oh, Lord! not I; I never read novels; I have something else to do."

Catherine, humbled and ashamed, was going to apologize for her question, but he prevented her by saying, "Novels are all so full of nonsense and stuff; there has not been a tolerably decent one come out since Tom Jones, except the Monk; I read that t'other day; but as for all the others, they are the stupidest things in creation.

"I think you must like Udolpho, if you were to read it; it is so very interesting."

"Not I, faith! No, if I read any, it shall be Mrs. Radcliffe's; her novels are amusing enough; they are worth reading; some fun and nature in *them*."

"Udolpho was written by Mrs. Radcliffe," said Catherine, with some hesitation, from the fear of mortifying him.

"No sure; was it? Aye, I remember, so it was; I was thinking of that other stupid book, written by that woman they make such a fuss about; she who married the French emigrant."

"I suppose you mean Camilla!"

"Yes, that's the book; such unnatural stuff!—An old man playing at see-saw! I took up the first volume once and looked it over, but I soon found it would not do; indeed I guessed what sort of stuff it must be before I saw it: as soon as I heard she had married an emigrant, I was sure I should never be able to get through it."

"I have never read it."

"You had no loss, I assure you; it is the horridest nonsense you can imagine; there is nothing in the world in it but an old man's playing at see-saw and learning Latin; upon my soul there is not."

from Chapter 14

The next morning was fair, and Catherine almost expected another attack from the assembled party. With Mr. Allen to support her, she felt no dread of the event: but she would gladly be spared a contest, where victory itself was painful; and was heartily rejoiced therefore at neither seeing nor hearing anything of them. The Tilneys called for her at the appointed time; and no new difficulty arising, no sudden recollection, no unexpected summons, no impertinent intrusion to disconcert their measures, my heroine was most unnaturally able to fulfil her engagement, though it was made with the hero himself. They determined on walking round Beechen Cliff, that noble hill, whose beautiful verdure and hanging coppice render it so striking an object from almost every opening in Bath.

"I never look at it," said Catherine, as they walked along the side of the river, "without thinking of the south of France."

"You have been abroad, then?" said Henry, a little surprized.

"Oh! no, I only mean what I have read about. It always puts me in mind of the country that Emily and her father travelled through, in 'The Mysteries of Udolpho.' But you never read novels, I dare say?"

"Why not?"

"Because they are not clever enough for you—gentlemen read better books."

"The person, be it gentleman or lady, who has not pleasure in a good novel, must be intolerably stupid. I have read all Mrs. Radcliffe's works, and most of them with great pleasure. 'The Mysteries of Udolpho,' when I had once begun it, I could not lay down again;—I remember finishing it in two days—my hair standing on end the whole time."

"Yes," added Miss Tilney, "and I remember that you undertook to read it aloud to me, and that when I was called away for only five minutes to answer a note, instead of waiting for me, you took the volume into the Hermitage-walk, and I was obliged to stay till you had finished it."

"Thank you, Eleanor;—a most honourable testimony. You see, Miss Morland, the injustice of your suspicions. Here was I, in my eagerness to get on, refusing to wait only five minutes for my sister; breaking the promise I had made of reading it aloud, and keeping her in suspense at a most interesting part, by running away with the volume, which, you are to observe, was her own, particularly her own. I am proud when I reflect on it, and I think it must establish me in your good opinion."

"I am very glad to hear it indeed, and now I shall never be ashamed of liking Udolpho myself. But I really thought before, young men despised novels amazingly."

"It is *amazingly*; it may well suggest *amazement* if they do—for they read nearly as many as women. I myself have read hundreds and hundreds. Do not imagine that you can cope with me in a knowledge of Julias and Louisas. If we proceed to particulars, and engage in the never-ceasing inquiry of 'Have you read this?' and 'Have you read that?' I shall soon leave you as far behind me as—what shall I say?—I want an appropriate simile;— as far as your friend Emily herself left poor Valancourt when she went with her aunt into Italy. Consider how many years I have had the start of you. I had entered on my studies at Oxford, while you were a good little girl working your sampler at home!"

"Not very good, I am afraid. But now really, do not you think Udolpho the nicest book in the world?"

"The nicest;—by which I suppose you mean the neatest. That must depend upon the binding."

"Henry," said Miss Tilney, "you are very impertinent. Miss Morland, he is treating you exactly as he does his sister. He is for ever finding fault with me, for some incorrectness of language, and now he is taking the same liberty with you. The word 'nicest', as you used it, did not suit him; and you had better change it as soon as you can, or we shall be overpowered with Johnson and Blair all the rest of the way."

"I am sure," cried Catherine, "I did not mean to say anything wrong; but it *is* a nice book, and why should not I call it so?"

"Very true," said Henry, "and this is a very nice day, and we are taking a very nice walk, and you are two very nice young ladies. Oh! it is a very nice word, indeed!—it does for everything. Originally perhaps it was applied only to express neatness, propriety, delicacy, or refinement;— people were nice in their dress, in their sentiments, or their choice. But now every commendation on every subject is comprised in that one word."

"While, in fact," cried his sister, "it ought only to be applied to you, without any commendation at all. You are more nice than wise. Come, Miss Morland, let us leave him to meditate over our faults in the utmost propriety of diction, while we praise Udolpho in whatever terms we like best. It is a most interesting work. You are fond of that kind of reading?"

"To say the truth, I do not much like any other."

PLAN OF A NOVEL

ACCORDING TO HINTS FROM VARIOUS QUARTERS
(undated)

Scene to be in the country. Heroine the daugher of a clergyman,[1] one who after having lived much in the world had retired from it and settled in a curacy with a very small fortune of his own. He, the most excellent man that can be imagined—perfect in character, temper, and manners—without the smallest drawback or peculiarity to prevent his being the most delightful companion to his daughter from one year's end to the other. Heroine a faultless[2] character herself—perfectly good, with much tenderness and sentiment, and not the least wit[3]—very highly accomplished,[4] understanding modern languages and (generally speaking) everything that the most accomplished young women learn, but particularly excelling in music— her favourite pursuit—and playing equally well on the pianoforte and harp— and singing in the first style. Her person quite beautiful—dark eyes and plump cheeks.[5] Book to open with the description of father and daughter— who are to converse in long speeches, elegant language, and a tone of high, serious sentiment. The father to be induced, at his daughter's earnest request, to relate to her the past events of his life. This narrative will reach through the greatest part of the first volume—as, besides all the circumstances of his attachment to her mother and their marriage, it will comprehend his going to sea as chaplain[6] to a distinguished naval character about the Court, his going afterwards to Court himself, which introduced him to a great variety of characters and involved him in many interesting situations, concluding with his opinion of the benefits to result from tithes being done away and his having buried his own mother (heroine's lamented grand-mother) in consequence of the high priest of the parish in which she died refusing to pay her remains the respect due to them. The father to be of a very literary turn, an enthusiast in literature, nobody's enemy but his own— at the same time most zealous in the discharge of his pastoral duties, the model of an exemplary parish priest.[7] The heroine's friendship to be sought

---

[1] Mr. Gifford.
[2] Fanny Knight.
[3] Mary Cooke.

[4] Fanny K.
[5] Mary Cooke.

[6] Mr. Clarke.
[7] Mr. Sherer.

after by a young woman in the same neighbourhood, of talents and shrewd-ness,[8] with light eyes and a fair skin; but having a considerable degree of wit, heroine shall shrink from the acquaintance. From this outset the story will proceed and contain a striking variety of adventures. Heroine and her father never above a fortnight together in one place,[9] *he* being driven from his curacy by the vile arts of some totally unprincipled and heartless young man, desperately in love with the heroine and pursuing her with unrelenting passion—no sooner settled in one country of Europe than they are necessi-tated to quit it and retire to another—always making new acquaintance and always obliged to leave them. This will of course exhibit a wide variety of characters—but there will be no mixture; the scene will be forever shifting from one set of people to another—but all the Good will be unexceptionable in every respect—[10] and there will be no foibles or weaknesses but with the wicked, who will be completely depraved and infamous, hardly a resemblance of humanity left in them. Early in her career, in the progress of her first removals, heroine must meet with the hero—all perfection of course—[11] and only prevented from paying his addresses to her by some excess of refinement. Wherever she goes, somebody falls in love with her, and she receives repeated offers of marriage—which she always refers wholly to her father, exceedingly angry that *he* should not be the first applied to.[12] Often carried away by the antihero, but rescued either by her father or the hero—often reduced to support herself and her father by her talents and work for her bread—continually cheated and defrauded of her hire, worn down to a skeleton, and now and then starved to death. At last, hunted out of civilized society, denied the poor shelter of the humblest cottage, they are compelled to retreat into Kamschatka, where the poor father, quite worn down, finding his end approaching, throws himself on the ground, and after four or five hours of tender advice and parental admonition to his miserable child, expires in a fine burst of literary enthusiasm, intermingled with invectives against holders of tithes. Heroine inconsolable for some time—but after-wards crawls back towards her former country—having at least twenty narrow escapes of falling into the hands of antihero—and at last in the very nick of time, turning a corner to avoid him, runs into the arms of the hero himself, who having just shaken off the scruples which fettered him before, was at the very moment setting off in pursuit of her. The tenderest and completest eclaircissement takes place, and they are happily united. Through-out the whole work, heroine to be in the most elegant society and living in high style.[13] The name of the work *not* to be *Emma*—[14] but of the same sort as S & S and P & P.[15]

---

[8] Mary Cooke.
[9] Many critics.
[10] Mary Cooke.
[11] Fanny Knight.

[12] Mrs. Pearse of Chilton-Lodge.
[13] Fanny Knight.
[14] Mrs. Craven.
[15] Mr. H. Sanford.

6

SIR WALTER SCOTT

(1771–1832)

Inspired by the success of Maria Edgeworth in her fictional presentation of the Irish scene, Sir Walter Scott utilized his native Scotland with equal patriotic fervor when he began "The Waverley Novels" with *Waverley, or 'Tis Sixty Years Since* (1814). His first nine novels—including *The Heart of Midlothian* (1818) and *Old Mortality* (1816), among his best—deal with Scotland. *Ivanhoe* (1820), which began Scott's European vogue, is the first of his novels to deal with a purely English subject.

When death came—after neither financial distress nor severe illness had slowed his rapid pen, he had produced thirty novels, covering a period of eight centuries. His unprecedented profits enabled him to rebuild Abbotsford, his baronial mansion, and to repay the enormous debts incurred through his association with the Ballantyne publishing firm. He had, in 1820, been made a baronet by George IV in honor of his literary accomplishments—the first author to be so honored. The international vogue of historical fiction in the nineteenth century can be traced to his tremendous influence on novelists in France, Italy, Russia, and the United States, as well as in Great Britain.

All of these achievements combined to help overcome lingering prejudice toward the novel and to establish it as a legitimate form of literature. Scott had no doubt about the artistic merit of the novel; he ranked historical fiction, when well done, with the epic. But he was, at first, uncertain of his success and hesitated to endanger his career as a lawyer by associating himself with fiction. So he published his novels anonymously, not acknowledging them formally until 1827. Before turning to prose fiction, he had already become famous as a narrative poet, yielding first place finally to Byron. And he was a prolific producer of biographies, histories, editions, and articles.

Writing novels in addition to other literature and combining a literary career with the duties attendant on his legal profession and the pleasures of overseeing the additions to Abbotsford necessitated a haste in writing and an unconcern for revision to which is traceable many of the technical weaknesses pointed out by critics. Lack of a preconceived plan led to false starts, tangential episodes, and awkward structure, such as the extension of the story to fill out a third volume in *The Heart of Midlothian*. At first Scott relied on his tenacious memory of stories, incidents, and characters from his early reading in ballads, folk tales, and books of adventure. Childhood illness had prevented his participation in an active life, but the reading he did as a substitute stimulated his imagination. When he came to write, his materials were in his mind, and he could write rapidly. Later, the pace slowed as he relied on research for his matter.

Even before he turned to fiction, Scott's literary productions were motivated by monetary profit. He needed it first for Abbotsford and later to pay off his part of the Ballantyne firm's debt. At the peak of his fictional career, the "Wizard of the North" was writing three novels a year—and these in the three-volume format that he helped impose on fiction for almost the remainder of the century. He has been criticized for lack of depth; certainly there is an objectivity, an absence of propaganda, and a lack of concern for exploring contemporary problems in fiction. He gave his readers thrilling adventure in dramatic episodes and an abundance and variety of character never before seen in the novel. *Kenilworth* (1821), the product of great research, combines an example of his notable characterization in the person of Queen Elizabeth I with his typical attainment of real tragedy as well as of melodrama. Here and elsewhere he achieved the balance of the realistic and the romantic that he sought.

Scott's voluminous writings contain more commentary on fiction than any of his predecessors had written. His theories were expressed in prefaces (although most of these pertain to the specific novel and its sources), book reviews, articles, dedicatory epistles, critical biographies in his *Lives of the Novelists* (1821–24), and his *Journal*.

The Introduction to *Waverley* stands at the beginning of his fictional career as a statement of his own proposed course, which sought to eschew the supernatural, sentimental, and fashionable schools that he characterized herein. Further discussion of his opinions on the Gothic may be found in his *Life of Walpole* and in his *Life of Mrs. Radcliffe*, his article "On the Supernatural in Fictitious Composition, and Particularly on the Works of Hoffman," and in his review of *Frankenstein* (1818), where he grants to this "class of fictitious narrations . . . the extraordinary postulates which the author demands as the foundation of his narrative, only on condition of his deducing the consequences with logical precision." Every one of Scott's own major works is marked by some traditional devices of the Gothic school.

Scott's admiration of Jane Austen's novels as a type he was incapable of writing recalls her own profession of an inability to write a historical romance. Together they stand as the greatest novelists in Britain between Fielding and Dickens. In his review of *Emma* (1815) Scott compares the newer modes of fiction with the older romance. Additional commentary on this distinction may be found in "An Essay on Romance," written for the *Encyclopedia Britannica*, where he restates the old distinction that novels deal with real life whereas romances are concerned with the marvelous and the uncommon. Although he was not consistent, Scott usually referred to his own books as romances.

Gratified by his success, Scott was nevertheless modest: "Perhaps I was, and have always been, the more indifferent to the degree of estimation in which I might be held as an author, because I did not put so high a value as many others upon what is termed literary reputation in the abstract, or at least upon the species of popularity which had fallen to my share; for though it were worse than affectation to deny that my vanity was satisfied at my success in the department in which chance had in some measure enlisted me, I was, nevertheless, far from thinking that the novelist or romance-writer stands high in the ranks of literature" (Preface to *The Abbot*, 1820). He pursues this topic in the Introductory Epistle to *The Fortunes of Nigel* (1822), where, in spite of the notable part he had already played in improving the status of fiction, he shows none of Jane Austen's insistence on it. Here also he speaks of the creative process, financial return, and moral utility. On the last point he is more explicit in his *Life of Richardson*.

Other aspects of his theory include the requirements for a novelist, discussed in his *Life of Fielding* and his *Life of Smollett*, where he says: "Every successful novelist must be more or less a poet, even although he may never have written a line of verse. The quality of imagination is absolutely indispensable to him; his accurate power of examining and embodying human character and human passion, as well as the external face of nature, is not less essential; and the talent of describing well what he feels with acuteness, added to the above requisites, goes far to complete the poetic character." Another concern is structure, discussed in the Introduction to *The Monastery* (1820). The relative emphasis on character and incident is the subject of his review (1826) of John Galt's *The Omen*, where Scott considers character more important. And a comparison of the novel with the drama includes this statement from his *Life of Fielding*: "Hence it follows, that though a good acting play may be made, by selecting a plot and characters from a novel, yet scarce any effect of genius could render a play into a narrative romance." The use of history in fiction and the relationship of the hero to the plot is the subject of his review (1817) of his own *Tales of My Landlord*. In these thoroughgoing comments, as well as in many others treating these and other aspects of fiction, Scott proved to be a thoughtful critic, recognizing excellence as well as weakness.

FROM *WAVERLEY, OR 'TIS SIXTY YEARS SINCE*
(1814)

Chapter 1

The title of this work has not been chosen without the grave and solid deliberation which matters of importance demand from the prudent. Even its first or general denomination was the result of no common research or selection, although, according to the example of my predecessors, I had only to seize upon the most sounding and euphonic surname that English history or topography affords, and elect it at once as the title of my work and the name of my hero. But, alas! what could my readers have expected from the chivalrous epithets of Howard, Mordaunt, Mortimer, or Stanley, or from the softer and more sentimental sounds of Belmour, Belville, Belfield, and Belgrave, but pages of inanity similar to those which have been so christened for half a century past? I must modestly admit I am too diffident of my own merit to place it in unnecessary opposition to preconceived associations; I have, therefore, like a maiden knight with his white shield, assumed for my hero, WAVERLEY, an uncontaminated name, bearing with its sound little of good or evil excepting what the reader shall hereafter be pleased to affix to it. But my second, or supplemental, title was a matter of much more difficult election, since that, short as it is, may be held as pledging the author to some special mode of laying his scene, drawing his characters, and managing his adventures. Had I, for example, announced in my frontispiece, "Waverley: a Tale of other Days," must not every novel-reader have anticipated a castle scarce less than that of Udolpho, of which the eastern wing had long been uninhabited, and the keys either lost or consigned to the care of some aged butler or housekeeper, whose trembling steps, about the middle of the second volume, were doomed to guide the hero or heroine to the ruinous precincts? Would not the owl have shrieked and the cricket cried in my very title page? And could it have been possible for me, with a moderate attention to decorum, to introduce any scene more lively than might be produced by the jocularity of a clownish but faithful valet, or the garrulous narrative of the heroine's *fille-de-chambre*, when rehearsing the stories of blood and horror which she had heard in the servants' hall? Again, had my title borne "Waverley: a Romance from the German," what head so obtuse as not to image forth a profligate abbot, an oppressive duke, a secret and mysterious association of Rosicrucians and Illuminati,[1] with all their properties of black cowls, caverns, daggers, electrical machines, trap-doors, and dark-lanterns? Or if I had rather chosen to call my work a "Sentimental Tale," would it not have been a sufficient presage of a heroine with a profusion of auburn hair, and a harp, the soft solace of her solitary hours, which she fortunately finds always the means of transporting from castle to cottage, although she herself be sometimes obliged to jump out of a two-pair-of-stairs window, and is more than once bewildered on her journey, alone and on foot, without any guide but a blowzy peasant girl whose jargon she hardly can understand? Or, again, if my Waverley had been entitled, "A Tale of the Times," wouldst thou not, gentle reader, have demanded from me a dashing sketch of the fashionable world, a few anecdotes of private scandal thinly veiled, and if lusciously painted so much the better,—a heroine from Grosvenor Square, and a hero from the Barouche Club or the Four-in-Hand, with a set of subordinate characters from the elegantes of Queen Anne Street East, or the dashing heroes of the Bow Street Office?[2] I could proceed in proving the importance of a titlepage, and displaying at the same time my own intimate knowledge of the particular ingredients necessary to the composition of romances and novels of various descriptions; but it is enough, and I scorn to tyrannize longer over the impatience of my reader, who is doubtless already anxious to know the choice made by an author so profoundly versed in the different branches of his art.

By fixing, then, the date of my story Sixty Years before this present 1st November, 1805, I would have my readers understand that they will meet in the following pages neither a romance of chivalry nor a tale of modern manners; that my hero will neither have iron on his shoulders, as of yore, nor on the heels of his boots, as is the present fashion of Bond Street; and that my damsels will neither be clothed "in purple and in pall," like the Lady Alice of an old ballad, nor reduced to the primitive nakedness of a modern fashionable at a rout. From this my choice of an era the understanding critic may farther presage that the object of my tale is more a description of men than manners. A tale of manners, to be interesting, must either refer to antiquity so great as to have become venerable, or it must bear a vivid reflection of those scenes which are passing daily before our eyes, and are interesting from their novelty. Thus the coat-of-mail of our ancestors, and the triple-furred pelisse of our modern beaux, may, though for very different reasons, be equally fit for the array of a fictitious character; but who, meaning the costume of his hero to be impressive, would willingly attire him in the court dress of George the Second's reign, with its no collar, large sleeves, and low pocket-holes? The same may be urged, with equal

---

[1] Secret societies associated with occult practices and religious reform.

[2] Grosvenor Square, London, was the center of fashion; the Four-in-Hand or Barouche Club was an aristocratic group practicing coachmanship; the Bow Street Office was that of the Metropolitan Police.

truth, of the Gothic hall, which, with its darkened and tinted windows, its elevated and gloomy roof, and massive oaken table garnished with boar's-head and rosemary, pheasants and peacocks, cranes and cygnets, has an excellent effect in fictitious description. Much may also be gained by a lively display of a modern *fête*, such as we have daily recorded in that part of a newspaper entitled the *Mirror of Fashion*, if we contrast these, or either of them, with the splendid formality of an entertainment given Sixty Years since; and thus it will be readily seen how much the painter of antique or of fashionable manners gains over him who delineates those of the last generation.

Considering the disadvantages inseparable from this part of my subject, I must be understood to have resolved to avoid them as much as possible, by throwing the force of my narrative upon the characters and passions of the actors,—those passions common to men in all stages of society, and which have alike agitated the human heart whether it throbbed under the steel corselet of the fifteenth century, the brocaded coat of the eighteenth, or the blue frock and white dimity waistcoat of the present day. Upon these passions it is no doubt true that the state of manners and laws casts a necessary colouring; but the bearings,—to use the language of heraldry,—remain the same, though the tincture may be not only different, but opposed in strong contradistinction. The wrath of our ancestors, for example, was coloured *gules*; it broke forth in acts of open and sanguinary violence against the objects of its fury. Our malignant feelings, which must seek gratification through more indirect channels, and undermine the obstacles which they cannot openly bear down, may be rather said to be tinctured *sable*. But the deep-ruling impulse is the same in both cases; and the proud peer who can now only ruin his neighbour according to law, by protracted suits, is the genuine descendant of the baron who wrapped the castle of his competitor in flames, and knocked him on the head as he endeavoured to escape from the conflagration. It is from the great book of Nature, the same through a thousand editions, whether of black-letter, or wire-wove and hot-pressed, that I have venturously essayed to read a chapter to the public. Some favourable opportunities of contrast have been afforded me by the state of society in the northern part of the island at the period of my history, and may serve at once to vary and to illustrate the moral lessons which I would willingly consider as the most important part of my plan; although I am sensible how short these will fall of their aim if I shall be found unable to mix them with amusement,—a task not quite so easy in this critical generation as it was "Sixty Years since."

FROM "EMMA; A NOVEL"
(*Quarterly Review*, October, 1815)

There are some vices in civilized society so common that they are hardly acknowledged as stains upon the moral character, the propensity to which is nevertheless carefully concealed, even by those who most frequently give way to them; since no man of pleasure would willingly assume the gross epithet of a debauchee or a drunkard. One would almost think that novel-reading fell under this class of frailties, since among the crowds who read little else, it is not common to find an individual of hardihood sufficient to avow his taste for these frivolous studies. A novel, therefore, is frequently "bread eaten in secret"; and it is not upon Lydia Languish's toilet alone that Tom Jones and Peregrine Pickle are to be found ambushed behind works of a more grave and instructive character. And hence it has happened, that in no branch of composition, not even in poetry itself, have so many writers, and of such varied talents, exerted their powers. It may perhaps be added, that although the composition of these works admits of being exalted and decorated by the higher exertions of genius; yet such is the universal charm of narrative, that the worst novel ever written will find some gentle reader content to yawn over it, rather than to open the page of the historian, moralist, or poet. We have heard, indeed, of one work of fiction so unutterably stupid, that the proprietor, diverted by the rarity of the incident, offered the book, which consisted of two volumes in duodecimo, handsomely bound, to any person who would declare, upon his honour, that he had read the whole from beginning to end. But although this offer was made to the passengers on board an Indiaman, during a tedious outward-bound voyage, the 'Memoirs of Clegg the Clergyman,' (such was the title of this unhappy composition,) completely baffled the most dull and determined student on board, and bid fair for an exception to the general rule above-mentioned,—when the love of glory prevailed with the boatswain, a man of strong and solid parts, to hazard the attempt, and he actually conquered and carried off the prize!

The judicious reader will see at once that we have been pleading our own cause while stating the universal practice, and preparing him for a display of more general acquaintance with this fascinating department of literature, than at first sight may seem consistent with the graver studies to which we are compelled by duty: but in truth, when we consider how many hours of languor and anxiety, of deserted age and solitary celibacy, of pain even and poverty, are beguiled by the perusal of these light volumes, we cannot austerely condemn the source from which is drawn the alleviation of such a portion of human misery, or consider the regulation of this department as beneath the sober consideration of the critic.

If such apologies may be admitted in judging the labours of ordinary novelists, it becomes doubly the duty of the critic to treat with kindness as well as candour works which, like this before us, proclaim a knowledge of the human heart, with the power and resolution to bring that knowledge to the service of honour and virtue. The author is already known to the public by the two novels announced in her title-page, and both, the last especially, attracted, with justice, an attention from the public far superior to what is granted to the ephemeral productions which supply the regular demand of watering-places and circulating libraries. They belong to a class of fictions which has arisen almost in our own times, and which draws the characters and incidents introduced more immediately from the current of ordinary life than was permitted by the former rules of the novel.

In its first appearance, the novel was the legitimate child of the romance; and though the manners and general turn of the composition were altered so as to suit modern times, the author remained fettered by many peculiarities derived from the original style of romantic fiction. These may be chiefly traced in the conduct of the narrative, and the tone of sentiment attributed to the fictitious personages. On the first point, although

> The talisman and magic wand were broke,
> Knights, dwarfs, and genii vanish'd into smoke,

still the reader expected to peruse a course of adventures of a nature more interesting and extraordinary than those which occur in his own life, or that of his next-door neighbours. The hero no longer defeated armies by his single sword, clove giants to the chine, or gained kingdoms. But he was expected to go through perils by sea and land, to be steeped in poverty, to be tried by temptation, to be exposed to the alternate vicissitudes of adversity and prosperity, and his life was a troubled scene of suffering and achievement. Few novelists, indeed, adventured to deny to the hero his final hour of tranquillity and happiness, though it was the prevailing fashion never to relieve him out of his last and most dreadful distress until the finishing chapters of his history; so that although his prosperity in the record of his life was short, we were bound to believe it was long and uninterrupted when the author had done with him. The heroine was usually condemned to equal hardships and hazards. She was regularly exposed to being forcibly carried off like a Sabine virgin by some frantic admirer. And even if she escaped the terrors of masked ruffians, an insidious ravisher, a cloak wrapped forcibly around her head, and a coach with the blinds up driving she could not conjecture whither, she had still her share of wandering, of poverty, of obloquy, of seclusion, and of imprisonment, and was frequently extended upon a bed of sickness, and reduced to her last shilling before the author condescended to shield her from persecution. In all these dread contingencies the mind of the reader was expected to sympathize, since by incidents so much beyond the bounds of his ordinary experience, his wonder and interest ought at once to be excited. But gradually he became familiar with the land of fiction, the adventures of which he assimilated not with those of real life, but with each other. Let the distress of the hero or heroine be ever so great, the reader reposed an imperturbable confidence in the talents of the author, who, as he had plunged them into distress, would in his own good time, and when things, as Tony Lumkin says, were in a concatenation accordingly, bring his favourites out of all their troubles. Mr. Crabbe has expressed his own and our feelings excellently on this subject.

> For should we grant these beauties all endure
> Severest pangs, they've still the speediest cure;
> Before one charm be wither'd from the face,
> Except the bloom which shall again have place,
> In wedlock ends each wish, in triumph all disgrace.
> And life to come, we fairly may suppose,
> One light bright contrast to these wild dark woes.[3]

In short, the author of novels was, in former times, expected to tread pretty much in the limits between the concentric circles of probability and possibility; and as he was not permitted to transgress the latter, his narrative, to make amends, almost always went beyond the bounds of the former. Now, although it may be urged that the vicissitudes of human life have occasionally led an individual through as many scenes of singular fortune as are represented in the most extravagant of these fictions, still the causes and personages acting on these changes have varied with the progress of the adventurer's fortune, and do not present that combined plot, (the object of every skilful novelist,) in which all the more interesting individuals of the dramatis personæ have their appropriate share in the action and in bringing about the catastrophe. Here, even more than in its various and violent changes of fortune, rests the improbability of the novel. The life of man rolls forth like a stream from the fountain, or it spreads out into tranquillity like a placid or stagnant lake. In the latter case, the individual grows old among the characters with whom he was born, and is contemporary,— shares precisely the sort of weal and woe to which his birth destined him, —moves in the same circle,—and, allowing for the change of seasons, is influenced by, and influences the same class of persons by which he was originally surrounded. The man of mark and of adventure, on the contrary, resembles, in the course of his life, the river whose mid-current and discharge into the ocean are widely removed from each other, as well as from the

---

[3] George Crabbe, *The Borough*, Letter XX: Ellen Orford, ll. 113–19.

rocks and wild flowers which its fountains first reflected; violent changes of time, of place, and of circumstances, hurry him forward from one scene to another, and his adventures will usually be found only connected with each other because they have happened to the same individual. Such a history resembles an ingenious, fictitious narrative, exactly in the degree in which an old dramatic chronicle of the life and death of some distinguished character, where all the various agents appear and disappear as in the page of history, approaches a regular drama, in which every person introduced plays an appropriate part, and every point of the action tends to one common catastrophe.

We return to the second broad line of distinction between the novel, as formerly composed, and real life,—the difference, namely, of the sentiments. The novelist professed to give an imitation of nature, but it was, as the French say, *la belle nature*. Human beings, indeed, were presented, but in the most sentimental mood, and with minds purified by a sensibility which often verged on extravagance. In the serious class of novels, the hero was usually

> "A knight of love, who never broke a vow."[4]

And although, in those of a more humorous cast, he was permitted a license, borrowed either from real life or from the libertinism of the drama, still a distinction was demanded even from Peregrine Pickle, or Tom Jones; and the hero, in every folly of which he might be guilty, was studiously vindicated from the charge of infidelity of the heart. The heroine was, of course, still more immaculate; and to have conferred her affections upon any other than the lover to whom the reader had destined her from their first meeting, would have been a crime against sentiment which no author, of moderate prudence, would have hazarded, under the old *régime*.

Here, therefore, we have two essential and important circumstances, in which the earlier novels differed from those now in fashion, and were more nearly assimilated to the old romances. And there can be no doubt that, by the studied involution and extrication of the story, by the combination of incidents new, striking and wonderful beyond the course of ordinary life, the former authors opened that obvious and strong sense of interest which arises from curiosity; as by the pure, elevated, and romantic cast of the sentiment, they conciliated those better propensities of our nature which loves to contemplate the picture of virtue, even when confessedly unable to imitate its excellences.

But strong and powerful as these sources of emotion and interest may be, they are, like all others, capable of being exhausted by habit. The imitators who rushed in crowds upon each path in which the great masters of the art

---

4 Dryden's version of the anonymous "The Flower and the Leaf" includes the lines:
But those who wear the Woodbine on their Brow
Were Knights of Love, who never broke their Vow:
—ll. 521–22.

had successively led the way, produced upon the public mind the usual effect of satiety. The first writer of a new class is, as it were, placed on a pinnacle of excellence, to which, at the earliest glance of a surprized admirer, his ascent seems little less than miraculous. Time and imitation speedily diminish the wonder, and each successive attempt establishes a kind of progressive scale of ascent between the lately deified author, and the reader, who had deemed his excellence inaccessible. The stupidity, the mediocrity, the merit of his imitators, are alike fatal to the first inventor, by showing how possible it is to exaggerate his faults and to come within a certain point of his beauties.

Materials also (and the man of genius as well as his wretched imitator must work with the same) become stale and familiar. Social life, in our civilized days, affords few instances capable of being painted in the strong dark colours which excite surprize and horror; and robbers, smugglers, bailiffs, caverns, dungeons, and mad-houses, have been all introduced until they ceased to interest. And thus in the novel, as in every style of composition which appeals to the public taste, the more rich and easily worked mines being exhausted, the adventurous author must, if he is desirous of success, have recourse to those which were disdained by his predecessors as unproductive, or avoided as only capable of being turned to profit by great skill and labour.

Accordingly a style of novel has arisen, within the last fifteen or twenty years, differing from the former in the points upon which the interest hinges; neither alarming our credulity nor amusing our imagination by wild variety of incident, or by those pictures of romantic affection and sensibility, which were formerly as certain attributes of fictitious characters as they are of rare occurrence among those who actually live and die. The substitute for these excitements, which had lost much of their poignancy by the repeated and injudicious use of them, was the art of copying from nature as she really exists in the common walks of life, and presenting to the reader, instead of the splendid scenes of an imaginary world, a correct and striking representation of that which is daily taking place around him.

In adventuring upon this task, the author makes obvious sacrifices, and encounters peculiar difficulty. He who paints from *le beau idéal*, if his scenes and sentiments are striking and interesting, is in a great measure exempted from the difficult task of reconciling them with the ordinary probabilities of life: but he who paints a scene of common occurrence, places his composition within that extensive range of criticism which general experience offers to every reader. The resemblance of a statue of Hercules we must take on the artist's judgment; but every one can criticize that which is presented as the portrait of a friend, or neighbour. Something more than a mere sign-post likeness is also demanded. The portrait must have spirit and character, as well as resemblance; and being deprived of all that, according to Bayes, goes "to elevate and surprize," it must make amends by displaying depth of knowledge and dexterity of execution. We, therefore, bestow no mean compliment upon the author of Emma, when we say that, keeping close to common incidents, and to such characters as occupy the ordinary walks of life, she has produced sketches of such spirit and originality, that we never miss the excitation which depends upon a narrative of uncommon events, arising from the consideration of minds, manners, and sentiments, greatly above our own. In this class she stands almost alone; for the scenes of Miss Edgeworth are laid in higher life, varied by more romantic incident, and by her remarkable power of embodying and illustrating national character. But the author of Emma confines herself chiefly to the middling classes of society; her most distinguished characters do not rise greatly above well-bred country gentlemen and ladies; and those which are sketched with most originality and precision, belong to a class rather below that standard. The narrative of all her novels is composed of such common occurrences as may have fallen under the observation of most folks; and her dramatis personæ conduct themselves upon the motives and principles which the readers may recognize as ruling their own and that of most of their acquaintances. The kind of moral, also, which these novels inculcate, applies equally to the paths of common life, as will best appear from a short notice of the author's former works, with a more full abstract of that which we at present have under consideration. . . .

THE FORTUNES OF NIGEL
(1822)

from Introductory Epistle

CAPTAIN CLUTTERBUCK TO THE REVEREND DR. DRYASDUST.

DEAR SIR,

I readily accept of, and reply to the civilities with which you have been pleased to honour me in your obliging letter, and entirely agree with your quotation, of "*Quam bonum et quam jucundum!*"[5] We may indeed esteem ourselves as come of the same family, or, according to our country proverb, as being all one man's bairns; and there needed no apology on your part,

---

[5] "*Quam bonum et quam jucundum!*" : How good and how pleasant!

reverend and dear sir, for demanding of me any information which I may be able to supply respecting the subject of your curiosity. The interview which you allude to took place in the course of last winter, and is so deeply imprinted on my recollection, that it requires no effort to collect all its most minute details.

You are aware that the share which I had in introducing the Romance, called THE MONASTERY, to public notice, has given me a sort of character in the literature of our Scottish metropolis. I no longer stand in the outer shop of our bibliopolists, bargaining for the objects of my curiosity with an unrespective shop-lad, hustled among boys who come to buy Corderies[6] and copy-books, and servant-girls cheapening a pennyworth of paper, but am cordially welcomed by the bibliopolist himself, with, "Pray, walk into the back-shop, Captain. Boy, get a chair for Captain Clutterbuck. There is the newspaper, Captain—today's paper"; or, "Here is the last new work—there is a folder, make free with the leaves"; or, "Put it in your pocket and carry it home"; or, "We will make a bookseller of you, sir, you shall have it at trade price." Or, perhaps, if it is the worthy trader's own publication, his liberality may even extend itself to—"Never mind booking such a trifle to *you*, sir—it is an over-copy. Pray, mention the work to your reading friends." I say nothing of the snug well-selected literary party arranged round a turbot, leg of five-year-old mutton, or some such gear, or of the circulation of a quiet bottle of Robert Cockburn's choicest black—nay, perhaps, of his best blue, to quicken our talk about old books, or our plans for new ones. All these are comforts reserved to such as are freemen of the corporation of letters, and I have the advantage of enjoying them in perfection.

But all things change under the sun; and it is with no ordinary feelings of regret, that, in my annual visits to the metropolis, I now miss the social and warm-hearted welcome of the quick-witted and kindly friend who first introduced me to the public; who had more original wit than would have set up a dozen of professed sayers of good things, and more racy humour than would have made the fortune of as many more. To this great deprivation has been added, I trust for a time only, the loss of another bibliopolical friend, whose vigorous intellect, and liberal ideas, have not only rendered his native country the mart of her own literature, but established there a Court of Letters, which must command respect, even from those most inclined to dissent from many of its canons. The effect of these changes, operated in a great measure by the strong sense and sagacious calculations of an individual, who knew how to avail himself, to an unhoped-for extent, of the various kinds of talent which his country produced, will probably appear more clearly to the generation which shall follow the present.

I entered the shop at the Cross, to enquire after the health of my worthy friend, and learned with satisfaction, that his residence in the south had

[6] Corderies: A Latin primer, called *The Colloquies of Corderius*, by Mathurin Cordier (1479-1564), and widely used in schools, was called a Cordery.

abated the rigour of the symptoms of his disorder. Availing myself, then, of the privileges to which I have alluded, I strolled onward in that labyrinth of small dark rooms, or *crypts*, to speak our own antiquarian language, which form the extensive back-settlements of that celebrated publishing-house. Yet, as I proceeded from one obscure recess to another, filled, some of them with old volumes, some with such as, from the equality of their rank on the shelves, I suspected to be the less saleable modern books of the concern, I could not help feeling a holy horror creep upon me, when I thought of the risk of intruding on some ecstatic bard giving vent to his poetical fury; or, it might be, on the yet more formidable privacy of a band of critics, in the act of worrying the game which they had just run down. In such a supposed case, I felt by anticipation the horrors of the Highland seers, whom their gift of deuteroscopy compels to witness things unmeet for mortal eye; and who, to use the expression of Collins,

> heartless, oft, like moody madness, stare
> To see the phantom train their secret work prepare.[7]

Still, however, the irresistible impulse of an undefined curiosity drove me on through this succession of darksome chambers, till, like the jeweller of Delhi in the house of the magician Bennaskar, I at length reached a vaulted room, dedicated to secrecy and silence, and beheld, seated by a lamp, and employed in reading a blotted *revise*,[8] the person, or perhaps I should rather say the Eidolon, or representative Vision, of the AUTHOR OF WAVERLEY. You will not be surprised at the filial instinct which enabled me at once to acknowledge the features borne by this venerable apparition, and that I at once bended the knee, with the classical salutation of, *Salve, magne parens!*[9] The vision, however, cut me short, by pointing to a seat, intimating at the same time, that my presence was not unexpected, and that he had something to say to me.

I sat down with humble obedience, and endeavoured to note the features of him with whom I now found myself so unexpectedly in society. But on this point I can give your reverence no satisfaction; for, besides the obscurity of the apartment, and the fluttered state of my own nerves, I seemed to myself overwhelmed by a sense of filial awe, which prevented my noting and recording what it is probable the personage before me might most desire to have concealed. Indeed, his figure was so closely veiled and wimpled, either with a mantle, morning-gown, or some such loose garb, that the verses of Spenser might well have been applied—

---

[7] William Collins, "An Ode on the Popular Superstitions of the Highlands of Scotland," ll. 68–69.

[8] *revise:* "The uninitiated must be informed, that a second proof-sheet is so called." [Scott]

[9] *Salve, magne parens!:* Hail, honored father; from *salve, magna parens:* Hail, honored mother—Virgil, *Georgics* 2. 173.

> Yet, certes, by her face and physnomy,
> Whether she man or woman only were,
> That could not any creature well descry.[10]

I must, however, go on as I have begun, to apply the masculine gender; for, notwithstanding very ingenious reasons, and indeed something like positive evidence, have been offered to prove the Author of Waverley to be two ladies of talent, I must abide by the general opinion, that he is of the rougher sex. There are in his writings too many things

> Quæ maribus sola tribuuntur,[11]

to permit me to entertain any doubt on that subject. I will proceed, in the manner of dialogue, to repeat as nearly as I can what passed betwixt us, only observing, that in the course of the conversation my timidity imperceptibly gave way under the familiarity of his address; and that, in the concluding part of our dialogue, I perhaps argued with fully as much confidence as was beseeming.

Author of Waverley. I was willing to see you, Captain Clutterbuck, being the person of my family whom I have most regard for, since the death of Jedediah Cleishbotham; and I am afraid I may have done you some wrong, in assigning to you the Monastery as a portion of my effects. I have some thoughts of making it up to you, by naming you godfather to this yet unborn babe—(he indicated the proof-sheet with his finger)—But first, touching The Monastery—How says the world—you are abroad and can learn?

Captain Clutterbuck. Hem! hem!—The enquiry is delicate—I have not heard any complaints from the Publishers.

Author. That is the principal matter; but yet an indifferent work is sometimes towed on by those which have left harbour before it, with the breeze in their poop.—What say the Critics?

Captain. There is a general—feeling—that the White Lady is no favourite.

Author. I think she is a failure myself; but rather in execution than conception. Could I have evoked an *esprit follet,*[12] at the same time fantastic and interesting, capricious and kind; a sort of wildfire of the elements, bound by no fixed laws, or motives of action; faithful and fond, yet teazing and uncertain——

Captain. If you will pardon the interruption, sir, I think you are describing a pretty woman.

Author. On my word, I believe I am. I must invest my elementary spirits with a little human flesh and blood—they are too fine-drawn for the present taste of the public.

---

[10] Spenser, *The Faerie Queene* 7. 7. 5.
[11] *Quæ maribus sola tribuuntur:* which are granted to men alone.
[12] *esprit follet:* a sprite, hobgoblin.

Captain.   They object, too, that the object of your Nixie ought to have been more uniformly noble—Her ducking the priest was no Naiad-like amusement.

Author.   Ah! they ought to allow for the capriccios of what is, after all, but a better sort of goblin. The bath into which Ariel, the most delicate creation of Shakspeare's imagination, seduces our jolly friend Trinculo, was not of amber or rose-water. But no one shall find me rowing against the stream. I care not who knows it—I write for general amusement; and, though I never will aim at popularity by what I think unworthy means, I will not, on the other hand, be pertinacious in the defence of my own errors against the voice of the public.

Captain.   You abandon, then, in the present work—(looking, in my turn, towards the proof-sheet)—the mystic, and the magical, and the whole system of signs, wonders, and omens? There are no dreams, or presages, or obscure allusions to future events?

Author.   Not a Cock-lane scratch, my son—not one bounce on the drum of Tedworth—not so much as the poor tick of a solitary death-watch in the wainscot. All is clear and above board—a Scots metaphysician might believe every word of it.

Captain.   And the story is, I hope, natural and probable; commencing strikingly, proceeding naturally, ending happily—like the course of a famed river, which gushes from the mouth of some obscure and romantic grotto—then gliding on, never pausing, never precipitating its course, visiting, as it were, by natural instinct, whatever worthy subjects of interest are presented by the country through which it passes—widening and deepening in interest as it flows on; and at length arriving at the final catastrophe as at some mighty haven, where ships of all kinds strike sail and yard?

Author.   Hey! hey! what the deuce is all this? Why, 'tis Ercles' vein, and it would require someone much more like Hercules than I, to produce a story which should gush, and glide, and never pause, and visit, and widen, and deepen, and all the rest on't. I should be chin-deep in the grave, man, before I had done with my task; and, in the meanwhile, all the quirks and quiddities which I might have devised for my reader's amusement, would lie rotting in my gizzard, like Sancho's suppressed witticisms, when he was under his master's displeasure.—There never was a novel written on this plan while the world stood.

Captain.   Pardon me—Tom Jones.

Author.   True, and perhaps Amelia also. Fielding had high notions of the dignity of an art which he may be considered as having founded. He challenges a comparison between the Novel and the Epic. Smollett, Le Sage, and others, emancipating themselves from the strictness of the rules he has laid down, have written rather a history of the miscellaneous adventures which befall an individual in the course of life, than the plot of a regular and connected epopeia, where every step brings us a point nearer to the final catastrophe. These great masters have been satisfied if they amused the reader upon the road; though the conclusion only arrived because the tale must have an end—just as the traveller alights at the inn, because it is evening.

Captain. A very commodious mode of travelling, for the author at least. In short, sir, you are of opinion with Bayes—"What the devil does the plot signify, except to bring in fine things?"

Author. Grant that I were so, and that I should write with sense and spirit a few scenes unlaboured and loosely put together, but which had sufficient interest in them to amuse in one corner the pain of body; in another, to relieve anxiety of mind; in a third place, to unwrinkle a brow bent with the furrows of daily toil; in another, to fill the place of bad thoughts, or to suggest better; in yet another, to induce an idler to study the history of his country; in all, save where the perusal interrupted the discharge of serious duties, to furnish harmless amusement,—might not the author of such a work, however inartificially executed, plead for his errors and negligences the excuse of the slave, who, about to be punished for having spread the false report of a victory, saved himself by exclaiming—"Am I to blame, O Athenians, who have given you one happy day?"

.   .   .   .

Captain. Respect to yourself, then, ought to teach caution.

Author. Ay, if caution could augment the chance of my success. But, to confess to you the truth, the works and passages in which I have succeeded, have uniformly been written with the greatest rapidity; and when I have seen some of these placed in opposition with others, and commended as more highly finished, I could appeal to pen and standish, that the parts in which I have come feebly off, were by much the more laboured. Besides, I doubt the beneficial effect of too much delay, both on account of the author and the public. A man should strike while the iron is hot, and hoist sail while the wind is fair. If a successful author keep not the stage, another instantly takes his ground. If a writer lie by for ten years ere he produces a second work, he is superseded by others; or, if the age is so poor of genius that this does not happen, his own reputation becomes his greatest obstacle. The public will expect the new work to be ten times better than its predecessor; the author will expect it should be ten times more popular, and 'tis a hundred to ten that both are disappointed.

Captain. This may justify a certain degree of rapidity in publication, but not that which is proverbially said to be no speed. You should take time at least to arrange your story.

Author. That is a sore point with me, my son. Believe me, I have not been fool enough to neglect ordinary precautions. I have repeatedly laid down my future work to scale, divided it into volumes and chapters, and endeavoured to construct a story which I meant should evolve itself gradually and strikingly, maintain suspense, and stimulate curiosity; and which, finally, should terminate in a striking catastrophe. But I think there is a demon who seats himself on the feather of my pen when I begin to write, and leads it astray from the purpose. Characters expand under my hand; incidents are multipled; the story lingers, while the materials increase; my regular mansion turns out a Gothic anomaly, and the work is closed long before I have attained the point I proposed.

Captain. Resolution and determined forbearance might remedy that evil.

Author. Alas! my dear sir, you do not know the force of paternal affection. When I light on such a character as Bailie Jarvie, or Dalgetty, my imagination brightens, and my conception becomes clearer at every step which I take in his company, although it leads me many a weary mile away from the regular road, and forces me to leap hedge and ditch to get back into the route again. If I resist the temptation, as you advise me, my thoughts become prosy, flat, and dull; I write painfully to myself, and under a consciousness of flagging which makes me flag still more; the sunshine with which fancy had invested the incidents, departs from them, and leaves everything dull and gloomy. I am no more the same author I was in my better mood, than the dog in a wheel, condemned to go round and round for hours, is like the same dog merrily chasing his own tail, and gambolling in all the frolic of unrestrained freedom. In short, sir, on such occasions, I think I am bewitched.

.   .   .   .

Captain. You are determined to proceed then in your own system? Are you aware that an unworthy motive may be assigned for this rapid succession of publication? You will be supposed to work merely for the lucre of gain.

Author. Supposing that I did permit the great advantages which must be derived from success in literature, to join with other motives in inducing me to come more frequently before the public,—that emolument is the voluntary tax which the public pays for a certain species of literary amusement—it is extorted from no one, and paid, I presume, by those only who can afford it, and who receive gratification in proportion to the expense. If the capital sum which these volumes have put into circulation be a very large one, has it contributed to my indulgences only? or can I not say to hundreds, from honest Duncan, the paper-manufacturer, to the most snivelling of the printer's devils, "Didst thou not share? Hadst thou not fifteen pence?" I profess I think our Modern Athens much obliged to me for having established such an extensive manufacture; and when universal suffrage comes in fashion, I intend to stand for a seat in the House on the interest of all the unwashed artificers connected with literature.

Captain. This would be called the language of a calico-manufacturer.

Author. Cant again, my dear son—there is lime in this sack, too— nothing but sophistication in this world! I do say it, in spite of Adam Smith and his followers, that a successful author is a productive labourer, and that his works constitute as effectual a part of the public wealth, as that which is created by any other manufacture. If a new commodity, having an actually intrinsic and commercial value, be the result of the operation, why are the author's bales of books to be esteemed a less profitable part of the public stock than the goods of any other manufacturer? I speak with reference to the diffusion of the wealth arising to the public, and the degree of industry which even such a trifling work as the present must stimulate and reward, before the volumes leave the publisher's shop. Without me it could not exist, and to this extent I am a benefactor to the country. As for my own emolument, it is won by my toil, and I account myself answerable to Heaven only for the mode in which I expend it. The candid may hope it is not all dedicated to selfish purposes; and, without much pretensions to merit in him who disburses it, a part may "wander, heaven-directed, to the poor."

Captain.   Yet it is generally held base to write from the mere motives of gain.

Author.   It would be base to do so exclusively, or even to make it a principal motive for literary exertion. Nay, I will venture to say, that no work of imagination, proceeding from the mere consideration of a certain sum of copy-money, ever did, or ever will, succeed. So the lawyer who pleads, the soldier who fights, the physician who prescribes, the clergyman—if such there be—who preaches, without any zeal for his profession, or without any sense of its dignity, and merely on account of the fee, pay, or stipend, degrade themselves to the rank of sordid mechanics. Accordingly, in the case of two of the learned faculties at least, their services are considered as unappreciable, and are acknowledged, not by any exact estimate of the services rendered, but by a *honorarium*, or voluntary acknowledgment. But let a client or patient make the experiment of omitting this little ceremony of the *honorarium*, which is *censé*[13] to be a thing entirely out of consideration between them, and mark how the learned gentleman will look upon his case. Cant set apart, it is the same thing with literary emolument. No man of sense, in any rank of life, is, or ought to be, above accepting a just recompense for his time, and a reasonable share of the capital which owes its very existence to his exertions. When Czar Peter wrought in the trenches, he took the pay of a common soldier; and nobles, statesmen, and divines, the most distinguished of their time, have not scorned to square accounts with their bookseller.

Captain.   (*Sings.*)

> Oh, if it were a mean thing,
> The gentles would not use it;
> And if it were ungodly,
> The clergy would refuse it.[14]

---

[13] *censé:* reputed.

[14] A variant of lines of a song entitled "The Fryer and the Nun," collected in *Wit and Mirth: or Pills to Purge Melancholy,* ed. Thomas D'Urfey (New York, 1959; facsimile reproduction of the 1876 reprint of the original edition of 1719–20), III, 176–78. Two stanzas read

Author. You say well. But no man of honour, genius, or spirit, would make the mere love of gain, the chief, far less the only, purpose of his labours. For myself, I am not displeased to find the game a winning one; yet while I pleased the public, I should probably continue it merely for the pleasure of playing; for I have felt as strongly as most folks that love of composition, which is perhaps the strongest of all instincts, driving the author to the pen, the painter to the pallet, often without either the chance of fame or the prospect of reward. Perhaps I have said too much of this. I might, perhaps, with as much truth as most people, exculpate myself from the charge of being either of a greedy or mercenary disposition; but I am not, therefore, hypocrite enough to disclaim the ordinary motives, on account of which the whole world around me is toiling unremittingly, to the sacrifice of ease, comfort, health, and life. I do not affect the disinterestedness of that ingenious association of gentlemen mentioned by Goldsmith, who sold their magazine for sixpence a-piece, merely for their own amusement.

Captain. I have but one thing more to hint—The world say you will run yourself out.

Author. The world say true; and what then? When they dance no longer, I will no longer pipe; and I shall not want flappers enough to remind me of the apoplexy.

.   .   .   .

I leave it to you to form your own opinion concerning the import of this dialogue, and I cannot but believe I shall meet the wishes of our common parent in prefixing this letter to the work which it concerns.

I am, reverend and dear Sir,
Very sincerely and affectionately

Yours, &c. &c.
CUTHBERT CLUTTERBUCK.

Kennaquhair,
1st April, 1822.

---

as follows:

> If it were Unlawful,
>   Then Lawyers were to blame:
> And if it were Ungodly,
>   To Priests it were a shame:
> For they no doubt do use it,
>   Tho' it a Vice they call;
> Yet Priests and Lawyers both will play
>   *At Up-tails all.* [Stanza 4]
> If it were a costly thing,
>   Then Beggars could not buy it;
> And if it were a Loathsom thing,
>   Then Genteels would defie it:
> But it is a sweet thing,
>   And pleasing unto all;
> There is not one but that will play
>   *At Up-tails all.* [Stanza 7 and last]

7

ROBERT P. WARD

(1765–1846)

Robert Ward had had a successful career as a lawyer and statesman when he turned to fiction writing at the age of sixty. His inclination toward politics culminated in a seat in the House of Commons in 1802, when he was of service to Pitt's new administration. Various other posts followed, including a seat on the admiralty board until 1811 and the position of clerk of the ordnance until 1823. In the latter situation he wrote numerous surveys and reports; as a lawyer he wrote extensively on legal matters, e.g., *An Inquiry into the Foundation and History of the Law of Nations in Europe . . .* (1795). Many short essays resulted from his travels, and he is sometimes criticized as more of an essayist than a novelist in manner.

Ward's close knowledge of the political and fashionable scene was manifested in the authenticity of his first novel, *Tremaine: or the Man of Refinement* (1825). A product of his leisure time over a two-year period, the anonymously published novel went through several editions. Although tiresome to a modern reader, the endless discussions of ethical and religious problems seem to have had a contemporary attraction, and they added an intellectual dimension to the silver-fork school of fiction. Witty language and character analysis are among Ward's characteristics.

When Ward capitalized on his success with *De Vere, or the Man of Independence* (1827), public opinion immediately identified the main character, an ambitious idealist, with George Canning, then about to become prime minister. Although this novel, too, was favorably received, Canning himself is reported to have said that Ward's law books were as pleasant as his novels, and his novels as dull as his law books. Declaring in his preface to *De Vere* that "no particular person is meant to be pourtrayed by any of the Dramatis Personae," Ward went on to make an interesting comparison between the novel and the drama.

PREFACE

DE VERE
OR THE MAN OF INDEPENDENCE
(1827)

That species of literary composition called the Novel has been carried to so consummate a pitch of perfection during the last twenty or thirty years, that, in its power of delineating, exciting, or soothing the human heart, it almost rivals the Drama itself. True, the Novel must ever want that great advantage of the Drama, which the name of the latter implies,—that of *representing by action*; and it is also inferior, inasmuch as it never can soar into poetry. This, however, cannot be done even by Rhetoric, with all its flowers; and both this species of writing, and Rhetoric itself, must always be content to be prose. And yet, as the Drama charms us in the closet without being acted, and also without being always poetry, there is no reason, *à priori*, why a Novel, founded on human nature, and not confined to *mere pictures* of things, should not assume as high a tone, and possess as much influence over us, as any *unacted* dramatic prose composition. As to representation, we are often more charmed with Shakspeare, in our libraries, than even upon the stage; and the plays of Miss Baillie, on the passions, speak to our minds as forcibly, and as beautifully, as if they were presented to the eye and ear by the best acting of Kemble or Siddons.

We allow, however, that the Novel being confined to prose, loses not only the elevation of poetry, but that inexpressible charm which arises from beautiful, measured, and lofty language. The subjects of the Novel, too, being for the most part busied with ordinary life, cannot entirely compare with the higher subjects of the Drama. In the Novel, whatever may have been done for it by exalted genius, we can scarcely expect to witness

> "Gorgeous Tragedy,
> In scepter'd pall, come sweeping by;"[1]

though the Author of Waverley has made even this almost doubtful.

---

[1] Sometime let gorgeous Tragedy
In sceptred pall come sweeping by,"
—Milton, "Il Penseroso," ll. 97–98.

A greater authority, indeed, than ours, carries its sentiments in favour of the Novel, as compared with the Drama, much farther than we do; for, in point of limit, and, as it were, in the abstract, it gives the preference to the Novel. "*There is no element* of dramatic composition," (says the Quarterly Review) "which may not be successfully employed in the Romantic; but the Drama being essentially a much more limited representation of life than the Romance, many sources of interest are open to the latter, from which the former is completely debarred." The writer adds, that "it is altogether out of the question *to limit in any manner whatever*, the dominion of the sister art," meaning novel-writing. Finally, he says, that "as to materials, the empire of Romance *includes* that of the Drama, and includes therein perhaps its finest province."[2]

These sentiments, as they regard the *subjects* of Romance, are certainly correct. But inasmuch as they do not even allude to the great if not the only reason for the superiority of dramatic composition, (distinct from its capability of representation,)—namely, that its vehicle is, or may be, Poetry,—they are abstractedly perhaps not quite so just as they were intended to be. With this exception, however, the argument of the masterly article in the Review is unanswerable.

Take Poetry from the Drama, and, from its limited range, it becomes instantly inferior to Romance; for even in point of language, its superiority is lost. To this latter fact, our few tragedies in prose bear testimony. In regard to Comedy, too, even though sustained by dialogue and visible action, there is no reason (except as drawn from the merits of the respective writers) why it should bear the palm from the narrative mode of composition.

We have mentioned the Author of Waverley. What dramatist, except Shakspeare, surpasses him? Who else can even approach him in his delineations of character; his knowledge of the human heart and mind; the beauty, variety, and magnificence of his descriptions? Waverley, Old Mortality, Kenilworth, Ivanhoe, Quentin Durward, Rob Roy, and the Heart of Mid-Lothian, produce all the effect of perfect Dramas, except that they are in prose. The first (but for this exception) might rank even as an epic poem. Yet all these are Novels.

As to knowledge of mankind, nothing forbids (on the contrary, every-thing requires) that the novelist should be at least as consummate an observer of the passions as the writer of dramatic poetry. There is, perhaps, more knowledge of the heart, and more acuteness of observation in Gil Blas, than in all the plays of all nations put together, save only those of Shakspeare. If, therefore, "the proper study of mankind is man," the Novel should never have lost its relative consequence in comparison with the Drama. It did lose it, however, after Fielding and Richardson were no more; and, with the exception of the Vicar of Wakefield, some few other elegant compositions, and

---

[2] "See *Quarterly Review* for Sept. 1826, p. 364—'Lives of the Novelists.' " [Ward]

the Novels of Smollett, (which are broad satires, rather than pictures of mankind,) this species of writing dwindled into trash, in the hands of feeble men or of mere fanciful women.

For the honour of the sex, however, it was Woman that restored the Novel to its usefulness, and therefore to its consequence. Witness Madame D'Arblay, who led the way; and Miss Edgeworth, who pursued it with an effect, an attraction, and a success which all admit. The last, indeed, showed that the sunken and despised Novel, might, when restored to its vigour, be converted even into an instrument of a nation's good. If the love, the respect, and often the admiration which their English fellow-subjects now feel for them, are of any value to the Irish, in exchange for the cold and most unjust disparagement with which the Irish character was once treated here, I will venture to hazard an opinion, that to this change Miss Edgeworth has very much contributed. To both nations, therefore, she may be considered as an amiable benefactress.

In all these respects, then, the descriptions of character (by which I do not mean mere passing manners), to be found in such novelists as I have mentioned, may be not unworthy the moral philosopher himself; and if History is, as it has been called, Philosophy teaching by examples, so also may be the Romance, if properly conducted. The difference, indeed, appears at first sight to be a marked one; for History is busy with real, Romance with imaginary events. But the difference is only seeming; for, if the imaginary events are (what they ought to be) perfectly consonant with nature, the lesson is the same. Who inquires whether the workings of Macbeth's mind on the stage—his half resolves—his fear and remorse, and final surrender of himself to wickedness,—who inquires whether these are true or false in regard to the Macbeth of history? Most probably they were all imaginary, and only *conceived* in that wonderful brain which had observed them elsewhere.

All this eulogy, however, of the species of writing we are upon, only increases the difficulty which the Author has to encounter, in introducing his own work to the public: for, in proportion as the line of writing he has chosen, is important, his responsibility for pursuing it must be perilous; and it would, perhaps, have been better policy not to have extolled an art, in which, on that very account, he may only be found the more wanting. Nevertheless, his respect for many professors of it is so great that he could not resist this tribute to it, considering how much it formerly was undervalued.

With regard to the following work, as it has taken Ambition for its subject, one would think little would be necessary to explain if farther. We all of us know this to be one of the great passions, if not the greatest passion of the human mind. It has, at least, been the cause of most of the great crimes of mankind; and most materially, therefore, is it interwoven with the happiness and the actions of men. He, indeed, is either more or less than man, who has not at one time or other, felt its power. It, therefore, generally shows itself by producing great situations, ending in great events.

And yet those who expect such events and situations here—who look for the consequences of ambition, as they appeared in the prominent characters of history, such as Cæsar, or Cromwell, Wolsey, or Richelieu, Buckingham, or the Guises—will be disappointed: for the tale, though not of the present, is comparatively of modern times, and of a civilized nation; and the effect of high civilization, like that of politeness in private life, is to reduce everything as much as possible to a smooth surface and to comparative tranquillity. In times like these, there can be no very dazzling or over-powering virtues; no very atrocious crimes to record; in such times, we should in vain wish with Sallust, *"præclari facinoris famam quærere."* [3]

It follows, therefore, that the kind of ambition which is here chosen for a subject, must be totally wanting in splendour, and that the work, in point of events, can have little imposing belonging to it. Nevertheless, the human heart remains the same, under all appearances, and the study of it will ever excite our first and best interest. The less fertile, therefore, the time in great events, and the greater the refinement which manners assume, the greater may be the nicety required to unmask the heart, and unfold its operations; and thus it may become, in itself, a matter of more subtle interest. Still, where there is nothing to record but the common occurrences of a peaceable, civilized æra, there will undoubtedly be more difficulty in awakening the passions of the reader, than where his attention hangs on the grandeur of kingdoms, the fate of princes, and

"The grappling vigour and rough frown of war." [4]

The action, however, in this work, is not confined to ambition. There is another passion, (if it may be called a passion), in the pride of independence of De Vere, which challenges attention: for it bears up the hero under all his little reverses, and is the main cause of much of the action.

As to the public characters mentioned, it is a pleasure to think that the unfavourable specimens of them are drawn from what men have been, not what they are. To look into the accounts formerly given by public men of themselves, as well as of each other, makes us tremble; and we are only consoled by the conviction that such accounts are deserved no longer. Were Halifax, therefore, or Bolingbroke, Swift, Chesterfield, Doddington, and Lord Orford, and (would we were not forced to add to these!) that pattern of a high-minded gentleman, Lord Waldegrave; if these were to revive, they would look in vain among our public characters for the prototypes from which they drew their portraits. The whole Walpolian and Pelham school is at an end, and the spirit in which the present work closes, includes no

[3] *"præclari facinoris famam quærere"*: to seek the fame of a celebrated deed.
[4] Shakespeare, *King John* 3. 1. 104.

greater eulogy than may be said to be deserved by all our statesmen of later times.

But the mention of this part of the subject, brings us to topics of fearful consequence, should they be viewed and judged of by prejudice rather than candour: for the production of ministers and public men on the scene, however ideal, or removed from the passing time, or even however distant from real likeness to individual character at any time, can hardly fail to produce effects which may be made most painful to the Author's feelings. He is aware that throughout the scenes of the work, (and they are many) which are occupied with political ambition, he steps upon dangerous ground, *"Per ignes suppositos doloso cineri."* [5] He therefore desires most seriously, distinctly, and without a reserve, to declare in the outset, once and for ever, that no particular person is meant to be pourtrayed by any of the Dramatis Personæ of this work. He declares once, and for ever, that he knows no such individuals as Wentworth or Beaufort; Mowbray or Cleveland; Lord Oldcastle or Clayton.

But it may be said that certain known traits and anecdotes have been introduced, in connexion with particular characters; and that these characters, therefore, must surely be intended to represent the persons (whether alive or dead), to whom the anecdotes actually apply.

From this imputation, the Author can hardly expect to escape, when he recollects, that because the real name of Corporal Trim was stated to be James Butler, the world immediately fastened upon Sterne the design of representing the Duke of Ormond. Yet surely a real anecdote of one person may be engrafted on the history of another, without identifying the two; and to suppose the contrary, is as illogical as it may be uncharitable. A sufficiently striking illustration of this may be found in the present work, where an anecdote of the late Mr. Windham is made applicable to such a person as Clayton. Mr. Windham was, as is known, expressing his fears, that he was too downright for a public man; and Dr. Johnson, in jest, observed, "Never fear, Sir; I dare say, in time, you will make a very pretty rascal!" But Mr. Windham was all honour; Clayton, all deceit. Will, then, the application of the anecdote fix upon the author an intention of making the two characters the same?

But there is a chronology, if not directly set forth, yet at least made cognizable by anecdotes and quotations, so that the reader may fix nearly the very year when some of the events happened.

This could scarcely have been avoided; and the Author trusts to the candour of the reader, that he will not fix this upon him as a proof of things which he did not intend. All events must be in time; and if an imaginary story touch upon occurrences of a public nature, it will naturally fix its

---

[5] *"Per ignes suppositos doloso cineri"*: while over hidden fires the treacherous foot-tracks lead.

—Horace, *Odes* 2. 1. 7–8.

own chronology. But hard, indeed, would it be, that what is purely imaginary, must therefore be incrusted with a real body; and that a character (perhaps even the most opposite to that really deserved) should be allotted to any individual person. Some latitude ought surely to be allowed to an author in these respects, and he should be read only in the spirit in which he has written.

To apply this, and have done. A searcher of dates may be able to say, that the epoch of De Vere is about the time of Lord Chatham's last administration; nay, that the resignation, from illness, and the hints in respect to *former* glory, plainly show that he himself is intended.[6]

But though the last years of Lord Chatham's life may afford useful lessons to English ambition, all that the Author intended, in introducing a retiring great Minister upon the scene, was to paint generally, the intrigues which, *according to the characters in his work*, might be expected to follow such an event; not that those intrigues or characters were actually the same as in history.

In the same manner it is necessary, in the work, to introduce a Chancellor, for the purpose of a solemn judgment; and a critic might, by the help of a political index, and an attention to the anecdotes scattered up and down the book, discover, that Lord Camden was probably Chancellor at the time; but still Lord Camden was not meant, for all that.

These inconveniences, however great, are from the nature of the subject, unavoidable, while the scene is at home, and the time, from internal evidence, specified. It is, therefore, against the improper use of this specification that the Author asks leave to protest; he lays a claim which he hopes will be allowed, to be permitted to use illustrative anecdotes, or emphatic dicta, as mere general materials without being tied down to the consequences of their being specifically and incorrectly applied. Such applications might have been eluded, by laying the scene in another country, and in no specified æra; but the ambition and the persons described, would not then have been English ambition, or English persons; and though the inconveniences might be cured, the advantages would be lost. To remedy the inconvenience, and preserve the advantage, can only be accomplished through the candour of the reader, pondering the truth of these explanations.

---

[6] "Most unhappily for himself, his friends, and for the world, and to the Author's own grief, while almost in the act of writing the above, another severe illness, of another good and great person has also occurred, in a manner as unexpected as lamentable; and this illness may possibly lead to a most important resignation in the present time. It might really, therefore, require some candour, if left unexplained, to believe that what is described of the same nature, in the work, may not have been intended with particular allusions to the present day. All that can be said upon it is, that the scene in the book was finished fourteen months ago, and actually in the press, before this last most sudden as well as unhappy event could have been even contemplated." [Ward]

8

MRS. CATHERINE G. GORE

(*1799–1861*)

Although Thackeray's parody of Mrs. Gore's novels of high society in "Lords and Liveries," one of his *Novels by Eminent Hands*, dramatized what he felt to be their deficiencies, the fact that he did parody her work testifies to her popularity. Further evidence of this, if not of her talents, is the praise of her novel *Women as They Are, or The Manners of the Day* (1830) by George IV as the best bred and most amusing novel published in his recollection. A passage of dialog taken from this book, between Lady Isabella (a frivolous lady of fashion) and Lord Willersdale (the heroine's reserved middle-aged husband), indicates Mrs. Gore's awareness that although the vogue of the silver-fork novel was passing its values justified its existence.

Versatile—Mrs. Gore produced plays, poems, and music, as well as novels. In 1831 "The School for Coquettes," a five-act comedy, ran for thirty nights at the Haymarket Theatre. Prolific—she produced some seventy works in nearly two hundred volumes, as well as ten children.

After her early fiction, including *Theresa Marchmont, or the Maid of Honour* (1824) and *Hungarian Tales* (1829), she became a reliable source of supply of the novel of fashionable life for the circulating libraries. Although she conformed to their insistence on the three-volume format and accepted the censorship they exerted by virtue of their standards of selection, she was among the first to denounce these forms of tyranny over novelists practiced especially by Mudie's Circulating Library.

Even though she used the names of actual merchants in her works, she protested in the preface to *Pin Money* (1831) against any such interpretation in that work and went on to summarize her object:

It has become so much the custom to connect every character introduced into a work of fiction with some living original, that the writer of PIN MONEY feels it necessary to declare its incidents and personages to be wholly imaginary. Exhibiting an attempt to transfer the familiar narrative of Miss Austin [*sic.*] to a higher sphere of society, it is, in fact, a Novel of the simplest kind, addressed by a woman to readers of her own sex; by whom as well as by the professional critics, its predecessor, "The Manners of the Day," was received with too much indulgence not to encourage a further appeal to their favour.

Other better-known novels by Mrs. Gore are: *Cecil, or the Adventures of a Coxcomb* (1841), published, like so many of her works, anonymously; its sequel, *Cecil, A Peer* (1841); *Mothers and Daughters* (1831), also issued anonymously; and *Mrs. Armytage, or Female Domination* (1836). All are marked by a satiric tone, an insight into character, and a faithful portrayal of upper-class life which fulfills the claim made for the historical value of this kind of fiction in Lord Willersdale's speech from *Women as They Are.*

WOMEN AS THEY ARE
OR THE MANNERS OF THE DAY
(1830)

from Volume II, Chapter 9

"I see you have a volume or two of French memoirs; matter-of-fudge books,—as I always call such as are not matter-of-fact;—and those you must lend to *me*. I consider one of the truest luxuries of civilized winter life, to be a warm dressing-room,—with an easy chair, a *douillette ouatée*,[1] a new novel steaming from the press, and a sufficiently sharp mother-of-pearl paper-knife!"

"Your ladyship forgot to particularize that the work should be *Parisian*. An English novel insures the heaviness of boards, and the *mauvaise odeur*[2] of sour paste," said Lord Willersdale sarcastically.

"Oh, as to an English modern novel, with its my Lord Dukes, and Sir Harrys, and caricatures of the *beau monde*, I hold its vulgarity and bad taste as secondary only to that of the columns of your newspapers after a drawing-room;—which announce to admiring Europe, that Lady Alberville wore a train of Pomona green; and that some old withered Marchioness, who has been morally defunct these twenty years, arose from the catacombs in the identical robe of crimson velvet which ought to have been covering her coffin."

"We have perhaps had more than enough of fashionable novels," replied Lord Willersdale; "but as the amber which serves to preserve the ephemeral modes and caprices of the passing day, they have their value. They will prove to a following generation what the comedies of Congreve, and Cibber, and Farquhar, have proved to ourselves. It is from the ashes of our long extinguished high-life comedy, that this swarm of triflers has arisen; but it was the bent of the public taste which originally called it into existence."

"The worst fault of such productions," observed the bland and smiling Mr. Vyvyan, "is the distortion of their portraiture; the writers or painters generally move in so base a sphere, that their upturned and wondering eyes necessarily disfigure the objects of their art. Were it not for Lady Mary

---

[1] *douillette ouatée:* quilted coat.
[2] *mauvaise odeur:* bad odor.

Wortley's contemporary letters, we should accept Richardson's Lovelace as the *beau idéal* of the fine gentleman of his day; whereas we learn that the whole M. family were regarded at the time as a vulgar outrage upon fashionable life. And lately, the Memoirs of Richelieu, and others of the court of Louis XV, have assured us that the heroes of Marmontel, airy and graceful as they are, have not the slightest affinity with the originals they were intended to delineate."

"That Richardson from his shop, and Marmontel from his *mansarde*,[3] may have viewed the world of fashion in a disproportionate light, I can well conceive. But ours is the age of aristocratic literature; and such novels as Tremaine, Granby, Pelham—"[4]

"Tremaine!—that moralizing driveller!" interrupted Lady Isabella.

"A driveller of *aqua fortis!*"[5] replied Lord Willersdale.

"And Pelham!—with its sparkling conceits, that blind one, as though the pages were dried with diamond dust!"

"You did not conclude your observation," said Mr. Edwards, to Lord Willersdale, perceiving that Florence had been an attentive listener.

"Such novels, and many others, form a mere reflexion of the scenes hourly passing around their writers; and are a valuable addition to our lighter literature. Were the author of Anastasius[6] to favour us with a modern novel, for instance—its truth would necessarily equal its miraculous graphic force. A novel of fashionable life does not pre-suppose a tissue of puerile vulgarity."

"We never hear Miss Edgeworth's 'Vivian,' or 'Absentee' classed among fashionable novels," observed Mr. Edwards. "Conveying a great moral lesson, we *feel* their end and aim, and are regardless of the scenery of the drama."

"You are growing too didactic for *me*," exclaimed Lady Isabella, escaping from the group. "Florence my dear, some music. Captain Mordaunt, pray take her to the harp, or the harp to her; for I have only a quarter of an hour to listen to her syrenship, before I go home to be scolded.— And now, my dear Lady Willersdale, admit me back to a corner of your sofa; that I may whisper my adieus under cover of Miss Dudley's preliminary *arpeggio*.[7] My last and most potent argument in favour of our ball, still remains unspoken."

---

[3] *mansarde:* attic.

[4] *Tremaine* (1825), by Robert P. Ward; *Granby* (1826), by Thomas H. Lister; and *Pelham* (1828), by Bulwer-Lytton.

[5] *aqua fortis:* nitric acid.

[6] *Anastasius* (1819), a popular, picaresque romance set in the eighteenth century, by Thomas Hope.

[7] *arpeggio:* the notes of a chord played in quick succession instead of simultaneously.

9

FREDERICK MARRYAT

(1792–1848)

Robert Louis Stevenson and Joseph Conrad were both inspired by the vivid tales of the sea spun by Frederick Marryat, Captain in the Royal Navy. Like Smollett before him, Captain Marryat successfully translated his own twenty-five years of naval service into exciting, vigorous fiction; twelve of his sixteen novels for adults deal with the sea. Such are *Peter Simple* (1834), *Jacob Faithful* (1834), and *Mr. Midshipman Easy* (1836). Retiring on a pension at the age of thirty-eight, he produced enough fiction and miscellaneous articles to fill twenty-nine volumes in the standard edition. Finding children's stories a particularly dependable source of income, during his last eight years, he produced some of the best ever written.

"Fiction, when written for young people, should, at all events, be based upon truth," he wrote in his preface to *Masterman Ready* (1842), the first and most popular of his books for juveniles. Certainly his own experience, if not strict truth, was the basis for all Marryat's fiction. Some of his letters, included in his daughter's *Life and Letters of Captain Marryat* (1872), help to reveal additional attitudes to fiction. Thus, in 1837 and 1839, he frankly admits writing for money. His comparatively low repute with critics, in spite of continued popularity with readers, stems from his lack of concern with characterization and plot. In the opening chapter of *Newton Forster* (1832), he reminds us of Trollope: "I never have made any arrangement of plot when I commenced a work of fiction, and often finish a chapter without having the slightest idea of what materials the ensuing one is to be constructed." Yet he prides himself on his claim in Chapter 36 of *Snarleyyow, or the Dog Fiend* (1837), a supernatural tale, that his novel is unique in observing the unities. In the main, Captain Marryat was a spinner of yarns, with only a general conformity in practice to the tried and true maxim that "the great end of literature is to instruct and amuse, to make mankind wiser and better" (*Life and Letters*, II, 199).

That Marryat could succeed in novels other than nautical is evident in the popular regard for his picaresque *Japhet in Search of a Father* (1836). That he could succeed in nonliterary work is evident in his election as a fellow of the Royal Society (1819) and his receipt of the cross of the Legion of Honor from France (1833) for composing *A Code of Signals for the Use of Vessels Employed in the Merchant Service* (1817). He also published *A Diary in America, with remarks on its Institutions* (1839) after a tour of the United States and Canada in 1837–38. His editorship of the *Metropolitan Magazine* (1832–35), which he owned and in which some of his best novels first appeared, also deserves mention.

Among Marryat's own contributions to the *Metropolitan* in 1833 are two skits, later collected in the three volumes of *Olla Podrida*, a miscellany published in 1840. One, "How to Write a Fashionable Novel," is a parody of the work of Isaac Disraeli and Bulwer-Lytton. Another, "How to Write a Romance," is a parody of the Gothic romance. His attitudes toward the two types of fiction are implied in the ridicule.

HOW TO WRITE A FASHIONABLE NOVEL
(1833)

SCENE.—*Chamber in Lincoln's Inn. Arthur Ansard at a briefless table, tête-à-tête with his wig on a block. A. casts a disconsolate look upon his companion, and soliloquizes.*

Yes, there you stand, "partner of my toils, my feelings, and my fame." We do not *suit*, for we never gained a *suit* together. Well, what with reporting for the bar, writing for the Annuals and the Pocket-books, I shall be able to meet all demands except those of my tailor; and, as his bill is most characteristically long, I think I shall be able to make it stretch over till next term, by which time I hope to fulfil my engagements with Mr. C., who has given me an order for a fashionable novel, written by a "nobleman." But how I, who was never inside of an aristocratical mansion in my life, whose whole idea of Court is comprised in the Court of King's Bench, am to complete my engagement, I know no more than my companion opposite, who looks so placidly stupid under my venerable wig. As far as the street door, the footman and carriage, and the porter are concerned, I can manage well enough; but as to what occurs within doors I am quite abroad. I shall never get through the first chapter; yet that tailor's bill must be paid. (*Knocking outside.*) Come in, I pray.

Enter BARNSTAPLE.

B. Merry Christmas to you, Arthur.

A. Sit down, my dear fellow; but don't mock me with merry Christmas. He emigrated long ago. Answer me seriously: do you think it possible for a man to describe what he never saw?

B. (*putting his stick up to his chin*). Why, 'tis possible; but I would not answer for the description being quite correct.

A. But suppose the parties who read it have never seen the thing described?

B. Why then it won't signify whether the description be correct or not.

A. You have taken a load off my mind; but still I am not quite at ease. I have engaged to furnish C. with a fashionable novel.

B. What do you mean to imply by a fashionable novel?

A. I really can hardly tell. His stipulations were, that it was to be a "fashionable novel in three volumes, each volume not less than three hundred pages."

B. That is to say, that you are to assist him in imposing on the public.

A. Something very like it, I'm afraid; as it is further agreed that it is to be puffed as coming from a highly talented nobleman.

B. You should not do it, Ansard.

A. So conscience tells me, but my tailor's bill says Yes; and that is a thing out of all conscience. Only look here. (*Displays a long bill.*)

B. Why, I must acknowledge, Ansard, that there is some excuse. One needs must, when the devil drives; but you are capable of better things.

A. I certainly don't feel great capability in this instance. But what can I do? The man will have nothing else—he says the public will read nothing else.

B. That is to say, that because one talented author astonished the public by style and merits peculiarly his own, and established, as it were, a school for neophytes, his popularity is to be injured by contemptible imitators. It is sufficient to drive a man mad, to find that the tinsel of others, if to be purchased more cheaply, is to be palmed upon the public instead of his gold; and more annoying still, that the majority of the public cannot appreciate the difference between the metal and the alloy. Do you know, Ansard, that by getting up this work, you really injure the popularity of a man of great talent?

A. Will he pay my tailor's bill?

B. No; I daresay he has enough to do to pay his own. What does your tailor say?

A. He is a stanch reformer, and on March the 1st he declares that he will have the bill, the whole bill, and nothing but the bill—carried to my credit. Mr. C., on the 10th of February, also expects the novel, the whole novel, and nothing but the novel, and that must be a fashionable novel. Look here, Barnstaple. (*Shows his tailor's bill.*)

B. I see how it is. He "pays your poverty, and not your will."

A. And by your leave, I thus must pay my bill (*bowing*).

B. Well, well, I can help you: nothing more difficult than to write a good novel, and nothing more easy than to write a bad one. If I were not above the temptation, I could pen you a dozen of the latter every ordinary year, and thirteen, perhaps, in the bissextile. So banish that Christmas cloud from your brow; leave off nibbling your pen at the wrong end, and clap a fresh nib to the right one. I have an hour to spare.

A. I thank you: that spare hour of yours may save me many a spare day. I'm all attention—proceed.

B. The first point to be considered is the *tempus*, or time; the next the *locus*, or place; and lastly the *dramatis personæ*; and thus, chapter upon chapter, will you build a novel.

A. Build!

B.   Yes, build; you have had your dimensions given, the interior is
left to your own decoration. First, as to the opening. Suppose we introduce
the hero in his dressing-room. We have something of the kind in "Pelham;"
and if we can't copy his merits, we must his peculiarities. Besides, it always is
effective: a dressing-room or boudoir of supposed great people, is admitting
the vulgar into the arcana which they delight in.

A.   Nothing can be better.

B.   Then, as to time; as the hero is still in bed, suppose we say four
o'clock in the afternoon?

A.   In the morning you mean.

B.   No; the afternoon. I grant you that fashionable young men in real
life get up much about the same time as other people; but in a fashionable
novel your real exclusive never rises early. The very idea makes the tradesman's wife lift up her eyes. So begin. "It was about thirty-three minutes
after four, *post meridian*——"

A.   Minute—to a minute!

B.   "That the Honourable Augustus Bouverie's finely chiselled——"

A.   Chiselled!

B.   Yes, great people are always chiselled, common people are only
cast.—"Finely chiselled head was still recumbent upon his silk-encased
pillow. His luxuriant and Antinous-like curls were now confined in *papillotes* [1]
of the finest satin paper, and the *tout ensemble* [2] of his head——"

A.   *Tout ensemble!*

B.   Yes; go on.—"Was greatly compressed by a caul of the finest
network, composed of the threads spun from the beauteous production of the
Italian worm."

A.   Ah! now I perceive—a silk nightcap. But why can't I say at once
a silk nightcap?

B.   Because you are writing a fashionable novel.—"With the fore-
finger of his gloved left hand——"

A.   But he's not coming in from a walk—he's not yet out of bed.

B.   You don't understand it.—"Gloved left hand he applied a gentle
friction to the portal of his right eye, which unclosing at the silent summons,
enabled him to perceive a repeater studded with brilliants, and ascertain
the exact minute of time, which we have already made known to the reader,
and at which our history opens."

A.   A very grand opening indeed!

B.   Not more than it ought to be for a fashionable novel.—"At the
sound of a silver *clochette*, [3] his faithful Swiss valet Coridon, who had for some
time been unperceived at the door, waiting for some notice of his master
having thrown off the empire of Somnus, in his light pumps, covered with

[1] *papillotes:* curl papers.
[2] *tout ensemble:* the whole.
[3] *clochette:* a small bell.

beaver, moved with noiseless step up to the bedside, like the advance of eve stealing over the face of nature."

A. Rather an incongruous simile.

B. Not for a fashionable novel.—"There he stood, like Taciturnity bowing at the feet of proud Authority."

A. Indeed, Barnstaple, that is too *outré*.[4]

B. Not a whit: I am in the true "Cambyses' vein."—"Coridon having softly withdrawn the rose-coloured gros de Naples bed curtains, which by some might have been thought to have been rather too extravagantly fringed with the finest Mechlin lace, exclaimed with a tone of tremulous deference and affection, '*Monsieur a bien dormi?*'[5] 'Coridon,' said the Honourable Augustus Bouverie, raising himself on his elbow in that eminently graceful attitude for which he was so remarkable when reclining on the ottomans at Almack's——"

A. Are you sure they have ottomans there?

B. No; but your readers can't disprove it.—" 'Coridon,' said he, surveying his attendant from head to foot, and ultimately assuming a severity of countenance, 'Coridon, you are becoming gross, if not positively what the people call *fat*.' The Swiss attendant fell back in graceful astonishment three steps, and arching his eyebrows, extending his inverted palms forward, and raising his shoulders above the apex of his head, exclaimed, '*Pardon, milor, j'en aurais un horreur parfait.*'[6] 'I tell you,' replied our gracefully recumbent hero, 'that it is so, Coridon; and I ascribe it to your partiality for that detestable wine called Port. Confine yourself to Hock and Moselle, sirrah: I fear me, you have a base hankering after mutton and beef. Restrict yourself to salads, and do not sin even with an omelette more than once a week. Coridon must be visionary and diaphanous, or he is no Coridon for me. Remove my night-gloves, and assist me to rise: it is past four o'clock, and the sun must have, by this time, sufficiently aired this terrestrial globe.' "

A. I have it now; I feel I could go on for an hour.

B. Longer than that, before you get him out of his dressing-room. You must make at least five chapters before he is apparelled, or how can you write a fashionable novel, in which you cannot afford more than two incidents in the three volumes? Two are absolutely necessary for the editor of the —— *Gazette* to extract as specimens, before he winds up an eulogy. Do you think that you can proceed now for a week without my assistance?

A. I think so, if you will first give me some general ideas. In the first place, am I always to continue in this style?

B. No; I thought you knew better. You must throw in patches of philosophy every now and then.

---

[4] *outré*: exaggerated, extreme.

[5] *Monsieur a bien dormi?*: Monsieur has slept well?

[6] *Pardon, milor, j'en aurais un horreur parfait*: Pardon, your lordship, I would have a Perfect horror of that.

A.   Philosophy in a fashionable novel?

B.   Most assuredly, or it would be complained of as trifling; but a piece, now and then, of philosophy, as unintelligible as possible, stamps it with deep thought. In the dressing-room, or boudoir, it must be occasionally Epicurean; elsewhere, especially in the open air, more Stoical.

A.   I'm afraid that I shall not manage that without a specimen to copy from. Now I think of it, Eugene Aram says something very beautiful on a starry night.

B.   He does; it is one of the most splendid pieces of writing in our language. But I will have no profanation, Arthur;—to your pen again, and write. We'll suppose our hero to have retired from the crowded festivities of a ball-room at some lordly mansion in the country, and to have wandered into a churchyard, damp and dreary with a thick London fog. In the light dress of fashion, he throws himself on a tombstone. "Ye dead!" exclaims the hero, "where are ye? Do your disembodied spirits now float around me, and, shrouded in this horrible veil of nature, glare unseen upon vitality? Float ye upon this intolerable mist, in yourself still more misty and intolerable? Hold ye high jubilee to-night? or do ye crouch behind these monitorial stones, gibbering and chattering at one who dares thus to invade your precincts? Here may I hold communion with my soul, and, in the invisible presence of those who could, but dare not to reveal. Away! it must not be."

A.   What mustn't be?

B.   That is the mystery which gives the point to his soliloquy. Leave it to the reader's imagination.

A.   I understand. But still the Honourable Augustus cannot lie in bed much longer, and I really shall not be able to get him out without your assistance. I do not comprehend how a man can get out of bed *gracefully*; he must show his bare legs, and the alteration of position is in itself awkward.

B.   Not half so awkward as you are. Do you not feel that he must not be got out of bed at all—that is, by description.

A.   How then?

B.   By saying nothing about it. Recommence as follows: " 'I should like the bath at seventy-six and a half, Coridon,' observed the Honourable Augustus Bouverie, as he wrapped his embroidered dressing-gown round his elegant form, and sank into a *chaise longue*, wheeled by his faithful attendant to the fire." There, you observe, he is out of bed, and nothing said about it.

A.   Go on, I pray thee.

B.   " 'How is the bath perfumed?' '*Eau de mille fleurs.*' '*Eau de mille fleurs!*'[7] Did not I tell you last week that I was tired of that villainous compound? It has been adulterated till nothing remains but its name. Get me another bath immediately *à la violette*[8]; and, Coridon, you may use that

---

[7] *Eau de mille fleurs:* fragrance of a thousand flowers.
[8] *à la violette:* of violet.

other scent, if there is any left, for the poodle; but observe, only when *you* take him an airing, not when he goes with *me*.' "

A. Excellent! I now feel the real merits of an exclusive; but you said something about dressing-room, or in-door philosophy.

B. I did; and now is a good opportunity to introduce it. Coridon goes into the ante-chamber to renew the bath, and of course your hero has met with a disappointment in not having the bath to his immediate pleasure. He must press his hands to his forehead. By-the-bye, recollect that his fore-head, when you describe it, must be high and white as snow; all aristocratical foreheads are—at least, are in a fashionable novel.

A. What! the women's and all?

B. The heroine's must be: the others you may lower as a contrast. But to resume with the philosophy. He strikes his forehead, lifts his eyes slowly up to the ceiling, and drops his right arm as slowly down by the side of the *chaise longue*; and then in a voice so low that it might have been con-sidered a whisper, were it not for its clear and brilliant intonation, he exclaims——

A. Exclaims in a whisper!

B. To be sure: you exclaim mentally; why should you not in a whisper?

A. I perceive—your argument is unanswerable.

B. Stop a moment; it will run better thus: "The Honourable Augustus Bouverie no sooner perceived himself alone, than he felt the dark shades of melancholy ascending and brooding over his mind, and enveloping his throbbing heart in their—their *adamantine* chains. Yielding to the over-whelming force, he thus exclaimed, 'Such is life—we require but one flower, and we are offered noisome thousands—refused that we wish, we live in loathing of that not worthy to be received—mourners from our cradle to our grave, we utter the shrill cry at our birth, and we sink in oblivion with the faint wail of terror. Why should we, then, ever commit the folly to be happy?' "

A. Hang me, but that's a poser!

B. Nonsense! hold your tongue; it is only preparatory to the end. " 'Conviction astonishes and torments—destiny prescribes and falsifies—attraction drives us away—humiliation supports our energies. Thus do we recede into the present, and shudder at the Elysium of posterity.' "

A. I have written that down, Barnstaple; but I cannot understand it, upon my soul!

B. If you had understood one particle, that particle I would have erased. This is your true philosophy of a fashionable novel, the extreme interest of which consists in its being unintelligible. People have such an opinion of their own abilities, that if they understood you they would despise you; but a dose like this strikes them with veneration for your talents.

A.   Your argument is unanswerable; but you said that I must describe the dressing-room.

B.   Nothing more easy; as a simile, compare it to the shrine of some favoured saint in a richly-endowed Catholic church. Three tables at least, full of materials in methodised confusion—all tending to the beautification of the human form divine. Tinted perfumes in every variety of cut crystal receivers, gold and silver. If at a loss, call at Bayley and Blew's, or Smith's in Bond Street. Take an accurate survey of all you see, and introduce your whole catalogue. You cannot be too minute. But, Arthur, you must not expect me to write the whole book for you.

A.   Indeed I am not so exorbitant in my demands upon your good nature; but observe, I may get up four or five chapters already with the hints you have given me, but I do not know how to move such a creation of the brain—so ethereal, that I fear he will melt away; and so fragile, that I am in terror lest he fall to pieces. Now only get him into the breakfast-room for me, and then I ask no more for the present. Only dress him, and bring him *downstairs*.

B.   There again you prove your incapability. Bring him downstairs! Your hero of a fashionable novel never ascends to the first floor. Bedroom, dressing-room, breakfast-room, library, and boudoir, all are upon a level. As for his dressing, you must only describe it as perfect when finished; but not enter into a regular detail, except that, in conversation with his valet, he occasionally asks for something unheard-of, or fastidious to a degree. You must not walk him from one chamber to another, but manage it as follows: "It was not until the beautiful airs of the French clock that decorated the mantelpiece had been thrice played, with all their variations, that the Honourable Augustus Bouverie entered his library, where he found his assiduous Coridon burning an aromatic pastille to disperse the compound of villainous exhalations arising from the condensed metropolitan atmosphere. Once more in a state of repose, to the repeated and almost affecting solicitations of his faithful attendant, who alternately presented to him the hyson of Pekoe, the bohea of Twankay, the fragrant berry from the Asiatic shore, and the frothing and perfumed decoction of the Indian nut, our hero shook his head in denial, until he at last was prevailed upon to sip a small liqueur glass of *eau sucrée*."[9] The fact is, Arthur, he is in love—don't you perceive? Now introduce a friend, who rallies him—then a resolution to think no more of the heroine—a billet on a golden salver—a counter resolution—a debate which equipage to order—a decision at last—hat, gloves, and furred great-coat—and by that time you will have arrived to the middle of the first volume.

A.   I perceive; but I shall certainly stick there without your assistance.

B.   You shall have it, my dear fellow. In a week I will call again, and

---

[9] *eau sucrée :* sugar water.

see how you get on. Then we'll introduce the heroine; that, I can tell you, requires some tact—*au revoir.*

A. Thanks, many thanks, my dear Barnstaple. Fare you well. (*Exit* BARNSTAPLE.)

A. (*looking over his memoranda*). It will do! (*Hopping and dancing about the room.*) Hurrah! my tailor's bill will be paid after all!

PART II

Mr. ARTHUR ANSARD'S *Chambers as before.* Mr. ANSARD *with his eyes fixed upon the wig block, gnawing the feather end of his pen. The table, covered with sundry sheets of foolscap, shows strong symptoms of the novel progressing.*

ANSARD (*solus*).

Where is Barnstaple? If he do not come soon, I shall have finished my novel without a heroine. Well, I'm not the first person who has been foiled by a woman. (*Continues to gnaw his pen in a brown study.*)

BARNSTAPLE *enters unperceived, and slaps* ANSARD *on the shoulder. The latter starts up.*

B. So, friend Ansard, making your dinner off your pen: it is not every novel-writer who can contrive to do that even in anticipation. Have you profited by my instructions?

A. I wish I had. I assure you that this light diet has not contributed, as might be expected, to assist a heavy head; and one feather is not sufficient to enable my genius to take wing. If the public knew what dull work it is to write a novel, they would not be surprised at finding them dull reading. *Ex nihilo nihil fit.*[10] Barnstaple, I am at the very bathos of stupidity.

B. You certainly were absorbed when I entered, for I introduced myself.

A. I wish you had introduced another personage with you—you would have been doubly welcome.

B. Who is that?

A. My heroine. I have followed your instructions to the letter. My hero is as listless as I fear my readers will be, and he is not yet in love. In fact, he is only captivated with himself. I have made him dismiss Coridon.

B. Hah! how did you manage that?

A. He was sent to ascertain the arms on the panel of a carriage. In his eagerness to execute his master's wishes, he came home with a considerable degree of perspiration on his brow, for which offence he was immediately put out of doors.

B. Bravo—it was unpardonable—but still——

A. Oh! I know what you mean—that is all arranged; he has an annuity of one hundred pounds per annum.

---

[10] *Ex nihilo nihil fit:* Nothing comes from nothing.

B. My dear Ansard, you have exceeded my expectations; but now for the heroine.

A. Yes, indeed; help me—for I have exhausted all my powers.

B. It certainly requires much tact to present your heroine to your readers. We are unfortunately denied what the ancients were so happy to possess,—a whole *cortége* of divinities that might be summoned to help any great personage in, or the author out of, a difficulty; but since we cannot command their assistance, like the man in the play who forgot his part, we will do without it. Now, have you thought of nothing new, for we must not plagiarise even from fashionable novels?

A. I have thought—and thought—and can find nothing new, unless we bring her in in a whirlwind: that has not yet been attempted.

B. A whirlwind! I don't know—that's hazardous. Nevertheless, if she were placed on a beetling cliff, overhanging the tempestuous ocean, lashing the rocks with its wild surge; of a sudden, after she has been permitted to finish her soliloquy, a white cloud rising rapidly and unnoticed—the sudden vacuum—the rush of mighty winds through the majestic and alpine scenery—the vortex gathering round her—first admiring the vast efforts of nature; then astonished; and lastly alarmed, as she finds herself compelled to perform involuntary gyrations, till at length she spins round like a well-whipped top, nearing the dangerous edge of the precipice. It is bold, and certainly quite novel—I think it will do. Portray her delicate little feet, peeping out, pointing downwards, the force of the elements raising her on her tiptoes, now touching, now disdaining the earth. Her dress expanded wide like that of Herbelé in her last and best pirouette—round, round she goes—her white arms are tossed frantically in the air. Corinne never threw herself into more graceful attitudes. Now is seen her diminishing ankle—now the rounded symmetry—mustn't go too high up, though—the wind increases—her distance from the edge of the precipice decreases—she has no breath left to shriek—no power to fall—threatened to be ravished by the wild and powerful god of the elements—she is discovered by the Honourable Augustus Bouverie, who has just finished his soliloquy upon another adjacent hill. He delights in her danger—before he rushes to her rescue, makes one pause for the purpose of admiration, and another for the purpose of adjusting his shirt collar.

A. The devil he does!

B. To be sure. The hero of a fashionable novel never loses caste. Whether in a storm, a whirlwind, up to his neck in the foaming ocean, or tumbling down a precipice, he is still the elegant and correct Honourable Augustus Bouverie. To punish you for your interruption, I have a great mind to make him take a pinch of snuff before he starts. Well—he flies to her assistance—is himself caught in the rushing vortex, which prevents him from getting nearer to the lady, and, despite of himself, takes to whirling in the opposite direction. They approach—they recede—she shrieks without being heard—holds out her arms for help—she would drop them in despair, but cannot, for they are twisted over her head by the tremendous force of the element. One moment they are near to each other, and the next they are separated; at one instant they are close to the abyss, and the waters below roar in delight of their anticipated victims, and in the next a favouring change of the vortex increases their distance from the danger—there they spin—and there you may leave them, and commence a new chapter.

A. But is not all this naturally and physically impossible?

B. By no means; there is nothing supernatural in a whirlwind, and the effect of a whirlwind is to twist everything round. Why should the heroine and the Honourable Augustus Bouverie not be submitted to the laws of nature? Besides, we are writing a fashionable novel. Wild and improbable as this whirlwind may appear, it is within the range of probability; whereas, that is not at all adhered to in many novels—witness the drinking scene in —— ——, and others equally *outrées*, in which the author, having turned probability out of doors, ends by throwing possibility out of the window— leaving folly and madness to usurp their place—and play a thousand antics for the admiration of the public, who, pleased with novelty, cry out, "How fine!"

A. Buy the book, and laud the author.

B. Exactly. Now, having left your hero and heroine in a situation peculiarly interesting, with the greatest nonchalance pass over to the Continent, rave on the summit of Mont Blanc, and descant upon the strata which compose the Mountains of the Moon in Central Africa. You have been philosophical, now you must be geological. No one can then say that your book is light reading.

A. That can be said of few novels. In most of them even smoke assumes the ponderosity of lead.

B. There is a metal still heavier, which they have the power of creating—gold—to pay a dunning tailor's bill.

A. But after being philosophical and geological, ought one not to be a little moral?

B. Pshaw! I thought you had more sense. The great art of novel-writing is to make the vices glorious, by placing them in close alliance with redeeming qualities. Depend upon it, Ansard, there is a deeper, more heart-felt satisfaction than mere amusement in novel reading—a satisfaction no less real, because we will not own it to ourselves—the satisfaction of seeing all our favourite and selfish ideas dressed up in a garb so becoming that we persuade ourselves that our false pride is proper dignity, our ferocity courage, our cowardice prudence, our irreligion liberality, and our baser appetites mere gallantry.

A. Very true, Barnstaple; but really I do not like this whirlwind.

B. Well, well, I give it up then; it was your own idea. We'll try again. Cannot you create some difficulty or dilemma, in which to throw her, so that the hero may come to her rescue with *éclat*?[11]

[11] *éclat*: glitter, pomp.

A. Her grey palfrey takes fright.

B. So will your readers; stale—quite stale!

A. A wild bull has his horns close to her, and is about to toss her.

B. As your book would be—away with contempt. Vapid—quite vapid!

A. A shipwreck—the waves are about to close over her.

B. Your book would be closed at the same moment—worn out—quite worn out.

A. In the dead of the night a fire breaks out—she is already in the midst of the flames——

B. Where your book would also be by the disgusted reader—worse and worse.

A. Confound it! you will not allow me to expose her to earth, air, fire, or water. I have a great mind to hang her in her garters, and make the hero come and cut her down.

B. You might do worse—and better.

A. What—hang myself?

B. That certainly would put an end to all your difficulties. But, Ansard, I think I can put your heroine in a situation really critical and eminently distressing, and the hero shall come to her relief, like the descent of a god to the rescue of a Greek or Trojan warrior.

A. Or of Bacchus to Ariadne in her distress.

B. Perhaps a better simile. The consequence will be, that eternal gratitude in the bosom of the maiden will prove the parent of eternal love, which eternity of passion will of course last until they are married.

A. I'm all attention.

B. Get up a splendid dinner-party for their first casual meeting. Place the company at table.

A. Surely you are not going to choke her with the bone of a chicken.

B. You surely are about to murder me, as Samson did the Philistines——

A. With the jawbone of a fashionable novel-writer, you mean.

B. Exactly. But to proceed:—they are seated at table: can you describe a grand dinner?

A. Certainly, I have partaken of more than one.

B. Where?

A. I once sat down three hundred strong at the Freemasons' Tavern.

B. Pshaw! a mere hog feed.

A. Well, then, I dined with the late lord mayor.

B. Still worse, my dear Ansard. It is, however, of no consequence. Nothing is more difficult to attain, yet nothing is more easy to describe, than a good dinner. I was once reading a very fashionable novel by a very fashionable bookseller, for the author is a mere nonentity, and was very much surprised at the accuracy with which a good dinner was described. The mystery was explained a short time afterwards, when casually taking up

Eustache Eude's book in Sams's library, I found that the author had copied it out exactly from the injunctions of that celebrated gastronome. You can borrow the book.

A. Well, we will suppose that done; but I am all anxiety to know what is the danger from which the heroine is to be rescued.

B. I will explain. There are two species of existence—that of mere mortal existence, which is of little consequence, provided, like Cæsar, the hero and heroine die decently; the other is of much greater consequence, which is fashionable existence. Let them once lose caste in that respect, and they are virtually dead, and one mistake, one oversight, is a death-blow for which there is no remedy, and from which there is no recovery. For instance, we will suppose, our heroine to be quite confounded with the appearance of our hero—to have become *distraite, rêveuse* [12]—and, in short, to have lost her recollection and presence of mind. She has been assisted to *filet de soles.* Say that the only sauce ever taken with them is *au macédoine* [13]—this is offered to her, and at the same time another, which to eat with the above dish would be unheard of. In her distraction she is about to take the wrong sauce—actually at the point of ruining herself for ever and committing suicide upon her fashionable existence, while the keen grey eyes of Sir Antinous Antibes, the arbiter of fashion, are fixed upon her. At this awful moment, which is for ever to terminate her fashionable existence, the Honourable Augustus Bouverie, who sits next to her, gently touches her *séduisante* [14] sleeve—blandly smiling, he whispers to her that the *other* is the sauce *macédoine.* She perceives her mistake, trembles at her danger, rewards him with a smile, which penetrates into the deepest recesses of his heart, helps herself to the right sauce, darts a look of contemptuous triumph upon Sir Antinous Antibes, and, while she is dipping her sole into the sauce, her soul expands with gratitude and love.

A. I see, I see. Many thanks; my heroine is now a fair counterpart of my hero.

> "Ah, sure a pair were never seen,
> So justly formed to meet by nature." [15]

B. And now I'll give you another hint, since you appear grateful. It is a species of clap-trap in a novel which always takes—to wit, a rich old uncle or misanthrope, who, at the very time that he is bitterly offended and disgusted with the hero, who is in awkward circumstances, pulls out a pocket-book and counts down say fifteen or twenty thousand pounds in bank-notes, to relieve him from his difficulties. An old coat and monosyllables will increase the interest.

---

[12] *distraite, rêveuse:* upset, distraught.
[13] *au macédoine:* a mixture.
[14] *séduisante:* charming, tempting.
[15] From the Song at the end of Act II, Scene ii of Richard Sheridan's *The Duenna.*

A. True. (*Sighing.*) Alas! there are no such uncles in real life; I wish there were.

B. I beg your pardon; I know no time in which *my uncle* forks out more bank-notes than at present.

A. Yes, but it is for value, or more than value, received.

B. That I grant; but I am afraid it is the only "uncle" left now; except in a fashionable novel. But you comprehend the value of this new auxiliary.

A. Nothing can be better. Barnstaple, you are really——, but I say no more. If a truly great man cannot be flattered with delicacy, it must not be attempted at all; silence then becomes the best tribute. Your advice proves you to be truly great. I am silent, therefore you understand the full force of the oratory of my thanks.

B. (*bowing*). Well, Ansard, you have found out the cheapest way of paying off your bills of gratitude I ever heard of. "Poor, even in thanks," was well said by Shakspeare; but you, it appears, are rich in having nothing at all wherewith to pay. If you could transfer the same doctrine to your tradesmen, you need not write novels.

A. Alas! my dear fellow, mine is not yet written. There is one important feature, nay, the most important feature of all—the style of language, the diction—on that, Barnstaple, you have not yet doctrinated.

B. (*pompously*). When Demosthenes was asked what were the principal attributes of eloquence, he answered, that the first was action; on being asked which was the second, he replied action; and the third, action; and such is the idea of the Irish *mimbers* in the House of Commons. Now there are three important requisites in the diction of a fashionable novel. The first, my dear fellow, is flippancy; the second, flippancy; and flippancy is also the third. With the dull it will pass for wit, with some it will pass for scorn, and even the witty will not be enabled to point out the difference, without running the risk of being considered invidious. It will cover every defect with a defect still greater; for who can call small-beer tasteless when it is sour, or dull when it is bottled and has a froth upon it?

A. The advice is excellent; but I fear that this flippancy is as difficult to acquire as the tone of true eloquence.

B. Difficult! I defy the writers of the silver-fork school to write out of the style flippant. Read but one volume of ——, and you will be saturated with it; but if you wish to go to the fountain-head, do as have done most of the late fashionable novel-writers, repair to their instructors—the lady's-maid, for flippancy in the vein *spirituelle*! to a London footman for the vein critical; but if you wish a flippancy of a still higher order, at once more solemn and more empty, which I would call the vein political, read the speeches of some of our members of Parliament. Only read them—I wish no man so ill as to inflict upon him the torture of hearing them—read them, I say, and you will have taken the very highest degree in the order of inane flippancy.

A. I see it at once. Your observations are as true as they are severe. When we would harangue geese, we must condescend to hiss; but still, my dear Barnstaple, though you have fully proved to me that in a fashionable novel all plot is unnecessary, don't you think there ought to be a catastrophe, or sort of a kind of an end to the work, or the reader may be brought up short, or, as the sailors say, "all standing," when he comes to the word "Finis," and exclaim with an air of stupefaction—"And then——"

B. And then, if he did, it would be no more than the fool deserved. I don't know whether it would not be advisable to leave off in the middle of a sentence, of a word, nay of a syllable, if it be possible: I am sure the winding up would be better than the lackadaisical running down of most of the fashionable novels. Snap the mainspring of your watch, and none but an ass can expect you to tell by it what it is o'clock; snap the thread of your narrative in the same way, and he must be an unreasonable being who would expect a reasonable conclusion. Finish thus, in a case of delicate distress; say, "The Honourable Mr. Augustus Bouverie was struck in a heap with horror. He rushed with a frantic grace, a deliberate haste, and a graceful awkwardness, and whispered in her ear these dread and awful words, 'IT IS TOO LATE!' " Follow up with a —— and Finis.

A. I see; the fair and agitated reader will pass a sleepless night in endeavouring to decipher the mutilated sentence. She will fail, and, consequently, call the book delightful. But should there not have been a marriage previously to this happy awful climax?

B. Yes; everything is arranged for the nuptials—carriages are sent home, jewellery received but not paid for, dresses all tried on, the party invited—nay, assembled in the blue-and-white drawing-room. The right reverend my lord bishop is standing behind the temporary altar—he has wiped his spectacles and thumbed his prayer-book—all eyes are turned towards the door, which opens not—the bride faints, for the bridegroom cometh not—he's not "i' the vein"—a something, as like nothing as possible, has given him a disgust that is insurmountable—he flings his happiness to the winds, though he never loved with more outrageous intensity than at the moment he discards his mistress; so he fights three duels with the two brothers and father. He wounds one of the young men dangerously, the other slightly; fires his pistol in the air when he meets her father—for how could he take the life of him who gave life to his adored one? Your hero can always hit a man just where he pleases—*vide* every novel in Mr. C.'s collection. The hero becomes misanthropical, the heroine maniacal. The former marries an antiquated and toothless dowager, as an escape from the imaginary disgust he took at the sight of a matchless woman; and the latter marries an old brute, who threatens her life every night, and puts her in bodily fear every morning, as an indemnity in full for the loss of the man of her affections. They are both romantically miserable; and then comes on your tantalising scene of delicate distress, and so the end of your third volume, and then finish without any end at all. *Verb. sap. sat.*[16] Or, if you like it better, kill the old dowager of a surfeit, and make the old brute who marries the heroine commit suicide; and after all these unheard-of trials, marry them as fresh and beautiful as ever.

A. A thousand thanks. Your *verba* are not thrown to a *sap.* Can I possibly do you any favour for all this kindness?

B. Oh, my dear fellow! the very greatest. As I see yours will be, at all points, a most fashionable novel, do me the inestimable favour *not* to ask me *to read it.*

---

[16] *Verb. sap. sat.: Verbum sapienti sat est:* A word to the wise is sufficient.

10

HARRIET MARTINEAU

(1802–1876)

"A Radical Victorian" is the subtitle of a recent biography of Harriet Martineau (R. K. Webb, *Harriet Martineau, A Radical Victorian*, London, 1960). So outspokenly radical in advocating social reform was she that, according to her *Autobiography*, her "writing about Egalité" offended the royal houses of Russia, Austria, and France, "and thus, I was personally excluded, before my Series was half done, from two of the three greatest countries in Europe, and in disfavor with the third . . . ."

The Series referred to was *Illustrations of Political Economy*, published in twenty-five monthly numbers between 1832–34. Her announced purpose was to overcome the difficulties associated with the science and make it understandable through a fictional presentation. As such, Miss Martineau is classified as a didactic novelist. Although the work is now characterized as "an unreadable mixture of fiction, founded on rapid cramming, with raw masses of the dismal science" (*D.N.B.*, XII, 1195), it was an immediate and a financial success. The latter consideration was important, for her family had become impoverished, and it was partly economic necessity that had led her to write reviews for the *Monthly Repository*. She became a close friend of the editor, W. J. Fox, and acquainted with the intellectuals, such as George Eliot, G. H. Lewes, and John Chapman, who were associated with the *Westminster Review*, for which she also wrote. Other literary celebrities with whom she was on close terms were Bulwer-Lytton and Wordsworth.

Throughout her life Miss Martineau suffered from poor health. She was afflicted by deafness and a total absence of the senses of taste and smell. Partly in search of health, she traveled widely. Her trip to America from 1834 to 1836 resulted in two books: *Society in America* (1837) and *A Retrospect of Western Travel* (1838). Her bibliography includes numerous articles, translations, and works of fiction. She considered her best work to be *Deerbrook*, a novel published in

77

1839. *The Hour and the Man* (1841) is a historical romance with Toussaint L'Ouverture as the hero.

About 1844 she turned to mesmerism as a cure, and it benefited her to the extent that she began traveling again, touring Egypt and Palestine in 1846 and making many excursions into the Lake District.

Aside from her preface to *Political Economy*, in which she declares that example is more effective than precept, she comments only occasionally on fiction. In a review of Charlotte Brontë's *Villette* (*Daily News*, 3 February 1853), she expressed approval of the autobiographical point of view. Although generally laudatory, this review made two objections to the book; first, "An atmosphere of pain hangs about the whole, forbidding that repose which we hold to be essential to the true presentment of any large portion of life and experience." Second, she objected to the assumption "that events and characters are to be regarded through the medium of one passion only." She protests, "It is not thus in real life. There are substantial, heartfelt interests for women of all ages, and under ordinary circumstances, quite apart from love . . . ." So also in her *Autobiography* (comp. 1855; pub. 1877), writing of her activities in 1833, it seemed to her "that every perfect plot in fiction is taken bodily from real life."

ILLUSTRATIONS OF POLITICAL ECONOMY
(1834)

from the Preface

The works already written on Political Economy almost all bear a reference to books which have preceded, or consist in part of discussions of disputed points. Such references and such discussions are very interesting to those whom they concern, but offer a poor introduction to those to whom the subject is new. There are a few, a very few, which teach the science systematically as far as it is yet understood. These too are very valuable: but they do not give us what we want—the science in a familiar, practical form. They give us its history; they give us its philosophy; but we want its *picture*. They give us truths, and leave us to look about us, and go hither and thither in search of illustrations of those truths. Some who have a wide range in society and plenty of leisure, find this all-sufficient; but there are many more who have neither time nor opportunity for such an application of what they learn. We cannot see why the truth and its application should not go together,—why an explanation of the principles which regulate society should not be made more clear and interesting at the same time by pictures of what those principles are actually doing in communities.

For instance: if we want to teach that security of property is necessary to the prosperity of a people, and to show how and in what proportion wealth increases where there is that security, and dwindles away where there is not, we may make the fact and the reasons very well understood by stating them in a dry, plain way: but the same thing will be quite as evident, and far more interesting and better remembered, if we confirm our doctrine by accounts of the hardships suffered by individuals, and the injuries by society, in such a country as Turkey, which remains in a state of barbarism chiefly through the insecurity of property. The story of a merchant in Turkey, in contrast with one of a merchant in England, will convey as much truth as any set of propositions on the subject, and will impress the memory and engage the interest in a much greater degree. This method of teaching Political Economy has never yet been tried, except in the instance of a short story or separate passage here and there.

This is the method in which we propose to convey the leading truths of Political Economy, as soundly, as systematically, as clearly and faithfully, as the utmost painstaking and the strongest attachment to the subject will enable us to do. We trust we shall not be supposed to countenance the practice of making use of narrative as a trap to catch idle readers, and make them learn something they are afraid of. We detest the practice, and feel ourselves insulted whenever a book of the *trap* kind is put into our hands. It is many years since we grew sick of works that pretend to be stories, and turn out to be catechisms of some kind of knowledge which we had much rather become acquainted with in its undisguised form. The reason why we choose the form of narrative is, that we really think it the best in which Political Economy can be taught, as we should say of nearly every kind of moral science. Once more we must apply the old proverb, "Example is better than precept." We take this proverb as the motto of our design. We declare frankly that our object is to teach Political Economy, and that we have chosen this method not only because it is new, not only because it is entertaining, but because we think it the most faithful and the most complete. There is no doubt that all that is true and important about any virtue,—integrity, for instance,—may be said in the form of a lecture, or written in a chapter of moral philosophy; but the faithful history of an upright man, his sayings and doings, his trials, his sorrows, his triumphs and rewards, teaches the same truths in a more effectual as well as more popular form. In like manner, the great principle of Freedom of Trade may be perfectly established by a very dry argument; but a tale of the troubles, and difficulties, and changes of good and evil fortune in a manufacturer and his operatives, or in the body of a manufacturing population, will display the same principle, and may be made very interesting besides; to say nothing of getting rid of the excuse that these subjects cannot be understood.

FROM *AUTOBIOGRAPHY*
(composed 1855; published 1877)

In planning my next story, *Berkeley the Banker*, I submitted myself to my reviewer's warning, and spared no pains in thoroughly incorporating the doctrine and the tale. I remember that, for two days, I sat over my materials from seven in the morning till two the next morning, with an interval of only twenty minutes for dinner. At the end of my plotting, I found that, after all, I had contrived little but relationships, and that I must trust to the uprising of new involutions in the course of my narrative. I had believed before, and I went on during my whole career of fiction-writing to be more and more thoroughly convinced, that the creating a plot is a task above human faculties.

It is indeed evidently the same power as that of prophecy: that is, if all human action is (as we know it to be) the inevitable result of antecedents, all the antecedents must be thoroughly comprehended in order to discover the inevitable catastrophe. A mind which can do this must be, in the nature of things, a prophetic mind, in the strictest sense; and no human mind is that. The only thing to be done, therefore, is to derive the plot from actual life, where the work is achieved for us: and, accordingly, it seems that every perfect plot in fiction is taken bodily from real life. The best we know are so derived. Shakspere's are so: Scott's one perfect plot (*the Bride of Lammermoor*) is so; and if we could know where Boccaccio and other old narrators got theirs, we should certainly find that they took them from their predecessors, or from the life before their eyes. I say this from no mortification at my own utter inability to make a plot. I should say the same (after equal study of the subject) if I had never tried to write a tale. I see the inequality of this kind of power in contemporary writers; an inequality wholly independent of their merits in other respects; and I see that the writers (often inferior ones) who have the power of making the best plots do it by their greater facility in forming analogous narratives with those of actual experience. They may be, and often are, so inferior as writers of fiction to others who cannot make plots that one is tempted to wish that they and their superiors could be rolled into one, so as to make a perfect novelist or dramatist. For instance, Dickens cannot make a plot,—nor Bulwer,—nor Douglas Jerrold, nor perhaps Thackeray; while Fanny Kemble's forgotten *Francis the First*, written in her teens, contains mines of plot, sufficient to furnish a groundwork for a score of fine fictions. As for me, my incapacity in this direction is so absolute that I always worked under a sense of despair about it. In *the Hour and the Man*, for instance, there are prominent personages who have no necessary connexion whatever with the story; and the personages fall out of sight, till at last, my hero is alone in his dungeon, and the story ends with his solitary death. I was not careless, nor unconscious of my inability. It was inability, "pure and simple." My only resource therefore was taking suggestion from facts, witnessed by myself, or gathered in any way I could. That tale of *Berkeley the Banker* owed its remarkable success, not to my hard work of those two days; but to my taking some facts from the crisis of 1825–6 for the basis of my story. The toil of those two days was not thrown away, because the amalgamation of doctrine and narrative was more complete than it would otherwise have been: but no protraction of the effort would have brought out a really good plot, any more than the most prodigious amount of labour in practicing would bring out good music from a performer unendowed with musical faculty.

11

SIR EDWARD G. BULWER-LYTTON

(1803–1873)

The Last Days of Pompeii (1834) enjoyed a popularity greater than that of any other novel since *Waverley*. Today, it is regarded as Bulwer-Lytton's masterpiece, but whereas he was one of the most widely read authors of his time, the rest of his sixty-odd novels are now largely neglected. Critics and readers alike have not subscribed to the judgment of Edgar Allan Poe that he was unsurpassed by any writer living or dead. Yet he does serve as a guide to the reading tastes of the middle part of the century, for, writing with an eye toward profit, he gave the public whatever was in fashion—historical romance: *Rienzi* (1835), *The Last Days of Pompeii*; the novel of crime: *Paul Clifford* (1830); scientific utopia: *The Coming Race* (1871); and supernatural mysticism: *A Strange Story* (1862).

Bulwer was subjected to much hostile criticism in his day. Thackeray, calling him "Bulwig," disliked the man and satirized his fiction. The list of his shortcomings that have relegated him to the second rank of British novelists is lengthy: an overcrowded canvas that he cannot control; a habit of over-writing marked by verbosity and of denying to the reader the opportunity of making his own analysis and interpretation; dialog that often neither character-izes the people nor advances the story; an excess of sentiment, coincidence, and authorial intrusion; a lack of humor and disregard for careful structure.

On the other hand, Lord Lytton had the highest regard for literature; in Parliament he devoted himself to questions affecting authors, such as copyright laws. He deplored the deprecatory attitude assumed by some authors toward fiction. For him, fiction was a vehicle for teaching and could be useful or harmful, depending on the author. Thus, following William Godwin's suggestion that he depict the life of highwaymen, he wrote *Paul Clifford*, a propagandist novel, condemning harsh criminal laws and suggesting that crime was a result of such laws. It is probable that this and other of his novels of crime were more influential in stimulating the "Newgate Novel," particularly in the hands of Ainsworth, than they were in promoting legal reform.

Fiction was a product of Bulwer's varied interests. He personally explored the ruins of Pompeii and gained for his book an accuracy of detail that recommends it as a guidebook even today. He lived with a gypsy band for a week to learn what they knew of astrology, palmistry, and the like, thus supplementing his experiments and reading by which his stories of the occult are given verisimilitude. He explored haunted houses and wrote one of the best ghost stories in the language: *The Haunters and the Haunted* (1859).

Bulwer's theories on the novel are expressed in prefaces and articles. The preface to *Night and Morning* (1845 edition) discusses instruction as an aim of fiction; the one to *Paul Clifford* defends a novelist's use of dialect. One of the most interesting of these introductory pieces is the dialog prefaced to *The Disowned* (1828), in which Mr. Pelham, the titular hero of Bulwer's previous novel, discusses with the "Author" the formula for a successful novel, the comparison between the novel and the drama, the advantages of a historical setting, and the supreme importance of the story.

Of his essays, those collected in *Caxtoniana: A Series of Essays on Life, Literature, and Manners* (1868) include specific, though scattered, commentary on fiction. More unified is his treatise "On Art in Fiction," which appeared anonymously in 1838 in *The Monthly Chronicle*, later reprinted in his *Pamphlets and Sketches*. When he wrote this, he had already written several novels. A modern scholar terms it "one of the most important critical documents of the period" (Richard Stang, *The Theory of the Novel in England 1850–1870*, New York, 1959, p. 11).

ON ART IN FICTION
(1838)

Art is that process by which we give to natural materials the highest excellence they are capable of receiving.

We estimate the artist, not only in proportion to the success of his labours, but in proportion to the intellectual faculties which are necessary to that success. Thus, a watch by Breguét is a beautiful work of art, and so is a tragedy by Sophocles:—The first is even more perfect of its kind than the last, but the tragedy requires higher intellectual faculties than the watch; and we esteem the tragedian above the watchmaker.

The excellence of art consists in the fitness of the object proposed with the means adopted. Art carried to its perfection would be the union of the most admirable object with the most admirable means; in other words, it would require a greatness in the conception correspondent to the genius in the execution. But as mechanical art is subjected to more definite and rigorous laws than intellectual art, so, in the latter, a comprehensive critic regards the symmetry of the whole with large indulgence towards blemishes in detail. We contemplate mechanical art with reference to its utility—intellectual art with reference to its beauty. A single defect in a watch may suffice to destroy all the value of its construction;—a single blemish in a tragedy may scarcely detract from its effect.

In regarding any work of art, we must first thoroughly acquaint ourselves with the object that the artist had in view. Were an antiquarian to set before us a drawing, illustrative of the costume of the Jews in the time of Tiberius, we should do right to blame him if he presented to our eye goblets in the fashion of the fifteenth century; but when Leonardo da Vinci undertook the sublime and moving representation of the Last Supper, we feel that his object is not that of an antiquary; and we do not regard it as a blemish that the apostles are seated upright instead of being recumbent, and that the loaves of bread are those of an Italian baker. Perhaps, indeed, the picture affected the spectators the more sensibly from their familiarity with the details; and the effect of art on the whole was only heightened by a departure from correctness in minutiæ. So, in an anatomical drawing that professed to give the exact proportions of man, we might censure the designer if the length of the limbs were disproportioned to the size of the trunk; but, when the sculptor of the Apollo Belvidere desired to convey to the human eye the ideal of the God of Youth, the length of the limbs contributed to give an additional and super-human lightness and elasticity to the form; and the excellence of the art was evinced and promoted by the sacrifice of mechanical accuracy in detail. It follows, therefore, that intellectual Art and technical Correctness are far from identical;—that one is sometimes proved by the disdain of the other. And, as this makes the distinction between mechanical and intellectual art, so is the distinction remarkable in proportion as that intellectual art is exercised in the highest degree,—in proportion as it realises the Ideal. For the Ideal consists not in the imitation, but the exaltation, of Nature; and we must accordingly inquire, not how far it resembles what we have seen so much as how far it embodies what we can imagine.

It is not till we have had great pictures, that we can lay down the rules of painting;—it is not till we have had great writers in a particular department of intellect, that we can sketch forth a code of laws for those who succeed them: For the theory of art resembles that of science; we must have data to proceed upon, and our inductions must be drawn from a vast store of experiments.

Prose fictions have been cultivated by modern writers of such eminence, and now form so wide and essential a part of the popular literature of Europe, that it may not be an uninteresting or an useless task to examine the laws by which the past may be tested, and the labours of future students simplified and abridged.

PROSE FICTIONS

The Novelist has three departments for his art: MANNERS, PASSIONS, CHARACTER.

MANNERS

The delineation of manners embraces both past and present; the Modern and the Historical Romance.

The Historical

We have a right to demand from the writer who professes to illustrate a former age, a perfect acquaintance with its characteristics and spirit. At the same time, as he intends rather to interest than instruct us, his art will be evinced in the illustrations he selects, and the skill with which they are managed. He will avoid all antiquarian dissertations not essentially necessary to the conduct of his tale. If, for instance, his story should have no connection with the mysteries of the middle ages, he will take care how he weary us with an episodical description that changes his character from that of a narrator into that of a lecturer. In the tale of Notre Dame de Paris, by Victor Hugo, the description of the cathedral of Notre Dame is not only apposite, but of the deepest interest; for the cathedral is, by a high effort of art, made an absolute portion of the machinery of the tale. But the long superfluous description of the spectacle with which the story opens is merely a parade of antiquarian learning, because the Scholars and the Mysteries have no proportionate bearing whatever in the future development of the tale.

The usual fault of the historical novelist is over minuteness in descriptions of dress and feasts, of pageants and processions. Minuteness is not accuracy. On the contrary, the more the novelist is minute, the more likely he is to mar the accurate effect of the whole, either by wearisome tameness or some individual error.

An over-antiquated phraseology is a common and a most inartistical defect: whatever diction the delineator of a distant age employs, can never be faithful to the language of the time, for if so, it would be unintelligible. So, in the German novels that attempt a classical subject, there is the prevalent vice of a cold imitation of a classic epistolary style. It is the very attempt at resemblance that destroys the illusion, as it is by the servility of a copy that we are most powerfully reminded of the difference between the copy and the original. The language of a former time should be presented to us in the freest and most familiar paraphrase we can invent. Thus the mind is relieved at once from the task of forming perpetual comparisons, and surrenders itself to the delusion the more easily, from the very candour with which the author makes demand on its credulity. In selecting a particular epoch for illustration, an artistical author will consider well what is the principal obstacle in the mind of his audience to the reception of his story. For instance, if he select a story of ancient Greece, the public will be predisposed to anticipate a frigid pedantry of style, and delineations of manners utterly different from those which are familiar to us now. The author will, therefore, agreeably surprise the reader, if he adopt a style as familiar and easy as that which a Greek would have used in common conversation; and show the classical spirit that pervades his diction, by the grace of the poetry, or the lightness of the wit, with which he can adorn his allusions and his dialogue. Thus, the very learning he must evince will only be but incidental and easy ornament. On the other hand, instead of selecting such specimens and modifications of human nature as are most different from, and unfamiliar to, the sympathies of modern times, he will rather prefer to appeal to the eternal sentiments of the heart, by showing how closely the men of one age resemble those of another. His hero, his lover, his epicure, his buffoon, his miser, his boaster, will be as close to the life as if they were drawn from the streets of London. The reader will be interested to see society different, yet men the same; and the Manners will be relieved from the disadvantage of unfamiliarity by an entire sympathy with the humours they mask, or the passions on which they play.

Again, if the author propose to carry his reader to the times of Richard the First or of Elizabeth, he will have to encounter an universal repugnance from the thought of an imitation of Ivanhoe or Kenilworth. An author who was, nevertheless, resolved to select such a period for his narrative would, accordingly, if an artist of sufficient excellence, avoid with care touching upon any of the points which may suggest the recollection of Scott. He would deeply consider all the features of the time, and select those neglected by his predecessor;—would carefully note all the deficiencies of the author of Kenilworth, and seize at once upon the ground which that versatile genius omitted to consecrate to himself.

To take the same epoch, the same characters, even the same narrative, as a distinguished predecessor, is perfectly allowable; and, if successful, a proof at once of originality and skill. But if you find the shadow of the previous work flinging itself over your own—if you have not thoroughly escaped the influence of the first occupant of the soil,—you will only invest your genius to unnecessary disadvantage, and build edifices, however graceful and laboured, upon the freehold of another.

In novels devoted to the delineation of existing manners, the young author will be surprised to find, that exact and unexaggerated fidelity has never been the characteristic of the greatest novelists of their own time. There would be, indeed, something inane and trifling, or mean and vulgar, in Dutch copies of the modern still life. We do not observe any frivolity in Walter Scott, when he describes with elaborate care the set of the ruffle, the fashion of the cloak of Sir Walter Raleigh, nor when he catalogues all the minutiæ of the chamber of Rowena. But to introduce your hero of May Fair with an exact portraiture of the colour of his coat, and the length of his pantaloons, to item all the commodes and fauteuils of the boudoir of a lady Caroline or Frances, revolts our taste as an effeminate attention to trifles.

In humbler life, the same rule applies with equal strength. We are willing to know how Gurth was dressed, or Esmeralda lodged; but we do not require the same minuteness in describing the smock-frock of a labourer, or the garret of the girl who is now walking upon stilts for a penny. The greatest masters of the novel of modern life have usually availed themselves of HUMOUR as the illustration of manners; and have, with a deep and true, but, perhaps, unconscious, knowledge of art, pushed the humour almost to the verge of caricature. For as the Serious Ideal requires a certain exaggeration in the proportions of the Natural, so also does the Ludicrous. Thus, Aristophanes, in painting the humours of his time, resorts to the most poetical extravagance of machinery, and calls the Clouds in aid of his ridicule of philosophy, or summons Frogs and Gods to unite in his satire on Euripides. The Don Quixote of Cervantes never lived, nor, despite the vulgar belief, ever could have lived, in Spain; but the art of the portrait is in the admirable exaltation of the Humorous by means of the Exaggerated. With more qualification, the same may be said of Parson Adams, of Sir Roger de Coverley, and even of the Vicar of Wakefield.

Where the author has not adopted the Humorous as the best vehicle for the delineation of manners, he has sometimes artfully removed the scene from the country that he seeks to delineate, so that he might place his portraitures at a certain, and the most advantageous, distance from the eye. Thus, Le Sage obtains his object, of a consummate and masterly picture of the manners of his own land, though he has taken Spain for the theatre of the adventures of Gil Blas; and Swift has transferred all that his experience or his malice could narrate of the intrigues of courts, the chimeras of philosophy, the follies and vices of his nation and his time, to the regions of Lilliput and Laputa.

It may be observed, that the delineation of Manners is usually the secondary object of a novelist of high power. To a penetrating mind, manners are subservient to the illustration of views of life, or the consummation of original character. In a few years the mere portraiture of manners is obsolete. It is the knowledge of what is durable in human nature that alone preserves the work from decay. Lilly and Shakspeare alike painted the prevailing and courtly mannerism of their age. The Euphues rests upon our shelves;—Don Armado will delight us as long as pedantry exists.

An author once said, "Give me a character, and I will find the play;" and, if we look to the most popular novels, we shall usually find, that where one reader speaks of the conduct of the story, a hundred readers will speak of the excellence of some particular character.

An author, before resolving on the characters he designs to portray, will do well to consider maturely, first, what part they are destined to play in his performance; and secondly, what is the precise degree of interest which he desires them to create. Having thus considered, and duly determined, he will take care that no other character in the work shall interfere with the effect each is intended to produce. Thus, if his heroine is to be drawn gentle and mild, no second heroine, with the same attributes, should distract the attention of the reader, a rule that may seem obvious, but which is usually overlooked. When the author feels that he has thoroughly succeeded in a principal and predominant character, he will even sacrifice others, nominally more important, to increase the interest of the figure in the foreground. Thus, in the tale of Ivanhoe, Rowena, professedly the heroine, is very properly sacrificed to Rebecca. The more interesting the character of Rowena, the more pathetic the position she had assumed, the more we should have lost our compassion and admiration of the Jewess; and the highest merit of the tale, its pathos, would have been diminished. The same remark will apply to the Clementina and Harriet Byron of Richardson.

The author will take care not to crowd his canvass. He will select as few characters as are compatible with the full agency of his design. Too many plants in a narrow compass destroy each other. He will be careful to individualise each; but, if aspiring to the highest order of art, he will yet tone down their colours by an infinite variety of shades. The most original characters are those most delicately drawn, where the individual peculiarity does not obtrude itself naked and unrelieved. It was a very cheap purchase of laughter in Sir Walter Scott, and a mere trick of farce, which Shakspeare and Cervantes would have disdained, to invest a favourite humorist with some cant phrase, which he cannot open his mouth without disgorging. This was so special a device (because so easy and popular a mode of producing a ludicrous effect) with Sir Walter Scott, that it was almost his invariable resource. The "Prodigious" of Dominie Sampson—the "My Father, the Baillie" of Nichol Jarvie—the *"Provant"* of Major Dalgettie—the *"Dejeuner* at Tillietudlem" of Lady Margaret Bellenden, &c., all belong to one source of humour, and that the shallowest and most hacknied. If your tale spread over a considerable space of time, you will take care that your readers may note the change of character which time has necessarily produced. You will quietly show the difference between the boy of eighteen and the man of forty;—you will connect the change in the character with the influence of the events you have narrated. In the novel of Anastasius, this art of composition is skilfully and delicately mastered; more so than in Gil Blas.

If you bend all your faculties to the developement of some single character, and you make us sensible that such is your object, the conduct of your story becomes but a minor consideration. Shakspeare, probably, cared but little whether the fencing scene in Hamlet was the best catastrophe he could invent: he took the incidents of the story as he found them; and lavished his genius on the workings of the mind, to which all external incidents on this side the grave had become trivial and uninfluential,—weary, unprofitable, stale.

It must rest entirely on the nature of the interest you desire it to effect, whether you seek clearly to place before us, or dimly to shadow out, each particular character. If you connect your hero with supernatural agency, if you introduce incidents not accounted for by purely human means, if you resort to the Legendary and Mysterious, for the interest that you identify with any individual character, it may be most artistical to leave such a character vague, shadowy, and half incompleted. Thus, very skilfully is the Master of Ravenswood, over whose head hang ominous and weird predictions, left a less distinct and palpable creation than the broad-shouldered and much-eating heroes, whom Scott usually conducts through a Labyrinth of adventures to marriage with a wealthy Ariadne.

The formation of characters improbable and grotesque is not very compatible with a high conception of art, unless the work be one that so avowedly deals with beings different from those we mix with, that our imagination is prepared as to the extent of the demand upon its faith. Thus, when Shakspeare introduces us at once to the Enchanted Island, and we see the wand of the magician, and hear the song of Ariel, we are fully prepared to consider Caliban a proper inhabitant of such a soil; or when the Faust opens with the Chorus of the Angels, and the black dog appears in the chamber of the solitary student, the imagination finds little difficulty in yielding assent to the vagaries of the witches, and the grotesque diablerie of the Hartz Mountains; but we are wholly unprepared to find a human Caliban in the bell-ringer of a Parisian cathedral; and we see no reason why Quasimodo should not have been as well shaped as other people. The use of the Grotesque in The Abbot, where Sir Percy Shafto is killed and revived, is an absurdity as gross and gratuitous as can well be conceived.

In the portraiture of evil and criminal characters lies the widest scope for an author profoundly versed in the philosophy of the human heart. In all countries, in all times, the delineation of crime has been consecrated to the highest order of poetry. For as the emotions of terror and of pity are those which it falls to the province of the sublimest genius to arouse, so it is chiefly, though not solely, in the machinations of guilt that may be found the source of the one, and in the misfortunes, sometimes of the victim of the guilt, nay, sometimes of the guilty agent himself, that we arrive at the fountain of the softer passion. Thus, the murder of Duncan rouses our compassion, through our admission to all the guilty doubts and aspirations of Macbeth; and our terror is of a far higher and more enthralling order, because it is reflected back upon us from the bared and struggling heart of the murderer, than it would have been if we had seen the physical death of the victim. It may be observed, indeed, that, in a fine tragedy, it is the preparation to the death that is to constitute the catastrophe that usually most sensibly excites the interest of terror, and that the blow of the murderer, and the fall of the victim, is but a release to the suspense of fear, and changes the whole current of our emotions. But the grandest combination is when the artist unites in one person the opposite passions of terror and pity—when we feel at once horror of the crime, yet compassion for the criminal. Thus, in the most stirring of all the ancient dramas, the moment that we discover that Œdipus has committed the crimes from which we most revolt, homicide and incest, is the very moment in which, to the deepest terror of the crimes is united the most intense compassion for the criminal. So, again, before the final catastrophe of the mystic fate of Macbeth, when evil predictions are working to their close, and we feel that his hour is come, Shakspeare has paused, to draw from the dark bosom of the fated murderer those moving reflections, "My way of life," &c. which steal from us insensibly our hatred of his guilt, and awaken a new and softer interest in the approaching consummation of the usurper's doom. Again, in the modern play of Virginius, when the scene opens, and discovers the avenging father upon the body of the murdered Appius, it is in Virginius, at once criminal and childless, that are concentrated our pity and our terror.

In the portraiture of crime, however dark, the artist will take care to throw some redeeming light. The veriest criminal has some touch and remnant of human goodness; and it is according as this sympathy between the outcast and ourselves is indicated or insinuated, that the author profanes or masters the noblest mysteries of his art. Where the criminal be one, so resolute and hardened, so inexorable and preter-human, in his guilt, that he passes the bounds of flesh-and-blood inconsistencies and sympathies, a great artist will bring forth intellectual qualities to balance our disgust at the moral. Thus, in Richard III, it is with a masterly skill that Shakspeare relieves us from the revolting contemplation of unmingled crime by enlisting our involuntary and unconscious admiration on the side of the address, the subtle penetration into character, the affluent wit, the daring energy, the royal will, with which the ruthless usurper moves through the bloody scenes of his treachery. And, at the last, it is, if not by a relic of human virtue, at least by a relic of human weakness, by the working conscience, and the haunted pillow, that we are taught to remember that it is a man who sins and suffers, not a beast that ravages and is slain. Still, despite all the subtle shadings in the character of Richard, we feel that the guilt is overdrawn— that the dark spirit wants a moral as well as intellectual relief. To penetrating critics, it has always, therefore, been the most coarse of all the creations of Shakspeare; and will never bear a comparison, as a dissection of human nature, with the goaded and writhing wickedness of Macbeth.

In the delineation of a criminal, the author will take care to show us the motives of the crimes—the influences beneath which the character has been formed. He will suit the nature of the criminal to the state of society in which he is cast. Thus, he will have occasions for the noblest morality. By concentrating in one focus the vicious influences of any peculiar error in the social system, he will hold up a mirror to nations themselves.

As the bad man will not be painted as thoroughly and unredeemedly bad, so he, whom you represent as good, will have his foibles or infirmities. You will show where even the mainspring of his virtues sometimes calls into play a counter vice. Your just man will be sometimes severe—your generous man will be sometimes careless of the consequences of generosity. It is true that, in both these applications of art, you will be censured by shallow critics and pernicious moralists. It will be said of you in the one case, "He seeks to interest us in a murderer or a robber, an adulterer or a parricide;"— it will be said of you in the other, "And this man whom he holds up to us as an example, whom he calls wise and good, is a rascal, who indulges such an error, or commits such an excess." But no man can be an artist who does not prefer experience and human nature to all criticism; and, for the rest, he must be contented to stand on the same ground, or to have filled his urn from the same fountains, as Shakspeare and Boccaccio, as Goethe and Schiller, Fielding and Le Sage. If it be, however, necessary to your design to paint some character as almost faultless, as exempt from our common infirmities and errors, you will act skilfully if you invest it with the attributes of old age. When all the experience of error has been dearly bought, when the passions are laid at rest, and the mind burns clear as the night deepens, virtue does, in fact, become less and less wavering and imperfect. But youth without a fault would be youth without a passion;

and such a portrait would make us despair of emulation, and arm against reverence and esteem all the jealousies of self-love.

Delineation of passions is inseparable from the delineation of character. A novel, admirable in character, may, indeed, be drawn, in which the passions are but coldly and feebly shadowed forth: Gil Blas is an example. But either such novels are intended as representations of external life, not of the metaphysical operations of the inner man, or they deal with the humours and follies, not the grave and deep emotions, of our kind, and belong to the *Comedy* of Romance.

But if a novel of character can be excellent without passion, it would be impossible to create a novel of passion without character. The elementary passions themselves, like the elements, are few: it is the modifications they take in passing through different bodies that give us so inexhaustible a variety of lights and shadows, of loveliness and glory.

The passion of Love is not represented by a series of eloquent rhapsodies, or even of graceful sentiments. It is represented, in fiction, by its effects on some particular character: the same with Jealousy, Avarice, Revenge, &c. Therefore, in a certain sense of the word, all representations of passion in fiction may be considered *typical*. In Juliet, it is not the picture of love solely and abstractedly—it is the picture of love in its fullest effect on *youth*. In Anthony, it is love as wild, and as frantic, and as self-sacrificing; but it is love, not emanating from the enthusiasm of youth, but already touched with something of the blindness and infirmity of dotage.

In Macbeth, it is not the mere passion of ambition that is portrayed,— it is ambition operating on a man physically daring, and morally irresolute; a man whom the darkest agencies alone can compel, and whom the fullest triumphs of success cannot reconcile, to crime. So, if we review all the passionate characters of Shakspeare, we shall find that the passion is individualised and made original by the mould in which the fiery liquid is cast. Nor is the language of that passion declamation upon the passion itself, but the revelation of the effect it produces on a single subject. It is, accordingly, in the perfect harmony that exists between the character and the passion that the abstract and bodiless idea finds human force and corporeal interest. If you would place the passion before us in a new light, the character that represents it must be original. An artistical author, taking advantage of the multiform inconsistencies of human nature, will often give to the most hacknied passion a thoroughly new form, by placing it in a character where it could least be looked for. For instance, should you desire to portray avarice, you will go but on worn-out ground, if you resort to Plautus and to Molière for your model. But if you find in history the record of a brilliant courtier, a successful general, marked and signalised by the vice of Harpagon, the vice itself takes a new hue, and your portraiture will be a new addition to our knowledge of the mysteries of our kind. Such a representation, startling, untouched, and truthful, might be taken from the character of the Duke of Marlborough, the hero of Blenheim. In portraying the effect of a passion, the rarest art of the novelist is to give it its due weight and no more. Thus, in love novels, we usually find nothing but love; as if, in the busy and complicated life of man, there were no other spring to desire and action but

"Love, love — eternal love."

Again, if an author portrays a miser, he never draws him otherwise than as a miser. He makes him, not the avaricious miser, but abstract avarice itself. Not so Shakspeare, when he created Shylock. Other things, other motives, occupy the spirit of the Jew besides his gold and his argosies: he is a grasping and relentless miser, yet he can give up avarice to revenge. He has sublime passions, that elevate his mean ones.

If your novel be devoted to love and its effects, you will act more consistently with the truths of life, if you throw the main interest of the passion in the heroine. In the hero, you will increase our sense of the power of the passion, if you show us all the conflicting passions with which in men it usually contends—ambition, or honour, or duty: the more the effect of the love is shown by the obstacles it silently subdues, the more triumphant will be your success. You will recollect that in the novel, as in the drama, it is in the *struggle* of emotions that the science of the heart is best displayed; and, in the delineation of such struggles, there is ground little occupied hitherto by the great masters of English fiction. It was not in the province of Fielding or Smollett; and Scott but rarely indulges, and still more rarely succeeds, in the metaphysical operations of stormy and conflicting feelings. He rather seems to have made it a point of art to imitate the ancient painter, and throw a veil over passions he felt inadequate to express. Thus, after the death and burial of Lucy, it is only by the heavy and unequal tread of Ravenswood, in his solitary chamber, that his agonies are to be conjectured. But this avoidance of the internal man, if constant and systematic, is but a clever trick to hide the want of power.

THE SENTIMENT

The SENTIMENT that pervades a book is often its most effective moral, and its most universal charm. It is a pervading and indescribable harmony, in which the heart of the author himself seems silently to address our own. Through creations of crime and vice, there may be one pervading sentiment of virtue; through the humblest scenes, a sentiment of power and glory. It is the sentiment of Wordsworth of which his disciples speak, when they enlarge upon attributes of holiness and beauty, which detached passages, however exquisite, do not suffice to justify; for the sentiment of a work is felt, not in its parts, but as a whole: it is undefinable and indefinite—it escapes while you seek to analyse it. Of all the qualities of fiction, the sentiment is that which we can least subject to the inquiries or codes of criticism. It emanates from the moral and predominant quality of the author,—the perfume from his genius; and by it he unconsciously reveals himself. The sentiment of Shakspeare is in the strong sympathies with all that is human. In the sentiment of Swift, we see the reflection of a spirit discontented and malignant. Mackenzie, Goldsmith, Voltaire, Rousseau, betray their several characters as much in the prevalent sentiment of their writings as if they had made themselves the heroes. Of all writers of great genius, Shakspeare has the most sentiment, and, perhaps Smollett and Defoe the least. The student will distinguish between a work of sentiment and a sentimental work. As the charm of sentiment in a fiction is that it is latent and indefinite, so the charm vanishes the instant it becomes obtruding and importunate. The mistake of Kotzebue and many of the Germans, of Metastasio, and a feeble and ephemeral school of the Italians, was in the confounding sentiment with passion.

Sentiment is capable of many classifications and subdivisions. The first and finest is that touched upon—the sentiment of the whole work: a sentiment of beauty or of grandeur—of patriotism or of benevolence—of veneration, of justice, or of piety. This may be perfectly distinct from the characters or scenes portrayed: it evinces itself insensibly and invisibly; and we do not find its effect till we sum up all the effects that the work has bequeathed. The sentiment is, therefore, often incorporated and identified with the moral tendency of the fiction.

There is also a sentiment that belongs to style, and gives depth and colouring to peculiar passages. For instance, in painting a pastoral life in the heart of lonely forests, or by the side of unpolluted streams, the language and thoughts of the author glide into harmony with the images he creates; and we feel that he has, we scarcely know by what art, penetrated himself and us with the Sentiment of Repose.

A sentiment of this nature will be felt at once by the lovers of Spenser, and of Ariosto and Tasso. In the entrance to the Domains of Death, Milton breathes over the whole description the Sentiment of Awe.

The Sentiments are distinct from the Passions: sometimes they are most eloquent in the utter absence of passion itself; as the sentiment that pervades the poem of The Castle of Indolence;—at other times they are the neighbours, the intervening shades, between one passion and another; as the Sentiment of a Pleasing Melancholy. Regret and Awe are sentiments: Grief and Terror, passions.

As there is a sentiment that belongs to description, so there are characters in which sentiment supplies the place of passion. The character of Jacques, in As You like It, is purely one of sentiment. Usually, sentiment is, in character, most effective when united with humour, as in Uncle Toby and Don Quixote, and, to quote a living writer, some of the masterly creations of Paul de Kock. For the very delicacy of the sentiment will be most apparent by the contrast of what seems to us at first the opposite quality; as the violet we neglect in a flower-bed enchants us in the hollow of a rock.

In a succeeding paper it is proposed to enter upon the construction of the fiction itself—the distinctions between the Drama and the Novel—and the mechanism, conduct, and catastrophe of the different species of Invented Narrative. [This "succeeding paper" was Part 2, beginning here.]

THE CONCEPTION

A story may be well constructed, yet devoid of interest; on the other hand, the construction may be faulty and the interest vivid. This is the case even with the drama. Hamlet is not so well constructed a story as the Don Carlos of Alfieri; but there is no comparison in the degree of interest excited in either tragedy. Still, though we ought not to consider that excellence in the technical arrangement of incidents as a certain proof of the highest order of art, it is a merit capable of the most brilliant effects, when possessed by a master. An exquisite mechanism in the construction of the mere story, not only gives pleasure in itself, but it displays other and loftier beauties to the best advantage. It is the setting of the jewels.

It is common to many novelists to commence a work without any distinct chart of the country which they intend to traverse—to suffer one chapter to grow out of another, and invention to warm as the creation grows. Scott had confessed to this mode of novel-writing[1] but Scott, with all his genius, was rather a great mechanist than a great artist. His execution was infinitely superior to his conception. It may be observed, indeed, that his conceptions are often singularly poor and barren, compared with the vigour with which they are worked out. He conceives a story with the design of telling it as well as he can, but is wholly insensible to the high and true aim of art, which is rather to consider for what objects the story should be told. Scott never appears to say to himself, "Such a tale will throw a new light upon human passions, or add fresh stores to human wisdom: for that reason I select it." He seems rather to consider what picturesque effects it will produce, what striking scenes, what illustrations of mere manners. He regards the story with the eye of the *property man*, though he tells it with the fervour of the poet. It is not thus that the greatest authorities in fiction have composed. It is clear to us that Shakspeare, when he selected the tale which he proposed to render χτῆμά ἐς ἀεί,—the everlasting possession of mankind,[2] made it his first and paramount object to work out certain passions, or affections of the mind, in the most complete and profound form. He did not so much consider how the incidents might be made most striking,

---

[1] "See Mr. Lockhart's Life of Scott, vol. vi. p. 232. 'In writing I never could lay down a plan,' etc. Scott, however, has the candour to add, 'I would not have young writers imitate my carelessness.' " [Bulwer-Lytton]

[2] Lit. "a possession forever"
—Thucydides, *History of the Peloponnesian War* 1. 22.

as how the truths of the human heart might be made most clear. And it is a remarkable proof of his consummate art, that though in his best plays we may find instances in which the mere incidents might be made more probable, and the theatrical effects more vivid, we can never see one instance in such plays where the passion he desired to represent, could have been placed in a broader light, or the character he designed to investigate, could have been submitted to a minuter analysis. We are quite sure that Othello and Macbeth were not written without the clear and deep and pre-meditated CONCEPTION of the story to be told us. For with Shakspeare the conception itself is visible and gigantic from the first line to the last. So in the greatest works of Fielding a very obtuse critic may perceive that the author sat down to write in order to embody a design previously formed. The perception of moral truths urged him to the composition of his fictions. In Jonathan Wild, the finest prose satire in the English language, Fielding, before he set pen to paper, had resolved to tear the mask from False Greatness. In his conception of the characters and histories of Blifil and Jones, he was bent on dethroning that popular idol—False Virtue. The scorn of hypocrisy in all grades, all places, was the intellectual passion of Fielding; and his masterpieces are the results of intense convictions. That many incidents never contemplated would suggest themselves as he proceeded —that the technical plan of events might deviate and vary, according as he saw new modes of enforcing his aims, is unquestionable. But still Fielding always commenced *with* a plan—with a conception—with a moral end, to be achieved by definite agencies, and through the medium of certain characters pre-formed in his mind. If Scott had no preconcerted story when he com-menced Chapter the First of one of his delightful tales, it was because he was deficient in the highest attributes of art, viz., its philosophy and its ethics. He never seems to have imagined that the loftiest merit of a tale rests upon the effect it produces, not on the fancy, but on the intellect and the passions. He had no grandeur of conception, for he had no strong desire to render palpable and immortal some definite and abstract truth.

It is a sign of the low state of criticism in this country that Scott has been compared to Shakspeare. No two writers can be more entirely opposed to each other in the qualities of their genius, or the sources to which they applied. Shakspeare ever aiming at the development of the secret man, and half disdaining the mechanism of external incidents; Scott painting the ruffles and the dress, and the features and the gestures—avoiding the movements of the heart, elaborate in the progress of the incident. Scott never caught the mantle of Shakspeare, but he improved on the dresses of his wardrobe, and threw artificial effects into the scenes of his theatres.

Let us take an example: we will select one of the finest passages in Sir Walter Scott: a passage unsurpassed for its mastery over the PICTURESQUE. It is that chapter in "Kenilworth," where Elizabeth has discovered Amy, and formed her first suspicions of Leicester.

"Leicester was at this moment the centre of a splendid group of lords and ladies, assembled together under an arcade or portico, which closed the alley. The company had drawn together in that place, to attend the commands of her majesty when the hunting party should go forward, and their astonishment may be imagined, when instead of seeing Elizabeth advance towards them with her usual measured dignity of motion, they beheld her walking so rapidly, that she was in the midst of them ere they were aware; and then observed with fear and surprise, that her features were flushed betwixt anger and agitation, that her hair was loosened by her haste of motion, and that her eyes sparkled as they were wont when the spirit of Henry VIII. mounted highest in his daughter. Nor were they less astonished at the appearance of the pale, extenuated, half-dead, yet still lovely female, whom the queen upheld by main strength with one hand, while with the other she waved aside the ladies and nobles, who pressed towards her, under the idea that she was taken suddenly ill. 'Where is my Lord of Leicester?' she said, in a tone that thrilled with astonishment all the courtiers who stood around — 'Stand forth, my Lord of Leicester!'

"If, in the midst of the most serene day of summer, when all is light and laughing around, a thunderbolt were to fall from the clear blue vault of heaven, and rend the earth at the very feet of some careless traveller, he could not gaze upon the smouldering chasm which so unexpectedly yawned before him, with half the astonishment and fear which Leicester felt at the sight that so suddenly presented itself. He had that instant been receiving, with a political affectation of disavowing and mis-understanding their meaning, the half-uttered, half-intimated congratulations of the courtiers upon the favour of the queen, carried apparently to its highest pitch during the interview of that morning; from which most of them seemed to augur, that he might soon arise from their equal in rank to become their master. And now, while the subdued yet proud smile with which he disclaimed those inferences was yet curling his cheek, the queen shot into the circle, her passions excited to the uttermost; and, supporting with one hand, and apparently without an effort, the pale and sinking form of his almost expiring wife, and pointing with the finger of the other to her half-dead features, demanded in a voice that sounded to the ears of the astounded statesman like the last dread trumpet-call, that is to summon body and spirit to the judgment seat, 'Knowest thou this woman?'"

The reader will observe that the whole of this splendid passage is devoted to external effects: the loosened hair and sparkling eyes of Elizabeth —the grouping of the courtiers—the proud smile yet on the cheek of Leicester—the pale and sinking form of the wife. Only by external effects do we guess at the emotions of the agents. Scott is thinking of the costume and postures of the actors, not the passions they represent. Let us take a parallel passage in Shakspeare; parallel, for, in each, a mind disturbed with jealousy is the real object placed before the reader. It is thus that Iago describes Othello, after the latter has conceived *his* first suspicions:

> "Look where he comes! Not poppy, nor mandragora,
>   Nor all the drowsy syrups of the world,
>   Shall ever medicine thee to that sweet sleep
>   Which thou ow'dst yesterday.
>   *Othello.*   Ha! ha! false to me?"

Here the reader will observe that there is no attempt at the Picturesque
—no sketch of the outward man. It is only by a reference to the woe that
kills sleep that we can form any notion of the haggard aspect of the Moor.
So, if we compare the ensuing dialogue in the romance with that in the
tragedy, we shall remark that Elizabeth utters only bursts of shallow passion,
which convey none of the deep effects of the philosophy of jealousy; none of
the sentiments that "inform us what we are." But every sentence uttered by
Othello penetrates to the very root of the passion described: the farewell to
fame and pomp, which comes from a heart that, finding falsehood in the
prop it leaned on, sees the world itself, and all its quality and circumstance,
crumbled away; the burst of vehement incredulity; the sudden return to
doubt; the intense revenge proportioned to the intense love; the human
weakness that must seek faith somewhere, and, with the loss of Desdemona,
casts itself upon her denouncer; the mighty knowledge of the heart exhibited
in those simple words to Iago, "I greet *thy* love;"—compare all this with the
mere words of Elizabeth, which have no force in themselves, but are made
effective by the picturesque grouping of the scene, and you will detect at
once the astonishing distinction between Shakspeare and Scott. Shakspeare
could have composed the most wonderful plays from the stories in Scott;
Scott could have written the most excellent stage directions to the plays of
Shakspeare.

If the novelist be contented with the secondary order of Art in Fiction,
and satisfied if his incidents be varied, animating, and striking, he may write
from chapter to chapter, and grope his way to a catastrophe in the dark;
but if he aim at loftier and more permanent effects, he will remember that
to execute grandly we must conceive nobly. He will suffer the subject he
selects to lie long in his mind, to be revolved, meditated, brooded over,
until from the chaos breaks the light, and he sees distinctly the highest end
for which his materials can be used, and the best process by which they can
be reduced to harmony and order.

If, for instance, he found his tale upon some legend, the author, inspired
with a great ambition, will consider what will be, not the most vivid interest,
but the loftiest and most durable *order* of interest he can extract from the
incidents. Sometimes it will be in a great truth elicited by the catastrophe;
sometimes by the delineation of one or more characters; sometimes by the
mastery over, and development of, some complicated passion. Having
decided what it is that he designs to work out, he will mould his story
accordingly; but before he begin to execute, he will have clearly informed
his mind of the conception that induces the work itself.

INTEREST

No fiction can be first-rate if it fail to create INTEREST. But the merit
of the fiction is not, by any means, proportioned to the *degree* of excitement
it produces, but to the *quality* of the excitement. It is certainly some merit

to make us weep; but the great artist will consider from what sources our
tears are to be drawn. We may weep as much at the sufferings of a beggar
as at the agonies of Lear; but from what sublime sympathies arise our tears
for the last! what commonplace pity will produce the first! We may have
our interest much more acutely excited by the "Castle of Udolpho" than
by "Anastasius;" but in the one, it is a melodramatic arrangement of
hair-breadth escapes and a technical skill in the arrangement of vulgar
mysteries—in the other, it is the consummate knowledge of actual life,
that fascinates the eye to the page. It is necessary, then, that every novel
should excite interest; but one novel may produce a much more gradual,
gentle, and subdued interest than another, and yet have infinitely more
merit in the *quality* of the interest it excites.

TERROR AND HORROR

True art never disgusts. If, in descriptions intended to harrow us, we
feel sickened and revolted by the very power with which the description is
drawn, the author has passed the boundary of his province; he does not
appal—he shocks. Thus, nothing is more easy than to produce a feeling of
intense pain by a portrait of great bodily suffering. The vulgarest mind
can do this, and the mistaken populace of readers will cry, "See the power
of this author!" But all sympathy with bodily torture is drawn from our
basest infirmities; all sympathy with mental torture from our deepest
passions and our most spiritual nature. HORROR is generally produced by
the one, TERROR by the other. If you describe a man hanging by a breaking
bough over a precipice—if you paint his starting eyeballs, his erect hair,
the death-sweat on his brow, the cracking of the bough, the depth of the
abyss, the sharpness of the rock, the roar of the cataract below, you may
make us dizzy and sick with sympathy; but you operate on the physical
nerves, and our sensation is that of coarse and revolting pain. But take a
moral abyss: Œdipus, for instance, on the brink of learning the awful secret
which proclaims him an incestuous parricide. Show the splendour of his
power, the depth of his wisdom, the loftiness of his pride, and then gradually,
step by step, reveal the precipice on which he stands—and you work not on
the body but the mind; you produce the true tragic emotion, *terror*. Even
in this, you must stop short of all that could make terror revolt while it thrills
us. This, Sophocles has done by one of those fine perceptions of nature
which open the sublimest mysteries of art; we are not allowed time to
suffer our thoughts to dwell upon the incest and self-assault of Œdipus,
or upon the suicide of Jocasta, before, by the introduction of the Children,
terror melts into pity, and the parricide son assumes the new aspect of the
broken-hearted father. A modern French writer, if he had taken this subject,
would have disgusted us by details of the incest itself, or forced us from the
riven heart to gaze on the bloody and eyeless sockets of the blind king;
and the more he disgusted us the more he would have thought that he

excelled the tragedian of Colonos. Such of the Germans, on the contrary, as follow the School of Schiller, will often stop as far short of the true boundaries of Terror as the French romanticists would go beyond it. Schiller held it a principle of art never to leave the complete and entire effects of a work of art one of pain. According to him, the pleasure of the art should exceed the sympathy with the suffering. He sought to vindicate this principle by a reference to the Greek drama, but in this he confounded the sentiments with which we, moderns, read the works of Æschylus and Sophocles, with the sentiments with which *a Greek* would have read them. No doubt, to a Greek religiously impressed with the truth and reality of the woes or the terror depicted, the "Agamemnon" of Æschylus, the "Œdipus Tyrannus" of Sophocles, and the "Medea" of Euripides, would have left a far more unqualified and overpowering sentiment of awe and painful sympathy than we now can entertain for victims, whom we believe to be shadows, to deities and destinies that we know to be chimeras. Were Schiller's rule universally adopted, we should condemn Othello and Lear.

Terror may then be carried up to its full extent, provided that it work upon us through the mind, not the body, and stop short of the reaction of recoil and disgust.

DESCRIPTION

One of the greatest and most peculiar arts of the Novelist is DESCRIPTION. It is in this that he has a manifest advantage over the dramatic poet. The latter will rarely describe scenery, costume, *personals*, for they ought to be placed before the eyes of the audience by the theatre and the actors. When he does do so, it is generally understood by an intelligent critic, to be an episode introduced for the sake of some poetical beauty, which, without absolutely carrying on the plot, increases the agreeable and artistical effect of the whole performance. This is the case with the description of Dover cliff, in "Lear," or with that of the chasm which adorns, by so splendid a passage, the monstrous tragedy of "The Cenci." In the classical French theatre, as in the Greek, Description, it is true, becomes an essential part of the play itself since the catastrophe is thrown into description. Hence the celebrated picture of the death of Hippolyte, in the "Phedre" of Racine— of the suicide of Hæmon in the "Antigone" of Sophocles. But it may be doubted whether both Sophocles and his French imitator did not, in this transfer of action to words, strike at the very core of dramatic art, whether ancient or modern; for it may be remarked—and we are surprised that it has not been remarked before, that Æschylus preferred placing the catastrophe before the eyes of the reader; and he who remembers the sublime close of the Prometheus, the storm, the lightning, the bolt, the shivered rock, and the mingled groans and threats of the Titan himself, must acknowledge that the effect is infinitely more purely tragical than it would have been if we had been told how it all happened by the Aggelos or Messenger. So in the

"Agamemnon" of the same sublime poet, though we do not see the blow given, the scene itself, opening, places before us the murderess and the corpse. No messenger intervenes—no description is required for the action. "I stand where I struck him," says Clytæmnestra. "The deed is done!" [3]

But without recurring farther to the Drama of other nations, we may admit at once that in our own it is the received and approved rule that Action, as much as possible, should dispense with Description. With Narrative Fiction it is otherwise: the novel writer is his own scene painter; description is as essential to him as canvass is to the actor—description of the most various character.

In this art, none ever equalled Scott. In the comparison we made between him and Shakspeare, we meant not to censure the former for indulging in what the latter shunned; each did that which his art required. We only lament that Scott did not combine with external description an equal, or, at least, not very inferior, skill in metaphysical analysis. Had he done so, he would have achieved all of which the novelist is capable.

In the description of natural scenery, the author will devote the greatest care to such landscapes as are meant for the localities of his principal events. There is nothing, for instance, very attractive in the general features of a common; but if the author lead us through a common, on which, in a later portion of his work, a deed of murder is to be done, he will strive to fix deeply in our remembrance the character of the landscape, the stunted tree, or the mantling pool, which he means to associate in our minds with an act of terror.

If the duration of time in a fiction be limited to a year, the author may be enabled artfully to show us the progress of time by minute descriptions of the gradual change in the seasons. This is attempted to be done in the tale of "Eugene Aram": instead of telling us when it is July, and when it is October, the author of that fiction describes the signs and characteristics of the month, and seeks to identify our interest in the natural phenomena, with the approaching fate of the hero, himself an observer and an artist of the "clouds that pass to and fro," and the "herbs that wither and are renewed." Again, in description, if there be any natural objects that will bear upon the catastrophe, if, for instance, the earthquake or the inundation be intended as an agent in the fate of those whose history the narrative relates, incidental descriptions of the state of the soil, frequent references to the river or the sea, will serve to make the elements themselves minister to the interest of the plot; and the final catastrophe will be made at once more familiar, yet more sublime, if we have been prepared and led to believe that you have from the first designed to invoke to your aid the awful agencies of Nature herself. Thus, in the Œdipus at Colonos, the Poet, at the very opening of the tragedy, indulges in the celebrated description of the seats

[3] "Even Sophocles, in one of his finest tragedies, has not scrupled to suffer the audience to witness the last moments of Ajax." [Bulwer-Lytton]

of the Dread Goddesses, because the place, and the deities themselves, though invisible, belong yet more essentially to the crowning doom of the wanderer than any of the characters introduced.

The description of *feelings* is also the property of the novelist. The dramatist throws the feelings into dialogue,—the novelist goes at once to the human heart, and calmly scrutinises, assorts, and dissects them. Few, indeed, are the writers who have hitherto attempted this—the master mystery of the hierophant! Godwin has done so the most elaborately; Goëthe the most skilfully. The first writer is, indeed, so minute, that he is often frivolous—so lengthened, that he is generally tedious; but the cultivator of the art, and not the art itself, is to be blamed for such defects. A few words will often paint the precise state of emotion as faithfully as the most voluminous essay; and in this department condensation and brevity are to be carefully studied. Conduct us to the cavern, light the torch, and startle and awe us by what you reveal; but if you keep us all day in the cavern, the effect is lost, and our only feeling is that of impatience and desire to get away.

ARRANGEMENT OF INCIDENTS

Distinctions between the Novel and the Drama

In the arrangement of incidents, the reader will carefully study the distinctions between the novel and the drama—distinctions the more important, because they are not, at the first glance, very perceptible.

In the first place, the incidents of a play must grow, progressively, out of each other. Each scene should appear the necessary consequence of the one that precedes it. This is far from being the case with the novel; in the last, it is often desirable to go back instead of forward—to wind, to vary, to shift the interest from person to person—to keep even your principal hero, your principal actor, in the background. In the novel, you see more of Frank Osbaldistone than you do of Rob Roy; but bring Rob Roy on the stage, and Frank Osbaldistone must recede at once into a fifth-rate personage.

In our closets we should be fatigued with the incessant rush of events that we desire when we make one of a multitude. Oratory and the drama in this resemble each other—that the things best to hear are not always the best to read. In the novel, we address ourselves to the one person—on the stage we address ourselves to a crowd: more rapid effects, broader and more popular sentiments, more condensed grasp of the universal passions are required for the last. The calm advice which persuades our friend would only tire out the patience of the crowd. The man who writes a play for Covent Garden ought to remember that the Theatre is but a few paces distant from the Hustings: success at either place, the Hustings or the Theatre, will depend upon a mastery over feelings, not perhaps the most commonplace, but the most commonly felt. If with his strong effects on the stage, the dramatic poet can, like Shakspeare, unite the most delicate and subtle refinement, like Shakspeare he will be a consummate artist. But the refinement will not do without the effects. In the novel it is different: the most enchanting and permanent kind of interest, in the latter, is often gentle, tranquillising, and subdued. The novelist can appeal to those delicate and subtle emotions, which are easily awakened when we are alone, but which are torpid and unfelt in the electric contagion of popular sympathies. The most refining amongst us will cease to refine when placed in the midst of a multitude.

There is a great distinction between the plot of a novel and that of a play; a distinction which has been indicated by Goëthe in the "Wilhelm Meister." The novel allows *accident*, the drama never. In the former, your principal character may be thrown from his horse, and break his neck; in the latter, this would be a gross burlesque on the first laws of the drama; for in the drama the incidents must bring about the catastrophe; in the novel, there is no such necessity. Don Quixote at the last falls ill and dies in his bed; but in order that he should fall ill and die in his bed, there was no necessity that he should fight windmills, or mistake an inn for a castle. If a novelist had taken for his theme the conspiracy of Fiesco, he might have adhered to history with the most perfect consistency to his art. In the history, as Fiesco, after realising his ambitious projects, is about to step into the ship, he slips from the plank, and the weight of his armour drowns him. This is accident, and this catastrophe would not only have been admissible in the novel, but would have conveyed, perhaps, a sublimer moral than any that fiction could invent. But when Schiller adapted Fiesco for the stage, he felt that accident was not admissible,[4] and his Fiesco falls by the hand of the patriot Verrina. The whole dialogue preceding the fatal blow is one of the most masterly adaptations of moral truth to the necessity of historical infidelity, in European literature.

In the "Bride of Lammermoor," Ravenswood is swallowed up by a quicksand. This catastrophe is singularly grand in romance; it could not be allowable on the stage; for this again is *accident*, and not *result*.

The distinctions, then, between the novel and the drama, so far as the management of incidents is concerned, are principally these: that in the one the interest must always progress—that in the other, it must often go back and often halt; that dealing with human nature in a much larger scale in the novel, you will often introduce events and incidents, not necessarily growing one out of the other, though all conducing to the completeness of the whole; that in the drama you have more impatience to guard against—you are addressing men in numbers, not the individual man; your effects must be more rapid and more startling; that in the novel you may artistically have recourse to accident for the working out of your design—in the drama, never.

[4] " 'The nature of the Drama,' observes Schiller, in his preface to Fiesco, and in excuse for his corruption of history, 'does not admit the hand of Chance.' " [Bulwer-Lytton]

The ordinary faults of a play by the novelist,[5] and of a novel by the play-writer, will serve as an illustration of the principles which have insensibly regulated each. The novelist will be too diffuse, too narrative, and too refined in his efforts for the stage; the play-writer will be too condensed, abrupt, and, above all, too exaggerated, for our notions of the Natural when we are in the closet. Stage effect is a vice in the novel; but, how can we expect a man trained to write for the stage to avoid what on the stage is a merit? A certain exaggeration of sentiment is natural, and necessary, for sublime and truthful effects when we address numbers; it would be ludicrous uttered to our friend in his easy chair. If Demosthenes, urging a young Athenian to conduct himself properly, had thundered out[6] that sublime appeal to the shades of Marathon, Platea, and Salamis, which thrilled the popular assembly, the young Athenian would have laughed in his face. If the dialogue of "Macbeth" were the dialogue of a romance on the same subject, it would be equally good in itself, but it would seem detestable bombast. If the dialogue in "Ivanhoe," which is matchless of its kind for spirit and fire, were shaped into blank verse, and cut up into a five-act play, it would be bald and pointless. As the difference between the effective oration and the eloquent essay—between Pitt so great to hear, and Burke so great to read, so is the difference between the writing for the eye of one man, and the writing for the ears of three thousand.

---

[5] " 'Why is it that a successful novelist never has been a successful play-writer?' This is a question that has been so often put, that we have been frightened out of considering whether the premises involved in the question are true or not. It is something like the schoolboy question, 'Why is a pound of feathers heavier than a pound of lead?' It is long before Tom or Jack ask, 'Is it heavier?' *Is* it true that a successful novelist never has been a successful play-writer? We will not insist on Goldsmith, whose comedy of 'She Stoops to Conquer,' and whose novel of the 'Vicar of Wakefield,' are alike among the greatest ornaments of our language. But was not Goëthe a great play-writer and a great novelist? Who will decide whether the palm in genius should be given to the 'Tasso' or the 'Wilhelm Meister' of that all-sided genius? Is not the 'Ghost-seer' a successful novel? Does it not afford the highest and most certain testimony of what Schiller could have done as a writer of narrative fiction, and are not 'Wallenstein,' and 'Fiesco,' and 'Don Carlos,' great plays by the same author? Are not 'Candide' and 'Zadig' imperishable masterpieces in the art of the novelist? And are not 'Zaire' and 'Mahomet' equally immortal? The three greatest geniuses that, in modern times, the Continent has produced, were both novelists and dramatists—equally great in each department. In France, at this day, Victor Hugo, who, with all his faults, is immeasurably the first writer in the school he has sought to found, is both the best novelist and the most powerful dramatist. That it has not happened *oftener* that the same man has achieved equal honour in the novel and the play is another question. But we might just as well ask why it has not happened oftener that the same man has been equally successful in tragedy and epic—in the ode and the didactic—why he who is sublime as a poet is often tame as a prose writer, and *vice versâ*—why the same artist who painted the 'Transfiguration' did not paint the 'Last Day.' Nature, circumstance, and education have not fitted many men to be great, except in one line. And least of all are they commonly great in two lines which, though seemingly close to each other, run in parallel directions. The more subtle the distinctions between the novel and the play, the more likely are they to be everlooked by him who attempts both. It is the same with all departments of art; the closer the approximation of the boundaries, the more difficult the blending." [Bulwer-Lytton]

[6] "Dem. de Cor." [Bulwer-Lytton]

MECHANISM AND CONDUCT

The MECHANISM AND CONDUCT OF THE STORY ought to depend upon the nature of the preconceived design. Do you desire to work out some definite end, through the passions or through the characters you employ? Do you desire to carry on the interest less through character and passion than through incident? Or, do you rather desire to entertain and instruct by a general and wide knowledge of living manners or human nature? or, lastly, would you seek to incorporate all these objects? As you are faithful to your conception, will you be attentive to, and precise in, the machinery you use. In other words, your *progress* must depend upon the order of interest you mean to be predominant. It is by not considering this rule that critics have often called that episodical or extraneous, which is in fact a part of the design. Thus, in "Gil Blas," the object is to convey to the reader a complete picture of the surface of society; the manners, foibles, and peculiarities of the time; elevated by a general, though not very profound, knowledge of the more durable and universal elements of human nature in the abstract. Hence, the numerous tales and nouvelletes scattered throughout the work, though episodical to the adventures of Gil Blas, are not episodical to the design of Le Sage. They all serve to complete and furnish out the conception, and the whole would be less rich and consummate in its effect without them. They are not passages which lead to nothing, but conduce to many purposes we can never comprehend, unless we consider well for what end the building was planned. So if you wish to bring out all the peculiarities of a certain character, you will often seem to digress into adventures which have no palpable bearing on the external plot of incident and catastrophe. This is constantly the case with Cervantes and Fielding; and the critic who blames you for it, is committing the gross blunder of judging the novel by the laws of the drama.

But as an ordinary rule, it may be observed that, since, both in the novel and the play, human life is represented by an epitome, so in both it is desirable that all your characters should more or less be brought to bear on the conclusions you have in view. It is not necessary in the novel that they should bear on the physical events; they may sometimes bear on the mental and interior changes in the minds and characters of the persons you introduce. For instance, if you design in the life of your hero to illustrate the Passion of Jealousy upon a peculiar conformation of mind, you may introduce several characters and several incidents, which will serve to ripen his tendencies, but not have the least bearing on the actual catastrophe in which those tendencies are confirmed into deeds. This is but fidelity to real life, in which it seldom happens that they who foster the passion are the witnesses or sufferers of the effects. This distinction between interior and external agencies will be made apparent by a close study of the admirable novel of Zeluco.

In the mechanism of external incidents, Scott is the greatest model that fiction possesses; and if we select from his works that in which this mechanism is most artistical, we instance not one of his most brilliant and popular, but one in which he combined all the advantages of his multiform and matured experience in the craft: we mean the *Fair Maid of Perth*. By noting well the manner in which, in this tale, the scene is ever varied at the right moment, and the exact medium preserved between abruptness and *longueur*; how all the incidents are complicated, so as to appear inextricable, yet the solution obtained by the simplest and shortest process, the reader will learn more of the art of *mechanical* construction, than by all the rules that Aristotle himself, were he living, could lay down.

DIVISIONS OF THE WORK

In the Drama, the DIVISIONS of the plot into *Acts* are of infinite service in condensing and simplifying the design of the author. The novelist will find it convenient to himself to establish analogous divisions in the conduct of his story. The division into volumes is but the affair of the printer, and affords little help to the intellectual purposes of the author. Hence, most of our greatest novelists have had recourse to the more definite sub-partition of the work into *Books*; and if the student use this mode of division, not from capricious or arbitrary pleasure, but with the same purposes of art, for which, in the drama, recourse is had to the division into Acts, he will find it of the greatest service. Properly speaking, each Book should be complete in itself, working out the exact and whole purpose that the author meditates in that portion of his work. It is clear, therefore, that the number of his Books will vary according to the nature of his design. Where you have shaped your story after a dramatic fashion, you will often be surprised to find how greatly you serve to keep your construction faithful to your design by the mere arrangement of the work into the same number of sub-divisions as are adopted in the drama, viz., five books instead of five acts. Where, on the other hand, you avoid the dramatic construction, and lead the reader through great varieties of life and action, meaning, in each portion of the history of your hero, to illustrate separate views of society or human nature, you will probably find a much greater number of subdivisions requisite. This must depend upon your design. Another advantage in these divisions consists in the rules that your own common sense will suggest to you with respect to the introduction of Characters. It is seldom advisable to admit any new character of importance, after the interest has arrived at a certain point of maturity. As you would not introduce a new character of consequence to the catastrophe, in the fifth act of a play, so, though with more qualification and reserve, it will be inartistical to make a similar introduction in the corresponding portion of a novel. The most illustrious exception to this general rule is in "Clarissa," in which the Avenger, the brother of the heroine, and the executioner of Lovelace, only appears at the close of the story, and for the single purpose of revenge; and here the effect is heightened by the lateness and suddenness of the introduction of the very person to whom the catastrophe is confided.

THE CATASTROPHE

The distinction between the novel and the drama is usually very visible in the Catastrophe. The stage effect of bringing all the characters together in the closing chapter, to be married or stabbed as the thing may require, is, to a fine taste, eminently displeasing in a novel. It introduces into the very place where we most desire verisimilitude, a clap-trap and theatrical effect. For it must be always remembered, that in prose fiction we require more of the Real than we do in the drama (which belongs, of right, to the regions of pure poetry), and if the very last effect bequeathed to us be that of palpable delusion and trick, the charm of the whole work is greatly impaired. Some of Scott's romances may be justly charged with this defect.

Usually, the author is so far aware of the inartist-like effect of a final grouping of all the characters before the fall of the curtain, that he brings but few of the agents he has employed to be *present* at the catastrophe, and follows what may be called the wind-up of the main interest, by one or more epilogical chapters, in which we are told how Sir Thomas married and settled at his country seat, how Miss Lucy died an old maid, and how the miser Grub was found dead on his money chest; disposing in a few sentences of the lives and deaths of all to whom we have been presented—a custom that we think might now give place to less hacknied inventions.

The drama will bear but one catastrophe; the novel will admit of more. Thus, in "Ivanhoe," the more vehement and apparent catastrophe is the death of Bois Guilbert; but the marriage of Ivanhoe, the visit of Rebecca to Rowena, and the solemn and touching farewell of the Jewess, constitute, properly speaking, a catastrophe no less capital in itself, and no less essential to the completion of the incidents. So also there is often a moral catastrophe, as well as a physical one, sometimes identified each with the other, sometimes distinct. If you have been desirous to work out some conception of a principle or a truth, the design may not be completed till after the more violent effects which form the physical catastrophe. In the recent novel of "Alice, or the Mysteries," the external catastrophe is in the vengeance of Cæsarini and the death of Vargrave, but the complete *denouement* and completion of the more typical meanings and ethical results of the fiction are reserved to the moment when Maltravers recognises the Natural to be the true Ideal, and is brought, by the faith and beauty of simple goodness, to affection and respect for mankind itself. In the drama, it would be necessary to incorporate in one scene all the crowning results of the preceding events. We could not bear a new interest after the death of Bois Guilbert; and a new act of mere dialogue between Alice and Maltravers, after the death of Vargrave, would be insufferably tame and frigid. The perfection of a catastrophe is not so much in the power with which it is told, as in the feeling of completeness which it should leave on the mind. On closing the work, we ought to feel that we have read a *whole*—that there is an harmonious unity in all its parts—that its close, whether it be pleasing or painful, is that which is essentially appropriate to all that has gone before; and not only the mere isolated thoughts in the work, but the unity of the work itself, ought to leave its single and deep impression on the mind. The book itself should be a thought.

There is another distinction between the catastrophe of a novel and that of a play. In the last, it ought to be the most permanent and striking events that lead to the catastrophe; in the former, it will often be highly artistical to revive for the consummating effect, many slight details—incidents the author had but dimly shadowed out—mysteries, that you had judged, till then, he had forgotten to clear up; and to bring a thousand rivulets, that had seemed merely introduced to relieve or adorn the way, into the rapid gulf which closes over all. The effect of this has a charm not derived from mere trick, but from its fidelity to the natural and lifelike order of events. What more common in the actual world than that the great crises of our fate are influenced and coloured, not so much by the incidents and persons we have deemed most important, but by many things of remote date, or of seeming insignificance. The feather the eagle carelessly sheds by the way-side plumes the shaft that transfixes him. In this management and combination of incidents towards the grand end, knowledge of Human Nature can alone lead the student to the knowledge of Ideal Art.

These remarks form the summary of the hints and suggestions that, after a careful study of books, we submit to the consideration of the student in a class of literature now so widely cultivated, and hitherto almost wholly unexamined by the critic. We presume not to say that they form an entire code of laws for the art. Even Aristotle's immortal treatise on Poetry, were it bequeathed to us complete, would still be but a skeleton; and though no poet could read that treatise without advantage, the most glorious poetry might be, and has been, written in defiance of nearly all its laws. Genius will arrive at fame by the light of its own star; but Criticism can often serve as a sign-post to save many an unnecessary winding, and indicate many a short way. He who aspires to excel in that fiction which is the glass of truth, may learn much from books and rules, from the lecturer and the critic; but he must be also the Imaginer, the Observer. He will be ever examining human life in its most catholic and comprehensive aspects. Nor is it enough to observe, —it is necessary to feel. We must let the heart be a student as well as the head. No man who is a passionless and cold spectator, will ever be an accurate analyst, of all the motives and springs of action. Perhaps, if we were to search for the true secret of CREATIVE GENIUS, we should find that secret in the intenseness of its SYMPATHIES.

12

CHARLES DICKENS

(1812–1870)

"I can now only take the reader into one confidence more," wrote Charles Dickens in the Preface to *David Copperfield* (1868–70 edition). "Of all my books, I like this the best. It will be easily believed that I am a fond parent to every child of my fancy, and that no one can ever love that family as dearly as I love them." Thus he expresses the close relationship existing between himself and his readers, on the one hand, and between himself and his characters, on the other. He strengthened the first bond by giving readings from his works in his later years before rapturous audiences in England, Scotland, and the United States. No novelist was ever closer to his public, and he took account of its reactions as he wrote for serial publication.

Dickens' affection for his characters reflects the affection he felt for the masses, whose condition he desired to elevate. In a speech at a banquet held in Boston for him, on 1 February 1842, he stated that his purpose had been to show the virtue present in low and unfortunate life. In another speech, some years later, he claimed that literature cannot be too faithful to the people, cannot too ardently advocate the cause of their advancement, happiness, and prosperity (Birmingham, 6 January 1853). Thus Dickens developed into a reformer, and his novels are unified by their attacks on governmental inadequacy, legal shortcomings, organizations such as trade unions, and penal laws. His panacea was brotherly love and trust in philanthropic benevolence. His method was melodrama, replete with sentiment.

Personal interest and knowledge provided Dickens with his subjects and his techniques. As a journalist he had come to know intimately the London that he wrote about; later he took field trips to gain up-to-date impressions of the scene. Journalistic reporting gave him an eye for detail and the ability to portray that detail in vivid language. The hardships of his early life served as a personal incentive to seek reform. His experiences in the theater gave him a knowledge of effective scene setting, melodrama, and an ability to characterize

109

through dialog and speech "tags." Aware of his predecessors in fiction, he borrowed and adapted techniques as he gradually developed his own methods.

Over a thirty-year writing career, Dickens produced fifteen novels; together with plays, Christmas books, sketches, and travel accounts, his works fill twenty volumes. Just as there are extremes of good and bad among the various novels, so there are weaknesses within his best books. Yet, now that his reputation has been firmly restored after the temporary loss of critical regard at the turn of the century, we distinguish several great books, including *Martin Chuzzlewit* (1843–44), *Dombey and Son* (1846–48), *David Copperfield* (1849–50), *Bleak House* (1852–53), *Great Expectations* (1860–61), *Our Mutual Friend* (1864–65), and his historical novel, *A Tale of Two Cities* (1859).

Today it is not the social note, the melodrama, the sentiment, nor the close relationship of author to reader that attracts us to Dickens. Rather, it is his ability to interest us in commonplace things by romanticizing them and his creation of memorable characters, especially the comic ones. His characters have been called caricatures, with a tone of detraction. But must there not be character before there can be caricature? Micawber is, to some, unbelievable because of exaggerated features, but Dickens' own father served as his model. In the Preface to the first edition of *Nicholas Nickleby* (1838–39), Dickens protested: "It is remarkable that what we call the world, which is so very credulous in what professes to be true, is most incredulous in what professes to be imaginary; and that while everyday in real life it will allow in one man no blemishes, and in another no virtues, it will seldom admit a very strongly-marked character, either good or bad, in a fictitious narrative, to be within the limits of probability." Regardless of his detractors, Micawber still remains one of the most memorable humorous creations in the long history of the novel.

Dickens' comments on the theory of the novel and on specific techniques are brief and sporadic. Possibly Bradford Booth is correct in writing that "Dickens thought all such explanations superogatory, and he consistently avoided formal criticism" ("Trollope on the Novel," *Essays Critical and Historical* . . . , Berkeley and Los Angeles, 1950, p. 219). Perhaps the answer is simply that Dickens was too busy writing novels to write about the art. Some of his letters do touch on specific questions. Thus, he rejects "that canon of fiction which forbids the interposition of accident in such a case as Madame Defarge's death. Where the accident is inseparable from the passion and emotion of the character, where it is strictly consistent with the whole design, and arises out of some culminating proceeding on the part of the character which the whole story has led up to, it seems to me to become, as it were, an act of divine justice" (Letter to Bulwer, 5 June 1860).

The letter to Mrs. Brookfield of 20 February 1866 argues that a story is best told through the characters and points out the necessity for a special structure for serialization. A more extended discussion, pertaining to one of his novels but expressing his general moral and social purpose in depicting criminal life in fiction, is his Preface to the third edition (1841) of *Oliver Twist* (1837–39).

PREFACE

OLIVER TWIST
(1841 Edition)

I saw no reason, when I wrote this book, why the very dregs of life, so long as their speech did not offend the ear, should not serve the purpose of a moral, at least as well as its froth and cream. Nor did I doubt that there lay festering in Saint Giles's as good materials towards the truth as any flaunting in Saint James's.

In this spirit, when I wished to show, in little Oliver, the principle of Good surviving through every adverse circumstance, and triumphing at last; and when I considered among what companions I could try him best, having regard to that kind of men into whose hands he would most naturally fall; I bethought myself of those who figure in these volumes. When I came to discuss the subject more maturely with myself, I saw many strong reasons for pursuing the course to which I was inclined. I had read of thieves by scores—seductive fellows (amiable for the most part), faultless in dress, plump in pocket, choice in horseflesh, bold in bearing, fortunate in gallantry, great at a song, a bottle, pack of cards or dice-box, and fit companions for the bravest. But I had never met (except in Hogarth) with the miserable reality. It appeared to me that to draw a knot of such associates in crime as really do exist; to paint them in all their deformity, in all their wretchedness, in all the squalid poverty of their lives; to show them as they really are, for ever skulking uneasily through the dirtiest paths of life, with the great, black, ghastly gallows closing up their prospects, turn them where they may; it appeared to me that to do this, would be to attempt a something which was greatly needed, and which would be a service to society. And therefore I did it as I best could.

In every book I know, where such characters are treated of at all, certain allurements and fascinations are thrown around them. Even in the Beggar's Opera, the thieves are represented as leading a life which is rather to be envied than otherwise; while Macheath, with all the captivations of command, and the devotion of the most beautiful girl and only pure character in the piece, is as much to be admired and emulated by weak beholders, as any fine gentleman in a red coat who has purchased, as Voltaire says, the right to command a couple of thousand men, or so, and to affront death at their head. Johnson's question, whether any man will turn thief because Macheath is reprieved, seems to me beside the matter. I ask myself, whether any man will be deterred from turning thief because of his being sentenced to death, and because of the existence of Peachum and Lockit; and remembering the captain's roaring life, great appearance, vast success, and strong advantages, I feel assured that nobody having a bent that way will take any warning from him, or will see anything in the play but a very flowery and pleasant road, conducting an honourable ambition in course of time, to Tyburn Tree.

In fact, Gay's witty satire on society had a general object, which made him careless of example in this respect, and gave him other, wider, and higher aims. The same may be said of Sir Edward Bulwer's admirable and most powerful novel of Paul Clifford, which cannot be fairly considered as having, or being intended to have, any bearing on this part of the subject, one way or other.

What manner of life is that which is described in these pages, as the everyday existence of a Thief? What charms has it for the young and ill-disposed, what allurements for the most jolter-headed of juveniles? Here are no canterings upon moonlit heaths, no merrymakings in the snuggest of all possible caverns, none of the attractions of dress, no embroidery, no lace, no jack-boots, no crimson coats and ruffles, none of the dash and freedom with which "the road" has been, time out of mind, invested. The cold, wet, shelterless midnight streets of London; the foul and frowsy dens, where vice is closely packed and lacks the room to turn; the haunts of hunger and disease, the shabby rags that scarcely hold together; where are the attractions of these things? Have they no lesson, and do they not whisper something beyond the little-regarded warning of a moral precept?

But there are people of so refined and delicate a nature, that they cannot bear the contemplation of these horrors. Not that they turn instinctively from crime; but that criminal characters, to suit them, must be, like their meat, in delicate disguise. A Massaroni in green velvet is quite an enchanting creature; but a Sikes in fustian is insupportable. A Mrs. Massaroni, being a lady in short petticoats and a fancy dress, is a thing to imitate in tableaux and have in lithograph on pretty songs; but a Nancy, being a creature in a cotton gown and cheap shawl, is not to be thought of. It is wonderful how Virtue turns from dirty stockings; and how Vice, married to ribbons and a little gay attire, changes her name, as wedded ladies do, and becomes Romance.

Now, as the stern and plain truth, even in the dress of this (in novels) much exalted race, was a part of the purpose of this book, I will not, for these readers, abate one hole in the Dodger's coat, or one scrap of curl-paper in the girl's dishevelled hair. I have no faith in the delicacy which cannot bear to look upon them. I have no desire to make proselytes among such people. I have no respect for their opinion, good or bad; do not covet their approval; and do not write for their amusement. I venture to say this without reserve; for I am not aware of any writer in our language having a respect for himself, or held in any respect by his posterity, who ever has descended to the taste of this fastidious class.

On the other hand, if I look for examples, and for precedents, I find them in the noblest range of English literature. Fielding, De Foe, Goldsmith, Smollett, Richardson, Mackenzie—all these for wise purposes, and especially the two first, brought upon the scene the very scum and refuse of the land. Hogarth, the moralist, and censor of his age—in whose great works the times in which he lived, and the characters of every time, will never cease to be reflected—did the like, without the compromise of a hair's breadth; with a power and depth of thought which belonged to few men before him, and will probably appertain to fewer still in time to come. Where does this giant stand now in the estimation of his countrymen? And yet, if I turn back to the days in which he or any of these men flourished, I find the same reproach levelled against them every one, each in his turn, by the insects of the hour, who raised their little hum, and died, and were forgotten.

Cervantes laughed Spain's chivalry away, by showing Spain its impossible and wild absurdity. It was my attempt, in my humble and far-distant sphere, to dim the false glitter surrounding something which really did exist, by showing it in its unattractive and repulsive truth. No less consulting my own taste, than the manners of the age, I endeavoured, while I painted it in all its fallen and degraded aspects, to banish from the lips of the lowest character I introduced, any expression that could by possibility offend; and rather to lead to the unavoidable inference that its existence was of the most debased and vicious kind, than to prove it elaborately by words and deeds. In the case of the girl, in particular, I kept this intention constantly in view. Whether it is apparent in the narrative, and how it is executed, I leave my readers to determine.

It has been observed of this girl, that her devotion to the brutal house-breaker does not seem natural, and it has been objected to Sikes in the same breath—with some inconsistency, as I venture to think—that he is surely overdrawn, because in him there would appear to be none of those redeeming traits which are objected to as unnatural in his mistress. Of the latter objection I will merely say, that I fear there are in the world some insensible and callous natures that do become, at last, utterly and irredeemably bad. But whether this be so or not, of one thing I am certain: that there are such men as Sikes, who, being closely followed through the same space of time, and through the same current of circumstances, would not give, by one look or action of a moment, the faintest indication of a better nature. Whether every gentler human feeling is dead within such bosoms, or the proper chord to strike has rusted and is hard to find, I do not know; but that the fact is so, I am sure.

It is useless to discuss whether the conduct and character of the girl seems natural or unnatural, probable or improbable, right or wrong. It is true. Every man who has watched these melancholy shades of life knows it to be so. Suggested to my mind long ago—long before I dealt in fiction—by what I often saw and read of, in actual life around me, I have, for years, tracked it through many profligate and noisome ways, and found it still the same. From the first introduction of that poor wretch, to her laying her bloody head upon the robber's breast, there is not one word exaggerated or over-wrought. It is emphatically God's truth, for it is the truth He leaves in such depraved and miserable breasts; the hope yet lingering behind; the last fair drop of water at the bottom of the dried-up weed-choked well. It involves the best and worst shades of our common nature; much of its ugliest hues, and something of its most beautiful; it is a contradiction, an anomaly, an apparent impossibility, but it is a truth. I am glad to have had it doubted, for in that circumstance I find a sufficient assurance that it needed to be told.

Devonshire Terrace, *April*, 1841.

LETTER TO MRS. BROOKFIELD
(20 February 1866)

OFFICE OF ALL THE YEAR ROUND
Tuesday, Twentieth February, 1866

My dear Mrs. Brookfield,—Having gone through your MS. (which I should have done sooner, but that I have not been very well), I write these few following words about it. Firstly, with a limited reference to its unsuitability to these pages. Secondly, with a more enlarged reference to the merits of the story itself.

If you will take a part of it and cut it up (in fancy) into the small portions into which it would have to be divided here for only a month's supply, you will (I think) at once discover the impossibility of publishing it in weekly parts. The scheme of the chapters, the manner of introducing the people, the progress of the interest, the places in which the principal places fall, are all hopelessly against it. It would seem as though the story were never coming, and hardly ever moving. There must be a special design to overcome that specially trying mode of publication, and I cannot better express the difficulty and labour of it than by asking you to turn over any two weekly numbers of A Tale of Two Cities, or Great Expectations, or Bulwer's story, or Wilkie Collins', or Reade's, or At the Bar, and notice how patiently and expressly the thing has to be planned for presentation in these fragments, and yet for afterwards fusing together as an uninterrupted whole.

Of the story itself I honestly say that I think highly. The style is particularly easy and agreeable, infinitely above ordinary writing, and sometimes reminds me of Mrs. Inchbald at her best. The characters are remarkably well observed, and with a rare mixture of delicacy and truthfulness. I observe this particularly in the brother and sister, and in Mrs. Neville. But it strikes me that you constantly hurry your narrative (and yet without getting on) *by telling it, in a sort of impetuous breathless way, in your own person, when the people should tell it and act it for themselves.* My notion always is, that when I have made the people to play out the play, it is, as it were, their business to do it, and not mine. Then, unless you really have led up to a great situation like Basil's death, you are bound in art to make more of it. Such a scene should form a chapter of itself. Impressed upon the reader's memory, it would go far to make the fortune of the book. Suppose yourself telling that affecting incident in a letter to a friend. Wouldn't you describe how you went through the life and stir of the streets and roads to the sick-room? Wouldn't you say what kind of room it was, what time of day it was, whether it was sunlight, starlight, or moonlight? Wouldn't you have a strong impression on your mind of how you were received, when you first met the look of the dying man, what strange contrasts were about you and struck you? I don't want you, in a novel, to present *yourself* to tell such things, but I want the things to be there. You make no more of the situation than the index might, or a descriptive playbill might in giving a summary of the tragedy under representation.

As a mere piece of mechanical workmanship, I think all your chapters should be shorter; that is to say, that they should be subdivided. Also, when you change from narrative to dialogue, or *vice versa*, you should make the transition more carefully. Also, taking the pains to sit down and recall the principal landmarks in your story, you should then make them far more elaborate and conspicuous than the rest. Even with these changes I do not believe that the story would attract the attention due to it, if it were published even in such monthly portions as the space of "Fraser" would admit of. Even so brightened, it would not, to the best of my judgment, express itself piecemeal. It seems to me to be so constituted as to require to be read "off the reel." As a book in two volumes I think it would have good claims to success, and good chances of obtaining success. But I suppose the polishing I have hinted at (not a meretricious adornment, but positively necessary to good work and good art) to have been first thoroughly administered.

Now, don't hate me, if you can help it. I can afford to be hated by some people, but I am not rich enough to put you in possession of that luxury. —Ever faithfully yours.

13

WILLIAM MAKEPEACE THACKERAY

(1811–1863)

When William Makepeace Thackeray published his first full-length novel, *Barry Lyndon*, in 1844, Dickens, with several years of novel writing already to his credit, was beginning to produce his masterpieces. Thackeray's masterpiece, *Vanity Fair* (1847–48), placed him alongside Dickens at the head of British fiction. Both writers maintained a close relationship with their readers. Beginning with his earliest work, Thackeray constantly addressed his public in essay-like digressions and entertained and instructed them in informal exposition mixed with narrative. His appeal was ever to a more intellectual public than were Dickens' admirers; in consequence, it was a more limited appeal. Thackeray was never so popular as Dickens, or even Bulwer, Ainsworth, or Lever.

Both Thackeray and Dickens wrote about the social group they knew from personal experience. Thus, Thackeray's upper-class scene was a complete contrast to that of Dickens. Yet his appeal to this more cultured group was not the result of flattery; on the contrary, his distinctive tone is satirical. Throughout, he is critical of hypocrisy, snobbery, pretense. The affectations of humanity, rather than the social ills of Dickens' world, concerned him. He never confused the function of the novelist with that of the social, political, or religious reformer: "Who is he, that he should assume the divine's office; or turn his desk into a preacher's pulpit?" (*The Newcomes*, Vol. I, Ch. 37). Yet the moralist speaks in numerous digressions and even in the title of his masterpiece.

As a social critic, if not a reformer, Thackeray strove for reality in his novels. In the opening of his historical novel, *Henry Esmond* (1852), he makes a plea for less of the heroic and more of the familiar. *Vanity Fair* avoids the romance ending: "I want to leave everybody dissatisfied and unhappy at the end of the story—we ought all to be with our own and all other stories" (letter to Robert Bell, 3 September 1848). In a letter to David Masson of ? 6 May 1851, paying tribute to Dickens, he objects to his unreal characters:

I quarrel with his Art in many respects: which I don't think represents Nature duly; for instance Micawber appears to me an exaggeration of a man, as his name is of a name. It is delightful and makes me laugh: but it is no more a real man than my friend Punch is: and in so far I protest against him—and against the doctrine quoted by my Reviewer from Goethe too—holding that the Art of Novels *is* to represent Nature: to convey as strongly as possible the sentiment of reality—in a tragedy or a poem or a lofty drama you aim at producing different emotions; the figures moving, and their words sounding, heroically: but in a drawing-room drama a coat is a coat to my ethics, not an embroidered tunic, nor a great red-hot instrument like the Pantomime weapon.

Thackeray did achieve reality in his characters. He gave them a sense of actuality and stability by tracing their genealogy, by carrying them over from one novel to another, by modeling them on actual people, and by combining faults and virtues in the same person. His range is limited, but we accept his characters as valid and true to life—as witness Becky Sharp, one of fiction's most memorable creations. Thackeray, like Dickens, believed in his characters. "Novel writers," he wrote in a letter to Mary Holmes, 10 August 1852, "should not be in a passion with their characters as I imagine, but describe them, good or bad, with a like calm—." However, he comments on the reality his characters have to him in his essay "De Finibus" (August, 1862) and expressed his reaction to characters in *Vanity Fair* in a letter to his mother of 2 July 1847:

Don't you see how odious all the people are in the book (with the exception of Dobbin)—behind whom all there lies a dark moral, I hope. What I want is to make a set of people living without God in the world (only that is a cant phrase)—greedy, pompous, mean, perfectly self-satisfied for the most part and at ease about their superior virtue. Dobbin and poor Briggs are the only two people with real humility as yet. Amelia's is to come, when her scoundrel of a husband is well dead with a ball in his odious bowels. . . .

Thackeray's theories on the novel are expressed in many places. Numerous, but usually brief, comments may be found throughout his letters. More extended commentary took the form of essays, such as "On Some French Fashionable Novels," published in *The Paris Sketch Book* (1840), wherein he compares favorably the values of the novel to those gained from history and personal experience. Thackeray's *Contributions to the Morning Chronicle* (ed. Gordon Ray, Urbana, 1955) "have the further value of revealing his developing views as to what fiction ought to be. Nowhere else does he speak so explicitly or at such length on this subject" (Ray, p. xvi). The contribution for 3 April 1845, "Lever's St. Patrick's Eve—Comic Politics," registers a protest against the use of the novel as a vehicle of political, economic, or religious morality.

Finally, Thackeray expressed his views on the novel in his prefaces, such as that to *Pendennis* (1848–50; Preface, 1850), containing his famous lament over the limitations imposed by his age on realistic portrayal. Similar protests are voiced in digressions in *The Virginians* (1857–59). The original version of Chapter 6 of *Vanity Fair* included a parody of the "genteel," "romantic," and "facetious" styles.

FROM "ON SOME FRENCH FASHIONABLE NOVELS WITH A PLEA FOR ROMANCES IN GENERAL"
(1840)

There is an old story of a Spanish court painter, who, being pressed for money, and having received a piece of damask, which he was to wear in a state procession, pawned the damask, and appeared, at the show, dressed out in some very fine sheets of paper, which he had painted so as exactly to resemble silk Nay, his coat looked so much richer than the doublets of all the rest, that the Emperor Charles, in whose honour the procession was given, remarked the painter, and so his deceit was found out.

I have often thought that, in respect of sham and real histories, a similar fact may be noticed; the sham story appearing a great deal more agreeable, life-like, and natural than the true one: and all who, from laziness as well as principle, are inclined to follow the easy and comfortable study of novels, may console themselves with the notion that they are studying matters quite as important as history, and that their favourite duodecimos are as instructive as the biggest quartos in the world.

If then, ladies, the big-wigs begin to sneer at the course of our studies, calling our darling romances foolish, trivial, noxious to the mind, enervators of intellect, fathers of idleness, and what not, let us at once take a high ground, and say,—Go you to your own employments, and to such dull studies as you fancy; go and bob for triangles, from the Pons Asinorum; go enjoy your dull black draughts of metaphysics; go fumble over history books, and dissert upon Herodotus and Livy; *our* histories are, perhaps, as true as yours; our drink is the brisk sparkling champagne drink, from the presses of Colburn, Bentley and Co.; our walks are over such sunshiny pleasure-grounds as Scott and Shakspeare have laid out for us; and if our dwellings are castles in the air, we find them excessively splendid and commodious;—be not you envious because you have no wings to fly thither. Let the big-wigs despise us; such contempt of their neighbours is the custom of all barbarous tribes; —witness, the learned Chinese: Tippoo Sultaun declared that there were not in all Europe ten thousand men: the Sklavonic hordes, it is said, so entitled themselves from a word in their jargon, which signifies "to speak;" the ruffians imagining that they had a monopoly of this agreeable faculty, and that all other nations were dumb.

Not so: others may be *deaf*; but the novelist has a loud, eloquent,

118

instructive language, though his enemies may despise or deny it ever so much. What is more, one could, perhaps, meet the stoutest historian on his own ground, and argue with him; showing that sham histories were much truer than real histories; which are, in fact, mere contemptible catalogues of names and places, that can have no moral effect upon the reader.

As thus:—

> Julius Cæsar beat Pompey, at Pharsalia.
> The Duke of Marlborough beat Marshal Tallard, at Blenheim.
> The Constable of Bourbon beat Francis the First, at Pavia.

And what have we here?—so many names, simply. Suppose Pharsalia had been, at that mysterious period when names were given, called Pavia; and that Julius Cæsar's family name had been John Churchill;—the fact would have stood, in history, thus:—

> "Pompey ran away from the Duke of Marlborough at Pavia."

And why not?—we should have been just as wise. Or it might be stated, that—

> "The tenth legion charged the French infantry at Blenheim; and Cæsar, writing home to his mamma, said, '*Madame, tout est perdu fors l'honneur.*'"[1]

What a contemptible science this is, then, about which quartos are written, and sixty-volumed Biographies Universelles, and Lardner's Cabinet Cyclopædias, and the like! the facts are nothing in it, the names everything; and a gentleman might as well improve his mind by learning Walker's "Gazetteer," or getting by heart a fifty-years-old edition of the "Court Guide."

Having thus disposed of the historians, let us come to the point in question—the novelists.

On the title-page of these volumes the reader has, doubtless, remarked, that among the pieces introduced, some are announced as "copies" and "compositions." Many of the histories have, accordingly, been neatly stolen from the collections of French authors (and mutilated, according to the old saying, so that their owners should not know them); and, for compositions, we intend to favour the public with some studies of French modern works, that have not as yet, we believe, attracted the notice of the English public.

Of such works there appear many hundreds yearly, as may be seen by the French catalogues; but the writer has not so much to do with works political, philosophical, historical, metaphysical, scientifical, theological, as with those for which he has been putting forward a plea—novels, namely; on which he has expended a great deal of time and study. And passing from novels in general to French novels, let us confess, with much humiliation, that we borrow from these stories a great deal more knowledge of French society than from our own personal observation we ever can hope to gain: for, let a gentleman who has dwelt two, four, or ten years in Paris (and has not gone thither for the purpose of making a book, when three weeks are

---

[1] *Madame, tout est perdu fors l'honneur:* Madame, all is lost except honor.

sufficient)—let an English gentleman say, at the end of any given period, how much he knows of French society, how many French houses he has entered, and how many French friends he has made?—He has enjoyed, at the end of the year, say—

> At the English Ambassador's, so many soirées.
> At houses to which he has brought letters, so many tea-parties.
> At cafés, so many dinners.
> At French private houses, say three dinners, and very lucky too.

He has, we say, seen an immense number of wax candles, cups of tea, glasses of orgeat, and French people, in best clothes, enjoying the same; but intimacy there is none; we see but the outsides of the people. Year by year we live in France, and grow grey, and see no more. We play écarté with Monsieur de Trêfle every night; but what know we of the heart of the man—of the inward ways, thoughts, and customs of Trêfle? If we have good legs, and love the amusement, we dance with Countess Flicflac, Tuesdays and Thursdays, ever since the Peace; and how far are we advanced in acquaintance with her since we first twirled her round a room? We know her velvet gown, and her diamonds (about three-fourths of them are sham, by the way); we know her smiles, and her simpers, and her rouge—but no more: she may turn into a kitchen wench at twelve on Thursday night, for aught we know; her *voiture*, a pumpkin; and her *gens*, so many rats: but the real, rougeless, *intime* Flicflac, we know not. This privilege is granted to no Englishman: we may understand the French language as well as Monsieur de Levizac, but never can penetrate into Flicflac's confidence: our ways are not her ways; our manners of thinking, not hers: when we say a good thing, in the course of the night, we are wondrous lucky and pleased; Flicflac will trill you off fifty in ten minutes, and wonder at the *bêtise* of the Briton, who has never a word to say. We are married, and have fourteen children, and would just as soon make love to the Pope of Rome as to any one but our own wife. If you do not make love to Flicflac, from the day after her marriage to the day she reaches sixty, she thinks you a fool. We won't play at écarté with Trêfle on Sunday nights; and are seen walking, about one o'clock (accompanied by fourteen red-haired children, with fourteen gleaming prayer-books), away from the church. "Grand Dieu!" cries Trêfle, "is that man mad? He won't play at cards on a Sunday; he goes to church on a Sunday: he has fourteen children!"

Was ever Frenchman known to do likewise? Pass we on to our argument, which is, that with our English notions and moral and physical constitution, it is quite impossible that we should become intimate with our brisk neighbours; and when such authors as Lady Morgan and Mrs. Trollope, having frequented a certain number of tea-parties in the French capital, begin to prattle about French manners and men,—with all respect for the talents of those ladies, we do believe their information not to be worth a sixpence; they speak to us, not of men, but of tea-parties. Tea-parties are the same all the world over; with the exception that, with the French, there are more lights and prettier dresses; and with us, a mighty deal more tea in the pot.

There is, however, a cheap and delightful way of travelling, that a man may perform in his easy-chair, without expense of passports or post-boys. On the wings of a novel, from the next circulating library, he sends his imagination a-gadding, and gains acquaintance with people and manners whom he could not hope otherwise to know. Twopence a volume bears us whithersoever we will;—back to Ivanhoe and Cœur de Lion, or to Waverley and the Young Pretender, along with Walter Scott; up to the heights of fashion with the charming enchanters of the silver-fork school; or, better still, to the snug inn-parlour, or the jovial tap-room, with Mr. Pickwick and his faithful Sancho Weller. I am sure that a man who, a hundred years hence, should sit down to write the history of our time, would do wrong to put that great contemporary history of "Pickwick" aside as a frivolous work. It contains true character under false names; and, like "Roderick Random," an inferior work, and "Tom Jones" (one that is immeasurably superior), gives us a better idea of the state and ways of the people than one could gather from any more pompous or authentic histories. . . .

LEVER'S ST. PATRICK'S EVE—COMIC POLITICS
(1845)

Since the days of Æsop, comic philosophy has not been cultivated so much as at present. The chief of our pleasant writers—Mr. Jerrold, Mr. Dickens, Mr. Lever—are assiduously following this branch of writing; and the first-named jocular sage, whose apologues adorned our spelling-books in youth, was not more careful to append a wholesome piece of instruction to his fable than our modern teachers now are to give their volumes a moral ballast. To some readers—callous, perhaps, or indifferent to virtue or to sermons—this morality is occasionally too obtrusive. Such sceptics will cry out—We are children no longer; we no longer want to be told that the fable of the dog in the manger is a satire against greediness and envy; or that the wolf and the lamb are types of Polk gobbling up a meek Aberdeen,[2] or

[2] "The Earl of Aberdeen, Foreign Secretary in Peel's cabinet, had replied in a reasonable and conciliatory fashion to the belligerent remarks about the northwestern boundary of the United States made by President Polk in his inaugural address of 5 March 1845. During the following year a treaty was concluded settling the Oregon problem to the satisfaction of both nations." [Ray]

innocence being devoured by oppression. These truths have been learned by us already. If we want instruction, we prefer to take it from fact rather than from fiction. We like to hear sermons from his reverence at church; to get our notions of trade, crime, politics, and other national statistics, from the proper papers and figures; but when suddenly, out of the gilt pages of a pretty picture book, a comic moralist rushes forward, and takes occasion to tell us that society is diseased, the laws unjust, the rich ruthless, the poor martyrs, the world lop-sided, and *vice versâ*, persons who wish to lead an easy life are inclined to remonstrate against this literary ambuscadoe. You may be very right, the remonstrant would say, and I am sure are very hearty and honest, but as these questions you propound here comprehend the whole scheme of politics and morals, with a very great deal of religion, I am, I confess, not prepared at the present moment to enter into them. Without wishing to be uncomplimentary, I have very shrewd doubts as to your competency to instruct upon all these points; at all events, I would much rather hear you on your own ground—amusing by means of amiable fiction, and instructing by kindly satire, being careful to avoid the discussion of abstract principles, beyond those of the common ethical science which forms a branch of all poets and novelists' business—but, above all, eschewing questions of politics and political economy, as too deep, I will not say for your comprehension, but for your readers'; and never, from their nature, properly to be discussed in any, the most gilded, story-book. Let us remember, too, how loosely some of our sentimental writers have held to political creeds:—thus, we all know that the great philospher, Mrs. Trollope, who, by means of a novel in shilling numbers,[3] determined to write down the poor-laws, somewhere towards the end of her story came to a hitch in her argu-ment, and fairly broke down with a confession that facts had come to light, subsequent to the commencement of her story, which had greatly altered her opinions regarding the law; and so the law was saved for that time. Thus, too, we know that the famous author of "Coningsby," before he propounded the famous New England philosophy, had preached many other respectable doctrines, viz., the Peel doctrines, the Hume doctrines, &c.: all this Sir Robert Peel himself took the pains to explain to the House of Commons the other night, when the great philospher alluded to called the right honourable baronet an organised hypocrite.[4]

The moral of this is (for we wish to show that newspaper critics can make morals as well as successful novelists) that as a Trollope and a Disraeli, persons of a fiery and poetical imagination, have gone astray when treading the crabbed labyrinths of political controversy; and not only gone astray,

[3] "*Jessie Phillips: a Tale of the New Poor Law*, which appeared in eleven shilling parts between 31 December 1842 and 30 November 1843." [Ray]

[4] "When Disraeli made the celebrated accusation that 'a Conservative Government is an organized hypocrisy' in his speech of 17 March 1845, Peel replied by outlining the incon-sistencies of Disraeli's political career (William Flavelle Monypenny, *The Life of Benjamin Disraeli, Earl of Beaconsfield*, three volumes, New York, 1913–4, II, 320–2)." [Ray]

but, as it were, tripped, stumbled, broken their noses, and scratched them-selves in an entirely ludicrous and undignified manner; other imaginative writers should take warning by the fate of these illustrious victims, nor venture into quagmires where they may flounder beyond their depth.

It is but fair to say that the above moral dissertation has been occasioned, not by Mr. Lever's moral story alone, but by other moral tales of other moral writers of great wit and merit, who have adopted the didactic tone. Mr. Lever is by far the most gentle of the comic satirists: he is not only gentle and kindly in his appreciation of the poor man, but kindly and gentle in regard to the rich, whom certain of Mr. Lever's brother moralists belabour so hardly; and if occasion is here taken of one of his stories to enter a protest against senti-mental politics altogether, it is not because this author is more sinful on this score than any other, but because the practice amongst novelists is pro-digiously on the increase, and can tend, as we fancy, to little good. You cannot have a question fairly debated in this way. You can't allow an author to invent incidents, motives, and characters, in order that he may attack them subsequently. How many Puseyite novels, Evangelical novels, Roman Catholic novels have we had, and how absurd and unsatisfactory are they. Monsieur Eugène Sue, for instance, has lately set all France against the Jesuits, because he has chosen to invent a story in which two or three most monstrous scoundrels, belonging to that order, are made to swindle and otherwise oppress several personages, equally imaginary, of the most interest-ing virtue and beauty. The Jesuits are, no doubt, bad enough: but they are not to be exterminated on account of M. Sue's *Rodin*. The landlords may be wickedly to blame; the monsters get two per cent. for their land; they roll about in carriages, do nothing, and drink champagne; while the poor labourer remains at home and works and starves;—but we had better have some other opinion than that of the novelist to decide upon the dispute between them. He can exaggerate the indolence and luxury of the one, or the miseries and privations of the other, as his fancy leads him. In the days of Marmontel and Florian it was the fashion to depict shepherds and shepherdesses in pink ribbons and laced petticoats, piping to their flocks all day, and dancing and serenading all night; in our time writers give a very different view of the peasant. Crime, poverty, death, pursue him: the game-keeper shoots him or banishes him from his home and little ones; the agent grinds him down; the callous landlord pockets the rent which has been squeezed out of the vitals of his victim, and goes home and drinks a cool bottle of claret after church. Much of this may be true as regards the luckless peasant of the present time—but what remedy or contrast has the political novelist to propose? An outcry against the landlords. His easy philosophy has led him no farther. Has any sentimental writer organised any feasible scheme for bettering the poor? Has any one of them, after weeping over poor Jack, and turning my lord to ridicule, devised anything for the substantial benefit of the former. At the conclusion of these tales, when the poor hero or heroine has been bullied enough—when poor Jack has been put off the murder he was meditating, or poor Polly has been rescued from the town on which she was about to go—there somehow arrives a misty reconciliation between the poor and the rich; a prophecy is uttered of better times for the one, and better manners in the other; presages are made of happy life, happy marriage and children, happy beef and pudding for all time to come; and the characters make their bow, grinning, in a group, as they do at the end of a drama when the curtain falls, and the blue fire blazes behind the scenes. This is not the way in which men seriously engaged and interested in the awful question between rich and poor meet and grapple with it. When Cobden thunders against the landlords, he flings figures and facts into their faces, as missiles with which he assails them; he offers, as he believes, a better law than theirs as a substitute for that which they uphold. When Sir Robert Peel resists or denies or takes up the standard which he has planted, and runs away, it is because he has cogent prudential reasons for his conduct of the day. But on one side and the other it is a serious contest which is taking place in the press and Parliament over the "Condition of England question."[5] The novelist as it appears to us, ought to be a noncombatant. But if he persists in taking a side, don't let him go into the contest unarmed; let him do something more effectual than call the enemy names. The cause of either party in this great quarrel requires a stronger championship than this, and merits a more earnest warfare.

We have said that the landlords in Ireland are by no means maltreated by Mr. Lever; indeed his remedy for the national evils is of the mildest sort and such as could not possibly do harm to that or any other afflicted country. The persons who, it is proposed, shall administer the prescribed remedies, viz., the absentees, who are called upon to return to Tipperary and elsewhere, might not at first relish the being brought so near the patient; but for the sick man himself, there can be no doubt that the application of a landlord would not injure him, any more than that of a leech in a case of apoplexy, or of a teaspoon full of milk and water in a fever. That the medicine would be sufficiently powerful is another question. It has been proposed by many persons: by Miss Edgeworth, by Mr. Carleton, and others, as well as Mr. Lever; but we fancy it would not answer one-hundredth part of the purpose for which it is intended; besides that, the landlords obstinately decline being put forward for the experiment.

The aim of our author's book is, he says, to show that absentees should return; that "prosperity has as many duties as adversity has sorrows; and that those to whom Providence has accorded many blessings are but the stewards of heaven's bounty to the poor."

As a general proposition none can be more amiable and undeniable than this; but we deny that Mr. Lever has worked it well, or has so con-

[5] "The title of chapter one of Carlyle's *Chartism* (1840)." [Ray]

structed his story as especially to illustrate this simple moral. His purpose is very good, but his end, when he defines it, is frequently entirely preposterous. For instance, in the following passage, the author pleads eloquently against absenteeism:—

"Alas! no; Mr. Leslie, when not abroad, lived in England. Of his Irish estates he knew nothing, save through the half-yearly accounts of his agent. He was conscious of excellent intentions; he was a kind, even a benevolent man; and, in the society of his set, remarkable for more than ordinary sympathies with the poor. To have ventured on any reflection on a landlord before him, would have been deemed a downright absurdity.

"He was a living refutation of all such calumnies; yet how was it that, in the district he owned, the misery of the people was a thing to shudder at? That there were hovels excavated in the bogs, within which human beings lingered on between life and death, their existence like some terrible passage in a dream? That beneath these frail roofs famine and fever dwelt, until suffering, and starvation itself, had ceased to prey upon minds on which no ray of hope ever shone? Simply, he did not know of these things; he saw them not; he never heard of them. He was aware that seasons of unusual distress occurred, and that a more than ordinary degree of want was experienced by a failure of the potato-crop; but on these occasions he read his name, with a subscription of a hundred pounds annexed, and was not that a receipt in full for all the claims of conscience? He ran his eyes over a list in which royal and princely titles figured, and he expressed himself grateful for so much sympathy with Ireland! But did he ask himself the question whether, if he had resided among his people, such necessities for almsgiving had ever arisen? Did he inquire how far his own desertion of his tenantry—his ignorance of their state—his indifference to their condition—had fostered these growing evils? Could he acquit himself of the guilt of deriving all the appliances of his ease and enjoyment from those whose struggles to supply them were made under the pressure of disease and hunger?"

This is strong enough as against the landlord, but is not the following a little too strong in favour of the tenant?—

"Had the landlord been a resident on his property—acquainting himself daily and hourly with the condition of his tenants—holding up examples for their imitation —rewarding the deserving—discountenancing the unworthy—extending the benefits of education among the young—and fostering habits of order and good conduct among all, Owen would have striven among the first for a place of credit and honour, and speedily have distinguished himself above his equals. But alas! no."

Surely it is somewhat ultra-sentimental to set up victims of this sort. In Mr. Lever's story, the hero (a tenant) in the first place gets a farm *for nothing*. He does not better himself; but takes to drink and idleness, and the landlord is rebuked because he is not there to be kind and didactic to him, and teach him how he should go.

In the second part of the story the tenant is turned out of his farm, drinks worse than ever, and finally agrees to *murder* the landlord's agent; but before this crime is committed the landlord returns, the tenant marries the young person to whom he is attached, all parties are reconciled, and all live happily ever after.

Now, have we not a right to protest against morals of this kind, and to put in a word for the landlord, just for novelty's sake? A man gets a farm for nothing (a gentleman surely cannot well let his ground for *less*), and who but the landlord is blamed because his idle tenant does not prosper? The tenant determines on murdering the agent, and the argument is, "Poor fellow! why was not the landlord there to teach him better?" Writers who mount the bench as judges in the great philanthropic suit now pending, have surely no right to deliver such preposterous sentences as these. Here we have an Irish judge convicting the landlords of "*guilt*, in deriving all the appliances of his ease and enjoyment from those whose struggles to supply them were made under the pressure of disease and hunger." Why not hunger? Without hunger there would be no work. We have just seen Mr. Lever's peasant, idling and drinking when he got his farm for nothing, and when he is to pay his landlord, the latter is straightway brought in *guilty*. What a verdict is this! All property may similarly be declared iniquitous, and all capital criminal. Let fund-holders and manufacturers look out—Judge Jerrold will show them no favour, Chief Baron Boz has charged dead against them, and so we see it has been ruled in Ireland by the chief authority of the literary bench.

A friend who comes in, and has read both "Saint Patrick's Eve" and the above observations, declares that the story has nothing to do with politics; that no critic has a right to judge it in a political sense; and that it is to be tested by its descriptive, its humorous, its pathetic, or romantic merits.

If such be the case (and we have our doubts), a great deal may be said in praise, and a little in blame of Mr. Lever's new story. In the first place, the writing is often exceedingly careless. The printer or some one else has somehow left out a verb in the very first sentence, by which the whole fabric falls to pieces; and the stops are so woefully disarranged in page 2, as to cause the greatest confusion. Periods are violently torn asunder. Accusatives are wrenched from their guardian verbs, which are left atrociously mangled. A regard for that mother whom the critic and the novelist ought to revere equally, the venerable English grammar, binds us to protest against this careless treatment of her. In regard of the merits, the narrative has the animated, rapid, easy style which is the charm of the author's writing, the kindly and affectionate humour (which appears in this volume to greater advantage, because it is not *over laughed* by the boisterous jocularity which we find in some of his other works), and the gay and brilliant manner of depicting figure and landscape, which distinguishes Mr. Lever's dexterous and facile hand. Parts of the tale are told with exceeding pathos and sweetness; and he who begins must needs go through it, with interest and with unabated pleasure. Great praise must also be bestowed upon the charming, faithful, and picturesque designs with which Mr. Brown has illustrated this brilliant little volume.

PREFACE

THE HISTORY OF PENDENNIS
(1850)

If this kind of composition, of which the two years' product is now laid before the public, fail in art, as it constantly does and must, it at least has the advantage of a certain truth and honesty, which a work more elaborate might lose. In his constant communication with the reader, the writer is forced into frankness of expression, and to speak out his own mind and feelings as they urge him. Many a slip of the pen and the printer, many a word spoken in haste, he sees and would recall as he looks over his volume. It is a sort of confidential talk between writer and reader, which must often be dull, must often flag. In the course of his volubility, the perpetual speaker must of necessity lay bare his own weaknesses, vanities, peculiarities. And as we judge of a man's character, after long frequenting his society, not by one speech, or by one mood or opinion, or by one day's talk, but by the tenor of his general bearing and conversation; so of a writer, who delivers himself up to you perforce unreservedly, you say, Is he honest? Does he tell the truth in the main? Does he seem actuated by a desire to find out and speak it? Is he a quack, who shams sentiment, or mouths for effect? Does he seek popularity by claptraps or other arts? I can no more ignore good fortune than any other chance which has befallen me. I have found many thousands more readers than I ever looked for. I have no right to say to these, You shall not find fault with my art, or fall asleep over my pages; but I ask you to believe that this person writing strives to tell the truth. If there is not that, there is nothing.

Perhaps the lovers of "excitement" may care to know, that this book began with a very precise plan, which was entirely put aside. Ladies and gentlemen, you were to have been treated, and the writer's and the publishers' pocket benefited, by the recital of the most active horrors. What more exciting than a ruffian (with many admirable virtues) in St. Giles's visited constantly by a young lady from Belgravia? What more stirring than the contrasts of society? the mixture of slang and fashionable language? the escapes, the battles, the murders? Nay, up to nine o'clock this very morning, my poor friend, Colonel Altamont, was doomed to execution, and the author only relented when his victim was actually at the window.

The "exciting" plan was laid aside (with a very honourable forbearance on the part of the publishers) because, on attempting it, I found that I failed from want of experience of my subject; and never having been intimate with any convict in my life, and the manners of ruffians and gaol-birds being quite unfamiliar to me, the idea of entering into competition with M. Eugène Sue was abandoned. To describe a real rascal, you must make him so horrible that he would be too hideous to show; and unless the painter paints him fairly, I hold he has no right to show him at all.

Even the gentlemen of our age—this is an attempt to describe one of them, no better nor worse than most educated men—even these we cannot show as they are, with the notorious foibles and selfishness of their lives and their education. Since the author of *Tom Jones* was buried, no writer of fiction among us has been permitted to depict to his utmost power a MAN. We must drape him, and give him a certain conventional simper. Society will not tolerate the Natural in our Art. Many ladies have remonstrated and subscribers left me, because, in the course of the story, I described a young man resisting and affected by temptation. My object was to say, that he had the passions to feel, and the manliness and generosity to overcome them. You will not hear—it is best to know it—what moves in the real world, what passes in society, in the clubs, colleges, mess-rooms,—what is the life and talk of your sons. A little more frankness than is customary has been attempted in this story; with no bad desire on the writer's part, it is hoped, and with no ill consequence to any reader. If truth is not always pleasant; at any rate truth is best, from whatever chair—from those whence graver writers or thinkers argue, as from that at which the story-teller sits as he concludes his labour, and bids his kind reader farewell.

KENSINGTON, *Nov.* 26, 1850.

THE VIRGINIANS
(1859)

from Volume II, Chapter 9

People were still very busy in Harry Warrington's time (not that our young gentleman took much heed of the controversy) in determining the relative literary merits of the ancients and the moderns; and the learned, and the world with them, indeed, pretty generally pronounced in favour of the former. The moderns of that day are the ancients of ours, and we speculate upon them in the present year of grace, as our grandchildren, a hundred years hence, will give their judgment about us. As for your book-learning, O respectable ancestors (though, to be sure, you have the mighty Gibbon with you), I think you will own that you are beaten, and could point to a couple of professors at Cambridge and Glasgow who know more Greek than was to be had in your time in all the universities of Europe, including that of Athens, if such an one existed. As for science, you were scarce more advanced than those heathen to whom in literature you owned yourselves inferior. And in public and private morality? Which is the better, this actual year 1858, or its predecessor a century back? Gentlemen of Mr. Disraeli's House of Commons! has every one of you his price, as in Walpole's or Newcastle's time,—or (and that is the delicate question) have you almost all of you had it? Ladies, I do not say that you are a society of Vestals; but the chronicle of a hundred years since contains such an amount of scandal, that you may be thankful you did not live in such dangerous times. No; on my conscience I believe that men and women are both better; not only that the Susannahs are more numerous, but that the Elders are not nearly so wicked. Did you ever hear of such books as "Clarissa," "Tom Jones," "Roderick Random"; paintings by contemporary artists, of the men and women, the life and society, of their day? Suppose we were to describe the doings of such a person as Mr. Lovelace, or my Lady Bellaston, or that wonderful "Lady of Quality" who lent her memoirs to the author of "Peregrine Pickle." How the pure and outraged Nineteenth Century would blush, scream, run out of the room, call away the young ladies, and order Mr. Mudie never to send one of that odious author's books again. You are fifty-eight years old, Madam, and it may be that you are too squeamish, that you cry out before you are hurt, and when nobody had any intention of offending your ladyship. Also, it may be that the novelist's art is injured by the restraints put upon him, as many an honest, harmless statue at St. Peter's and the Vatican is spoiled by the tin draperies in which ecclesiastical old women have swaddled the fair limbs of the marble. But in your prudery there is reason. So there is in the state censorship of the Press. The page may contain matter dangerous to *bonos mores*. Out with your scissors, censor, and clip off the prurient paragraph! We have nothing for it but to submit. Society, the despot, has given his imperial decree. We may think the statue had been seen to greater advantage without the tin drapery: we may plead that the moral were better might we recite the whole fable. Away with him—not a word! I never saw the piano-fortes in the United States with the frilled muslin trousers on their legs; but, depend on it, the muslin covered some of the notes as well as the mahogany, muffled the music, and stopped the player.

To what does this prelude introduce us? I am thinking of Harry Warrington, Esquire, in his lodgings in Bond Street, London, and of the life which he and many of the young bucks of fashion led in those times, and how I can no more take my fair young reader into them, than Lady Squeams can take her daughter to Cremorne Gardens on an ordinary evening. My dear Miss Diana (psha! I know you are eight-and-thirty, although you are so wonderfully shy, and want to make us believe you have just left off school-room dinners and a pinafore), when your grandfather was a young man about town, and a member of one of the Clubs at "White's," and dined at Pontac's off the feasts provided by Braund and Lebeck, and rode to Newmarket with March and Rockingham, and toasted the best in England with Gilly Williams and George Selwyn (and *didn't* understand George's jokes, of which, indeed, the flavour has very much evaporated since the bottling)—the old gentleman led a life of which your noble aunt (author of "Legends of the Squeams's; or, Fair Fruits off a Family Tree") has not given you the slightest idea.

from Volume II, Chapter 27

IN WHICH WE ARE TREATED TO A PLAY

The real business of life, I fancy, can form but little portion of the novelist's budget. When he is speaking of the profession of arms, in which men can show courage or the reverse, and in treating of which the writer naturally has to deal with interesting circumstances, actions, and characters, introducing recitals of danger, devotedness, heroic deaths, and the like, the novelist may perhaps venture to deal with actual affairs of life; but otherwise, they scarcely can enter into our stories. The main part of Ficulnus's life, for instance, is spent in selling sugar, spices, and cheese; of Causidicus's in poring over musty volumes of black-letter law; of Sartorius's in sitting, cross-legged, on' a board after measuring gentlemen for coats and breeches. What can a story-teller say about the professional existence of these men? Would a real rustical history of hobtails and eighteenpence a-day be endurable? In the days whereof we are writing, the poets of the time chose to represent a shepherd in pink breeches and a chintz waistcoat, dancing before his flocks, and playing a flageolet tied up with a blue satin ribbon. I say, in reply to some objections which have been urged by potent and friendly critics, that of the actual affairs of life the novelist cannot be expected to treat—with the almost single exception of war before named. But law, stock-broking, polemical theology, linen-drapery, apothecary-business, and the like, how can writers manage fully to develop these in their stories? All authors can do, is to depict men *out* of their business—in their passions, loves, laughters, amusements, hatreds, and what not—and describe these as well as they can, taking the business-part for granted, and leaving it as it were for subaudition.

Thus, in talking of the present or the past world, I know I am only dangling about the theatre-lobbies, coffee-houses, *ridottos*, pleasure-haunts, fair-booths, and feasting and fiddling rooms of life; that, meanwhile, the great serious past or present world is plodding in its chambers, toiling at its humdrum looms, or jogging on its accustomed labours, and we are only seeing our characters away from their work. Corydon has to cart the litter and thresh the barley, as well as to make love to Phyllis; Ancillula has to dress and wash the nursery, to wait at breakfast and on her misses, to take the children out, etc., before she can have her brief sweet interview through the area-railings with Boopis, the policeman. All day long have his heels to beat the stale pavement before he has the opportunity to snatch the hasty kiss or the furtive cold pie. It is only at moments, and away from these labours, that we can light upon one character or the other; and hence, though most of the persons of whom we are writing have doubtless their grave employments and avocations, it is only when they are disengaged and away from their work, that we can bring them and the equally disengaged reader together. . . .

VANITY FAIR
(1847–48)

from Chapter 6

VAUXHALL

I know that the tune I am piping is a very mild one, (although there are some terrific chapters coming presently,) and must beg the good-natured reader to remember, that we are only discoursing at present about a stock-broker's family in Russell Square, who are taking walks, or luncheon, or dinner, or talking and making love as people do in common life, and without a single passionate and wonderful incident to mark the progress of their loves. The argument stands thus—Osborne, in love with Amelia, has asked an old friend to dinner and to Vauxhall—Jos Sedley is in love with Rebecca. Will he marry her? That is the great subject now in hand.

We might have treated this subject in the genteel, or in the romantic, or in the facetious manner. Suppose we had laid the scene in Grosvenor Square, with the very same adventures—would not some people have listened? Suppose we had shown how Lord Joseph Sedley fell in love, and the Marquis of Osborne became attached to Lady Amelia, with the full consent of the Duke, her noble father: or instead of the supremely genteel, suppose we had resorted to the entirely low, and described what was going on in Mr. Sedley's kitchen;—how black Sambo was in love with the cook (as indeed he was), and how he fought a battle with the coachman in her behalf; how the knife-boy was caught stealing a cold shoulder of mutton, and Miss Sedley's new *femme de chambre* refused to go to bed without a wax candle; such incidents might be made to provoke much delightful laughter, and be supposed to represent scenes of "life." Or if, on the contrary, we had taken a fancy for the terrible, and made the lover of the new *femme de chambre* a professional burglar, who bursts into the house with his band, slaughters black Sambo at the feet of his master, and carries off Amelia in her night-dress, not to be let loose again till the third volume, we should easily have constructed a tale of thrilling interest, through the fiery chapters of which the reader should hurry, panting. Fancy this chapter having been headed

THE NIGHT ATTACK

The night was dark and wild—the clouds black—black—ink-black. The wild wind tore the chimney-pots from the roofs of the old houses and sent the tiles whirling and crashing through the desolate streets. No soul braved that tempest—the watchmen shrank into their boxes, whither the searching rain followed them—where the crashing thunderbolt fell and destroyed them—one had so been slain opposite the Foundling. A scorched gabardine, a shivered lantern, a staff rent in twain by the flash, were all that remained of stout Will Steadfast. A hackney coachman had been blown off his coach-box, in Southampton Row—and whither? But the whirlwind tells no tidings of its victim, save his parting scream as he is borne onwards! Horrible night! It was dark, pitch dark; no moon, No, no. No moon, Not a star. Not a little feeble, twinkling, solitary star. There had been one at early evening, but he showed his face, shuddering, for a moment in the black heaven, and then retreated back.

One, two, three! It is the signal that Black Vizard had agreed on.

"Mofy! is that your snum?" said a voice from the area. "I'll gully the dag and bimbole the clicky in a snuffkin."

"Nuffle your clod, and beladle your glumbanions," said Vizard, with a dreadful oath. "This way, men; if they screak, out with your snickers and slick! Look to the pewter room, Blowser. You, Mark, to the old gaff's mopus box! and I," added he, in a lower but more horrible voice, "I will look to Amelia!"

There was a dead silence. "Ha!" said Vizard "was that the click of a pistol?"

Or suppose we adopted the genteel rose-water style. The Marquis of Osborne has just despatched his *petit tigre* with a *billet-doux* to the Lady Amelia.

The dear creature has received it from the hands of her *femme de chambre*, Mademoiselle Anastasie.

Dear Marquis! what amiable politeness! His lordship's note contains the wished-for invitation to D—— House!

"Who is that monstrous fine girl," said the *Semillant* Prince G—rge of

C—mbr—dge, at a mansion in Piccadilly the same evening (having just arrived from the omnibus at the opera.) "My dear Sedley, in the name of all the Cupids introduce me to her!"

"Her name, *Monseigneur*," said Lord Joseph, bowing gravely, "is Sedley."

"*Vous avez alors un bien beau nom*," said the young Prince, turning on his heel rather disappointed, and treading on the foot of an old gentleman who stood behind, in deep admiration of the beautiful Lady Amelia.

"*Trente mille tonnerres!*" shouted the victim, writhing under the *agonie du moment*.

"I beg a thousand pardons of your Grace," said the young *étourdi*, blushing, and bending low his fair curls. He had trodden on the toe of the great Captain of the age!

"Oh, D——!" cried the young Prince, to a tall and good-natured nobleman, whose features proclaimed him of the blood of the Cavendishes. "A word with you! Have you still a mind to part with your diamond necklace?"

"I have sold it for two hundred and fifty thousand pounds, to Prince Esterhazy here."

"*Und das war gar nicht theuer, potztausend!*" exclaimed the princely Hungarian, &c., &c., &c. . . . .

Thus you see, ladies, how this story *might* have been written, if the author had but a mind; for, to tell the truth, he is just as familiar with Newgate as with the palaces of our revered aristocracy, and has seen the outside of both. But as I don't understand the language or manners of the Rookery, nor that polygot conversation which, according to the fashionable novelists, is spoken by the leaders of *ton*; we must, if you please, preserve our middle course modestly, amidst those scenes and personages with which we are most familiar.

In a word, this chapter about Vauxhall would have been so exceeding short but for the above little disquisition, that it scarcely would have deserved to be called a chapter at all. And yet it is a chapter, and a very important one too. Are not there little chapters in everybody's life, that seem to be nothing, and yet affect all the rest of the history?

14

CHARLOTTE BRONTË

(1816–1855)

The only member of the Brontë family who seems to have written down some theories on fiction, Charlotte Brontë is best known for *Jane Eyre* (1847). Like her sister Emily's *Wuthering Heights* (1847), a romantic anachronism in the Victorian Age, its popularity has not diminished since the day it was published. Charlotte's father, Patrick Prunty, who assumed a popular name to conceal his Irish origin, wrote and published several volumes of tales and poetry—none of which ever attracted attention. Her brother, Patrick Branwell, the colorful profligate, wrote much and published nothing. Both may have had an influence on her theory and practice. Certainly, Charlotte, Patrick, Emily, and Anne shared not only in the composition of the childhood stories they wove about the imaginary kingdom Angria but also in the development of their mature fiction.

The rejection of *The Professor*, Charlotte's first novel, by six publishers required her to make modifications in her belief that a novelist should confine himself to "Truth and Nature," "the plain and homely." *Jane Eyre* had enough "startling incident" and "thrilling excitement" to suit a publisher's opinion of what the circulating libraries demanded. Thus, when she sought enlightenment on her dilemma from G. H. Lewes, corresponding with him under her pseudonym "Currer Bell," she was more inclined to blame public taste than to question the validity of her own theory.

Part of the solution to this conflict between personal preference and public demand came with her recognition of a muse that replaced the conscious mind during times of literary creativity. In consequence she came to believe that she could write only when the mood was on her (See letter to George Smith, 28 November 1851). In her preface to Emily's *Wuthering Heights* she pays tribute to this mystical quality in seeking a neutral position.

Another facet of her creed is reminiscent of Jane Austen, whose work

Charlotte did not admire. She insisted on defining the limits of her art by her own experience. When she enlarged upon it, as in *Shirley* (1849), she was less successful. Returning to it in *Villette* (1853), a reworking of *The Professor*, which was ultimately published posthumously in 1857, and applying the point of view and subjective intensity developed in *Jane Eyre*, she achieved her second-best novel.

LETTER TO G. H. LEWES
(6 November 1847)

Dear Sir,

Your letter reached me yesterday. I beg to assure you that I appreciate fully the intention with which it was written, and I thank you sincerely both for its cheering commendation and valuable advice.

You warn me to beware of melodrama, and you exhort me to adhere to the real. When I first began to write, so impressed was I with the truth of the principles you advocate, that I determined to take Nature and Truth as my sole guides, and to follow to their very footprints; I restrained imagination, eschewed romance, repressed excitement; over-bright colouring, too, I avoided, and sought to produce something which should be soft, grave, and true.

My work (a tale in one volume) being completed, I offered it to a publisher. He said it was original, faithful to nature, but he did not feel warranted in accepting it; such a work would not sell. I tried six publishers in succession; they all told me it was deficient in "startling incident" and "thrilling excitement," that it would never suit the circulating libraries, and as it was on those libraries the success of works of fiction mainly depended, they could not undertake to publish what would be overlooked there.

Jane Eyre was rather objected to at first, on the same grounds, but finally found acceptance.

I mention this to you, not with a view of pleading exemption from censure, but in order to direct your attention to the root of certain literary evils. If, in your forthcoming article in *Fraser*, you would bestow a few words of enlightenment on the public who support the circulating libraries, you might, with your powers, do some good.

You advise me, too, not to stray far from the ground of experience, as I become weak when I enter the region of fiction; and you say "real experience is perennially interesting, and to all men."

I feel that this also is true; but, dear sir, is not the real experience of each individual very limited? And, if a writer dwells upon that solely or principally, is he not in danger of repeating himself, and also becoming an egotist? Then, too, imagination is a strong, restless faculty, which claims to be heard and exercised: are we to be quite deaf to her cry, and insensate to her struggles? When she shows us bright pictures, are we never to look at them, and try to reproduce them? And when she is eloquent, and speaks rapidly and urgently in our ear, are we not to write to her dictation?

I shall anxiously search the next number of *Fraser* for your opinions on these points.—Believe me, dear sir, yours gratefully,

C. BELL

LETTER TO G. H. LEWES
(12 January 1848)

Dear Sir,

I thank you, then, sincerely for your generous review; and it is with the sense of double content I express my gratitude, because I am now sure the tribute is not superfluous or obtrusive. You were not severe on *Jane Eyre*; you were very lenient. I am glad you told me my faults plainly in private, for in your public notice you touch on them so lightly, I should perhaps have passed them over, thus indicated, with too little reflection.

I mean to observe your warning about being careful how I undertake new works; my stock of materials is not abundant, but very slender; and besides, neither my experience, my acquirements, nor my powers are sufficiently varied to justify my ever becoming a frequent writer. I tell you this because your article in *Fraser* left in me an uneasy impression that you were disposed to think better of the author of *Jane Eyre* than that individual deserved; and I would rather you had a correct than a flattering opinion of me, even though I should never see you.

If I ever *do* write another book, I think I will have nothing of what you call "melodrama"; I *think* so, but I am not sure. I *think*, too, I will endeavour to follow the counsel which shines out of Miss Austen's "mild eyes", "to finish more and be more subdued"; but neither am I sure of that. When authors write best, or, at least, when they write most fluently, an influence seems to waken in them, which becomes their master—which will have its own way— putting out of view all behests but its own, dictating certain words, and insisting on their being used, whether vehement or measured in their nature; new-moulding characters, giving unthought-of turns to incidents, rejecting carefully elaborated old ideas, and suddenly creating and adopting new ones.

Is it not so? And should we try to counteract this influence? Can we indeed counteract it?

I am glad that another work of yours will soon appear; most curious shall I be to see whether you will write up to your own principles, and work out your own theories. You did not do it altogether in *Ranthorpe*—at least, not in the latter part; but the first portion was, I think, nearly without fault; then it had a pith, truth, significance in it which gave the book sterling value; but to write so one must have seen and known a great deal, and I have seen and known very little.

Why do you like Miss Austen so very much? I am puzzled on that point. What induced you to say that you would have rather written *Pride and Prejudice* or *Tom Jones*, than any of the Waverley Novels?

I had not seen *Pride and Prejudice* till I read that sentence of yours, and then I got the book. And what did I find? An accurate daguerreotyped portrait of a commonplace face; a carefully fenced, highly cultivated garden, with neat borders and delicate flowers; but no glance of a bright, vivid physiognomy, no open country, no fresh air, no blue hill, no bonny beck. I should hardly like to live with her ladies and gentlemen, in their elegant but confined houses. These observations will probably irritate you, but I shall run the risk.

Now I can understand admiration of George Sand; for though I never saw any of her works which I admired throughout (even *Consuelo*, which is the best, or the best that I have read, appears to me to couple strange extravagance with wondrous excellence), yet she has a grasp of mind which, if I cannot fully comprehend, I can very deeply respect: she is sagacious and profound; Miss Austen is only shrewd and observant.

Am I wrong; or were you hasty in what you said? If you have time I should be glad to hear further on this subject; if not, or if you think the question frivolous, do not trouble yourself to reply.—I am yours respectfully,

C. Bell

WUTHERING HEIGHTS
(1850 Edition)

from the Editor's Preface

Whether it is right or advisable to create beings like Heathcliff, I do not know: I scarcely think it is. But this I know: the writer who possesses the creative gift owns something of which he is not always master—something that, at times, strangely wills and works for itself. He may lay down rules and devise principles, and to rules and principles it will perhaps for years lie in subjection; and then, haply without any warning of revolt, there comes a time when it will no longer consent to "harrow the valleys, or be bound with a band in the furrow"—when it "laughs at the multitude of the city, and regards not the crying of the driver"—when, refusing absolutely to make ropes out of sea-sand any longer, it sets to work on statue-hewing, and you have a Pluto or a Jove, a Tisiphone or a Psyche, a Mermaid or a Madonna, as Fate or Inspiration direct. Be the work grim or glorious, dread or divine, you have little choice left but quiescent adoption. As for you—the nominal artist—your share in it has been to work passively under dictates you neither delivered nor could question—that would not be uttered at your prayer, nor suppressed nor changed at your caprice. If the result be attractive, the World will praise you, who little deserve praise; if it be repulsive, the same World will blame you, who almost as little deserve blame.

—CURRER BELL

LETTER TO GEORGE SMITH
(30 October 1852)

My Dear Sir,

You must notify honestly what you think of *Villette* when you have read it. I can hardly tell you how I hunger to hear some opinion beside my own, and how I have sometimes desponded, and almost despaired, because there was no one to whom to read a line, or of whom to ask a counsel. *Jane Eyre* was not written under such circumstances, nor were two-thirds of *Shirley*. I got so miserable about it, I could bear no allusion to the book. It is not finished yet; but now I hope. As to the anonymous publication, I have this to say: If the withholding of the author's name should tend materially to injure the publisher's interest, to interfere with booksellers' orders, etc., I would not press the point; but if no such detriment is contingent I should be much thankful for the sheltering shadow of an incognito. I seem to dread the advertisements—the large-lettered "Currer Bell's New Novel," or "New Work by the author of *Jane Eyre*." These, however, I feel well enough, are the transcendentalisms of a retired wretch; so you must speak frankly. . . . I shall be glad to see *Colonel Esmond*. My objection to the second volume lay here: I thought it contained decidedly too much History—too little Story.

You will see that *Villette* touches on no matter of public interest. I cannot write books handling the topics of the day; it is of no use trying. Nor can I write a book for its moral. Nor can I take up a philanthropic scheme, though I honour philanthropy; and voluntarily and sincerely veil my face before such a mighty subject as that handled in Mrs. Beecher Stowe's work, *Uncle Tom's Cabin*. To manage these great matters rightly they must be long and practically studied—their bearings known intimately, and their evils felt genuinely; they must not be taken up as a business matter and a trading speculation. I doubt not Mrs. Stowe had felt the iron of slavery enter into her heart, from childhood upwards, long before she ever thought of writing books. The feeling throughout her work is sincere and not got up. Remember to be an honest critic of *Villette*, and tell Mr. Williams to be unsparing: not that I am likely to alter anything, but I want to know his impressions and yours.

PREFACE

THE PROFESSOR
(1857)

This little book was written before either *Jane Eyre* or *Shirley*, and yet no indulgence can be solicited for it on the plea of a first attempt. A first attempt it certainly was not, as the pen which wrote it had been previously worn a good deal in a practice of some years. I had not indeed published anything before I commenced *The Professor*, but in many a crude effort, destroyed almost as soon as composed, I had got over any such taste as I might once have had for ornamented and redundant composition, and come to prefer what was plain and homely. At the same time I had adopted a set of principles on the subject of incident, etc., such as would be generally approved in theory, but the result of which, when carried out into practice, often procures for an author more surprise than pleasure.

I said to myself that my hero should work his way through life as I had seen real living men work theirs—that he should never get a shilling he had not earned—that no sudden turns should lift him in a moment to wealth and high station; that whatever small competency he might gain, should be won by the sweat of his brow; that, before he could find so much as an arbour to sit down in, he should master at least half the ascent of "the Hill of Difficulty"; that he should not even marry a beautiful girl or a lady of rank. As Adam's son he should share Adam's doom, and drain throughout life a mixed and moderate cup of enjoyment.

In the sequel, however, I found that publishers in general scarcely approved of this system, but would have liked something more imaginative and poetical—something more consonant with a highly wrought fancy, with a taste for pathos, with sentiments more tender, elevated, unworldly. Indeed until an author has tried to dispose of a manuscript of this kind, he can never know what stores of romance and sensibility lie hidden in breasts he would not have suspected of casketing such treasures. Men in business are usually thought to prefer the real; on trial the idea will be often found fallacious; a passionate preference for the wild, wonderful, and thrilling—the strange, startling, and harrowing—agitates divers souls that show a calm and sober surface.

Such being the case, the reader will comprehend that to have reached him in the form of a printed book, this brief narrative must have gone through some struggles—which indeed it has. And after all, its worst struggle and strongest ordeal is yet to come; but it takes comfort—subdues fear—leans on the staff of a moderate expectation—and mutters under its breath, while lifting its eye to that of the public,

"He that is low need fear no fall."[1]

CURRER BELL

[1] An adaptation of "He that is down needs fear no fall"—Bunyan, *Pilgrim's Progress*, Part II.

15

WILLIAM WILKIE COLLINS

(1824–1889)

The inscription on Wilkie Collins' tombstone includes the words: "Author of 'The Women in White' and other works of fiction." Since he wrote the epitaph himself, Collins obviously regarded this as his best novel; when serialized in 1859–60 simultaneously in London, New York, and Paris, it brought him international fame. A ten-year apprenticeship in fiction had preceded this success, beginning with a historical romance, *Antonina, or the Fall of Rome* (1850), the preface to which sets forth principles similar to those held by Scott.

With *Basil: A Story of Modern Life* (1852), Collins initiated the sensation novel, perfected in *The Woman in White*. Utilizing devices and properties once the province of the Gothic romance, but seeking to make them plausible, Collins wrote of premonitory dreams, blood-chilling curses, and pervading mystery. His novels, most of which were serialized in popular magazines (six in Dickens' periodicals), were numerous and popular.

As in the Brontës, nature is atmosphere and symbol at once. Rain and darkness presage trouble; trees and forests suggest death. The son of a successful society painter, Collins had dabbled in painting himself; these associations had made him sensitive to the values of landscape. But nature serves also as a tool of fate, to which constant reference is made. As in Hardy, it is always triumphant, in spite of the efforts of the characters to circumvent it. Collins' influence on subsequent mystery and detective fiction can hardly be overstated. *The Moonstone* (1868), according to Dorothy L. Sayers, is "the very finest detective story ever written." It became the model for this type of fiction.

The Dedication to *Basil* makes a close comparison between the novel and the play—they "are twins in fiction." Collins had acted in some of the amateur theatricals produced by Dickens, his close friend. He seemed to think of himself as writing drama in novel form. In his later career, turning to the novel of purpose, he discussed the relative values of character and dramatic situation in the Preface to *Heart and Science* (1882–83), an antivivisection novel.

As a means of fulfilling his purpose of writing entertaining fiction, Collins built his sensation novels on skillfully constructed plots. Reviewers called them Chinese puzzles, but Hardy and Trollope were among those who ranked him first for his ingenuity in telling a story. Perhaps his major influence on Dickens was in this aspect. At the same time, Collins insisted that character creation was one of his chief concerns, and his Preface to *The Woman in White* finds no incompatibility between his "opinion that the primary object of a work of fiction should be to tell a story" and his belief in the importance of "the delineation of character."

PREFACE

ANTONINA
OR THE FALL OF ROME
(1850)

The remarkable historical events which have been chosen, to originate the following story, are amply and brilliantly detailed in the "Decline and Fall of the Roman Empire." The origin and progress of the Gothic invasion of Italy under Alaric; those social and political convulsions within the Empire, which concurred with the attacks from without in ultimately producing the memorable overthrow of the whole Roman power; those occurrences attending the first barbarian siege of the Imperial City, which the present Romance is intended to reproduce, and which essentially mark the commencing epoch of the "Fall of Rome;" will all be found by the reader who may not be previously acquainted with the subject, in the pages of the great history already mentioned.

Whenever it has been thought probable that some desire might be felt to test the historical accuracy of particular passages, the proper notes have been inserted at the foot of the page, where little more than a reference to chapter and book was requisite; but where some extent of quotation appeared necessary, the reader is referred to the Appendix at the end of each Volume.

Believing that the work of Gibbon would be more easily attainable to all classes of readers than any of the other ancient and modern authorities which he had consulted the Author has taken care to refer, on all possible occasions, to the "Decline and Fall of the Roman Empire," except in cases where the introduction of minute historical particulars, which importantly influenced the story, seemed to require the production of the various historical sources (mostly ancient) from which they had been drawn.

It will be observed, that the only two historical personages introduced in the following pages, (the Emperor Honorius and Alaric,) appear as characters of secondary importance, as regards the conduct of the story. Upon consideration of the principle on which he should write, the Author doubted the propriety (in *his* case, at least,) of selecting heroes and heroines from the real personages of the period. He feared, on this plan, that while he was necessarily adding from invention to what was actually known, *his* fiction might be placed in unfavourable contrast with truth, and that he might be unable to carry out his story, written upon such a system, without confusing or falsifying dates; thus failing in one main object of his anxiety, viz., to make his plot invariably arise, and proceed out of, the great historical events of the era, exactly in the order in which they occurred.

Under these circumstances, he thought that by forming all his principal characters from imagination, he should be able to mould them as he pleased to the main necessities of the story; to display them, without any impropriety, as influenced in whatever manner appeared most strikingly interesting by its minor incidents; and, further, to make them on all occasions, without trammel or hindrance, the practical exponents of the spirit of the age, of all the various historical illustrations of the period which the Author's researches among conflicting but equally important authorities, had enabled him to garner up. While, at the same time, the appearance of verisimilitude necessary to an historical romance might, he imagined, be successfully preserved by the occasional introduction of the living characters of the period, in those portions of the plot comprising events with which they had been remarkably connected.

Some discrepancy in the length of the different chapters of the romance may also be noticed. One chapter may be considered as extended unnecessarily to fifty or sixty pages, while another is arbitrarily shortened to twenty or thirty. This is, however, not the result of accident or carelessness. Knowing that his work must be arranged in divisions, the author thought it best to let the plot divide itself; to end each chapter only when a pause naturally occurred in the events that it related; and each Book and Volume, only when each portion of the story reached its grand climax, in preference to preserving arithmetical symmetry by giving to every division of the narrative an equal number of pages. By this plan, it was thought that the different passages in the story might be most forcibly contrasted one with another, that each scene, while it preserved its separate interest to the mind of the reader, might most clearly appear to be combining to form one complete whole; that, in the painter's phrase, the "effects" might thus be best "massed," and the "lights and shadows" most harmoniously "balanced" and "discriminated."

The author hopes that his motives in making these explanations will not be misunderstood. They are not obtruded on the reader from any desire to present them as worthy of attention in themselves, but solely as tending to prove that he did not enter on his undertaking, such as it was, without some thought, some plan of arrangement by which he should proceed. He is well aware that he has ventured greatly in appearing before the public as the writer of a romance, at a period when so much that is admirable in fiction is already addressed to them, and he is anxious for this very reason to be permitted to explain—whatever the reception which may be accorded to his book—that he did not begin to write it without careful consideration of the task he was imposing on himself, or without forming a system to work on, which whether good or bad, was at any rate the best that his ingenuity could invent.

There are other matters connected with many passages in the present work, which might be referred to in these pages of introduction, but to notice them now would, it is feared, be to make too large a demand upon the reader's patience. If the book cannot of itself appeal to some of his sympathies, it is useless to attempt to awaken them here—if it can, it is most fit and most desirable that it should be left to speak on its own merits.

LONDON,
February 21, 1850.

DEDICATION

BASIL: A STORY OF MODERN LIFE
(1852)

To CHARLES JAMES WARD, Esq.

It has long been one of my pleasantest anticipations to look forward to the time when I might offer to you, my old and dear friend, some such acknowledgment of the value I place on your affection for me, and of my grateful sense of the many acts of kindness by which that affection has been proved, as I now gladly offer in this place. In dedicating the present work to you, I fulfil therefore a purpose which, for some time past, I have sincerely desired to achieve; and, more than that, I gain for myself the satisfaction of knowing that there is one page, at least, of my book, on which I shall always look with unalloyed pleasure—the page that bears your name.

I have founded the main event out of which this story springs on a fact within my own knowledge. In afterwards shaping the course of the narrative thus suggested, I have guided it, as often as I could, where I knew by my own experience, or by experience related to me by others, that it would touch on something real and true in its progress. My idea was that the more of the Actual I could garner up as a text to speak from, the more certain I might feel of the genuineness and value of the Ideal which was sure to spring out of it. Fancy and Imagination, Grace and Beauty, all those qualities which are to the work of Art what scent and colour are to the flower, can only grow towards heaven by taking root in earth. Is not the noblest poetry of prose fiction the poetry of every-day truth?

Directing my characters and my story, then, towards the light of Reality wherever I could find it, I have not hesitated to violate some of the conventionalities of sentimental fiction. For instance, the first love-meeting of two of the personages in this book occurs (where the real love-meeting from which it is drawn occurred) in the very last place and under the very last circumstances which the artifices of sentimental writing would sanction. Will my lovers excite ridicule instead of interest, because I have truly represented them as seeing each other where hundreds of other lovers have first seen each other, as hundreds of people will readily admit when they read the passage to which I refer? I am sanguine enough to think not.

So again, in certain parts of this book where I have attempted to excite the suspense or pity of the reader, I have admitted as perfectly fit accessories to the scene the most ordinary street-sounds that could be heard, and the most ordinary street-events that could occur, at the time and in the place represented—believing that by adding to truth, they were adding to tragedy —adding by all the force of fair contrast—adding as no artifices of mere writing possibly could add, let them be ever so cunningly introduced by ever so crafty a hand.

Allow me to dwell a moment longer on the story which these pages contain.

Believing that the Novel and the Play are twin-sisters in the family of Fiction; that the one is a drama narrated, as the other is a drama acted; and that all the strong and deep emotions which the Play-writer is privileged to excite, the Novel-writer is privileged to excite also, I have not thought it either politic or necessary, while adhering to realities, to adhere to every-day realities only. In other words, I have not stooped so low as to assure myself of the reader's belief in the probability of my story by never once calling on him for the exercise of his faith. Those extraordinary accidents and events which happen to few men seemed to me to be as legitimate materials for fiction to work with—when there was a good object in using them—as the ordinary accidents and events which may, and do, happen to us all. By appealing to genuine sources of interest *within* the reader's own experience, I could certainly gain his attention to begin with; but it would be only by appealing to other sources (as genuine in their way) *beyond* his own experience that I could hope to fix his interest and excite his suspense, to occupy his deeper feelings, or to stir his nobler thoughts.

In writing thus—briefly and very generally (for I must not delay you too long from the story), I can but repeat, though I hope almost unnecessarily, that I am now only speaking of what I have *tried* to do. Between the purpose hinted at here, and the execution of that purpose contained in the succeeding pages, lies the broad line of separation which distinguishes between the will and the deed. How far I may fall short of another man's standard, remains to be discovered. How far I have fallen short of my own, I know painfully well.

One word more on the manner in which the purpose of the following pages is worked out—and I have done.

Nobody who admits that the business of fiction is to exhibit human life can deny that scenes of misery and crime must of necessity, while human nature remains what it is, form part of that exhibition. Nobody can assert that such scenes are unproductive of useful results when they are turned to a plainly and purely moral purpose. If I am asked why I have written certain scenes in this book, my answer is to be found in the universally-accepted truth which the preceding words express. I have a right to appeal to that truth; for I guided myself by it throughout. In deriving the lesson which the following pages contain, from those examples of error and crime which would most strikingly and naturally teach it, I determined to do justice to the honesty of my object by speaking out. In drawing the two characters whose actions bring about the darker scenes of my story, I did not forget that it was my duty, while striving to pourtray them naturally, to put them to a good moral use; and at some sacrifice, in certain places, of dramatic effect (though I trust with no sacrifice of truth to Nature), I have shown the conduct of the vile, as always, in a greater or less degree, associated with something that is selfish, contemptible, or cruel in motive. Whether any of my better characters may succeed in endearing themselves to the reader, I know not; but this I do certainly know: that I shall in no instance cheat him out of his sympathies in favour of the bad.

To those persons who dissent from the broad principles here adverted to; who deny that it is the novelist's vocation to do more than merely amuse them; who shrink from all honest and serious reference, in books, to subjects which they think of in private and talk of in public everywhere; who see covert implications where nothing is implied, and improper allusions where nothing improper is alluded to; whose innocence is in the word, and not in the thought; whose morality stops at the tongue, and never gets on to the heart—to those persons, I should consider it loss of time, and worse, to offer any further explanation of my motives than the sufficient explanation which I have given already. I do not address myself to them in this book, and shall never think of addressing myself to them in any other.

PREFACE

THE WOMAN IN WHITE
(1861 Edition)

"The Woman in White" has been received with such marked favour by a very large circle of readers, that this volume scarcely stands in need of any prefatory introduction on my part. All that it is necessary for me to say on the subject of the present edition—the first issued in a portable and popular form—may be summed up in few words.

I have endeavoured, by careful correction and revision, to make my story as worthy as I could of a continuance of the public approval. Certain technical errors which had escaped me while I was writing the book are here rectified. None of these little blemishes in the slightest degree interfered with the interest of the narrative—but it was as well to remove them at the first opportunity, out of respect to my readers; and in this edition, accordingly, they exist no more.

Some doubts having been expressed, in certain captious quarters, about the correct presentation of the legal "points" incidental to the story, I may be permitted to mention that I spared no pains—in this instance, as in all others—to preserve myself from unintentionally misleading my readers. A solicitor of great experience in his profession most kindly and carefully guided my steps, whenever the course of the narrative led me into the labyrinth of the Law. Every doubtful question was submitted to this gentleman, before I ventured on putting pen to paper; and all the proof-sheets which referred to legal matters were corrected by his hand before the story was published. I can add, on high judicial authority, that these precautions were not taken in vain. The "law" in this book has been discussed, since its publication, by more than one competent tribunal, and has been decided to be sound.

One word more, before I conclude, in acknowledgment of the heavy debt of gratitude which I owe to the reading public.

It is no affectation on my part to say that the success of this book has been especially welcome to me, because it implied the recognition of a literary principle which has guided me since I first addressed my readers in the character of a novelist.

I have always held the old-fashioned opinion that the primary object of a work of fiction should be to tell a story; and I have never believed that the novelist who properly performed this first condition of his art, was in danger, on that account, of neglecting the delineation of character—for this plain reason, that the effect produced by any narrative of events is essentially dependent, not on the events themselves, but on the human interest which is directly connected with them. It may be possible, in novel writing, to present character successfully without telling a story; but it is not possible to tell a story successfully without presenting characters: their existence, as recognizable realities, being the sole condition on which the story can be effectively told. The only narrative which can hope to lay a strong hold on the attention of readers, is a narrative which interests them about men and women—for the perfectly obvious reason that they are men and women themselves.

The reception accorded to "The Woman in White" has practically confirmed these opinions, and has satisfied me that I may trust to them in the future. Here is a novel which has met with a very kind reception, because it is a Story; and here is a story, the interest of which—as I know by the testimony, voluntarily addressed to me, of the readers themselves—is never disconnected from the interest of character. "Laura," "Miss Halcombe," and "Anne Catherick"; "Count Fosco," "Mr. Fairlie," and "Walter Hartright"; have made friends for me wherever they have made themselves known. I hope the time is not far distant when I may meet those friends again, and when I may try, through the medium of new characters, to awaken their interest in another story.

PREFACE

HEART AND SCIENCE
(1883)

TO READERS IN GENERAL

You are the children of Old Mother England, on both sides of the Atlantic; you form the majority of buyers and borrowers of novels; and you judge of works of fiction by certain inbred preferences, which but slightly influence the other great public of readers on the continent of Europe.

The two qualities in fiction which hold the highest rank in your estimation are: Character and Humour. Incident and dramatic situation only occupy the second place in your favour. A novel that tells no story, or that blunders perpetually in trying to tell a story—a novel so entirely devoid of all sense of the dramatic side of human life, that not even a theatrical thief can find anything in it to steal—will nevertheless be a work that wins (and keeps) your admiration, if it has humour which dwells on your memory, and characters which enlarge the circle of your friends.

I have myself always tried to combine the different merits of a good novel, in one and the same work; and I have never succeeded in keeping an equal balance. In the present story you will find the scales inclining, on the whole, in favour of character and humour. This has not happened accidentally.

Advancing years, and health that stands sadly in need of improvement, warn me—if I am to vary my way of work—that I may have little time to lose. Without waiting for future opportunities, I have kept your standard of merit more constantly before my mind, in writing this book, than on some former occasions.

Still persisting in telling you a story—still refusing to get up in the pulpit and preach, or to invade the platform and lecture, or to take you by the buttonhole in confidence and make fun of my Art—it has been my chief effort to draw the characters with a vigour and breadth of treatment, derived from the nearest and truest view that I could get of the one model, Nature. Whether I shall at once succeed in adding to the circle of your friends in the world of fiction—or whether you will hurry through the narrative, and only discover on a later reading that it is the characters which have interested you in the story—remains to be seen. Either way, your sympathy will find me grateful; for, either way, my motive has been to please you.

During its periodical publication correspondents, noting certain passages in *Heart and Science*, inquired how I came to think of writing this book. The question may be readily answered in better words than mine. My book has been written in harmony with opinions which have an indisputable claim to respect. Let them speak for themselves.

SHAKESPEARE'S OPINION.—"It was always yet the trick of our English nation, if they have a good thing, to make it too common." (*King Henry IV., Part II.*)

WALTER SCOTT'S OPINION.—"I am no great believer in the extreme degree of improvement to be derived from the advancement of Science; for every study of that nature tends, when pushed to a certain extent, to harden the heart." (*Letter to Miss Edgeworth.*)

FARADAY'S OPINION.—"The education of the judgment has for its first and its last step—Humility." (*Lecture on Mental Education at the Royal Institution.*)

Having given my reasons for writing the book, let me conclude by telling you what I have kept out of the book.

It encourages me to think that we have many sympathies in common; and among them, that most of us have taken to our hearts domestic pets. Writing under this conviction, I have not forgotten my responsibility towards you, and towards my Art, in pleading the cause of the harmless and affectionate beings of God's creation. From first to last, you are purposely left in ignorance of the hideous secrets of Vivisection. The outside of the laboratory is a necessary object in my landscape—but I never once open the door and invite you to look in. I trace, in one of my characters, the result of the habitual practice of cruelty (no matter under what pretense) in fatally deteriorating the nature of man—and I leave the picture to speak for itself. My own personal feeling has throughout been held in check. Thankfully accepting the assistance rendered to me by Miss Frances Power Cobbe, by Mrs. H. M. Gordon, and by Surgeon-General Gordon, C.B., I have borne in mind (as they have borne in mind) the value of temperate advocacy to a good cause.

With this, your servant withdraws, and leaves you to the story.

16

GEORGE ELIOT (MARY ANN EVANS)

(1819–1880)

In the same year that Darwin's *Origin of the Species* (1859) substituted natural science for history as the chief intellectual interest of the English people, George Eliot's first full-length novel, *Adam Bede*, marked a shift in the direction of fiction. From then until the 1880's, when interest in plot and incident was revived for the last two decades of the century, the novel became intellectual. Fiction conveyed philosophical concepts; character analysis catered to psychological interests.

Critical attention to George Eliot's ideas and techniques has reached a high point one hundred years after she began writing novels; however, her popularity with the general reader has never been what it was when, in her later career, she was compared with Shakespeare, Dante, and Goethe. *Adam Bede* was a best seller in the same year that Thackeray's *Virginians* finished serial publication and Meredith's *Ordeal of Richard Feverel* appeared. For the Victorians, neither her intellectualism, her didactic undertone, nor her authorial intrusions were matters for objection. On the other hand, her "faithful representing of commonplace things" gave a nostalgic appeal to *Adam Bede* and to *The Mill on the Floss* (1860). The personal experience reflected in these first novels invested them with a vitality which is lacking in her historical novel, *Romola* (1862–63), and her psychological masterpiece, *Middlemarch* (1871–72). Like her favorite poet, Wordsworth, she sought elemental values in humble life in her earlier fiction and explained her position in Chapter 17 of *Adam Bede*.

George Eliot's theories on the novel are not, as a whole, consistent with her practice. Scattered throughout her numerous letters are comments reflecting her own problems and attitudes. An early letter of 16 March 1839, to her governess, amuses us with its expression of distrust of fiction. Twenty years later she is concerned with technique: "Beginnings are always troublesome" (letter to Sara Hennell, 15 August 1859) and "Conclusions are the weak point of most authors" (letter to John Blackwood, 1 May 1857). In 1873 she is theorizing: "I have always exercised a severe watch against anything that could be called preaching, and if I have ever allowed myself in dissertation or in dialogue [anything] which is not part of the *structure* of my books, I have there sinned against my own laws" (letter to John Blackwood, 12 November 1873). Of course, one of the most frequent charges brought against George Eliot is her habit of analyzing and interpreting instead of simply providing the reader with the materials to make his own deductions.

George H. Lewes, critic, philospher, and George Eliot's common-law husband, was among the first to warn her against this tendency to substitute exposition for dramatic representation. She became acquainted with him as one of the intellectuals producing *The Westminster Review*, an organ of the radicals. He influenced her thinking with his positivist ideas, and she began to contribute critical articles and reviews to the magazine and became an assistant editor in 1851. One such article, "Silly Novels by Lady Novelists" (1856), is noteworthy in showing that before she began writing fiction she had become exasperated by the careless techniques and general "silliness" of some contemporary writers. By this time her critical perception was developing into theory, frequently implied in subsequent reviews of novels. At this point Lewes encouraged her own creative efforts, and she entered the ranks of novel writers a mature woman with a developed philosophy and thoughtful theories. A brief essay on "Story-Telling," published posthumously as *Leaves from a Notebook* (1884), explores the problem of order in narrative.

FROM "SILLY NOVELS BY LADY NOVELISTS"
(1856)

Silly Novels by Lady Novelists are a genus with many species, determined by the particular quality of silliness that predominates in them—the frothy, the prosy, the pious, or the pedantic. But it is a mixture of all these —a composite order of feminine fatuity, that produces the largest class of such novels, which we shall distinguish as the *mind-and-millinery* species. The heroine is usually an heiress, probably a peeress in her own right, with perhaps a vicious baronet, an amiable duke, and an irresistible younger son of a marquis as lovers in the foreground, a clergyman and a poet sighing for her in the middle distance, and a crowd of undefined adorers dimly indicated beyond. Her eyes and her wit are both dazzling; her nose and her morals are alike free from any tendency to irregularity; she has a superb *contralto* and a superb intellect; she is perfectly well-dressed and perfectly religious; she dances like a sylph, and reads the Bible in the original tongues. Or it may be that the heroine is not an heiress—that rank and wealth are the only things in which she is deficient; but she infallibly gets into high society, she has the triumph of refusing many matches and securing the best, and she wears some family jewels or other as a sort of crown of righteousness at the end. Rakish men either bite their lips in impotent confusion at her repartees, or are touched to penitence by her reproofs, which, on appropriate occasions, rise to a lofty strain of rhetoric; indeed, there is a general propensity in her to make speeches, and to rhapsodize at some length when she retires to her bedroom. In her recorded conversations she is amazingly eloquent, and in her unrecorded conversations, amazingly witty. She is understood to have a depth of insight that looks through and through the shallow theories of philosophers, and her superior instincts are a sort of dial by which men have only to set their clocks and watches, and all will go well. The men play a very subordinate part by her side. You are consoled now and then by a hint that they have affairs, which keeps you in mind that the working-day business of the world is somehow being carried on, but ostensibly the final cause of their existence is that they may accompany the heroine on her "starring" expedition through life. They see her at a ball, and are dazzled; at a flower-show, and they are fascinated; on a riding excursion, and they are witched by her noble horsemanship; at church, and they are awed by the sweet solemnity of her demeanour. She is the ideal woman in feelings, faculties, and flounces. For all this, she as often as not marries the wrong person to begin with, and she suffers terribly from the plots and intrigues of the vicious baronet; but even death has a soft place in his heart for such a paragon, and remedies all mistakes for her just at the right moment. The vicious baronet is sure to be killed in a duel, and the tedious husband dies in his bed requesting his wife, as a particular favour to him, to marry the man she loves best, and having already dispatched a note to the lover informing him of the comfortable arrangement. Before matters arrive at this desirable issue our feelings are tried by seeing the noble, lovely, and gifted heroine pass through many *mauvais moments*, but we have the satisfaction of knowing that her sorrows are wept into embroidered pocket-handkerchiefs, that her fainting form reclines on the very best upholstery, and that whatever vicissitudes she may undergo, from being dashed out of her carriage to having her head shaved in a fever, she comes out of them all with a complexion more blooming and locks more redundant than ever.

We may remark, by the way, that we have been relieved from a serious scruple by discovering that silly novels by lady novelists rarely introduce us into any other than very lofty and fashionable society. We had imagined that destitute women turned novelists, as they turned governesses, because they had no other "lady-like" means of getting their bread. On this supposition, vacillating syntax and improbable incident had a certain pathos for us, like the extremely supererogatory pincushions and ill-devised nightcaps that are offered for sale by a blind man. We felt the commodity to be a nuisance, but we were glad to think that the money went to relieve the necessitous, and we pictured to ourselves lonely women struggling for a maintenance, or wives and daughters devoting themselves to the production of "copy" out of pure heroism,—perhaps to pay their husband's debts, or to purchase luxuries for a sick father. Under these impressions we shrank from criticising a lady's novel: her English might be faulty, but, we said to ourselves, her motives are irreproachable; her imagination may be uninventive, but her patience is untiring. Empty writing was excused by an empty stomach, and twaddle was consecrated by tears. But no! This theory of ours, like many other pretty theories, has had to give way before observation. Women's silly novels, we are now convinced, are written under totally different circumstances. The fair writers have evidently never talked to a tradesman except from a carriage window; they have no notion of the working-classes except as "dependents"; they think five-hundred-a-year a miserable pittance; Belgravia and "baronial halls" are their primary truths; and they have no idea of feeling interest in any man who is not at least a great landed proprietor, if not a prime minister. It is clear that they write in elegant boudoirs, with violet-coloured ink and a ruby pen; that they must be entirely indifferent to publishers' accounts, and inexperienced in every form of poverty except poverty of brains. It is true that we are constantly struck with the want of verisimilitude in their representations of the high society in which they seem to live; but then they betray no closer acquaintance with any other form of life. If their peers and peeresses are improbable, their literary men, tradespeople, and cottagers are impossible; and their intellect seems to have the peculiar impartiality of reproducing both what they *have* seen and heard, and what they have *not* seen and heard, with equal unfaithfulness.

.   .   .   .

[Here Eliot illustrates her points on "the mind-and-millinery species" of fiction by detailed reference to, and quotations from, *Compensation, Laura Gay,* and *Rank and Beauty.*]

Writers of the mind-and-millinery school are remarkably unanimous in their choice of diction. In their novels, there is usually a lady or gentleman who is more or less of a upas tree:[1] the lover has a manly breast; minds are redolent of various things; hearts are hollow; events are utilized; friends are consigned to the tomb; infancy is an engaging period; the sun is a luminary that goes to his western couch, or gathers the rain-drops into his refulgent bosom; life is a melancholy boon; Albion and Scotia are conversational epithets. There is a striking resemblance, too, in the character of their moral comments, such, for instance, as that "It is a fact, no less true than melancholy, that all people, more or less, richer or poorer, are swayed by bad example"; that "Books, however trivial, contain some subjects from which useful information may be drawn"; that "Vice can too often borrow the language of virtue"; that "Merit and nobility of nature must exist, to be accepted, for clamour and pretension cannot impose upon those too well read in human nature to be easily deceived"; and that, "In order to forgive, we must have been injured." There is, doubtless, a class of readers to whom these remarks appear peculiarly pointed and pungent; for we often find them doubly and trebly scored with the pencil, and delicate hands giving in their determined adhesion to these hardy novelties by a distinct *très vrai*, emphasized by many notes of exclamation. The colloquial style of these novels is often marked by much ingenious inversion, and a careful avoidance of such cheap phraseology as can be heard every day. Angry young gentlemen exclaim—"''Tis ever thus, methinks"; and in the half-hour before dinner a young lady informs her next neighbour that the first day she read Shakspeare she "stole away into the park, and beneath the shadow of the greenwood tree, devoured with rapture the inspired page of the great magician." But the most remarkable efforts of the mind-and-millinery writers lie in their philosophic reflections. The authoress of "Laura Gay," for example, having married her hero and heroine, improves the event by observing that "if those sceptics, whose eyes have so long gazed on matter that they can no longer see aught else in man, could once enter with heart and soul into such bliss as this, they would come to say that the soul of man and the polypus are not of

---

[1] A Javanese tree whose bark yields a milky juice used to poison arrows; thus, a poisonous or harmful influence.

common origin, or of the same texture." Lady novelists, it appears, can see something else besides matter; they are not limited to phenomena, but can relieve their eyesight by occasional glimpses of the *noumenon*, and are, therefore, naturally better able than any one else to confound sceptics, even of that remarkable, but to us unknown school, which maintains that the soul of man is of the same texture as the polypus.

The most pitiable of all silly novels by lady novelists are what we may call the *oracular* species—novels intended to expound the writer's religious, philosophical, or moral theories. There seems to be a notion abroad among women, rather akin to the superstition that the speech and actions of idiots are inspired, and that the human being most entirely exhausted of common sense is the fittest vehicle of revelation. To judge from their writings, there are certain ladies who think that an amazing ignorance, both of science and of life, is the best possible qualification for forming an opinion on the knottiest moral and speculative questions. Apparently, their recipe for solving all such difficulties is something like this:—Take a woman's head, stuff it with a smattering of philosophy and literature chopped small, and with false notions of society baked hard, let it hang over a desk a few hours every day, and serve up hot in feeble English, when not required. You will rarely meet with a lady novelist of the oracular class who is diffident of her ability to decide on theological questions,—who has any suspicion that she is not capable of discriminating with the nicest accuracy between the good and evil in all church parties,—who does not see precisely how it is that men have gone wrong hitherto,—and pity philosophers in general that they have not had the opportunity of consulting her. Great writers, who have modestly contented themselves with putting their experience into fiction, and have thought it quite a sufficient task to exhibit men and things as they are, she sighs over as deplorably deficient in the application of their powers. "They have solved no great questions"—and she is ready to remedy their omission by setting before you a complete theory of life and manual of divinity, in a love story, where ladies and gentlemen of good family go through genteel vicissitudes, to the utter confusion of Deists, Puseyites, and ultra-Protestants, and to the perfect establishment of that particular view of Christianity which either condenses itself into a sentence of small caps, or explodes into a cluster of stars on the three hundred and thirtieth page. It is true, the ladies and gentlemen will probably seem to you remarkably little like any you have had the fortune or misfortune to meet with, for, as a general rule, the ability of a lady novelist to describe actual life and her fellow-men, is in inverse pro- portion to her confident eloquence about God and the other world, and the means by which she usually chooses to conduct you to true ideas of the in- visible is a totally false picture of the visible.

·　·　·　·　·　·　·　·　·　·　·　·　·

[Eliot here makes detailed references to *The Enigma* as typical of "the oracular kind" of fiction.]

A more numerous class of silly novels than the oracular, (which are generally inspired by some form of High Church, or transcendental Christianity,) is what we may call the *white neck-cloth* species, which represent the tone of thought and feeling in the Evangelical party. This species is a kind of genteel tract on a large scale, intended as a sort of medicinal sweet-meat for Low Church young ladies; an Evangelical substitute for the fashionable novel, as the May Meetings are a substitute for the Opera. Even Quaker children, one would think, can hardly have been denied the indulgence of a doll; but it must be a doll dressed in a drab gown and a coal-scuttle bonnet—not a wordly doll, in gauze and spangles. And there are no young ladies, we imagine,—unless they belong to the Church of the United Brethren, in which people are married without any love-making— who can dispense with love stories. Thus, for Evangelical young ladies there are Evangelical love stories, in which the vicissitudes of the tender passion are sanctified by saving views of Regeneration and the Atonement. These novels differ from the oracular ones, as a Low Churchwoman often differs from a High Churchwoman: they are a little less supercilious, and a great deal more ignorant, a little less correct in their syntax, and a great deal more vulgar.

The Orlando of Evangelical literature is the young curate, looked at from the point of view of the middle class, where cambric bands are under-stood to have as thrilling an effect on the hearts of young ladies as epaulettes have in the classes above and below it. In the ordinary type of these novels, the hero is almost sure to be a young curate, frowned upon, perhaps, by worldly mammas, but carrying captive the hearts of their daughters, who can "never forget *that* sermon"; tender glances are seized from the pulpit stairs instead of the opera-box; *tête-à-têtes* are seasoned with quotations from Scripture, instead of quotations from the poets; and questions as to the state of the heroine's affections are mingled with anxieties as to the state of her soul. The young curate always has a background of well-dressed and wealthy, if not fashionable society;—for Evangelical silliness is as snobbish as any other kind of silliness; and the Evangelical lady novelist, while she explains to you the type of the scapegoat on one page, is ambitious on another to represent the manners and conversation of aristocratic people. Her pictures of fashion-able society are often curious studies considered as efforts of the Evangelical imagination; but in one particular the novels of the White Neck-cloth School are meritoriously realistic,—their favourite hero, the Evangelical young curate is always rather an insipid personage.

·   ·   ·   ·   ·   ·   ·   ·   ·   ·   ·   ·   ·   ·

[Eliot makes references to *The Old Grey Church* to exemplify her points about "the white neck-cloth species" of fiction.]

But, perhaps, the least readable of silly women's novels, are the *modern-antique* species, which unfold to us the domestic life of Jannes and Jambres, the private love affairs of Sennacherib, or the mental struggles and ultimate conversion of Demetrius the silversmith. From most silly novels we can at least extract a laugh; but those of the modern antique school have a ponderous, a leaden kind of fatuity, under which we groan. What can be more demonstrative of the inability of literary women to measure their own powers, than their frequent assumption of a task which can only be justified by the rarest concurrence of acquirement with genius? The finest effort to reanimate the past is of course only approximate—is always more or less an infusion of the modern spirit into the ancient form,—

> Was ihr den Geist der Zeiten heisst,
> Das ist im Grund der Herren eigner Geist,
> In dem die Zeiten sich bespiegeln.[2]

Admitting that genius which has familiarized itself with all the relics of an ancient period can sometimes, by the force of its sympathetic divination, restore the missing notes in the "music of humanity," and reconstruct the fragments into a whole which will really bring the remote past nearer to us, and interpret it to our duller apprehension,—this form of imaginative power must always be among the very rarest, because it demands as much accurate and minute knowledge as creative vigour. Yet we find ladies constantly choosing to make their mental mediocrity more conspicuous, by clothing it in a masquerade of ancient names; by putting their feeble sentimentality into the mouths of Roman vestals or Egyptian princesses, and attributing their rhetorical arguments to Jewish high-priests and Greek philosophers.

.   .   .   .

[Eliot refers to *Adonijah, a Tale of the Jewish Dispersion* to exemplify "the modern-antique species."]

"Be not a baker if your head be made of butter," says a homely proverb, which, being interpreted, may mean, let no woman rush into print who is not prepared for the consequences. We are aware that our remarks are in a very different tone from that of the reviewers who, with a perennial recurrence of precisely similar emotions, only paralleled, we imagine, in the experience of monthly nurses, tell one lady novelist after another that they "hail" her productions "with delight." We are aware that the ladies at whom our criticism is pointed are accustomed to be told, in the choicest phraseology of puffery, that their pictures of life are brilliant, their characters well drawn, their style fascinating, and their sentiments lofty. But if they are inclined to resent our plainness of speech, we ask them to reflect for a moment on the chary praise, and often captious blame, which their panegyrists give to

---

[2] Was ihr den Geist der Zeiten . . . sich bespiegeln:
> What you call the spirit of the age
> Is, after all, the spirit of the people
> In which the age is reflected.
> —Goethe, *Faust* ll. 577–79.

writers whose works are on the way to become classics. No sooner does a woman show that she has genius or effective talent, than she receives the tribute of being moderately praised and severely criticised. By a peculiar thermometric adjustment, when a woman's talent is at zero, journalistic approbation is at the boiling pitch; when she attains mediocrity, it is already at no more than summer heat; and if ever she reaches excellence, critical enthusiasm drops to the freezing point. Harriet Martineau, Currer Bell, and Mrs. Gaskell have been treated as cavalierly as if they had been men. And every critic who forms a high estimate of the share women may ultimately take in literature, will, on principle, abstain from any exceptional indulgence towards the productions of literary women. For it must be plain to every one who looks impartially and extensively into feminine literature, that its greatest deficiencies are due hardly more to the want of intellectual power than to the want of those moral qualities that contribute to literary excellence —patient diligence, a sense of the responsibility involved in publication, and an appreciation of the sacredness of the writer's art. In the majority of women's books you see that kind of facility which springs from the absence of any high standard; that fertility in imbecile combination or feeble imitation which a little self-criticism would check and reduce to barrenness; just as with a total want of musical ear people will sing out of tune, while a degree more melodic sensibility would suffice to render them silent. The foolish vanity of wishing to appear in print, instead of being counterbalanced by any consciousness of the intellectual or moral derogation implied in futile authorship, seems to be encouraged by the extremely false impression that to write *at all* is a proof of superiority in a woman. On this ground, we believe that the average intellect of women is unfairly represented by the mass of feminine literature, and that while the few women who write well are very far above the ordinary intellectual level of their sex, the many women who write ill are very far below it. So that, after all, the severer critics are fulfilling a chivalrous duty in depriving the mere fact of feminine authorship of any false prestige which may give it a delusive attraction, and in recommending women of mediocre faculties—as at least a negative service they can render their sex—to abstain from writing.

The standing apology for women who become writers without any special qualification is, that society shuts them out from other spheres of occupation. Society is a very culpable entity, and has to answer for the manufacture of many unwholesome commodities, from bad pickles to bad poetry. But society, like "matter," and Her Majesty's Government, and other lofty abstractions, has its share of excessive blame as well as excessive praise. Where there is one woman who writes from necessity, we believe there are three women who write from vanity; and, besides, there is something so antiseptic in the mere healthy fact of working for one's bread, that the most trashy and rotten kind of feminine literature is not likely to have been produced under such circumstances. "In all labour there is profit"; but ladies' silly novels, we imagine, are less the result of labour than of busy idleness.

Happily, we are not dependent on argument to prove that Fiction is a department of literature in which women can, after their kind, fully equal men. A cluster of great names, both living and dead, rush to our memories in evidence that women can produce novels not only fine, but among the very finest;—novels, too, that have a precious speciality, lying quite apart from masculine aptitudes and experience. No educational restrictions can shut women out from the materials of fiction, and there is no species of art which is so free from rigid requirements. Like crystalline masses, it may take any form, and yet be beautiful; we have only to pour in the right elements —genuine observation, humour, and passion. But it is precisely this absence of rigid requirement which constitutes the fatal seduction of novel-writing to incompetent women. Ladies are not wont to be very grossly deceived as to their power of playing on the piano; here certain positive difficulties of execution have to be conquered, and incompetence inevitably breaks down. Every art which has its absolute *technique* is, to a certain extent, guarded from the intrusions of mere left-handed imbecility. But in novel-writing there are no barriers for incapacity to stumble against, no external criteria to prevent a writer from mistaking foolish facility for mastery. And so we have again and again the old story of La Fontaine's ass, who puts his nose to the flute, and, finding that he elicits some sound, exclaims, "Moi, aussi, je joue de la flute";—a fable which we commend, at parting, to the consideration of any feminine reader who is in danger of adding to the number of "silly novels by lady novelists."

ADAM BEDE
(1859)

from Chapter 17

"This Rector of Broxton is little better than a pagan!" I hear one of my readers exclaim. "How much more edifying it would have been if you had made him give Arthur some truly spiritual advice! You might have put into his mouth the most beautiful things—quite as good as reading a sermon."

Certainly I could, if I held it the highest vocation of the novelist to represent things as they never have been and never will be. Then, of course, I might refashion life and character entirely after my own liking; I might select the most unexceptionable type of clergyman, and put my own admirable opinions into his mouth on all occasions. But it happens, on the contrary, that my strongest effort is to avoid any such arbitrary picture, and to give a faithful account of men and things as they have mirrored themselves in my mind. The mirror is doubtless defective; the outlines will sometimes be disturbed, the reflection faint or confused; but I feel as much bound to tell you as precisely as I can what that reflection is, as if I were in the witness-box narrating my experience on oath.

Sixty years ago—it is a long time, so no wonder things have changed—all clergymen were not zealous; indeed there is reason to believe that the number of zealous clergymen was small, and it is probable that if one among the small minority had owned the livings of Broxton and Hayslope in the year 1799, you would have liked him no better than you like Mr. Irwine. Ten to one, you would have thought him a tasteless, indiscreet, methodistical man. It is so very rarely that facts hit that nice medium required by our own enlightened opinions and refined taste! Perhaps you will say, "Do improve the facts a little, then; make them more accordant with those correct views which it is our privilege to possess. The world is not just what we like; do touch it up with a tasteful pencil, and make believe it is not quite such a mixed entangled affair. Let all people who hold unexceptionable opinions act unexceptionably. Let your most faulty characters always be on the wrong side, and your virtuous ones on the right. Then we shall see at a glance whom we are to condemn, and whom we are to approve. Then we shall be able to admire, without the slightest disturbance of our prepossessions: we shall hate and despise with that true ruminant relish which belongs to undoubting confidence."

But, my good friend, what will you do then with your fellow-parishioner who opposes your husband in the vestry?—with your newly-appointed vicar, whose style of preaching you find painfully below that of his regretted predecessor?—with the honest servant who worries your soul with her one failing?—with your neighbour, Mrs. Green, who was really kind to you in your last illness, but has said several ill-natured things about you since your convalescence?—nay, with your excellent husband himself, who has other irritating habits besides that of not wiping his shoes? These fellow-mortals, everyone, must be accepted as they are: you can neither straighten their noses, nor brighten their wit, nor rectify their dispositions; and it is these people—amongst whom your life is passed—that it is needful you should tolerate, pity, and love; it is these more or less ugly, stupid, inconsistent people, whose movements of goodness you should be able to admire—for whom you should cherish all possible hopes, all possible patience. And I would not, even if I had the choice, be the clever novelist who could create a world so much better than this, in which we get up in the morning to do our daily work, that you would be likely to turn a harder, colder eye on the dusty streets and the common green fields—on the real breathing men and women, who can be chilled by your indifference or injured by your prejudice;

who can be cheered and helped onward by your fellow-feeling, your forbearance, your outspoken, brave justice.

So I am content to tell my simple story, without trying to make things seem better than they were; dreading nothing, indeed, but falsity, which, in spite of one's best efforts, there is reason to dread. Falsehood is so easy, truth so difficult. The pencil is conscious of a delightful facility in drawing a griffin—the longer the claws, and the larger the wings, the better; but that marvellous facility which we mistook for genius is apt to forsake us when we want to draw a real unexaggerated lion. Examine your words well, and you will find that even when you have no motive to be false, it is a very hard thing to say the exact truth, even about your own immediate feelings—much harder than to say something fine about them which is *not* the exact truth.

It is for this rare, precious quality of truthfulness that I delight in many Dutch paintings, which lofty-minded people despise. I find a source of delicious sympathy in these faithful pictures of a monotonous homely existence, which has been the fate of so many more among my fellow-mortals than a life of pomp or of absolute indigence, of tragic suffering or of world-stirring actions. I turn, without shrinking, from cloud-borne angels, from prophets, sibyls, and heroic warriors, to an old woman bending over her flower-pot, or eating her solitary dinner, while the noonday light, softened perhaps by a screen of leaves, falls on her mob-cap, and just touches the rim of her spinning-wheel, and her stone jug, and all those cheap common things which are the precious necessaries of life to her;—or I turn to that village wedding, kept between four brown walls, where an awkward bride-groom opens the dance with a high-shouldered, broad-faced bride, while elderly and middle-aged friends look on, with very irregular noses and lips, and probably with quart-pots in their hands, but with an expression of unmistakable contentment and goodwill. "Foh!" says my idealistic friend, "what vulgar details! What good is there in taking all these pains to give an exact likeness of old women and clowns? What a low phase of life!—what clumsy, ugly people!"

But bless us, things may be lovable that are not altogether handsome, I hope? I am not at all sure that the majority of the human race have not been ugly, and even among those "lords of their kind," the British, squat figures, ill-shapen nostrils, and dingy complexions are not startling exceptions. Yet there is a great deal of family love amongst us. I have a friend or two whose class of features is such that the Apollo curl on the summit of their brows would be decidedly trying; yet to my certain knowledge tender hearts have beaten for them, and their miniatures—flattering, but still not lovely—are kissed in secret by motherly lips. I have seen many an excellent matron, who could never in her best days have been handsome, and yet she had a packet of yellow love-letters in a private drawer, and sweet children showered kisses on her sallow cheeks. And I believe there have been plenty of young heroes, of middle stature and feeble beards, who have felt quite sure they could never love anything more insignificant than a Diana, and yet have found themselves in middle life happily settled with a wife who waddles. Yes! thank God; human feeling is like the mighty rivers that bless the earth: it does not wait for beauty—it flows with resistless force and brings beauty with it.

All honour and reverence to the divine beauty of form! Let us cultivate it to the utmost in men, women, and children—in our gardens and in our houses. But let us love that other beauty too, which lies in no secret of proportion, but in the secret of deep human sympathy. Paint us an angel, if you can, with a floating violet robe, and a face paled by the celestial light; paint us yet oftener a Madonna, turning her mild face upward and opening her arms to welcome the divine glory; but do not impose on us any æsthetic rules which shall banish from the region of Art those old women scraping carrots with their work-worn hands, those heavy clowns taking holiday in a dingy pot-house, those rounded backs and stupid weather-beaten faces that have bent over the spade and done the rough work of the world—those homes with their tin pans, their brown pitchers, their rough curs, and their clusters of onions. In this world there are so many of these common coarse people, who have no picturesque sentimental wretchedness! It is so needful we should remember their existence, else we may happen to leave them quite out of our religion and philosophy, and frame lofty theories which only fit a world of extremes. Therefore let Art always remind us of them; therefore let us always have men ready to give the loving pains of a life to the faithful representing of commonplace things—men who see beauty in these commonplace things, and delight in showing how kindly the light of heaven falls on them. There are few prophets in the world; few sublimely beautiful women; few heroes. I can't afford to give all my love and reverence to such rarities: I want a great deal of those feelings for my everyday fellow-men, especially for the few in the foreground of the great multitude, whose faces I know, whose hands I touch, for whom I have to make way with kindly courtesy. Neither are picturesque lazzaroni or romantic criminals half so frequent as your common labourer, who gets his own bread, and eats it vulgarly but creditably with his own pocket-knife. It is more needful that I should have a fibre of sympathy connecting me with that vulgar citizen who weighs out my sugar in a vilely-assorted cravat and waistcoat, than with the handsomest rascal in red scarf and green feathers;—more needful that my heart should swell with loving admiration at some trait of gentle goodness in the faulty people who sit at the same hearth with me, or in the clergyman of my own parish, who is perhaps rather too corpulent, and in other respects is not an Oberlin or a Tillotson, than at the deeds of heroes whom I shall never know except by hearsay, or at the sublimest abstract of all clerical graces that was ever conceived by an able novelist.

STORY-TELLING
(1884)

What is the best way of telling a story? Since the standard must be the interest of the audience, there must be several or many good ways rather than one best. For we get interested in the stories life presents to us through divers orders and modes of presentation. Very commonly our first awakening to a desire of knowing a man's past or future comes from our seeing him as a stranger in some unusual or pathetic or humourous situation, or manifesting some remarkable characteristics. We make inquiries in consequence, or we become observant and attentive whenever opportunities of knowing more may happen to present themselves without our search. You have seen a refined face among the prisoners picking tow in gaol; you afterwards see the same unforgettable face in a pulpit: he must be of dull fibre who would not care to know more about a life which showed such contrasts, though he might gather his knowledge in a fragmentary and unchronological way.

Again, we have heard much, or at least something not quite common, about a man whom we have never seen, and hence we look round with curiosity when we are told that he is present; whatever he says or does before us is charged with a meaning due to our previous hearsay knowledge about him, gathered either from dialogue of which he was expressly and emphatically the subject, or from incidental remark, or from general report either in or out of print.

These indirect ways of arriving at knowledge are always the most stirring even in relation to impersonal subjects. To see a chemical experiment gives an attractiveness to a definition of chemistry, and fills it with a significance which it would never have had without the pleasant shock of an unusual sequence, such as the transformation of a solid into gas, and *vice versa*. To see a word for the first time either as substantive or adjective in a connection where we care about knowing its complete meaning, is the way to vivify its meaning in our recollection. Curiosity becomes the more eager from the incompleteness of the first information. Moreover, it is in this way that memory works in its incidental revival of events; some salient experience appears in inward vision, and in consequence the antecedent facts are retraced from what is regarded as the beginning of the episode in which that experience made a more or less strikingly memorable part. "Ah! I remember addressing the mob from the hustings at Westminster,—you wouldn't have thought that I could ever have been in such a position. Well, how I came there was in this way"; and then follows a retrospective narration.

The modes of telling a story founded on these processes of outward and inward life derive their effectiveness from the superior mastery of images and pictures in grasping the attention—or, one might say with more fundamental accuracy, from the fact that our earliest, strongest impressions, our most intimate convictions, are simply images added to more or less of sensation. These are the primitive instruments of thought. Hence it is not surprising that early poetry took this way—telling a daring deed, a glorious achievement, without caring for what went before. The desire for orderly narration is a later, more reflective birth. The presence of the Jack in the box affects every child: it is the more reflective lad, the miniature philosopher, who wants to know how he got there.

The only stories life presents to us in an orderly way are those of our autobiography, or the career of our companions from our childhood upwards, or perhaps of our own children. But it is a great art to make a connected strictly relevant narrative of such careers as we can recount from the beginning. In these cases the sequence of associations is almost sure to overmaster the sense of proportion. Such narratives *ab ovo* are summer's-day stories for happy loungers; not the cup of self-forgetting excitement to the busy who can snatch an hour of entertainment.

But the simple opening of a story with a date and necessary account of places and people, passing on quietly towards the more rousing elements of narrative and dramatic presentation, without need of retrospect, has its advantages, which have to be measured by the nature of the story. Spirited narrative, without more than a touch of dialogue here and there, may be made eminently interesting, and is suited to the novelette. Examples of its charm are seen in the short tales in which the French have a mastery never reached by the English, who usually demand coarser flavours than are given by that delightful gaiety which is well described by La Fontaine as not anything that provokes fits of laughter, but a certain charm, an agreeable mode of handling which lends attractiveness to all subjects, even the most serious.[3] And it is this sort of gaiety which plays around the best French novelettes. But the opening chapters of the "Vicar of Wakefield" are as fine as anything that can be done in this way.

Why should a story not be told in the most irregular fashion that an author's idiosyncrasy may prompt, provided that he gives us what we can enjoy? The objections to Sterne's wild way of telling "Tristram Shandy" lie more solidly in the quality of the interrupting matter than in the fact of interruption. The dear public would do well to reflect that they are often bored from the want of flexibility in their own minds. They are like the topers of "one liquor."

[3] Translation of a sentence from Preface to La Fontaine's *Fables*.

17

CHARLES KINGSLEY

(1819–1875)

Writing novels was a sideline for Charles Kingsley, and his six volumes of adult fiction constitute only a portion of his total output and contribute nothing to the development of the genre. By profession an energetic country parson, Rector of Eversley, in Hampshire, he held the chair of Modern History at Cambridge from 1860 to 1869. His published work was vast and varied: sermons, lectures, articles, poetry, essays, and tales for children. It is for the latter that he is probably best remembered today: *Water Babies* (1863) and his idealized depiction of Elizabethan sea-rovers in *Westward Ho!* (1855), his most popular book at the time but now designated as juvenile reading.

Like Disraeli and Mrs. Gaskell, Kingsley regarded the novel primarily as an important vehicle for discussion: ". . . the novel, however charlatans may degrade it, and the lazy would love to have it degraded, is in idea, next to the drama, the highest organ of moral teaching, and in practice just now a far more powerful one" ("Sir E. B. Lytton and Mrs. Grundy," *Fraser's Magazine*, XLI, January, 1850, 111). Influenced by Carlyle's ideas, Kingsley was more concerned with social reform than with moral teaching. *Yeast, A Problem* (1848) expressed his sympathy for the suffering agricultural worker; *Alton Locke* (1850) is a similar treatise in fiction form on the problems of the London laborer. Poverty, starvation, excessive working hours, unsanitary conditions were all denounced in Kingsley's novels as unnecessary: labor organizations could improve the lot of the worker; simple humanity would enable the employer to recognize inequities and accept a peaceful profit-sharing. As one of the didactic "social novelists" of the period, Kingsley showed more enthusiasm than creative genius. But his denunciation of the indifference of clergy and aristocracy is eloquent, and his natural descriptions reflect his love of the countryside.

The problem of realism is the only aspect of the novel on which Kingsley expressed his views at any length. In a letter to George Brimley of 1857, he wrote: "Writing novels is a farce and a sham. If any man could write the simple life of a circle of five miles round his own house, as he knew, and could in many cases swear it to be, at that moment, no one would believe it; and least of all would those believe it who did believe it. Do you ask the meaning of the paradox? Those who know best that the facts are true, or might be true, would be those most interested in declaring them impossible" (*Charles Kingsley: His Letters and Memories of his Life*, ed. by his wife, London, 1901, III, 45). More detailed comment on this matter, together with a rather cavalier approach to the question of authorial intervention may be found in another letter to Brimley of the same year, quoted below, (*Letters and Memories*, III, 40–41).

LETTER TO GEORGE BRIMLEY
(1857)

Thanks for your excellent review of *Two Years Ago*, and your equally excellent letter. About Major Campbell you are, perhaps, right, portrait as he is.

About the canons of criticism I know little, and am trying to forget what I know. I think the latter part of your letter answers the question, and that photography *versus* painting does give the analogy which will have to be followed henceforth.

I look at it thus. The idea of self-evolution in a story, beautiful as it is, is just one of those logical systems which is too narrow for the transcendental variety of life and fact. It would stand good of a Greek tragedy, as of a Greek statue. It never has stood good for Christian art, either painting, drama, or aught else.

In the greatest Christian pictures you see figures thrown in ἐν παρέργῳ[1] which are not required by the subject, *e.g.* the Pope and St. Theresa in the Madonna di San Sisto. Their use, conscious or unconscious, is to connect the subject with the rest of the universe, even with the present time, and show that it does not stand alone, that it is not a world of itself (to which alone self-evolution would be completely applicable), but is connected with the rest of the world. That this is the case in the Shakespearian drama, all know. Not a play of Shakespeare's in which whole scenes, whole characters, might not be cut out without hurting the plot, and you will find, comparing his dramas with the Italian *novelle*, from which he took them, that these supernumeraries are his own, put in on purpose, while the mere *novella* is self-evolved, and consequently narrow, and without deep and broad human application.

Now in the modern novel you ought to have all this, if it is to be a picture of actual life. You must have people coming in, influencing your principal characters for awhile—as people do influence you and me, and then go on their way, and you see them no more, as John Bunyan has it, in the best (and therefore most successful) novel which ever was written, which ought to be a model for all novelists. You must have descriptions of everything which can possibly influence your characters, or make your readers picture them strongly to themselves, subordinated only to the development of human

---

[1] ἐν παρέργῳ: as subordinate.

170

character and the arousing of interest. You must, as you so well remark, have people talk, as people do in real life, about all manner of irrelevant things, only taking care that each man's speech shall show more of his character, and that the general tone shall be such as never to make the reader forget the main purpose of the book. Finally, you must have παραβάσεις,[2] isn't it? like those in the Greek romantic drama, where the author throws off the mask and speaks for himself. The Greeks found it necessary, so do we. People are too stupid and in too great a hurry, to interpret the most puzzling facts for themselves, and the author must now and then act as showman, and do it for them. Whether it's according to "Art" or not, I don't care a fig. What's "Art"? I never saw a little beast flying about with "Art" labelled on its back. Art ought to mean the art of pleasing and instructing, and, believe me, these passages in which the author speaks in his own person do so. Froude approveth of them, for I talked it over with him. Women like them better than any part of a book. They like to be taught a little now and then; to feel that the book is the work of a human person, speaking to them as human persons, and therefore I fear the * * * * hateth them—just because they are the parts of the book which have the real practical influence.

But I go on. What was artistic enough for Eupolis, Cratinus, Aristophanes, etc., will do for me; and I ask you to look at Bulwer's novels, and see whether the same use of παραβάσεις—what women call "delightful subjective bits"—has not been one of the secrets of his great success. Of course it is very easy for a reviewer who disagrees with the doctrine to call it an obtrusion of the author's self; but the author's business is to see that it is just not that—to speak, if he can, the thoughts of many hearts, to put into words for his readers what they would have said for themselves if they could; he will be paid at once in thanks and correspondence, and having the secrets of sad hearts opened to him: as last night, already, brought me one of the saddest and most interesting letters I ever read, from someone to whom reading *Two Years Ago* had awakened a new view of God. God grant that it may last, and give a new life.

But you are right about Marie and Stangrave, up to a certain point. They and their story were altogether an afterthought, and don't fit well. To have fitted perfectly, Marie ought to have been brought under Grace's influence (so, too, ought Lucia), as all the characters are under that of Tom Thurnall—then the parallelism of the book would have been complete. But I trusted to the making the war of two years ago influence both Marie and Stangrave's thoughts, as it does other people's. But I shall bore you. Good-bye, and many thanks.

---

[2] παραβάσεις: digression, an aside.

18

GEORGE MEREDITH

(1828–1909)

Oscar Wilde's discerning observation that Meredith could do everything
except tell a story sums up both the latter's accomplishments and his limitations.
In Meredith's eyes, "The art of writing novels is to present a picture of life . . ."
(Letter to F. H. Evans, 16 November 1883), and, as with Trollope, whose
definition was similar, narrative was important only as a means of exhibiting
characters in action. The most extreme example of this attitude is *The Egoist*
(1879), more of an ethical study of self than a novel, yet intellectually intriguing
with its philosophical basis, psychological analysis, and stylistic eccentricities.
Meredith's constant emphasis on character and corresponding unconcern with
plot seems inconsistent with his advice to Hardy to give more attention to the
latter aspect.

The "picture of life" drawn by Meredith is typically one that portrays a
problem. His first important novel, *The Ordeal of Richard Feverel* (1859), is one of
several concerned with the rearing of a young gentleman, in this case torn
between expanding human nature and his father's "System." Others of his
dozen-odd novels express conflicts that, similarly, became prominent in late
nineteenth-century life. The demand for equal social rights for women and for
more liberal divorce laws thus found a champion in Meredith with *Diana of
the Crossways* (1885), as well as several other books. Although he criticized
society in his novels, Meredith deprecated the didactic novel:

Sick as we are of "purpose" in novels, we do not ask for nothing but pleasure. If life
in the present is to be portrayed, some hard things must needs obtrude. The province of
Art is to subordinate and soften them down. There are few subjects not legitimate to
the novelist, but as we are happily constituted to shun and detest the sight of evil, it
should be the novelist's care not to give what is painful undue prominence, and
especially not to strike a doubtful chord in the mind. We look on life apprehending the
bad and searching for the good. In the picture of life, this search should be assisted

without compromising truth, and to do this, and not throw dust in our eyes, is to be a great and worthy artist.

—"Belles Lettres and Art," *Westminster Review,*
LXVII (April, 1857), 615.

Indifference to story, concern with problems, and an intellectual approach are characteristically coupled with an indirect, epigrammatic, and artificially clever style. The resultant obscurity poses unusual demands for a reader. The *Ordeal* appealed more to critics and to the intellectual elite than to a public that became enthusiastic over *Adam Bede* in the same year. The inferential method, abrupt transitions, abundant analogies, recondite allusions, and concentrated essence were the products of Meredith's native wit, poetic talent, and an idealistic concept of the nature and function of the novel. In a lecture entitled "The Idea of Comedy and the Uses of the Comic Spirit," delivered 1 February 1877 at the London Institution, he promulgated his theory that civilization can be promoted by cultivating a sense of proportion. With the senses dominated by the intellect, a reasoned perception of individual folly and social stupidity, of hypocrisy, prejudice, and conceit will result. Like Eliot, Meredith formulated a thorough philosophy of life.

By adopting this theory of the Comic Spirit for fiction, Meredith denoted his novels as instruments of civilization. He touches on this hope in a letter of 22 July 1887 to G. P. Baker. Elsewhere, also, Meredith anticipates a change in public taste that will effect a better understanding of his efforts. The importance of the trivia he employs as links will someday be recognized, he hopes in a digression in the *Ordeal*. In the same vein, he anticipates the eventual coming of age of the novel, in the opening chapter of *Diana*, where he enters a plea for a philosophical basis of fiction.

Brief passages in his book reviews published under the "Belles Lettres and Art" section of the *Westminster Review*, supplement his other expressions of theory. Herein he deplores the flood of personal record stories that seek in vain to emulate the achievements of Charlotte Brontë (Vol. LXVII, April, 1857). Undoubtedly, as a reader for thirty-five years of manuscripts submitted to the publishing firm of Chapman and Hall, Meredith later became even more surfeited with inferior works and was, perhaps, encouraged in his use of intellectual material and development of an erudite style. He finds Trollope "wanting in certain of the higher elements that make a great novelist. He does not exhibit much sway over the emotional part of our nature." And he praises the same writer for avoiding authorial intrusion: "In general our modern prose satirists spread their canvas for a common tale, out of which they start when the occasion suits, to harangue, exhort, and scold the world in person. Mr. Trollope entrusts all this to the individuals of his story" (Vol. LXVIII, October, 1857). Meredith's own lack of emotional appeal and his abundant interjections are, thus, evidence of further discrepancies between his theory and his own practice.

THE ORDEAL OF RICHARD FEVEREL
(1859)

from Chapter 25[1]

Now surely there will come an age when the presentation of science at war with Fortune and the Fates will be deemed the true epic of modern life; and the aspect of a scientific humanist who, by dint of incessant watchfulness, has maintained a System against those active forces, cannot be reckoned less than sublime, even though at the moment he but sit upon his horse, on a fine March morning such as this, and smile wistfully to behold the son of his heart, his System incarnate, wave a serene adieu to tutelage, neither too eager nor morbidly unwilling to try his luck alone for a term of two weeks. At present, I am aware, an audience impatient for blood and glory scorns the stress I am putting on incidents so minute, a picture so little imposing. An audience will come to whom it will be given to see the elementary machinery at work: who, as it were, from some slight hint of the straws, will feel the winds of March when they do not blow. To them will nothing be trivial, seeing that they will have in their eyes the invisible conflict going on around us, whose features a nod, a smile, a laugh of ours perpetually changes. And they will perceive, moreoever, that in real life all hangs together: the train is laid in the lifting of an eyebrow, that bursts upon the field of thousands. They will see the links of things as they pass, and wonder not, as foolish people now do, that this great matter came out of that small one.

Such an audience, then, will participate in the baronet's gratification at his son's demeanour, wherein he noted the calm bearing of experience not gained in the usual wanton way: and will not be without some excited apprehension at his twinge of astonishment, when, just as the train went sliding into swiftness, he beheld the grave, cold, self-possessed young man throw himself back in the carriage violently laughing. Science was at a loss to account for that. Sir Austin checked his mind from inquiring, that he might keep suspicion at a distance, but he thought it odd, and the jarring sensation that ran along his nerves at the sight, remained with him as he rode home.

[1] Originally Chapter 29; in the 1878 revision, the first four chapters were compressed into one and Chapter 22 was suppressed.

LETTER TO G. P. BAKER
(22 July 1887)

MY DEAR SIR,—When at the conclusion of your article on my works, you say that a certain change in public taste, should it come about, will be to some extent due to me, you hand me the flowering wreath I covet. For I think that all right use of life, and the one secret of life, is to pave ways for the firmer footing of those who succeed us; as to my works, I know them faulty, think them of worth only when they point and aid to that end. Close knowledge of our fellows, discernment of the laws of existence, these lead to great civilization. I have supposed that the novel, exposing and illustrating the natural history of man, may help us to such sustaining roadside gifts. But I have never started on a novel to pursue the theory it developed. The dominant idea in my mind took up the characters and the story midway.

You say that there are few scenes. Is it so throughout? My method has been to prepare my readers for a crucial exhibition of the personae, and then to give the scene in the fullest of their blood and brain under stress of a fiery situation.

Concerning style, thought is tough, and dealing with thought produces toughness. Or when strong emotion is in tide against the active mind, there is perforce confusion. Have you found that scenes of simple emotion or plain narrative were hard to view? When their author revised for the new edition, his critical judgment approved these passages. Yet you are not to imagine that he holds his opinion combatively against his critics. The verdict is with the observer.

In the Comedies, and here and there where a concentrated presentment is in design, you will find a "pitch" considerably above our common human; and purposely, for only in such a manner could so much be shown. Those high notes and condensings are abandoned when the strong human call is heard—I beg you to understand merely that such was my intention.

Again, when you tell me that Harvard has the works, and that Young Harvard reads them, the news is of a kind to prompt me to fresh productiveness and higher. In England I am encouraged but by a few enthusiasts. I read in a critical review of some verses of mine the other day that I was "a harlequin and a performer of antics." I am accustomed to that kind of writing, as our hustings orator is to the dead cat and the brickbat flung in his face—at which he smiles politely; and I too; but after many years of it my mind looks elsewhere. Adieu to you.—Most faithfully yours,

GEORGE MEREDITH

175

DIANA OF THE CROSSWAYS
(1885)

from Chapter 1

Diarists of amusing passages are under an obligation to paint us a realistic revival of the time, or we miss the relish. The odour of the roast, and more, a slice of it is required, unless the humorous thing be preternaturally spirited to walk the earth as one immortal among a number less numerous than the mythic Gods. "He gives good dinners," a candid old critic said, when asked how it was that he could praise a certain poet. In an island of chills and fogs, cœlum crebris imbribus ac nebulis fœdum,[2] the comic and other perceptions are dependent on the stirring of the gastric juices. And such a revival by any of us would be impolitic, were it a possible attempt, before our systems shall have been fortified by philosophy. Then may it be allowed to the Diarist simply to relate, and we can copy from him.

Then, ah! then, moreover, will the novelist's Art, now neither blushless infant nor executive man, have attained its majority. We can then be veraciously historical, honestly transcriptive. Rose-pink and dirty drab will alike have passed away. Philosophy is the foe of both, and their silly cancelling contest, perpetually renewed in a shuffle of extremes, as it always is where a phantasm falseness reigns, will no longer baffle the contemplation of natural flesh, smother no longer the soul issuing out of our incessant strife. Philosophy bids us to see that we are not so pretty as rose-pink, not so repulsive as dirty drab; and that instead of everlastingly shifting those barren aspects, the sight of ourselves is wholesome, bearable, fructifying, finally a delight. Do but perceive that we are coming to philosophy, the stride towards it will be a giant's—a century a day. And imagine the celestial refreshment of having a pure decency in the place of sham; real flesh; a soul born active, wind-beaten, but ascending. Honourable will fiction then appear; honourable, a fount of life, an aid to life, quick with our blood. Why, when you behold it you love it—and you will not encourage it?—or only when presented by dead hands? Worse than that alternative dirty drab, your recurring rose-pink is rebuked by hideous revelations of the filthy foul; for nature will force her way, and if you try to stifle her by drowning, she comes

---

[2] cœlum crebris imbribus ac nebulis fœdum: always damp with rains and overcast with clouds.—Tacitus, *Agricola* 12.

176

up, not the fairest part of her uppermost! Peruse your Realists—really your castigators for not having yet embraced Philosophy. As she grows in the flesh when discreetly tended, nature is unimpeachable, flower-like, yet not too decoratively a flower; you must have her with the stem, the thorns, the roots, and the fat bedding of roses. In this fashion she grew, says historical fiction; thus does she flourish now, would say the modern transcript, reading the inner as well as exhibiting the outer.

And how may you know that you have reached to Philosophy? You touch her skirts when you share her hatred of the sham decent, her derision of sentimentalism. You are one with her when—but I would not have you a thousand years older! Get to her, if in no other way, by the sentimental route:—that very winding path, which again and again brings you round to the point of original impetus, where you have to be unwound for another whirl; your point of original impetus being the grossly material, not at all the spiritual. It is most true that sentimentalism springs from the former, merely and badly aping the latter;—fine flower, or pinnacle flame-spire, of sensualism that it is, could it do other?—and accompanying the former it traverses tracts of desert here and there couching in a garden, catching with one hand at fruits, with another at colours; imagining a secret ahead, and goaded by an appetite, sustained by sheer gratifications. Fiddle in harmonics as it may, it will have these gratifications at all costs. Should none be discoverable, at once you are at the Cave of Despair, beneath the funereal orb of Glaucoma, in the thick midst of poniarded, slit-throat, rope-dependant figures, placarded across the bosom Disillusioned, Infidel, Agnostic, Miserrimus. That is the sentimental route to advancement. Spirituality does not light it; evanescent dreams are its oil-lamps, often with wick askant in the socket.

A thousand years! You may count full many a thousand by this route before you are one with divine Philosophy. Whereas a single flight of brains will reach and embrace her; give you the savour of Truth, the right use of the senses, Reality's infinite sweetness; for these things are in philosophy; and the fiction which is the summary of actual Life, the within and without of us, is, prose or verse, plodding or soaring, philosophy's elect handmaiden. To such an end let us bend our aim to work, knowing that every form of labour, even this flimsiest, as you esteem it, should minister to growth. If in any branch of us we fail in growth, there is, you are aware, an unfailing aboriginal democratic old monster that waits to pull us down; certainly the branch, possibly the tree; and for the welfare of Life we fall. You are acutely conscious of yonder old monster when he is mouthing at you in politics. Be wary of him in the heart; especially be wary of the disrelish of brainstuff. You must feed on something. Matter that is not nourishing to brains can help to constitute nothing but the bodies which are pitched on rubbish heaps. Brainstuff is not lean stuff; the brainstuff of fiction is internal history, and to suppose it dull is the profoundest of errors; how deep, you will understand when I tell you that it is the very football of the holiday-afternoon imps below. They kick it for pastime; they are intelligences perverted. The comic of it, the adventurous, the tragic, they make devilish, to kindle their Ogygian hilarity. But sharply comic, adventurous, instructively tragic, it is in the interwinding with human affairs, to give a flavour of the modern day reviving that of our Poet, between whom and us yawn Time's most hollow jaws. Surely we owe a little to Time, to cheer his progress; a little to posterity, and to our country. Dozens of writers will be in at yonder yawning breach, if only perusers will rally to the philosophic standard. They are sick of the woodeny puppetry they dispense, as on a race-course to the roaring frivolous. Well, if not dozens, half-dozens; gallant pens are alive; one can speak of them in the plural. I venture to say that they would be satisfied with a dozen for audience, for a commencement. They would perish of inanition, unfed, unapplauded, amenable to the laws perchance for an assault on their last remaining pair of ears or heels, to hold them fast. But the example is the thing; sacrifices must be expected. The example might, one hopes, create a taste. A great modern writer, of clearest eye and head, now departed, capable in activity of presenting thoughtful women, thinking men, groaned over his puppetry, that he dared not animate them, flesh though they were, with the fires of positive brainstuff. He could have done it, and he is of the departed! Had he dared, he would (for he was Titan enough) have raised the Art in dignity on a level with History, to an interest surpassing the narrative of public deeds as vividly as man's heart and brain in their union excel his plain lines of action to eruption. The everlasting pantomime, suggested by Mrs. Warwick in her exclamation to Perry Wilkinson, is derided, not unrighteously, by our graver seniors. They name this Art the pasture of idiots, a method for idiotizing the entire population which has taken to reading; and which soon discovers that it can write likewise, *that* sort of stuff at least. The forecast may be hazarded, that if we do not speedily embrace Philosophy in fiction, the Art is doomed to extinction, under the shining multitude of its professors. They are fast capping the candle, Instead, therefore, of objurgating the timid intrusions of Philosophy, invoke her presence, I pray you. History without her is the skeleton map of events: Fiction a picture of figures modelled on no skeleton-anatomy. But each, with Philosophy in aid, blooms, and is humanly shapely. To demand of us truth to nature, excluding Philosophy, is really to bid a pumpkin caper. As much as legs are wanted for the dance, Philosophy is required to make our human nature credible and acceptable. Fiction implores you to heave a bigger breast and take her in with this heavenly preservative helpmate, her inspiration and her essence. You have to teach your imagination of the feminine image you have set up to bend your civilized knees to, that it must temper its fastidiousness, shun the grossness of the overdainty. Or, to speak in the philosophic tongue, you must turn on *yourself*, resolutely track and seize that burrower, and scrub and cleanse him; by which process, during the course of it, you will arrive at the conception of the right heroical woman for *you* to worship: and if you prove to be of some spiritual stature, you may reach to an ideal of the heroical feminine type for the worship of mankind, an image as yet in poetic outline only, on our upper skies.

"So well do we know ourselves, that we one and all determine to know a purer," says the heroine of my columns. Philosophy in fiction tells, among various other matters, of the perils of this intimate acquaintance with a flattering familiar in the "purer"—a person who more than ceases to be of use to us after his ideal shall have led up men from their flint and arrowhead caverns to inter-communicative daylight. For when the fictitious creature has performed that service of helping to civilize the world, it becomes the most dangerous of delusions, causing first the individual to despise the mass, and then to join the mass in crushing the individual. Wherewith let us to our story, the froth being out of the bottle.

19

CHARLES READE

(1814–1884)

"I feign probabilities; I record improbabilities: the former are conjectures; the latter truths: mixed they make a thing not so true as Gospel nor so false as History: viz., Fiction." Thus wrote Charles Reade in the Preface to *The Autobiography of a Thief* (1858). His creed of fiction was that a novel should be based on facts, that it was a serious art form, that its best technique was the dramatic, and that it was an effective instrument for social protest. He is sometimes mentioned as an innovator, along with Wilkie Collins, of the sensation novel. Reade's conception of fiction was conditioned, in part, by his study of law, which he never practiced although he was admitted to the bar. It taught him the value of organized factual data:

> It has lately been objected to me, in studiously courteous terms of course, that I borrow from other books, and am a Plagiarist. To this I reply that I borrow facts from every accessible source, and am not a Plagiarist. The Plagiarist is one who borrows from a homogeneous work: for such a man borrows not ideas only, but their treatment. He who borrows only from heterogeneous works is not a Plagiarist. All fiction, worth a button, is founded on facts; and it does not matter one straw whether the facts are taken from personal experience, hearsay, or printed books; only those books must not be works of fiction.
>
> Ask your common sense man why a man writes better fiction at forty than he can at twenty. It is simply because he has gathered more facts from each of these three sources—experience, hearsay, print.
>
> —Preface to *A Simpleton* (1873)

As a lifelong Fellow of Magdalen College, Oxford, Reade had learned how to acquire facts through research. Preparing to write his masterpiece, *The Cloister and the Hearth* (1861), whose historical setting was better adapted to documentation than the contemporary subjects of most of his novels, he explained his two years of research:

180

You may well be surprised that I am so long over *Good Fight* [title for the first version], but the fact is, it is not the writing but the reading which makes me slow. It may perhaps give you an idea of the system in which I write fiction, if I set down the list of books I have read, skimmed, or studied to write this little misery [There follows a list of over 70 books].

This system, wasted on an old world story, has kept you and me apart some months, which I regret; but then I hope your time will come to benefit by it; for surely this *must be* the right method. Anyway, I shall apply the same diligence and research to the subject of our own day I am preparing for you, that I have expended, perhaps wasted, on a medieval tale.

> —Undated letter to his publishers, Ticknor and Fields, quoted in Annie Fields, "An Acquaintance with Charles Reade," *The Century Magazine* XXIX (November, 1884), 73.

Even *Hard Cash* (1863), his exposure of the scandalous conditions in insane asylums, was the product of arduous research:

Hard Cash, like *The Cloister and the Hearth*, is a matter-of-fact Romance; that is, a fiction built on truths; and these truths have been gathered by long, severe, systematic labour, from a multitude of volumes, pamphlets, journals, reports, blue-books, manuscript narratives, letters, and living people, whom I have sought out, examined, and cross-examined, to get at the truth on each main topic I have striven to handle.

> —Preface to *Hard Cash*

The description of Mr. Rolfe's study in *A Terrible Temptation* (1870–71) may be read as an autobiographical account of Reade's systematic organization of the quantities of materials he accumulated in his bid for realism.

As a realist—a contemporary of Zola—Reade objected to sentimentalized endings and to the contemporary practice of tracing the disposition of minor characters:

In compliance with a custom I despise, but have not the spirit to resist, I linger on the stage to pick up the smaller fragments of humanity I have scattered about, i.e., some of them, for the wayside characters have no claim on me; they have served their turn if they have persuaded the reader that Gerard travelled from Holland to Rome through human beings, and not through a population of dolls.

> —*The Cloister and the Hearth*, Ch. 100

He objected, too, to interpolated stories: "a story within a story is a frightful flaw in art . . ." (Preface to *The Autobiography of a Thief*).

Nor was character analysis a proper function of the novelist, according to Reade:

Her mind was in a whirl; and, were I to imitate those writers who undertake to dissect and analyze the heart at such moments, and put the exact result on paper, I should be apt to sacrifice truth to precision; I must stick to my old plan, and tell you what she did: that will surely be some index to her mind, especially with my female readers.

> —*Griffith Gaunt* (1866; Ch. 23)

He expresses an intention to "trust a little to our readers' intelligence" to make the proper deductions from his presentation. (*A Perilous Secret*, 1884, Ch. 5).

One particular problem discussed by Reade was the treatment of a period of time during which incidents are unequally distributed. Sometimes he resorts to summary as in Chapter 5 of *A Perilous Secret*; sometimes he describes a representative day, "the representative of many such days which now succeeded to it" (*The Cloister and the Hearth*, Ch. 30); and sometimes, as in *Hard Cash* (Vol. III, Ch. 11) he presents the problem and concludes: "I throw myself on the intelligence of my readers."

Throughout his works, in appendices, footnotes, and dedications, Reade comments, usually briefly, on both general and specific aspects of fiction. In his Appendix to *The Wandering Heir* (1872), he defines fiction, gives his prescription for success, and considers the artist as critic. In his Dedication "To My Male Readers," of *Love Me Little, Love Me Long* (1859), he objects to the confusion of characters' statements with authors' sentiments.

The melodramatic character of Reade's incidents and the climactic curtains reflect his experience and interest in the theater. A successful writer of several plays, he transformed one, "Masks and Faces" (1852), into a novel, *Peg Woffington* (1853), the story of an eighteenth-century actress who actually existed.

Reade produced about twenty-five volumes of essays, stories, and novels, of which only *The Cloister and the Hearth* is generally read today. He himself is said to have liked his historical fiction less well than his novels of contemporary life. In these he promoted causes and attacked abuses: *It is Never Too Late to Mend* (1856) deals with mismanagement of prisons and mistreatment of criminals. *The Eighth Commandment* (1860) culminates an attack on literary piracy begun in plays and pamphlets. *Put Yourself in His Place* (1870) attacks the trade unions. Even *The Cloister and the Hearth* was a crusade against the clerical rule of celibacy.

HARD CASH
(1863)

from Volume III, Chapter 1

No life was ever yet a play: I mean an unbroken sequence of dramatic incidents. Calms will come; unfortunately for the readers, happily for the read. And I remember seeing it objected to novelists, by a young gentleman just putting his foot for the first time into "Criticism," that the writers aforesaid suppress the small intermediate matters which in real life come by the score between each brilliant event, and so present the ordinary and the extraordinary parts of life in false proportions. Now, if this remark had been offered by way of contrast between events themselves and all mortal attempts to reproduce them upon paper or the stage, it would have been philosophical; but it was a strange error to denounce the practice as distinctive of fiction: for it happens to be the one trait the novelist and dramatist have in common with the evangelist. The gospels skip fifteen years of the most interesting life Creation has witnessed, relating Christ's birth in full, and hurrying from his boyhood to the more stirring events of his thirtieth and subsequent years. And all the inspired histories do much the same thing. The truth is, that epics, dramas, novels, histories, chronicles, reports of trials at law, in a word, all narratives true or fictitious, except those which true or fictitious nobody reads, abridge the uninteresting facts as Nature never did, and dwell as Nature never did on the interesting ones.

Can nothing, however, be done to restore, in the reader's judgment, that just balance of "the sensational" and "the soporific," which all writers, that have readers, disturb? Nothing, I think, without his own assistance. But surely something with it. And, therefore, I throw myself on the intelligence of my readers; and ask them to realize, that henceforth pages are no measure of time, and that to a year big with strange events, on which I have therefore dilated in this story, succeeded a year in which few brilliant things happened to the personages of this tale: in short, a year to be skimmed by chronicler or novelist, and yet (mind you) a year of three hundred and sixty-five days six hours, or thereabouts, and one in which the quiet, unobtrusive troubles of our friends' hearts, especially the female hearts, their doubts, divisions, distresses, did not remit, far from it. Now this year I propose to divide into topics, and go by logical, rather than natural, sequence of events.

A TERRIBLE TEMPTATION
(1871)

from Volume II, Chapter 8

So far, the room was romantic; but there was a prosaic corner to shock those, who fancy that fiction is the spontaneous overflow of a poetic fountain fed by nature only; between the fireplace and the window, and within a foot or two of the wall, stood a gigantic writing-table, with the signs of hard labour on it, and of severe system. Three plated buckets, each containing three pints full of letters to be answered, other letters to be pasted into a classified guard-book, loose notes to be pasted into various books and classified (for this writer used to sneer at the learned men who say, "I will *look among my papers for it*;" he held that every written scrap ought either to be burnt, or pasted into a classified guard-book, where it could be found by consulting the index); five things like bankers' bill-books, into whose several compartments MS. notes and newspaper cuttings were thrown, as a preliminary towards classification in books.

Underneath the table was a formidable array of note-books, standing upright, and labelled on their backs. There were about twenty large folios, of classified facts, ideas, and pictures; for the very wood-cuts were all indexed and classified on the plan of a tradesman's ledger; there was also the receipt-book of the year, treated on the same plan. Receipts on a file would not do for this romantic creature: if a tradesman brought a bill, he must be able to turn to that tradesman's name in a book, and prove in a moment whether it had been paid or not. Then there was a collection of solid quartos, and of smaller folio guard-books called Indexes. There was "Index rerum et journalium"—"Index rerum et librorum"—"Index rerum et hominum"— and a lot more: indeed so many that, by way of climax, there was a fat folio ledger, entitled "Index ad Indices."

By the side of the table were six or seven thick pasteboard cards, each about the size of a large portfolio, and on these the author's notes and extracts were collected from all his repertories into something like a focus, for a present purpose. He was writing a novel based on facts; facts, incidents, living dialogue, pictures, reflections, situations, were all on these cards to choose from, and arranged in headed columns; and some portions of the work he was writing on this basis of imagination and drudgery lay on the table in two forms, his own writing, and his secretary's copy thereof, the latter corrected for the press. This copy was half margin, and so provided for additions and improvements; but for one addition there were ten excisions, great and small.

Lady Bassett had just time to take in the beauty and artistic character of the place, and to realise the appalling drudgery that stamped it a workshop, when the author, who had dashed into his garden for a moment's recreation, came to the window, and furnished contrast No. 3; for he looked neither like a poet, nor a drudge, but a great fat country farmer. He was rather tall, very portly, smallish head, commonplace features, mild brown eye not very bright, short beard, and wore a suit of tweed all one colour. Such looked the writer of romances founded on fact. He rolled up to the window —for, if he looked like a farmer, he walked like a sailor—and stepped into the room.

THE WANDERING HEIR
(1872)

from the Appendix

To sum up—Fiction is the art of weaving fact with invention. If it were mere arrangement of fact, thousands could write it; if it were pure invention, the young would beat the elderly at it. Instead of that, the young, with all the advantage of their ardent imaginations and generous blood and elastic energy, write flimsy stuff for want of Fact. If Dickens appears an exception, that is only because Dickens ripened early, and was initiated into that sort of Fact which is good material for fiction ten years sooner than other writers.

Of Fact there are three sources—experience, hearsay, printed records.

An individual's personal experience is so narrow, that it can carry him but a little way in fiction. We none of us know much except from print.

In writing an historical tale, experience and hearsay dwindle, and the printed facts we have gathered, many of them unconsciously, become the main material.

To interweave these in fiction is the same intellectual operation as to interweave the facts we have seen and heard. Whoever denies this is a fool; whoever admits it, yet cannot realize it, and apply it to the question of plagiarism, is weak of mental digestion, and, though he may criticise all his life, will never be a critic. To borrow scenes and dialogues from a novel of Swift, and put them in a novel, would be plagiarism. But to transplant a few facts out of many in a heap collected by Swift, and then, by change of form and sequence, wield them with another topic into a heterogeneous work, this is not plagiarism; it is one of every true inventor's processes, and only an inventor can do it well. It is precisely the same intellectual crime I was guilty of, when I took the fact of the turf backgammon board, and the dice boy, from the lips of a friend, and wove it into my tale; or when in "A Simpleton" I interwove the numerous facts I had gathered at first-hand in auction-rooms.

Spawn and millet—millet and spawn—without the pair, nature cannot produce a single herring, nor art a single fiction worth its weight in sawdust.

And when Fiction adds to its difficulties, when it aspires to deal with the past, to raise the dead from their graves, and make them live, and move, and dress, and act, and speak, and feel again in a strong domestic story, then must ripe learning and keen invention meet, or gross failure ensue. Then must the spawn be more copious than ever, and the millet more strong and vivifying. To this occasion the words of Horace apply particularly—

> "Nec studium sine divite venâ
> Nec rude quid possit video ingenium; alterius sic
> Altera poscit opem res, et conjurat amice."[1]

An artist is seldom a critic, and you may think it presumptuous of me to lay down the law. Permit me to explain. I studied the great art of Fiction closely for fifteen years before I presumed to write a line of it. I was a ripe critic long before I became an artist. My critical knowledge has directed my art, but the practice of that art has not diminished my studies.

Forty years examination of masterpieces, and their true history, have qualified me to speak with some little authority.

---

[1] I see neither what study without rich native talents nor genius without art can do: so much does one require the aid of the other, and swears alliance with it.—Horace, *Ars Poetica* ll. 409–11.

20

CHARLES J. LEVER

(1806–1872)

Among the several novelists that Thackeray ridiculed in his parodies was Charles Lever, but the latter's shortcomings did not prevent Thackeray from visiting him in 1842 and dedicating his *Irish Sketch-Book* (1843) to him. Although born in Dublin, Lever was of English descent on both sides—his father had come from Manchester. Because of this foreign ancestry, he has never been credited with exhibiting the true Irish spirit, and Irishmen have objected to his presentation of lower-class peasants as typical of the Irish scene.

Lever was more than a writer of local color. After graduation from Trinity College in 1827, he spent some time in the American backwoods, even living among the Indians. He studied medicine in Germany, earning the Bachelor of Medicine degree. From 1845 until his death in 1872 he lived in various parts of the Continent, especially Florence. He was appointed to the nominal post of Consul at Trieste in 1867, where he died. One result of this extensive experience was a European-wide setting for his fiction. Characteristic is his *Tom Burke of "Ours"* (1843–44), wherein an Irish soldier of fortune provides the moving center of romantic episodes, military life, and a surface picture of the Continental scene.

In spite of his large output (37 volumes in the edition collected by his daughter) and the excellent sale of his novels, Lever has never been ranked as a major writer. Indeed, it was because he wrote so much that he had no time to plan or revise, and his fiction tends toward the episodic and the cavalier. His preface to his first novel, *The Confessions of Harry Lorrequer* (1837–40), admits his carelessness and testifies to his irresponsibility. And, writing to James Glashan on 20 September 1839, Lever said: "I sent you a week since, two chaps.—xliii and xliv of 'Harry Lorrequer.' God grant they have reached you, for I never can rewrite, and if lost, they break the chains, if there be any, in the narrative." In spite of its weaknesses, the novel was a financial success. Lever's extravagant habits, addiction to cards, and an expensive family motivated him to drift into

187

writing as a more lucrative source of income than his profession of a country doctor. When, in 1842, he assumed the editorship of the *Dublin University Magazine,* in which *Harry Lorrequer* first appeared serially, he abandoned his medical career.

Lever's novels are characterized by humor, anecdote, description, and vigor. On the other hand, they are formless, lacking in imagination, and devoid of any artistic instinct. His theories, insofar as his guidelines may be termed theories, are more implied than expressed; but there are occasional brief expressions of these, such as his opinion on the introduction of extraneous incidents:

Tale writers are blamed for the introduction of incidents which have little bearing on the main story, or whose catastrophes are veiled in obscurity. But I would humbly ask, are not these exactly the very traits of real life? Is not every man's course chequered with incidents, and crossed by people who never affect his actual career?

—"Notice" to *Sir Jasper Carewe* (1855).

There is also an interesting comment on conclusions and the vitality of fictional characters:

There is nothing I find so hard in a story as the end. I never can put the people to bed with the propriety that I wish. Some won't come for their night-cap; some won't lie down; and some will run about in their shirts when I want to extinguish the candle. In fact—absurd as it may seem—one's creatures have a will of their own, and the unhappy author of their being is as much tormented by their vagaries and caprices as if they were his flesh-and-blood children going into debt, and making bad matches and the rest of it.

—Letter to John Blackwood, 19 August 1866.

Lever's prefaces, composed in 1871–72 for a new edition of his novels, usually pertain to the origin of his ideas and the originals of his characters. The preface to his most popular novel, *Charles O'Malley, the Irish Dragoon* (1840–41), is no exception; it serves to suggest his theories on fictional material and character creation.

PREFACE

CHARLES O'MALLEY
THE IRISH DRAGOON
(1871–72 Edition)

The success of *Harry Lorrequer* was the reason for writing *Charles O'Malley*. That I myself was in nowise prepared for the favour the public bestowed on my first attempt is easily enough understood. The ease with which I strung my stories together—in reality the *Confessions of Harry Lorrequer* are little more than a note-book of absurd and laughable incidents—led me to believe that I could draw on this vein of composition without any limit whatever. I felt, or thought I felt, an inexhaustible store of fun and buoyancy within me, and I began to have a misty half-confused impression that Englishmen generally laboured under a sad-coloured temperament, and were proportionately grateful to anyone who would rally them, even passingly, out of their despondency, and give them a laugh without much trouble for going in search of it.

When I set to work to write *Charles O'Malley*, I was, as I have ever been, very low with fortune, and the success of a new venture was pretty much as eventful to me as the turn of the right colour at *rouge-et-noir*. At the same time, I had then an amount of spring in my temperament, and a power of enjoying life, which I can honestly say I never found surpassed. The world had for me all the interest of an admirable comedy, in which the part allotted to myself, if not a high or a foreground one, was eminently suited to my taste, and brought me, besides, sufficiently often on the stage to enable me to follow all the fortunes of the piece. Brussels (where I was then living) was adorned at the period with most agreeable English society. Some leaders of the fashionable world of London had come there to refit and recruit, both in body and estate. There were several pleasant people, and a great number of pretty people; and so far as I could judge, the fashionable dramas of Belgrave Square and its vicinity were being performed in the Rue Royale and the Boulevard de Waterloo with very considerable success. There were dinners, balls, *déjeûners*, and picnics in the Bois de Cambre, excursions to Waterloo, and select little parties to Boisfort (a charming little resort in the forest), whose intense Cockneyism became perfectly inoffensive, being in a foreign land and remote from the invasion of home-bred vulgarity.

I mention these things to show the adjuncts by which I was aided, and the rattle of gaiety by which I was, as it were, "accompanied" when I tried my voice.

The soldier element tinctured our society strongly, and, I will add, most agreeably. Amongst those whom I remember best were several old Peninsulars. Lord Combermere was of this number; and another of our set was an officer who accompanied—if indeed he did not command—the first boat party who crossed the Douro. It is needless to say how diligently I cultivated a society so full of all the storied details I was eager to obtain, and how generously disposed were they to give me all the information I needed. On topography especially were they valuable to me, and with such good result that I have been more than once complimented on the accuracy of my descriptions of places which I have never seen.

When, therefore, my publishers asked me could I write a story in the Lorrequer vein,—a story in which active service and military adventure could figure more prominently than mere civilian life, and where achievements of a British army might form the staple of the narrative,—I was ready to reply: "*Not one, but fifty.*"

Do not mistake me, and suppose that any overweening confidence in my literary powers would have emboldened me to make this reply: my whole strength lay in the fact that I could not recognise anything like literary effort in the matter. If the world would only condescend to read that which I wrote precisely as I was in the habit of talking, nothing could be easier. Not alone was it easy, but it was intensely interesting and amusing to myself to be so engaged.

The success of *Harry Lorrequer* had been freely wafted across the German Ocean: it was very intoxicating incense, and I set to work on my second book with a thrill of hope as regards the world's favour which—and it is no small thing to say it—I can yet recall.

I can recall, too,—and I am afraid more vividly still,—some of the difficulties of my task when I endeavoured to form anything like an accurate or precise idea of some campaigning incident, or some passage of arms, from the narratives of two distinct and separate "eye-witnesses." What mistrust I conceived for all eye-witnesses from my own brief experience of their testimonies! What an impulse did it lend to me to study the nature and the temperament of the narrator as an indication of the peculiar colouring he might lend his narrative! And how it taught me to measure the force of the French epigram that it was the alternating popularity of Marshal Soult that decided whether he won or lost the battle of Toulouse!

While, however, I was sifting these evidences, and separating, as well as I might, the wheat from the chaff, I was in a measure training myself for what, without my then knowing it, was to become my career in life. My training was not without a certain amount of labour, but so light and pleasant was the labour, so full of picturesque peeps at characters and of humorous views of human nature, that it would be the rankest ingratitude if I did not own that I gained all my earlier experiences of the world in very pleasant company, highly enjoyable at the time and with matter for charming souvenirs long afterwards.

That certain traits of my acquaintances found themselves embodied in some of the characters of this story, I do not seek to deny. The principle of natural selection adapts itself to novels as well as to nature, and it would have demanded an effort above my strength to have disabused myself at the desk of all the impressions of the dinner-table, and to have forgotten features which interested or amused me.

One of the personages of my tale I drew, however, with very little aid from fancy. I would go so far as to say that I took him from the life, if my memory did not confront me with the lamentable inferiority of my picture to the great original which it was meant to portray.

With the exception of the quality of courage, I never met a man who contained within himself so many of the traits of Falstaff as the individual who furnished me with "Major Monsoon." But the Major—I must call him so, though that rank was far beneath his own—was a man of unquestionable bravery. His powers as a story-teller were to my thinking unrivalled; the peculiar reflections on life which he would passingly introduce—the wise apothegms—were of a morality essentially of his own invention; he would indulge in the unsparing exhibition of himself in situations such as other men would never have confessed,—all blended up with a racy enjoyment of life, dashed occasionally with sorrow that our tenure of it was short of patriarchal. All these idiosyncracies, accompanied by a face redolent of intense humour and a voice whose modulations were managed with the skill of a consummate artist, were above me to convey; nor indeed, as I re-read any of the adventures in which he figures, am I other than ashamed at the weakness of my drawing and the poverty of my colouring.

In order to show that I had a better chance to personify him than is usually the lot of a novelist,—that I possessed, so to say, a vested interest in his life and adventures,—I will relate a little incident; and my accuracy, if necessary, can be attested by another actor in the scene who yet survives.

I was living a bachelor life at Brussels—my family being at Ostend for the bathing—during the summer of 1840. The city was comparatively empty, all the so-called society being absent at the various spas or baths of Germany. One member of the British Legation, who remained at his post to represent the mission, and myself, making common cause of our desolation and ennui, spent much of our time together and dined *tête-à-tête* every day.

It chanced that one evening, as we were hastening through the park on our way to dinner, we espied the Major—as "Major" I must speak of him—lounging about with that half-careless, half-observant air which indicated a desire to be somebody's—anybody's—guest rather than to surrender himself to the homeliness of domestic fare.

"There's that confounded old Monsoon!" said my diplomatist friend. "It's all up if he sees us, and I can't endure him."

Now I must remark that my friend, though very far from being insensible to the humouristic side of the Major's character, was not always in the vein to enjoy it, and when he was so indisposed he could invest the object of his dislike with something little short of repulsiveness. "Promise me," said he, as Monsoon came towards us, "you'll not ask him to dinner." Before I could make any reply the Major was shaking a hand of either of us, rapturously expatiating over his good luck at meeting us. "Mrs. M.," said he, "has got a dreary party of old ladies to dine with her, and I have come out here to find some pleasant fellow to join me and take our mutton-chop together."

"We're behind our time, Major," said my friend. "Sorry to leave you so abruptly, but must push on. Eh. Lorrequer?" added he, to evoke corroboration from me.

"Harry says nothing of the kind," interrupted Monsoon. "He says, or he's going to say, 'Major, I have a nice bit of dinner waiting for me at home,—enough for two, will feed three; or, if there be a shortcoming, nothing easier than to eke out the deficiency by another bottle of Moulton. Come along with us then, Monsoon, and we shall be all the merrier for your company.'"

Repeating his words, "Come along, Monsoon," I passed my arm within his, and away we went. For a moment my friend tried to get free and leave me, but I held him fast and carried him along in spite of himself. He was, however, so chagrined and provoked that till the moment we reached my door he never uttered a word nor paid the slightest attention to Monsoon, who talked away in a vein that occasionally made gravity all but impossible.

Dinner proceeded drearily enough: the diplomatist's stiffness never relaxed for a moment, and my own awkwardness damped all my attempts at conversation. Not so, however, Monsoon; he ate heartily, approved of everything, and pronounced my wine to be exquisite. He gave us a discourse upon sherry and the Spanish wines in general; told us the secret of the Amontillado flavour; and explained the process of browning, by boiling down wine, which some are so fond of in England. At last he diverged into anecdote. "I was once fortunate enough," said he, "to fall upon some of that choice sherry from the St. Lucas Luentas which is always reserved for royalty. It was a pale wine, delicious in the drinking, and leaving no more flavour in the mouth than a faint dryness that seemed to say, 'Another glass.' shall I tell you how I came by it?" And scarcely pausing for a reply, he told the story of having robbed his own convoy and stolen the wine he was in charge of for safe conveyance.[1]

[1] This story is told in *Charles O'Malley*.

I wish I could give any, even the weakest, idea of how he narrated the incident,—the struggle between duty and temptation, and the apologetic tone of voice in which he explained that the frame of mind which succeeds to any yielding to seductive influences is often in the main more profitable to a man than is the vainglorious sense of having resisted a temptation. "Meekness is the mother of all virtues," said he, "and there "is no meekness without frailty." The story, told as he told it, was too much for the diplomatist's gravity, and at last he fairly roared with laughter.

As soon as I myself recovered from the effects of his drollery I said, "Major, I have a proposition to make. Let me tell that story in print and I'll give you five Naps."

"Are you serious, Harry?" said he. "Is this on honour?"

"On honour assuredly," I replied.

"Let me have the money down on the nail and I'll give you leave to have me and my whole life,—every adventure that ever befell me,—ay, and if you like, every moral reflection that my experiences have suggested."

"Done!" cried I. "I agree."

"Not so fast," said the diplomatist. "We must make a protocol of this: the high contracting parties must know what they give and what they receive. I'll draw out the treaty."

He did so, at full length, on a sheet of that solemn blue-tinted paper dedicated to despatch purposes, duly setting forth the concession and the consideration. Each of us signed the document; it was witnessed and sealed; and Monsoon pocketed my five Napoleons, filling a bumper to any success the bargain might bring me.

This document, along with my university degree, my commission in a militia regiment, and a vast amount of letters (very interesting to me), were seized by the Austrian authorities on the way from Como to Florence in the August of 1847, being deemed part of a treasonable correspondence— purposely allegorical in form,—and they were never restored to me. I freely own that I'd give all the rest willingly to repossess myself of the Monsoon treaty.

To show that I did not entirely fail in making my "Major" resemble the great original from whom I copied, I may mention that he was speedily recognised by the Marquis of Londonderry, the well-known Sir Charles Stuart of the Peninsular campaign. "I know that fellow well," said he. "He once sent me a challenge, and I had to make him a very humble apology. The occasion was this: I had been out with a single aide-de-camp to make a reconnaissance in front of Victor's division; and to avoid attracting any notice, we covered over our uniform with two common grey overcoats which reached to the feet, effectually concealing our rank. Scarcely, however, had we topped a hill which commanded a view of the French, when a shower of shells flew over and around us. Amazed to think that we had been so quickly noticed, I looked around me and discovered, quite close in my rear, your friend Monsoon with what he called his staff,—a popinjay set of rascals dressed out in green and gold, and with more plumes and feathers than ever the general staff boasted. Carried away by momentary passion at the failure of my reconnaissance, I burst out with some insolent allusion to the harlequin assembly which had drawn the French fire upon us. Monsoon saluted me respectfully and retired without a word; but I had scarcely reached my quarters when a 'friend' of his waited upon me with a message,—a categorical message it was, too: 'It must be a meeting or an ample apology.' I made the apology—a most full one—for the 'Major' was right and I had not a fraction of reason to sustain me. We have been the best of friends ever since."

I had heard the story before this from Monsoon, but I did not then accord it all the faith that was its due; and I admit that the accidental corroboration of this one event very often served to puzzle me afterwards, when I listened to tales in which the Major seemed to be a second Munchausen. It might be that he was amongst the truest and most matter-of-fact of historians. May the reader be not less embarrassed than myself! is my sincere, if not very courteous, prayer. I have no doubt that often in recounting some strange incident—a personal experience it always was—he was himself carried away by the credulity of his hearers and the amount of interest he could excite in them, rather than by the story. He possessed the true narrative style, and there was a marvellous instinct in the way in which he would vary a tale to suit the tastes of an audience, while his moralisings were almost certain to take the tone of a humouristic quiz of the company. Though fully aware that I was availing myself of the contract that delivered him into my hands, and though he dined with me two or three times a-week, he never lapsed into any allusion to his appearance in print, and *O'Malley* had been published some weeks when he asked me to lend him "that last thing"—he forgot the name of it—I was writing.

Of Frank Webber I have said elsewhere that he was one of my earliest friends, my chum at college, and in the very chambers in Old Trinity where I have located Charles O'Malley. He was a man of the highest order of abilities, with a memory that never forgot; but he was ruined and run to seed by the idleness that came of a discursive uncertain temperament. Capable of anything—he spent his youth in follies and eccentricities, every one of which, however, gave indications of a mind inexhaustible in resources and abounding in devices and contrivances. Poor fellow! he died young; and perhaps it is better it should have been so. Had he lived to a later day, he would most probably have been found a foremost leader of Fenianism; and from what I knew of him, I can say that he would have been a more dangerous enemy to English rule than any of those dealers in the petty larceny of rebellion we have lately seen amongst us.

Of Mickey Free I had not one, but one thousand, types. Indeed I am not quite sure that in my late visit to Dublin I did not chance on a living specimen of the "Free" family, much readier in repartee, quicker at an *apropos*, and droller in illustration, than my own Mickey. The fellow was "boots" at a great hotel in Sackville Street; and he afforded me more amusement and some heartier laughs than it has always been my fortune to enjoy in a party of wits. His criticisms on my sketches of Irish character were about the shrewdest and the best I ever listened to; and that I am not bribed to this opinion by any flattery, I may remark that they were often more severe than complimentary, and that he hit every blunder of image, every mistake in figure, of my peasant characters with an acuteness and correctness which made me very grateful to know that his daily occupations were limited to the blacking of boots and not to the "polishing off" of authors.

I should like to own that *Charles O'Malley* was the means of according me a more heartfelt glow of satisfaction, a more gratifying sense of pride, than anything I ever have written. My brother, at that time the rector of an Irish parish, once forwarded to me a letter from a lady, unknown to him, who had heard that he was the brother of "Harry Lorrequer," and who addressed him not knowing where a letter might be directed to myself. The letter was the grateful expression of a mother, who said: "I am the widow of a field-officer, and with an only son, for whom I obtained a presentation to Woolwich; but seeing in my boy's nature certain traits of nervousness and timidity which induced me to hesitate on embarking him in the career of a soldier, I became very unhappy, and uncertain which course to decide upon. While in this state of uncertainty I chanced to make him a birthday present of *Charles O'Malley*, the reading of which seemed to act like a charm on his whole character, inspiring him with a passion for movement and adventure, and spiriting him on to an eager desire for a military life. Seeing that this was no passing enthusiasm but a decided and determined bent, I accepted the cadetship for him, and his career has been not alone distinguished as a student, but one which has marked him out for an almost hare-brained courage and for a dash and heroism that give high promise for his future. Thank your brother for me," she continued,—"a mother's thanks for the welfare of an only son, and say how I wish that my best wishes for him and his could recompense him for what I owe him."

I humbly hope that it may not be imputed to me as unpardonable vanity the recording of this incident. It gave me intense pleasure when I heard it; and now, as I look back on it, it invests the story for myself with an interest which nothing else that I have written can afford me.

21

ANTHONY TROLLOPE

(*1815–1882*)

"Have you ever read the novels of Anthony Trollope?" asked Nathaniel Hawthorne. "They precisely suit my taste; solid, substantial, written on strength of beef and through the inspiration of ale, and just as real as if some giant had hewn a great lump out of the earth and put it under a glass case, with all its inhabitants going about their daily business, and not suspecting that they were made a show of." Thus, for one reader at least, Trollope realized his definition of the novel—"a picture of common life enlivened by humour and sweetened by pathos." He possessed the knack of making conventional life interesting—as had Jane Austen, with whom he has more in common than he has with many of his contemporaries.

After several, unsuccessful, initial attempts in fiction, Trollope scored with *The Warden* (1855), which Henry James liked most of all his novels. The ensuing Barsetshire, or Cathedral, Series, from *Barchester Towers* (1857) to *The Last Chronicle of Barset* (1867), incorporates his best work. Among his nearly fifty works of fiction are social satires, historical fiction, political novels, and novels of manners. Popular during his lifetime, they were neglected after his death, partly because of the disillusioning account in his posthumously published *Autobiography* (1883) of the mechanical formulae that produced them. But he had earned almost £70,000 from his writing up to 1879, and today virtually all of his novels are in print and are reported by libraries to be in great demand.

From 1834, when he obtained a clerkship, until his retirement in 1867 as an inspector, Trollope's professional career was in the Postal Service. His travels throughout the world to survey postal systems led to his writing of travel books and provided time to write, for he prided himself on being able to write at any time and in any place. His account of *North America* (1862) helped to counteract the bad impressions produced by his author-mother, Mrs Frances Trollope, in her *Domestic Manners of the Americans* (1832). Although Trollope's civil service career gave him access to information such as that which helped him to write *The Three Clerks* (1858), it was never the basis for his fiction.

Bradford Booth characterized Trollope's criticism as "of unequal merit . . . His approach was always that of the practicing novelist who knows what elements constitute successful fiction . . ." ("Trollope on the Novel," *Essays Critical and Historical*, Berkeley and Los Angeles, 1950). Certainly his view of art was a material one. "The primary object of a novelist is to please," he wrote in his *Autobiography* (Ch. 13). He opposed the sensationalism of the Dickens' school; he eschewed the use of fiction as a vehicle for reform or as a platform for philosophy. Even in his Barsetshire series, the first to make Cathedral life a subject of fiction, there is no great concern over Church controversies or spiritual issues. The value of his work lies in his depiction of the outward aspects of contemporary England.

Trollope's specific means to this fidelity to fact lies not in his plots, which are indifferent because they are, to him, only a vehicle; not in his manner, which lacks subtlety and insists on a complete confidence between writer and reader that permits no surprises; but in his characterizations, which are thoroughly consistent. "The canvas should be crowded with real portraits, not of individuals known to the world or to the author, but of created personages impregnated with traits of characters which are known" (*Autobiography*, Ch. VII). His theory on the use of ordinary, rather than heroic, characters is expressed at the end of *Ralph the Heir* (1870–71), together with his belief in the inevitability of moralizing.

Throughout his novels Trollope discussed aspects of his art in brief digressions. His *Autobiography*, written between 1875 and 1876, contains more extended commentary; in particular, Chapter XII, entitled "On Novels and the Art of Writing Them," should be noted. Much of this chapter is taken from his lecture, "On English Prose Fiction as a Rational Amusement," delivered at Edinburgh on 28 January 1870. A final version of this discussion was published as an article in the *Nineteenth Century* for January, 1879, under the title "Novel-Reading: The Works of Charles Dickens; The Works of W. Makepeace Thackeray." It vindicates the novel, disputes attempts to divide fiction into the sensational and the realistic, deals with the treatment of love, and insists on the necessity of reality in characterization.

RALPH THE HEIR
(1871)

from Volume III, Chapter 18

And with the same grey horses shall the happy bride and bridegroom be bowled out of our sight also. The writer of this story feels that some apology is due to his readers for having endeavoured to entertain them so long with the adventures of one of whom it certainly cannot be said that he was fit to be delineated as a hero. It is thought by many critics that in the pictures of imaginary life which novelists produce for the amusement, and possibly for the instruction of their readers, none should be put upon the canvas but the very good, who by their noble thoughts and deeds may lead others to nobility, or the very bad, who by their declared wickedness will make iniquity hideous. How can it be worth one's while, such critics will say,—the writer here speaks of all critical readers, and not of professional critics,—how can it be worth our while to waste our imaginations, our sympathies, and our time upon such a one as Ralph, the heir of the Newton property? The writer, acknowledging the force of these objections, and confessing that his young heroes of romance are but seldom heroic, makes his apology as follows.

The reader of a novel,—who has doubtless taken the volume up simply for amusement, and who would probably lay it down did he suspect that instruction, like a snake in the grass, like physic beneath the sugar, was to be imposed upon him,—requires from his author chiefly this, that he shall be amused by a narrative in which elevated sentiment prevails, and gratified by being made to feel that the elevated sentiments described are exactly his own. When the heroine is nobly true to her lover, to her friend, or to her duty, through all persecution, the girl who reads declares to herself that she also would have been a Jeannie Deans had Fate and Fortune given her an Effie as a sister. The bald-headed old lawyer,—for bald-headed old lawyers do read novels,—who interests himself in the high-minded, self-devoting chivalry of a Colonel Newcombe, believes he would have acted as did the Colonel had he been so tried. What youth in his imagination cannot be as brave, and as loving, though as hopeless in his love, as Harry Esmond? Alas, no one will wish to be as was Ralph Newton! But for one Harry Esmond, there are fifty Ralph Newtons,—five hundred and fifty of them; and the very youth whose bosom glows with admiration as he reads of Harry,—who exults in the idea that as Harry did, so would he have done,—lives as

Ralph lived, is less noble, less persistent, less of a man even than was Ralph Newton.

It is the test of a novel writer's art that he conceals his snake-in-the-grass; but the reader may be sure that it is always there. No man or woman with a conscience,—no man or woman with intellect sufficient to produce amusement, can go on from year to year spinning stories without the desire of teaching; with no ambition of influencing readers for their good. Gentle readers, the physic is always beneath the sugar, hidden or unhidden. In writing novels we novelists preach to you from our pulpits, and are keenly anxious that our sermons shall not be inefficacious. Inefficacious they are not, unless they be too badly preached to obtain attention. Injurious they will be unless the lessons taught be good lessons.

What a world this would be if every man were a Harry Esmond, or every woman a Jeannie Deans! But then again, what a world if every woman were a Beckie Sharp and every man a Varney or a Barry Lyndon! Of Varneys and Harry Esmonds there are very few. Human nature, such as it is, does not often produce them. The portraits of such virtues and such vices serve no doubt to emulate and to deter. But are no other portraits necessary? Should we not be taught to see the men and women among whom we really live,— men and women such as we are ourselves,—in order that we should know what are the exact failings which oppress ourselves, and thus learn to hate, and if possible to avoid in life the faults of character which in life are hardly visible, but which in portraiture of life can be made to be so transparent.

Ralph Newton did nothing, gentle reader, which would have caused thee greatly to grieve for him, nothing certainly which would have caused thee to repudiate him, had he been thy brother. And gentlest, sweetest reader, had he come to thee as thy lover, with sufficient protest of love, and with all his history written in his hand, would that have caused thee to reject his suit? Had he been thy neighbour, thou well-to-do reader, with a house in the country, would he not have been welcome to thy table? Wouldst thou have avoided him at his club, thou reader from the West End? Has he not settled himself respectably, thou grey-haired, novel-reading paterfamilias, thou materfamilias, with daughters of thine own to be married? In life would he have been held to have disgraced himself,—except in the very moment in which he seemed to be in danger? Nevertheless, the faults of a Ralph Newton, and not the vices of a Varney or a Barry Lyndon, are the evils against which men should in these days be taught to guard themselves;—which women also should be made to hate. Such is the writer's apology for his very indifferent hero, Ralph the Heir.

NOVEL-READING
(1879)

The Works of Charles Dickens.

The Works of W. Makepeace Thackeray.

In putting at the head of this paper the names of two distinguished English novelists whose tales have been collected and republished since their death,[1] it is my object to review rather the general nature of the work done by English novelists of latter times than the contributions specially made by these two to our literature. Criticism has dealt with them, and public opinion has awarded to each his own position in the world of letters. But it may be worth while to inquire what is and what will be the result of a branch of reading which is at present more extended than any other, and to which they have contributed so much. We used to regard novels as ephemeral; and a quarter of a century since were accustomed to consider those by Scott, with a few others which, from *Robinson Crusoe* downwards, had made permanent names to themselves, as exceptions to this rule. Now we have collected editions of one modern master of fiction after another brought out with all circumstances of editorial luxury and editorial cheapness. The works of Dickens are to be bought in penny numbers; and those of Thackeray are being at the present moment reissued to the public with every glory of paper, print, and illustration, at a proposed cost to the purchaser of 33*l.* 12*s.*, for the set. I do not in the least doubt that the enterprising publishers will find themselves justified in their different adventures. The popular British novel is now so popular that it can be neither too cheap nor too dear for the market.

> Æquo pulsat pede pauperum tabernas
> Regumque turres.[2]

I believe it to be a fact that of no English author has the sale of the works been at the same time so large and so profitable for the first half-dozen years after his death as of Dickens; and I cannot at the moment remember any edition so costly as that which is now being brought out of Thackeray's novels, in proportion to the amount and nature of the work. I have seen it

---

[1] *The Collected Works of Charles Dickens.* In 20 volumes. Chapman & Hall. *The Collected Works of W. M. Thackeray.* In 22 volumes. Smith, Elder, & Co. [Trollope]

[2] It strikes equally the huts of the poor and the palaces of the rich.—Horace, *Odes* I. 4. 13–14.

asserted that the three English authors whose works are most to be found in the far-off homes of our colonists—in Australia, Canada, and South Africa— are Shakespeare, Macaulay, and Dickens. Shakespeare no doubt is there, as he is in the houses of so many of us not so far off, for the sake of national glory. Macaulay and Dickens, perhaps, share between them the thumbs of the family, but the marks of affection bestowed on the novelist will be found to be the darker.

With such evidence before us of the wide-spread and enduring popularity of popular novels, it would become us to make up our minds whether this coveted amusement is of its nature prone to do good or evil. There cannot be a doubt that the characters of those around us are formed very much on the lessons which are thus taught. Our girls become wives, and our wives mothers, and then old women, very much under these inspirations. Our boys grow into manhood, either nobly or ignobly partly as they may teach, and in accordance with such teaching will continue to bear their burdens gallantly or to repudiate them with cowardly sloth.

Sermons have been invented, coming down to us from the Greek Chorus, and probably from times much antecedent to the Greek dramatists, in order that the violence of the active may be controlled by the prudence of the inactive, and the thoughtlessness of the young by the thoughtfulness of the old. And sermons have been very efficacious for these purposes. There are now among us preachers influencing the conduct of many, and probably delighting the intellectual faculties of more. But it is, we think, felt that the sermon which is listened to with more or less of patience once or twice a week does not catch a hold of the imagination as it used to do, so as to enable us to say that those who are growing up among us are formed as to their character by the discourses which they hear from the pulpit. Teaching to be efficacious must be popular. The birch has, no doubt, saved many from the uttermost depth of darkness, but it never yet made a scholar. I am inclined to think that the lessons inculcated by the novelists at present go deeper than most others. To ascertain whether they be good or bad, we should look not only to the teaching but to that which has been taught,—not to the masters only but the scholars. To effect this thoroughly, an essay on the morals of the people would be necessary,—of such at least of the people as read sufficiently for the enjoyment of a novel. We should have to compare the conduct of the present day with that of past years, and our own conduct with that of other people. So much would be beyond our mark. But something may be done to show whether fathers and mothers may consider themselves safe in allowing to their children the latitude in reading which is now the order of the day, and also in giving similar freedom to themselves. It is not the daughter only who now reads her *Lord Aimworth* without thrusting him under the sofa when a strange visitor comes, or feels it necessary to have Fordyce's sermons open on the table. There it is, unconcealed, whether for good or bad, patent to all and established, the recognised amusement of our lighter hours, too often our mainstay in literature, the former of our morals, the code by which we rule ourselves, the mirror in which we dress ourselves, the *index expurgatorius* of things held to be allowable in the ordinary affairs of life. No man actually turns to a novel for a definition of honour, nor a woman for that of modesty; but it is from the pages of many novels that men and women obtain guidance both as to honour and modesty. As the writer of the leading article picks up his ideas of politics among those which he finds floating about the world, thinking out but little for himself and creating but little, so does the novelist find his ideas of conduct, and then create a picture of that excellence which he has appreciated. Nor does he do the reverse with reference to the ignoble or the immodest. He collects the floating ideas of the world around him as to what is right and wrong in conduct, and reproduces them with his own colouring. At different periods in our history, the preacher, the dramatist, the essayist, and the poet have been efficacious over others;—at one time the preacher, and at one the poet. Now it is the novelist. There are reasons why we would wish it were otherwise. The reading of novels can hardly strengthen the intelligence. But we have to deal with the fact as it exists, deprecating the evil as far as it is an evil, but acknowledging the good if there be good.

Fond as most of us are of novels, it has to be confessed that they have had a bad name among us. Sheridan, in the scene from which we have quoted, has put into Lydia's mouth a true picture of the time as it then existed. Young ladies, if they read novels, read them on the sly, and married ladies were not more free in acknowledging their acquaintance with those in English than they are now as to those in French. That freedom was growing then as is the other now. There were those who could read unblushingly; those who read and blushed; and those who sternly would not read at all. At a much later date than Sheridan's it was the ordinary practice in well-conducted families to limit the reading of novels. In many houses such books were not permitted at all. In others Scott was allowed, with those probably of Miss Edgeworth and Miss Austen. And the amusement, though permitted, was not encouraged. It was considered to be idleness and a wasting of time. At the period of which we are speaking,—say forty years ago,—it was hardly recognised by any that much beyond amusement not only might be, but must be, the consequence of such reading. Novels were ephemeral, trivial,—of no great importance except in so far as they might perhaps be injurious. As a girl who is, as a rule, duly industrious, may be allowed now and then to sit idle over the fire, thinking as nearly as possible of nothing,—thus refreshing herself for her daily toils; as a man may, without reproach, devote a small portion of his day to loafing and lounging about his club; so in those perhaps healthier days did a small modicum of novel-reading begin to be permitted. Where now is the reading individual for whom a small modicum suffices?

And very evil things have been said of the writers of novels by their brethren in literature; as though these workers, whose work has gradually become so efficacious for good or evil, had done nothing but harm in the world. It would be useless, or even ungenerous now, to quote essayists, divines, and historians who have written of novelists as though the mere providing of a little fleeting amusement,—generally of pernicious amusement,—had been the only object in their view. But our readers will be aware that if such criticism does not now exist, it has not ceased so long but that they remember its tone. The ordinary old homily against the novel, inveighing against the frivolities, the falsehood, and perhaps the licentiousness, of a fictitious narrative, is still familiar to our ears. Though we may reckon among our dearest literary possessions the pathos of this story, the humour of another, the unerring truth to nature of a third; though we may be aware of the absolute national importance to us of a *Robinson Crusoe* or *Tom Jones*, of an *Ivanhoe* or an *Esmond*; though each of us in his own heart may know all that a good novel has done for him,—still there remains something of the bad character which for years has been attached to the art.

> Quo semel est imbuta recens, servabit odorem
> Testa diu.[3]

Even though it be true that the novels of the present day have in great measure taken the place of sermons, and that they feed the imagination too often in lieu of poetry, still they are admitted to their high functions not without forebodings, not without remonstrances, not without a certain sense that we are giving up our young people into the hands of an Apollyon. Is this teacher an Apollyon; or is he better because stronger, and as moral—as an archbishop?

It is certainly the case that novels deal mainly with one subject,—that, namely, of love; and equally certain that love is a matter in handling which for the instruction or delectation of the young there is much danger. This is what the novelist does daily, and, whatever may be the danger, he is accepted. We quite agree with the young lady in the *Hunchback* who declared that Ovid was a fool. "To call that thing an art which art is none."

> No art but taketh time and pains to learn.
> Love comes with neither.[4]

So much the novelist knows as well as Sheridan Knowles's young lady, and therefore sets about his work with descriptive rather than didactic lessons. His pupils would not accept them were he to tell them that he came into the house as a tutor in such an art. But still as a tutor he is accepted. What can be of more importance to us than to know whether we who all of us encourage such tutors in our houses, are subjecting those we love to good teaching or to

---

[3] A cask will long preserve the flavor with which when new it was once impregnated.—Horace, *Epistles* I. 2. 69–70.

[4] . . . Love an art! No art
But taketh time and pains to learn. Love comes
With neither!—Knowles, *The Hunchback* IV. i. 46–48.

ill? We do not dare to say openly to those dear ones, but we confess it to ourselves, that the one thing of most importance to them is whether they shall love rightly or wrongly. The sweet, innocent, bashful girl, who never to her dearest bosom friend dares to talk upon the matter, knows that it must be so for herself. Will it be her happy future to be joined to some man who, together with the energy necessary for maintaining her and her children, shall also have a loving heart and a sweet temper?—or shall she, through dire mistake, in this great affair of her life fall into some unutterable abyss of negligence, poverty, and heartless indifference? All this is vague, though still certain, to the girl herself. But to the mother it is in no way vague. Night and morning it must be her dearest prayer that the man who shall take her girl from her shall be worthy of her girl. And the importance to the man, though not so strongly felt, is equal. As it is not his lot to rise and fall in the world as his partner may succeed or the reverse, the image of a wife does not force itself upon his thoughts so vividly as does that of a husband on the female mind; but, as she is dependent on him for all honour, so he is on her for all happiness. It suits us to speak of love as a soft, sweet, flowery pastime, with many roses and some thorns, in which youth is apt to disport itself; but there is no father, no mother, no daughter, and should be no son, blind to the fact that, of all matters concerning life, it is the most important. That Ovid's *Art of Love* was nothing, much worse than nothing, we admit. But nevertheless the art is taught. Before the moment comes in which heart is given to heart, the imagination has been instructed as to what should accompany the gift, and what should be expected in accompaniment; in what way the gift should be made, and after what assurance; for how long a period silence should be held, and then how far speech should be unguarded.

By those who do not habitually read at all, the work is done somewhat roughly,—we will not say thoughtlessly, but with little of those precautions which education demands. With those who do read, all that literature gives them helps them somewhat in the operation of which we are speaking. History tells us much of love's efficacy, and much of the evil that comes from the want of it. Biography is of course full of it. Philosophy deals with it. Poetry is hardly poetry without it. The drama is built on it almost as exclusively as are the novels. But it is from novels that the crowd of expectant and ready pupils obtain that constant flow of easy teaching which fills the mind of all readers with continual thoughts of love. The importance of the teaching is mainly to the young, but the existence of the teaching is almost equally present to the old. Why is it that the judge when he escapes from the bench, the bishop even,—as we are told,—when he comes from his confirmation, the politician as he sits in the library of the House, the Cabinet Minister when he has a half-hour to himself, the old dowager in almost all the hours which she has to herself,—seek for distraction and reaction in the pages of a novel? It is because there is an ever-recurring delight in going back to the very rudiments of those lessons in love.

"My dear," says the loving but only half-careful mother to her daughter, "I wish you wouldn't devote so many of your hours to novel-reading. How far have you got with your Gibbon?" Whereupon the young lady reads a page or two of Gibbon, and then goes back to her novels. The mother knows that her girl is good, and does not make herself unhappy. Is she justified in her security by the goodness of the teaching? There is good and bad, no doubt. In speaking of good and bad we are not alluding to virtue and vice themselves, but to the representations made of them. If virtue be made ridiculous, no description of it will be serviceable. If vice be made alluring, the picture will certainly be injurious. Sydney Smith, as far as it went, did an injury to morality at large when he declared in one of his letters that the Prime Minister of the day was "faithful to Mrs. Percival." Desiring to make the Prime Minister ridiculous, he endeavoured to throw a stone at that domesticity which the Prime Minister was supposed to cherish, and doing so he taught evil. Gay did injury to morality when he persuaded all the town to sympathise with a thief. The good teaching of a novel may be evinced as much in displaying the base as the noble, if the base be made to look base as the noble is made to look noble.

If we look back to the earlier efforts of English novel writing, the lessons taught were too often bad. Though there was a wide world of British fiction before the time of Charles the Second, it generally took the shape of the drama, and of that, whether good or bad, in its results we have at present nothing to say. The prose romances were few in number, and entertained so limited an audience that they were not efficacious for good or evil. The people would flock to see plays, where plays could be produced for them, as in London,—but did not as yet care to feed their imaginations by reading. Then came the novelists of Charles the Second, who, though they are less profligate and also more stupid than is generally supposed of them, could certainly do no good to the mind of any reader. Of our novelists the first really known is Defoe, who, though he was born almost within the Commonwealth, did not produce his *Robinson Crusoe* till the time of George the First. *Robinson Crusoe* did not deal with love. Defoe's other stories, which are happily forgotten, are bad in their very essence. *Roxana* is an accurate sample of what a bad book may be. It relates the adventures of a woman thoroughly depraved, and yet for the most part successful,—is intended to attract by its licentiousness, and puts off till the end the stale scrap of morality which is brought in as a salve to the conscience of the writer. Putting aside *Robinson Crusoe*, which has been truly described as an accident, Defoe's teaching as a novelist has been altogether bad. Then, mentioning only the names which are well known to us, we come first to Richardson, who has been called the inventor of the modern English novel. It certainly was his object to write of love, so that young women might be profited by what he wrote,—and we may say that he succeeded. It cannot be doubted that he had a strong conscience in his work,—that he did not write only to please, or only for money, or only for reputation, nor for those three causes combined; but that he might do good to those for whom he was writing. In this respect he certainly was the inventor of the modern English novel. That his works will ever become popular again we doubt. Macaulay expressed an exaggerated praise for *Clarissa*, which brought forth new editions,—even an abridgment of the novel; but the tone is too melancholy, and is played too exclusively on a single string for the taste of a less patient age. Nor would his teaching, though it was good a hundred and thirty years ago, be good now. Against the horrors to which his heroine was subjected, it is not necessary to warn our girls in this safer age,—or to speak of them.

Of Fielding and Smollett,—whom, however, it is unfair to bracket,—it can hardly be said that their conscience was as clear in the matter of what they wrote as was that of Richardson, though probably each of them felt that the aim he had in view was to satirise vice. Defoe might have said the same. But when the satirist lingers lovingly over the vice which he castigates so as to allure by his descriptions, it may be doubted whether he does much service to morality. Juvenal was perhaps the sternest moral censor whom the world of letters has produced; but he was, and even in his own age must have been felt to be, a most lascivious writer. Fielding, who in the construction of a story and the development of a character is supreme among novelists, is, we think, open to the same reproach. That Smollett was so the readers of *Roderick Random* and his other stories are well aware; and in him the fault was more conspicuous than in Fielding,—without the great redeeming gifts. Novelists followed, one after another, whose tales were good enough to remain in our memories, though we cannot say that their work was effective for any special purpose. Among those Goldsmith was the first and the greatest. His *Vicar of Wakefield* has taken a hold on our national literature equalled perhaps by no other novel.

It is not my purpose to give a history of English fiction. Its next conspicuous phase was that of the awe-striking mysterious romances, such as the *Mysteries of Udolpho* and the *Italian*, by which we may say no such lessons were taught as those of which we are speaking, either for good or bad. The perusal of them left little behind beyond a slightly morbid tone of the imagination. They excited no passions, and created no beliefs. There was Godwin, a man whose mind was prone to revel in the injuries which an unfortunate might be subjected to by the injustice of the world; and Mrs. Inchbald, who longed to be passionate, though in the *Simple Story*, by which we know her, she hardly rose to the height of passion; and Miss Burney, who was a Richardson in petticoats, but with a woman's closer appreciation of the little details of life. After them, or together with them, and together also with the names which will follow them, flourished the Rosa Matilda school of fiction, than which the desire to have something to read has produced nothing in literature more vapid or more mean. Up to this time there was probably no recognised attempt on the part of the novelist himself, except by

Richardson, and perhaps by Miss Burney, to teach any lesson, to give out any code of morals, to preach as it were a sermon from his pulpit, as the parson preaches his sermon. The business was chance business,—the tendency being good if the tendency of the mind of the worker was good;—or bad if that was bad. Then came Miss Edgeworth and Miss Austen, who, the one in Ireland and the other in England, determined to write tales which should have a wholesome bearing. In this they were thoroughly successful, and were the first to convince the British matron that her darling girl might be amused by light literature without injury to her purity. For there had been about Miss Burney, in spite of her morality, a smell of the torchlights of iniquity which had been offensive to the nose of the ordinary British matron. Miss Edgeworth, indeed, did fall away a little towards the end of her long career; but, as we all know, a well-established character may bear a considerable strain. Miss Austen from first to last was the same,—with no touch of rampant fashion. Her young ladies indeed are very prone to look for husbands; but when this is done with proper reticence, with no flavour of gaslight, the British matron can excuse a little evil in that direction for the sake of the good.

Then Scott arose, who still towers among us as the first of novelists. He himself tells us that he was prompted to write Scotch novels by the success of Miss Edgeworth's Irish tales. "Without being so presumptuous as to hope to emulate the rich humour, pathetic tenderness, and admirable tact of my accomplished friend, I felt that something might be done for my own country of the same kind with that which Miss Edgeworth achieved for Ireland." It no doubt was the case that the success of Miss Edgeworth stimulated him to prose fiction; but we cannot but feel that there must have been present to him from first to last, through his long career of unprecedented success, a conviction of his duty as a teacher. In all those pages, in the telling of those incidents between men and women, in all those narratives of love, there is not a passage which a mother would feel herself constrained to keep from the eye of her daughter. It has been said that Scott is passionless in his descriptions of love. He moves us to our heart's core by his Meg Merrilies, his Edie Ochiltree, his Balfour of Burley, and a hundred other such characters; but no one sheds a tear over the sorrows of Flora Mac Ivor, Edith Bellenden, or Julia Mannering. When we weep for Lucy Ashton, it is because she is to be married to one she does not love, not because of her love. But in admitting this we ought to acknowledge at the same time the strain which Scott put upon himself so that he should not be carried away into the seducing language of ill-regulated passion. When he came to tell the story of unfortunate love, to describe the lot in life of a girl who had fallen,—when he created Effie Deans,—then he could be passionate. But together with this he possessed the greater power of so telling even that story, that the lesson from beginning to end should be salutary.

From Scott downwards I will mention no names till we come to those

which I have prefixed to this paper. There have been English novelists by
the score,—by the hundred we may say. Some of them have been very weak;
some utterly inefficacious for good or evil; some undoubtedly mischievous
in their tendencies. But there has accompanied their growth a general
conviction that it behoves the English novelist to be pure. As on the English
stage and with the English periodical press, both scurrility and lasciviousness
may now and again snatch a temporary success; so it is with English fiction.
We all know the writers who endeavour to be so nearly lascivious that they
may find an audience among those whose taste lies in that direction. But
such is not the taste of the nation at large; and these attempts at impropriety,
these longings to be as bold and wicked as some of our neighbours, do not
pay in the long run. While a true story of genuine love, well told, will win the
heart of the nation and raise the author to a high position among the
worthies of his country, the prurient dabbler in lust hardly becomes known
beyond a special class. The number of those who read novels have become
millions in England during the last twenty-five years. In our factories, with
our artisans, behind our counters, in third-class railway carriages, in our
kitchens and stables, novels are now read unceasingly. Much reaches those
readers that is poor. Much that is false in sentiment and faulty in art no
doubt finds its way with them. But indecency does not thrive with them,
and when there comes to them a choice of good or bad, they choose the better.
There has grown up a custom of late, especially among tea dealers, to give
away a certain number of books among their poorer customers. When so
much tea has been consumed, then shall be a book given. It came to my ears
the other day that eighteen thousand volumes of Dickens's works had just
been ordered for this purpose. The bookseller suggested that a little novelty
might be expedient. Would the benevolent tea-dealer like to vary his presents?
But no! The tradesman, knowing his business, and being anxious above all
things to attract, declared that Dickens was what he wanted. He had found
that the tea-consuming world preferred their Dickens.

In wide-spread popularity the novels of Charles Dickens have, I believe,
exceeded those of any other British novelist, though they have not yet
reached that open market of unrestricted competition which a book reaches
only when its copyright has run out. Up to this present time over 800,000
copies of *Pickwick* have been sold in this country, and the book is still copyright property. In saying this I make no invidious comparison between Scott
and Dickens. I may, indeed, be in error in supposing the circulation of
Waverley to have been less. As it is open to any bookseller to issue Scott's
novels, it would be difficult to arrive at a correct number. Our object is
simply to show what has been the circulation of a popular novel in Great
Britain. The circulation outside the home market has been probably as
great,—perhaps greater, as American readers are more numerous than the
English. Among the millions of those into whose hands these hundreds of
thousands of volumes have fallen, there can hardly be one who has not

received some lesson from what he has read. It may be that many dissent from the mode of telling which Dickens adopted in his stories, that they are indifferent to the stories themselves, that they question the taste, and fail to interest themselves in the melodramatic incidents and unnatural characters which it was his delight to portray. All that has no bearing on the issue which we now attempt to raise. The teaching of which we are speaking is not instruction as to taste, or art,—is not instruction as to style or literary excellence. By such lessons as Dickens taught will the young man learn to be honest or dishonest, noble or ignoble? Will the girl learn to be modest or brazen-faced? Will greed be engendered and self-indulgence? Will a taste for vicious pleasure be created? Will the young of either sex be taught to think it is a grand thing to throw off the conventional rules which the wisdom of the world has established for its guidance; or will they unconsciously learn from the author's pages to recognise the fact that happiness is to be obtained by obeying, and not by running counter to the principles of morality? Let memory run back for a few moments over those stories, and it will fail to find an immodest girl who has been made alluring to female readers, or an ill-conditioned youth whose career a lad would be tempted to envy. No ridicule is thrown on marriage constancy; no gilding is given to fictitious pleasure; no charm is added to idleness; no alluring colour is lent to de-bauchery. Pickwick may be softer, and Ralph Nickleby harder than the old men whom we know in the world; but the lessons which they teach are all in favour of a soft heart, all strongly opposed to hardness of heart. "What an impossible dear old duffer that Pickwick is!" a lady said to me the other day, criticising the character as I thought very correctly. Quite impossible, and certainly a duffer,—if I understand the latter phrase,—but so dear! That an old man, as he grows old, should go on loving everybody around him, loving the more the older he grows, running over with philanthropy, and happy through it all in spite of the susceptibility of Mrs. Bardell and the fallings off of Mr. Winkle! That has been the lesson taught by *Pickwick*; and though probably but few readers have so believed in Pickwick as to think that nature would produce such a man, still they have been unconsciously taught the sweetness of human love.

Such characters as those of Lord Frederick Veresopht and Sir Mulberry Hawk have often been drawn by dramatists and novelists,—too frequently with a dash of attractive fashion,—in a manner qualified to conceal in the mind of the unappreciating reader the vices of the men under the brightness of their trappings. Has any young man been made to wish that he should be such as Lord Frederick Veresopht, or should become such as Sir Mulberry Hawk? Kate Nickleby is not to us an entirely natural young woman. She lacks human life. But the girls who have read her adventures have all learnt to acknowledge the beauty and the value of modesty. It is not your daughter, my reader, who has needed such a lesson;—but think of the eight hundred thousands!

Of all Dickens's novels *Oliver Twist* is perhaps artistically the best, as in it the author adheres most tenaciously to one story, and interests us most thoroughly by his plot. But the characters are less efficacious for the teaching of lessons than in his other tales. Neither can Bill Sikes nor Nancy, nor can even the great Bumble, be credited with having been of much service by deterring readers from vice;—but then neither have they allured readers, as has been done by so many writers of fiction who have ventured to deal with the world's reprobates.

In *Martin Chuzzlewit*, in *David Copperfield*, in *Bleak House*, and *Little Dorrit*, the tendency of which I speak will be found to be the same. It is indeed carried through every work that he wrote. To whom has not kindness of heart been made beautiful by Tom Pinch, and hypocrisy odious by Pecksniff? The peculiar abominations of Pecksniff's daughters are made to be abominable to the least attentive reader. Unconsciously the girl-reader declares to herself that she will not at any rate be like that. This is the mode of teaching which is in truth serviceable. Let the mind be induced to sympathise warmly with that which is good and true, or be moved to hatred against that which is vile, and then an impression will have been made, certainly serviceable, and probably ineradicable. It may be admitted in regard to Dickens's young ladies that they lack nature. Dora, Nelly, Little Dorrit, Florence Dombey, and a host of others crowd upon our memory, not as shadows of people we have really known,—as do Jeanie Deans, for instance, and Jane Eyre;—but they have affected us as personifications of tenderness and gentle feminine gifts. We have felt each character to contain, not a woman, but something which will help to make many women. The Boythorns, Tulkinghorns, Cheerybles and Pickwicks, may be as unlike nature as they will. They are unlike nature. But they nevertheless charm the reader, and leave behind on the palate of his mind a sweet savour of humanity. Our author's heroes, down to Smike, are often outrageous in their virtues. But their virtues are virtues. Truth, gratitude, courage, and manly self-respect are qualities which a young man will be made not only to admire, but to like, by his many hours spent over these novels. And so it will be with young women as to modesty, reticence, and unselfish devotion.

The popularity of Thackeray has been very much less extended than that of Dickens, and the lessons which he has taught have not, therefore, been scattered afield so widely. Dickens, to use a now common phrase, has tapped a stratum lower in education and wealth, and therefore much wider, than that reached by his rival. The genius of Thackeray was of a nature altogether different. Dickens delighted much in depicting with very broad lines very well-known vices under impossible characters, but was, perhaps, still more thoroughly at home in representing equally well-known virtues after the same fashion. His Pinches and Cheerybles were nearer to him than his Ralph Nicklebys and his Pecksniffs. It seems specially to have been the work of Thackeray to cover with scorn the vices which in his hands were displayed in personages who were only too realistic. With him there is no touch of melodrama. From first to last you are as much at home with Barry Lyndon, the most complete rascal, perhaps, that ever was drawn, as with your wife, or your private secretary, if you have one, or the servant who waits upon you daily. And when he turns from the strength of his rascals to the weaker idiosyncrasies of those whom you are to love for their virtues, he is equally efficacious. Barry Lyndon was a man of infinite intellectual capacity, which is more than we can say for Colonel Newcome. But was there ever a gentleman more sweet, more lovable, more thoroughly a gentleman at all points, than the Colonel? How many a young lad has been taught to know how a gentleman should think, and how a gentleman should act and speak, by the thoughts and words and doings of the Colonel! I will not say that Barry Lyndon's career has deterred many from rascaldom, as such a career can only be exceptional; but it has certainly enticed no lad to follow it.

Vanity Fair, though not in my opinion the best, is the best known of Thackeray's works. Readers, though they are delighted, are not satisfied with it, because Amelia Sedley is silly, because Osborne is selfish, because Dobbin is ridiculous, and because Becky Sharp alone is clever and successful, —while at the same time she is as abominable as the genius of a satirist can make her. But let him or her who has read the book think of the lessons which have been left behind by it. Amelia is a true loving woman, who can love her husband even though he be selfish—loving, as a woman should love, with enduring devotion. Whatever is charming in her attracts; what is silly repels. The character of Osborne is necessary to that of Dobbin, who is one of the finest heroes ever drawn. Unselfish, brave, modest, forgiving, affectionate, manly all over,—his is just the character to teach a lesson. Tell a young man that he ought to be modest, that he ought to think more of the heart of the girl he loves than of his own, that even in the pursuit of fame he should sacrifice himself to others, and he will ridicule your advice and you too. But if you can touch his sentiment, get at him in his closet,—or perhaps rather his smoking-room,—without his knowing it, bring a tear to his eye and perhaps a throb to his throat, and then he will have learned something of that which your less impressive lecture was incapable of teaching. As for Becky Sharp, it is not only that she was false, unfeminine, and heartless. Such attributes no doubt are in themselves unattractive. But there is not a turn in the telling of the story which, in spite of her success, does not show the reader how little is gained, how much is lost, by the exercise of that depraved ingenuity.

Pendennis is an unsteady, ambitious, clever but idle young man, with excellent aspirations and purposes, but hardly trustworthy. He is by no means such a one as an anxious father would wish to put before his son as an example. But he is lifelike. Clever young men, ambitious but idle and vacillating, are met every day, whereas the gift of persistency in a young man is uncommon. The Pendennis phase of life is one into which clever young men are apt to run. The character if alluring would be dangerous. If reckless idle conceit had carried everything before it in the story,—if Pendennis had been made to be noble in the midst of his foibles,—the lesson taught would have been bad. But the picture which becomes gradually visible to the eyes of the reader is the reverse of this. Though Pendennis is, as it were, saved at last by the enduring affection of two women, the idleness and the conceit and the vanity, the littleness of the *soi-disant* great young man, are treated with so much disdain as to make the idlest and vainest of male readers altogether for the time out of love with idleness and vanity. And as for Laura, the younger of the two women by whom he is saved, she who becomes his wife, —surely no female character ever drawn was better adapted than hers to teach that mixture of self-negation, modesty and affection which is needed for the composition of the ideal woman whom we love to contemplate.

Of Colonel Newcome we have already spoken. Of all the characters drawn by Thackeray it is the most attractive, and it is so because he is a man *sans peur* and *sans reproche*. He is not a clever old man,—not half so amusing as that wordly old gentleman, Major Pendennis, with whom the reader of the former novel will have become acquainted,—but he is one who cannot lie, who cannot do a mean thing, who can wear his gown as a bedesman in the Grey Friars Hospital,—for to that he comes,—with all the honour that can hang about a judge's ermine.

Esmond is undoubtedly Thackeray's greatest work,—not only because in it his story is told with the directest purpose, with less of vague wandering than in the others,—but by reason also of the force of the characters portrayed. The one to which we will specially call attention is that of Beatrix, the younger heroine of the story. Her mother, Lady Castlewood, is an elder heroine. The term as applied to the personages of a modern novel,—as may be said also of hero,—is not very appropriate; but it is the word which will best convey the intended meaning to the reader. Nothing sadder than the story of Beatrix can be imagined,—nothing sadder though it falls so infinitely short of tragedy. But we speak specially of it here, because we believe its effect on the minds of girls who read it to be thoroughly salutary. Beatrix is a girl endowed with great gifts. She has birth, rank, fortune, intellect and beauty. She is blessed with that special combination of feminine loveliness and feminine wit which men delight to encounter. The novelist has not merely said that it is so, but has succeeded in bringing the girl before us with such vivid power of portraiture that we know her, what she is, down to her shoe-ties,—know her, first to the loving of her, and then to the hating of her. She becomes as she goes on the object of Esmond's love,—and could she permit her heart to act in this matter, she too would love him. She knows well that he is a man worthy to be loved. She is encouraged to love him by outward circumstances. Indeed, she does love him. But she has decided within her own bosom that the world is her oyster, which has to be opened by her, being a woman, not by her sword but by her beauty. Higher rank than her own, greater fortune, a bigger place in the world's eyes, grander jewels, have to be won. Harry Esmond, oh, how good he is; how fit to be the lord of any girl,—if only he were a duke, or such like! This is her feeling, and this is her resolve. Then she sets her cap at a duke, a real duke, and almost gets him,—would have got him only her duke is killed in a duel before she has been made a duchess. After that terrible blow she sinks lower still in her low ambition. A scion of banished royalty comes dangling after her, and she, thinking that the scion may be restored to his royal grandeur, would fain become the mistress of a king.

It is a foul career, the reader will say; and there may be some who would ask whether such is the picture which should be presented to the eyes of a young girl by those who are anxious, not only for the amusement of her leisure hours, but also for her purity and worth. It might be asked, also, whether the Commandments should be read in her ears, lest she should be taught to steal and to murder. Beautiful as Beatrix is, attractive, clever, charming,—prone as the reader is to sympathise with Esmond in his love for this winning creature,—yet by degrees the vileness becomes so vile, the ulcered sores are so revolting, the whited sepulchre is seen to be so foul within, that the girl who reads the book is driven to say, "Not like that; not like that! Whatever fate may have in store for me, let it not be like that." And this conviction will not come from any outward suffering,—not from poverty, ill-usage, from loss of beauty or youth. No condign punishment of that easy kind is inflicted. But the vice is made to be so ugly, so heartbreaking to the wretched victim who has encouraged it, that it strikes the beholder with horror. Vice is heartbreaking to its victim. The difficulty is to teach the lesson,—to bring the truth home. Sermons too often fail to do it. The little story in which Tom the naughty boy breaks his leg, while Jack the good boy gets apples, does not do it. The broken leg and the apples do not find credence. Beatrix in her misery is believed to be miserable.

I will not appeal to further instances of good teaching among later British novelists, having endeavoured to exemplify my meaning by the novels of two masters who have appeared among us in latter days, whose works are known to all of us, and who have both departed from among us; but I think that I am entitled to vindicate the character of the British novelist generally from aspersions often thrown upon it by quoting the works of those to whom I have referred. And I am anxious also to vindicate that public taste in literature which has created and nourished the novelist's work. There still exists the judgment,—prejudice, I think I may call it,—which condemns it. It is not operative against the reading of novels, as is proved by their general acceptance. But it exists strongly in reference to the appreciation in which they are professed to be held, and it robs them of much of that high character which they may claim to have earned by their grace, their honesty, and good teaching.

By the consent of all mankind who read, poetry takes the highest place in literature. That nobility of expression, and all but divine grace of words, which she is bound to attain before she can make her footing good, is not compatible with prose. Indeed, it is that which turns prose into poetry. When that has been in truth achieved, the reader knows that the writer has soared above the earth, and can teach his lessons somewhat as a god might teach. He who sits down to write his tale in prose makes no such attempt, nor does he dream that the poet's honour is within his reach. But his teaching is of the same nature, and his lessons tend to the same end. By either, false sentiment may be fostered, false notions of humanity may be engendered, false honour, false love, false worship may be created; by either, vice instead of virtue may be taught. But by each equally may true honour, true love, true worship, and true humanity be inculcated; and that will be the greatest teacher who will spread such truth the widest. At present, much as novels, as novels, are sought and read, there still exists an idea,—a feeling which is very prevalent,—that novels at their best are but innocent. Young men and women,—and old men and women too,—read more of them than they read of poetry because such reading is easier; but they read them as men eat pastry after dinner,—not without some inward conviction that the taste is vain if not vicious. We think that it is not vicious or vain,—unless indeed the employment be allowed to interfere with the graver duties of life.

A greater proportion of the teaching of the day than any of us have as yet acknowledged comes, no doubt, from the reading of these books. Whether the teaching be good or bad, that is the case. It is from them that girls learn what is expected from them, and what they are to expect when lovers come; and also from them that young men unconsciously learn what are, or should be, or may be, the charms of love. Other lessons also are taught. In these days, when the desire to be honest is pressed so hard on the heel by the ambition to be great, in which riches are the easiest road to greatness; when the temptations to which men are subjected dull their eyes to the perfected iniquities of others; when it is so hard for a man to decide vigorously that the pitch which so many are handling will defile him if it be touched,—men's conduct will be actuated much by that which is from day to day depicted to them as leading to glorious or inglorious results. The woman who is described as having obtained all that the world holds to be precious by lavishing her charms and caresses unworthily and heartlessly, will induce other women to do the same with theirs; as will she who is made interesting by exhibition of bold passion teach others to be spuriously passionate. The young man who in a novel becomes a hero,—perhaps a member of Parliament or almost a Prime Minister,—by trickery, falsehood, and flash cleverness, will have as many followers in his line as Jack Sheppard or Macheath will have in theirs; and will do, if not as wide, a deeper mischief.

To the novelist, thinking of all this, it must surely become a matter of deep conscience how he shall handle those characters by whose words and doings he hopes to interest his readers. It may frequently be the case that he will be tempted to sacrifice something for effect; to say a word or two here, or to draw a picture there, for which he feels that he has the power, and which, when spoken or drawn, would be alluring. The regions of absolute vice are foul and odious. The savour of them, till custom has hardened the palate and the nose, is disgusting. In these he will hardly tread. But there are outskirts on these regions in which sweet-smelling flowers seem to grow and grass to be green. It is in these border-lands that the danger lies. The novelist may not be dull. If he commit that fault, he can do neither harm nor good. He must please; and the flowers and the soft grass in those neutral territories sometimes seem to give too easy an opportunity of pleasing!

The writer of stories must please, or he will be nothing. And he must teach, whether he wish to teach or not. How shall he teach lessons of virtue, and at the same time make himself a delight to his readers? Sermons in themselves are not thought to be agreeable; nor are disquisitions on moral philosophy supposed to be pleasant reading for our idle hours. But the novelist, if he have a conscience, must preach his sermons with the same purpose as the clergyman, and must have his own system of ethics. If he can do this efficiently, if he can make virtue alluring and vice ugly, while he charms his reader instead of wearying him, then we think that he should not be spoken of generally as being among those workers of iniquity who do evil in their generation. So many have done so, that the English novelist as a class may, we think, boast that such has been the result of their work. Can any one, by search through the works of the fine writers whose names we have specially mentioned,—Miss Edgeworth, Miss Austen, Scott, Dickens, and Thackeray,—find a scene, a passage, or a word that could teach a girl to be immodest or a man to be dishonest? When men in their pages have been described as dishonest, or women as immodest, has not the reader in every instance been deterred by the example and its results? It is not for the novelist to say simply and baldly: "Because you lied here, or were heartless there; because you, Lydia Bennet, forgot the lessons of your honest home, or you, Earl Leicester, were false through your ambition, or you, Beatrix, loved too well the glitter of the world, therefore you shall be scourged with scourges either here or hereafter"; but it is for him to show, as he carries on his tale, that his Lydia, or his Leicester, or his Beatrix, will be dishonoured in the estimation of all by his or her vices. Let a woman be drawn clever, beautiful, attractive, so as to make men love her and women almost envy her; and let her be made also heartless, unfeminine, ambitious of evil grandeur, as was Beatrix,—what danger is there not in such a character! To the novelist who shall handle it, what peril of doing harm! But if at last it has been so handled that every girl who reads of Beatrix shall say: "Oh, not like that! let me not be like that!" and that every youth shall say: "Let me not have such a one as that to press to my bosom,—anything rather than that!" Then will not the novelist have preached his sermon as perhaps no other preacher can preach it?

Very much of a novelist's work, as we have said above, must appertain to the intercourse between young men and young women. It is admitted that a novel can hardly be made interesting or successful without love. Some few might be named in which the attempt has been made, but even in them it fails. *Pickwick* has been given as an exception to this rule, but even in *Pickwick* there are three or four sets of lovers whose amatory flutterings give a softness to the work. In this frequent allusion to the passion which most strongly stirs the imagination of the young, there must be danger, as the novelist is necessarily aware. Then the question has to be asked, whether the danger may not be so handled that good shall be the result, and to be answered. The subject is necessary to the novelist, because it is interesting to all; but as it is interesting to all, so will the lessons taught respecting it be widely received. Every one feels it, has felt it, or expects to feel it,—or else regrets it with an eagerness which still perpetuates the interest. If the novelist, therefore, can so treat his subject as to do good by his treatment of it, the good done will be very wide. If a writer can teach politicians and statesmen that they can do their work better by truth than by falsehood, he does a great service; but it is done in the first instance to a limited number of persons. But if he can make young men and women believe that truth in love will make them happy, then, if his writings be popular, he will have a very large class of pupils. No doubt that fear which did exist as to novels came from the idea that this matter of love would be treated in an inflammatory and unwholesome manner. "Madam," says Sir Anthony in the play, "a circulating library in a town is an evergreen tree of diabolical knowledge. It blossoms through the year; and, depend upon it, Mrs. Malaprop, they who are so fond of handling the leaves, will long for the fruit at last." Sir Anthony, no doubt, was right. But he takes it for granted that longing for the fruit is an evil. The novelist thinks differently, and believes that the honest love of an honest man is a treasure which a good girl may fairly hope to win, and that, if she can be taught to wish only for that, she will have been taught to entertain only wholesome wishes.

There used to be many who thought, and probably there are some who still think, that a girl should hear nothing of love till the time comes in which she is to be married. That was the opinion of Sir Anthony Absolute and of Mrs. Malaprop. But we doubt whether the old system was more favourable to purity of manners than that which we have adopted of late. Lydia Languish, though she was constrained by fear of her aunt to hide the book, yet had *Peregrine Pickle* in her collection. While human nature talks of love so forcibly, it can hardly serve our turn to be silent on the subject. "Naturam expelles furca, tamen usque recurret."[5] There are countries in which it has been in accordance with the manners of the upper classes that the girl should be brought to marry the man almost out of the nursery,—or rather, perhaps, out of the convent,—without having enjoyed any of that freedom of thought

[5] You may drive out nature with a yoke, yet it will ever return.—Horace, *Epistles* I. 10. 24.

which the reading of novels and poetry will certainly produce; but we do not know that the marriages so made have been thought to be happier than our own.

Among English novels of the present day, and among English novelists, a great division is made. There are sensational novels, and anti-sensational; sensational novelists, and anti-sensational; sensational readers, and anti-sensational. The novelists who are considered to be anti-sensational are generally called realistic. The readers who prefer the one are supposed to take delight in the elucidation of character. They who hold by the other are charmed by the construction and gradual development of a plot. All this we think to be a mistake,—which mistake arises from the inability of the inferior artist to be at the same time realistic and sensational. A good novel should be both,—and both in the highest degree. If a novel fail in either, there is a failure in art. Let those readers who fancy that they do not like sensational scenes, think of some of those passages from our great novelists which have charmed them most,—of Rebecca in the castle with Ivanhoe; of Burley in the cave with Morton; of the mad lady tearing the veil of the expectant bride in *Jane Eyre*; of Lady Castlewood as, in her indignation, she explains to the Duke of Hamilton Harry Esmond's right to be present at the marriage of his Grace with Beatrix. Will any one say that the authors of these passages have sinned in being over-sensational? No doubt a string of horrible incidents, bound together without truth in details, and told as affecting personages without character,—wooden blocks who cannot make themselves known to readers as men and women,—does not instruct, or amuse, or even fill the mind with awe. Horrors heaped upon horrors, which are horrors only in themselves, and not as touching any recognised and known person, are not tragic, and soon cease even to horrify. Such would-be tragic elements of a story may be increased without end and without difficulty. The narrator may tell of a woman murdered, murdered in the same street with you, in the next house; may say that she was a wife murdered by her husband, a bride not yet a week a wife. He may add to it for ever. He may say that the murderer burnt her alive. There is no end to it. He may declare that a former wife was treated with equal barbarity, and that the murderer when led away to execution declared his sole regret to be that he could not live to treat a third after the same fashion. There is nothing so easy as the creation and cumulation of fearful incidents after this fashion. If such creation and cumulation be the beginning and the end of the novelist's work,—and novels have been written which seem to be without other attraction,—nothing can be more dull and nothing more useless. But not on that account are we averse to tragedy in prose fiction. As in poetry, so in prose, he who can deal adequately with tragic elements is a greater artist, and reaches a higher aim, than the writer whose efforts never carry him above the mild walks of everyday life. The *Bride of Lammermoor* is a tragedy throughout in spite of its comic elements. The life of Lady Castlewood is a tragedy. Rochester's wretched thraldom to his mad wife in *Jane Eyre* is a tragedy. But these stories charm us, not simply because they are tragic, but because we feel that men and women with flesh and blood, creatures with whom we can sympathise, are struggling amidst their woes. It all lies in that. No novel is anything, for purposes either of comedy or tragedy, unless the reader can sympathise with the characters whose names he finds upon the page. Let the author so tell his tale as to touch his reader's heart and draw his reader's tears, and he has so far done his work well. Truth let there be,—truth of description, truth of character, human truth as to men and women. If there be such truth, I do not know that a novel can be too sensational.

22

OUIDA
(MARIE LOUISE
DE LA RAMÉE)

(1839–1908)

Any mention of the name Marie De La Ramée elicits only perplexed interrogation today; the addition of her penname produces only slight recognition. But mention of *Under Two Flags* (1867) or *A Dog of Flanders* (1872) revives memories of a cinema version, at least, of the first, and childhood affection for the second. In her lifetime, though, the authoress was as well known as her works. The glamorous, flamboyant novels were complemented by her eccentric, lavish style of living. "It is impossible not to laugh at Ouida," wrote G. K. Chesterton, "and equally impossible not to read her."

The only child of Louis Ramé, a French political reactionary who had married an Englishwoman and was employed to teach his native tongue, Marie Louise grew up in Bury St. Edmonds. After a brief period in Paris, where her father mysteriously disappeared, she eventually settled in London with her mother and grandmother in 1857. Her imaginative fiction and rebellion against the moral ideals purveyed in so many contemporary novels captured the attention of the reading public, and financial reward and literary popularity were immediate and immense. She responded with lavish receptions for fashionable society, became interested in politics, and adopted an extravagant manner suggested in the title of the biography by Yvonne ffrench, *Ouida: A Study in Ostentation* (London, 1938). A later biographer, Elizabeth Bigland, characterizes her in the title: *Ouida, The Passionate Victorian* (London, 1950). She embellished her surname with the prefatory "De La." Her nom de plume represents her childish corruption of the name "Louise."

In 1871 Ouida moved to Italy, where she settled in Florence for the rest of her life, the later years of which were spent in near poverty as a result of her earlier improvidence. But she continued to write fiction and left a total of thirteen volumes of short stories and thirty-one novels. Among the more popular of the latter, in addition to *Under Two Flags*, were *Held in Bondage* (1861–63), *Strathmore* (1863–65), and *Chandos* (1866).

Ouida's literary opinions were largely expressed in some of her essays, collected in three volumes. She objected to the prolixity of contemporary writing and rejoiced at the passing of the three-volume novel. She discussed the propriety of an author's changing a novel after its initial publication. She stressed the importance of a harmonious relationship of the parts of a novel:

Now, a well-constructed novel may please you or not, may be attractive or offensive, but it will always be accurately conceived and harmoniously balanced; and nothing animate or intimate will be introduced into it which has not some bearing direct or indirect upon the plot. Nothing can be more incorrect than to excite the expectations of the reader by indications which result in nothing, sign-posts on a road which do but lead to a blank wall.
—"The Italian Novels of Marion Crawford," *Critical Studies* (Leipzig, 1901), p. 98.

She had the highest praise for the abilities requisite to a novelist:

Reflect but a moment upon all the divers and numerous qualities which are of necessity existent in the creator of a fine novel before it can be produced; not only imagination but wit, not only wit but scholarship, not only scholarship but fancy, not only fancy but discrimination, observation, knowledge of the passions, sympathy with the most opposite temperaments, the power to call up character from the void, as the sculptor creates figures from the clay, and, for amalgamating, condensing, and vivifying all these talents, the mastery of an exquisite subtlety, force, and eloquence in language.
—"Le Secret Du Precepteur," *Critical Studies* (Leipzig, 1901), p. 120.

One of her essays, "Romance and Realism" (1883), is her reasoned reply to critics who leveled charges of unreality against the type of romanticized fiction that she practiced. The real, in her opinion, must not be so defined as to exclude all that is not commonplace.

ROMANCE AND REALISM
(1883)

I think the following story may interest your readers. I will not give the names of the persons concerned in it, but I vouch for the absolute truth of the narrative. Indeed, the little drama has been acted within a stone's throw of my gates. A cantatrice of obscure position had a lover in a Genoese gentleman, who not only had many claims on her fidelity by reason of his devotion to her, but also by the education which he had had her given when a poor girl, and the liberality which he had shown to her family; nevertheless, *telle est la femme*, she betrayed this generous lover, and carried on an intrigue with a young noble of the neighbourhood, a youth much younger than herself and very rich. For some time the Genoese gentleman, only able to visit her at intervals in the Tuscan village where she lived, was without much difficulty deceived; and when he did see the young noble, was assured that he was a relation of his *dama*. At last, however, his suspicions were fully aroused; instead of going back to Genoa he one day unexpectedly returned, and had full proofs of the worthlessness of his syren. Furious to be thus *canzonato* by a creature whom he had too ingenuously adored, he pursued his rival to his villa, and, failing to provoke him to a duel, swore that he would kill him. The Carabineers intervening, he found himself deprived of his just vengeance, and, in the madness of his despair and agony, shot himself by the river's side, while his faithless mistress jeered at him from her open window in the lovely stillness of the moonlit September eve. This was but a few nights ago; he is not dead, but still lies in great peril in a cottage near where he fell. The sympathy of the whole rural population is with this man, who at least knew how to love and how to avenge dishonour. The village populace were with trouble prevented from lynching his worthless *dama*; and the veteran Brigadier of the Guard wept like a child at the fate of this "*vittima d'amore.*" This is only one out of a thousand tragedies which yearly occur in this, the home of Romeo and Giulietta, where love is not a dead letter. Why are not those who can love and suffer thus as deserving of portrayal in fiction as the epicene beings who know no woes but a passing hysteria of conscience or a disillusion before the melting of a foggy and impalpable ideal? Because passion has never touched with its fire and its glory the prim life of the æsthetic prig, or the rotund Philistine, it is not for that reason perished off the face of the earth. It exists in the same force and

221

the same favour as in the days of Othello and Stradella; and, I confess, seems to me much more fitly a subject for the novelist or the dramatist than the fictitious "realism" of the spineless common-place. After all, there is no more vivid reality than love. The Genoese lover lying here now shot through the chest by his own hand, because his generous faith has been deceived by a heartless mistress, is every whit as "real" as the British prig going to his æsthetic afternoon teas or the British Philistine driving in an omnibus; therefore his story or its similitude presented in fiction would be as legitimate a centre of interest as Anthony Trollope's gossiping bishops or Henry James's heroines perplexed by a plethora or a paucity of proposals. The Tuscan villagers sorrowing by his bedside see nothing strange or unusual in a man of 25 years old giving up his life for love; but were it embodied in a romance that were printed and published the English reviewer would find his history "sensational" or pronounce it impossible. I remember when George Lawrence was told that the end of "Sword and Gown" was improbable, he answered, "Improbable. Oh, very likely; only, you see, it was true."

The *éternellement vrai* is as real as the *infiniment petit*. It may be well that there should exist painters of the latter as it may be well that there should exist carvers of cherry-stones, and men who give ten years of their existence to the production of a ladybird in ivory. But the Vatican Hermes is as "real" as the Japanese netzké, and the dome of St. Peter's is as real as the gasometer of East London; and I presume that the fact can hardly be disputed if I even assert that the passion flower is as real as the potato! I have, I believe, sometimes been accused of writing "fairy stories"; but is not life itself very often a fairy story, if too often, alas! one in which the evil genius preponderates, and the wishing cap is foolishly used by the unwise? To some of us, at least, a dreary and insipid story of an uneventful and unimpassioned life seems much more "unreal" (*i.e.*, unlike our own experiences) than the more romantic narrative conceived by the wildest fancy. To many of us—to myself, I confess, among the number—the world seems a marvellous union of tragedy and comedy, which run side by side like twin children; like a "web of Tyrian looms" with the gold threads crossing and recrossing on the dusky purple of its intricate meshes. But there are, no doubt, a number of good and tiresome people to whom it seems only a Quaker mute, a suit of homespun, a length of huckaback; they judge by what they have known themselves. How is one to persuade them that their knowledge is not the measure of the world? The amorous, magnificent, heroic life of Skobeleff would, no doubt, seem incredible to the London *littérateur* with his prim domesticities bound up in a duodecimo suburban villa, papered by Morris, or the rural clergyman solemnly pacing his treadmill of weekly monotonies; but Michael Skobeleff was just as "real" as are the modern Puff and Wormwood going up and down in their underground railway trains, or the Reverend Crawleys surrounded with their olive branches in muddy midland villages.

At this moment, fighting for the French flag at Tonquin, is a young man, the fame of whose *nom de plume* (were I to give it here) would be at once recognized as that of one of the masters of French fiction; this gallant sailor is also a great musician and an admirable artist, and he may very likely die in a barbarous country (as Henri Rivière died), burying with him his genius, his youth, and his marvellous and multitudinous powers. Well, is not this man every whit as "real" as Mr. Precisian Dulle, passing his life between a Civil Service desk and a house in South Kensington, or Mr. Smalle Joker penning his blameless fiction, which "never brings a blush on the cheek," &c., with his six daughters playing lawn-tennis in his back garden, and his physical and mental vision limited to the chimney pots?

No doubt, all the world over character creates circumstance; and the tortoise is not to blame if it cannot leap, only it need not disbelieve in the greyhound and the horse. No doubt "adventures are to the adventurous" in the most extended sense of the word; and romantic and brilliant lives will not fall to the lot of the dull and the mediocre. But such lives exist, nevertheless, and it is not true that a pale uniformity extends like a pall over the whole of the human race. Everyone, certainly, is not beautiful, but there are very beautiful people; and it is legitimate to describe beauty in fiction as it is legitimate to depict it in painting or reproduce it in sculpture. Everyone does not possess a great or beautiful house, but many people do. Why is not the palace as fit a subject for description as the hovel, or the "commodious dwelling" of advertising agents? A friend of mine never gives a reception without having 1,500 f. worth of wax candles lighted in his room; is he not as "real" as Jones or Brown whose housemaid lights his single gasalier? A little while ago I said to a well-known diplomatist, who is also a great virtuoso and a great artist, and who has also a most romantic personal history, "If you were 'put in a book,' as people say, nobody would believe in you." Let me beg to be distinctly understood; I do not object to realism in fiction; what I object to is the limitation of realism in fiction to what is commonplace, tedious, and bald—is the habit, in a word, of insisting that the potato is real and that the passion-flower is not. A novel is not necessarily any the more like real life because it is a story about nothing, leading to nowhere, which might meander on through half a century for any climax that it ever reaches. It is not correct to call this kind of writing miniature painting; the miniature may represent the hero as well as the infant, the court beauty as well as the white-coiffed peasant; on its few inches of ivory the miniature has borne the mature features of Napoleon as well as the baby face of the Roi de Rome. This pseudo-realistic literature, on the contrary, is rather similar to those small Dutch carvings in bone, which somewhat clumsily imitate the Japanese netzkés in ivory. When a novel is vapid, tedious, without any originality of circumstance or of character, and incapable of issuing out of one dead level of commonplace, it is very easy to praise it as "natural," but it does not in the least follow that it is so. The realistic novels of France are very fine of their kind, because they are not afraid to grapple with vice and depravity in its worst form; but the realistic novel of English or English-writing authors is no more real than the faded daguerreotypes of our grandmothers, where all the features are blurred into one indistinct brown cloud of shadow. I cannot suppose that my own experiences can be wholly exceptional ones, yet I have known very handsome people, I have known very fine characters, I have also known some very wicked ones, and I have also known many circumstances so romantic that were they described in fiction, they would be ridiculed as exaggerated and impossible; in real life there are coincidences so startling, mysteries so singular, destinies so strange, that no wise novelist could venture to portray them for fear of making his work appear too *bizarre* and too melodramatic. That "truth is stranger than fiction" is found at every turn in the world. The sunset on the Alps is as "real" as a Dutch cheese on a wooden platter; but the painter of the former will always be considered an idealist and the painter of the latter a realist. Again, if there be one thing more than another that is the most conspicuous note of our century, it is the number of great fortunes which are possessed in it; the extreme luxury and splendour of life in general, the self-indulgence and feverishness of society, the grace and ennui of existence. To describe great riches in a novel is surely therefore as legitimate as to describe middle-class competence, or the harshness of absolute poverty; the former has quite as much effect on the times as the latter, and infinitely more effect on the manners. Dunrobin or Belvoir, Chénonçeaux, &c., or the Trostberg, is surely as "real" as Westbourne Grove and Clapham, as Belleville or the crowded Trattnerhof; therefore, why is not a great house, similar to any one of the many great houses that exist in Europe, as legitimate a *venue* for the action of a romance, as a doctor's house in a square, or a grocer's villa in the *banlieue?*

A lecturer in the north of England, lecturing on my novels, remarked with *naïveté* and incredulity on the number of residences assigned in "Moths" to Prince Zouroff. Now, had the lecturer taken the trouble to inquire of anyone conversant with the world he would have learned that most great persons of all nationalities have three or four different residences at the least, and that a Russian noble is invariably extravagant in these matters. Indeed, is it ever possible to over-colour in fiction the expenditure and self-indulgence of what we call society in this day? The influences of the Second Empire are still with us all over Europe, but in English literature this is neither accurately traced or truthfully acknowledged. The world is not exclusively composed of the English middle class, varied with a few American young ladies. Would it not be well if lecturers or reviewers, before calling everything which seems strange to themselves unreal or unnatural, were visited with a wholesome doubt as to whether it might not be their own experiences which were limited? Allow me to conclude with a repetition of a passage which I wrote some years ago, and which is pertinent to this subject:—

"When the soldier dies at his post, unhonoured and unpitied, and out of sheer duty, is that unreal because it is noble? When the sister of charity hides her youth and her sex under a grey shroud, and gives up her whole life to woe and solitude, to sickness and pain, is that unreal because it is wonderful? A man paints a spluttering candle, a greasy cloth, a mouldy cheese, a pewter can; 'how real!' they cry. If he paints the spirituality of dawn, the light of the summer sea, the flame of arctic lights, of tropic woods, they are called unreal, though they exist no less than the candle and cloth, the cheese and the can. Ruy Blas is now condemned as unreal because the lovers kill themselves; the realists forget that there are lovers still to whom that death would be possible, would be preferable, to low intrigue and yet more lowering falsehood. They can only see the mouldy cheese, they cannot see the sunrise glory. All that is heroic, all that is sublime, impersonal, or glorious, is derided as unreal. It is a dreary creed. It will make a dreary world. Is not my Venetian glass with its iridescent hues of opal as real every whit as your pot of pewter? Yet the time is coming when everyone, morally and mentally at least, will be allowed no other than a pewter pot to drink out of, under pain of being 'writ down an ass'—or worse. It is a dreary prospect."

I put these words into the lips of Corrèze; and, by the by, will anyone be good enough to tell me why Corrèze has been considered an "impossible" character in a century which has known Mario, Marchese di Candia, and seen the women of Paris mad for a smile from Capoul?

23

SIR WALTER BESANT

(1836–1901)

Although Sir Walter Besant collaborated on several, long, romantic novels with James Rice, Editor of *Once a Week*, and produced over two dozen more after Rice's death in 1882, he made little reference to them or to fiction in his *Autobiography* (1902). One such infrequent comment in this book is his statement that "if I were asked for my opinion as to collaboration in fiction, it would be decidedly against it . . . an artist must necessarily stand alone." Fred W. Boege suggests that the lack of autobiographic comment on fiction, as well as the uneven quality of his novels, derives from Besant's failure to take "fiction seriously as an art that demanded all his devotion" ("Sir Walter Besant: Novelist," *Nineteenth Century Fiction*, XI, 1956, 59). The same critic writes:

. . . Besant was much more than a popular novelist. He moved his readers deeply, even to that rarely attained point of inducing them to part freely with their money. He was loved, revered, feared, and hated. In London a gigantic public building and the ecumenical Society of Authors survive to testify to his impact on his age. He was banqueted, lionized, knighted, institutionalized, being more in the public eye, perhaps, than any other author of his time. . . . For a period in the 'eighties Besant was in high repute; only Meredith and Hardy of the living novelists were ranked clearly above him. In his later years, however, he turned out a steady succession of inferior novels that eclipsed the merits of his better work.

—*Ibid.*, X, 249–50.

That Besant was more than a popular novelist is indicated by an unfinished topographical *Survey of London* in ten volumes (1902–12); his influence on copyright legislation in Great Britain, Canada, and the United States; and a period as a teacher in Mauritius. The building referred to by Boege was the People's Palace, opened by Victoria in 1887 and inspired by the "Palace of Delights," described in Besant's first independently-written novel, *All Sorts and Conditions of Men* (1882). The Society of Authors was founded with Besant's help in 1884, and he edited its journal until he died. He was knighted in 1895.

Besant's best fiction, including *Children of Gibeon* (1886), deals with life in London's East End. As if to confirm his opinion that novelists of the 1880's universally began writing with a conscious moral purpose, he urged education as the solution to the social evils he describes. His acceptance of moral teaching as a function of fiction is expressed as early as 1872 in "The Value of Fiction," a short article published in *Belgravia*; the concluding paragraph summarizes this and other values:

A great deal more might be said, but it suffices. Fiction lessens our anxieties, by preventing that perpetual brooding which magnifies them; it brightens our real world, by giving us an ideal one—more happy, more varied, more joyous, richer, and *fuller* than our own; it teaches us tolerance, by showing us the different ways in which our fellows live; and it perpetually, under a thousand new forms, impresses the good old maxim, that the "only way to be happy is by the narrow road."

Of the four contributions Besant made to symposia in the *New Review*, two were on literary topics: "Candour in English Fiction" (1890) and "The Science of Fiction" (1891). The former testified to the censorial power of the circulating libraries but supposed that average opinion set liberal enough limits; the latter entered a plea that fiction writing be taught in schools. More general and more important is Besant's lecture on "The Art of Fiction," delivered before the Royal Institution on 25 April 1884. Of this, Ernest Ball writes:

. . . his ideas on the art of the English novel are second to Fielding's only in time for their sound and enduring sense. They support the truism, that the most reliable philosopher on the art of the English novel will always be a practitioner.
　　—"Walter Besant on the Art of the Novel," *English Fiction in Transition*, II
　　　(Spring, 1959), 28.

The same author continues:

Besant's address is a classic; and, after the manner of a classic, it is remarkably filled with quotations. It is, to my knowledge, the first full statement made during the nineteenth century of the practices of the great novelists of the English humanitarian tradition. It preserves the essentials of that tradition: the need for faith in life as a whole, acceptance of a moral position, certainty in characterization, and an unqualified faith in the value of each individual life.
　　　　　　—*Ibid.*, p. 35.

Boege has this to say of Besant's lecture:

Besant had two main purposes: to plead for the recognition of fiction as one of the fine arts, the equal of any other, and to formulate some of the general laws of fiction comparable to those of harmony, perspective, and proportion in other arts. Besant's insistence on the first point, and James's gratitude to him for making it, remind us how seldom fiction was considered an art in 1884.
　　　　　　—*Op. cit.*, XI, 36–37.

FROM "THE ART OF FICTION"
(1884)

I desire, this evening, to consider Fiction as one of the Fine Arts. In order to do this, and before doing it, I have first to advance certain propositions. They are not new, they are not likely to be disputed, and yet they have never been so generally received as to form part, so to speak, of the national mind. These propositions are three, though the last two directly spring from the first. They are:—

1. That Fiction is an Art in every way worthy to be called the sister and the equal of the Arts of Painting, Sculpture, Music, and Poetry; that is to say, her field is as boundless, her possibilities as vast, her excellences as worthy of admiration, as may be claimed for any of her sister Arts.

2. That it is an Art which, like them, is governed and directed by general laws; and that these laws may be laid down and taught with as much precision and exactness as the laws of harmony, perspective, and proportion.

3. That, like the other Fine Arts, Fiction is so far removed from the mere mechanical arts, that no laws or rules whatever can teach it to those who have not already been endowed with the natural and necessary gifts.

These are the three propositions which I have to discuss. It follows as a corollary and evident deduction that, these propositions once admitted, those who follow and profess the Art of Fiction must be recognized as artists, in the strictest sense of the word, just as much as those who have delighted and elevated mankind by music and painting; and that the great Masters of Fiction must be placed on the same level as the great Masters in the other Arts. In other words, I mean that where the highest point, or what seems the highest point, possible in this Art is touched, the man who has reached it is one of the world's greatest men.

.   .   .   .

It [fiction] is then, first and before all, a real Art. It is the oldest, because it was known and practised long before Painting and her sisters were in existence or even thought of; it is older than any of the Muses from whose company she who tells stories has hitherto been excluded; it is the most widely spread, because in no race of men under the sun is it unknown, even though the stories may be always the same, and handed down from generation to generation in the same form; it is the most religious of all the Arts, because in every age until the present the lives, exploits, and sufferings of gods,

228

goddesses, saints, and heroes have been the favourite theme; it has always been the most popular, because it requires neither culture, education, nor natural genius to understand and listen to a story; it is the most moral, because the world has always been taught whatever little morality it possesses by way of story, fable, apologue, parable, and allegory. It commands the widest influence, because it can be carried easily and everywhere, into regions where pictures are never seen and music is never heard; it is the greatest teaching power, because its lessons are most readily apprehended and understood. All this, which might have been said thousands of years ago, may be said to-day with even greater force and truth. That world which exists not, but is an invention or an imitation—that world in which the shadows and shapes of men move about before our eyes as real as if they were actually living and speaking among us, is like a great theatre accessible to all of every sort, on whose stage are enacted, at our own sweet will, whenever we please to command them, the most beautiful plays: it is, as every theatre should be, the school in which manners are learned: here the majority of reading mankind learn nearly all that they know of life and manners, of philosophy and art; even of science and religion. The modern novel converts abstract ideas into living models; it gives ideas, it strengthens faith, it preaches a higher morality than is seen in the actual world; it commands the emotions of pity, admiration, and terror; it creates and keeps alive the sense of sympathy; it is the universal teacher; it is the only book which the great mass of reading mankind ever do read; it is the only way in which people can learn what other men and women are like; it redeems their lives from dulness, puts thoughts, desires, knowledge, and even ambitions into their hearts: it teaches them to talk, and enriches their speech with epigrams, anecdotes and illustrations. It is an unfailing source of delight to millions, happily not too critical. Why, out of all the books taken down from the shelves of the public libraries, four-fifths are novels, and of all those that are bought nine-tenths are novels. Compared with this tremendous engine of popular influence, what are all the other Arts put together? Can we not alter the old maxim, and say with truth, Let him who pleases make the laws if I may write the novels?

As for the field with which this Art of Fiction occupies itself, it is, if you please, nothing less than the whole of Humanity. The novelist studies men and women; he is concerned with their actions and their thoughts, their errors and their follies, their greatness and their meanness; the countless forms of beauty and constantly varying moods to be seen among them; the forces which act upon them; the passions, prejudices, hopes and fears which pull them this way and that. He has to do, above all, and before all, with men and women. No one, for instance, among novelists, can be called a landscape painter, or a painter of sea-pieces, or a painter of fruit and flowers, save only in strict subordination to the group of characters with whom he is dealing. Landscape, sea, sky, and air, are merely accessories

introduced in order to set off and bring into greater prominence the figures
on the stage. The very first rule in Fiction is that the human interest must
absolutely absorb everything else.

.   .   .   .

It is, therefore, the especial characteristic of this Art, that, since it deals
exclusively with men and women, it not only requires of its followers, but
also creates in readers, that sentiment which is destined to be a most mighty
engine in deepening and widening the civilization of the world. We call it
Sympathy, but it means a great deal more than was formerly understood by
the word. It means, in fact, what Professor Seeley once called the Enthusiasm
of Humanity, and it first appeared, I think, about a hundred and fifty years
ago, when the modern novel came into existence. You will find it, for
instance, conspicuous for its absence in Defoe. The modern Sympathy
includes not only the power to pity the sufferings of others, but also that of
understanding their very souls; it is the reverence for man, the respect for
his personality, the recognition of his individuality, and the enormous value
of the one man, the perception of one man's relation to another, his duties
and responsibilities. Through the strength of this newly-born faculty, and
aided by the guidance of a great artist, we are enabled to discern the real
indestructible man beneath the rags and filth of a common castaway, and
the possibilities of the meanest gutter-child that steals in the streets for its
daily bread. Surely that is a wonderful Art which endows the people—all the
people—with this power of vision and of feeling. Painting has not done it,
and could never do it; Painting has done more for nature than for humanity.
Sculpture could not to it, because it deals with situation and form rather
than action. Music cannot do it, because Music (if I understand rightly)
appeals especially to the individual concerning himself and his own aspirations. Poetry alone is the rival of Fiction, and in this respect it takes a lower
place, not because Poetry fails to teach and interpret, but because Fiction is,
and must always be, more popular.

Again, this Art teaches, like the others, by suppression and reticence.
Out of the great procession of Humanity, the *Comédie Humaine* which the
novelist sees passing ever before his eyes, single figures detach themselves
one after the other, to be questioned, examined, and received or rejected.
This process goes on perpetually. Humanity is so vast a field that to one who
goes about watching men and women, and does not sit at home and evolve
figures out of inner consciousness, there is not, and can never be, any end or
limit to the freshness and interest of these figures. It is the work of the artist
to select the figures, to suppress, to copy, to group, and to work up the
incidents which each one offers. The daily life of the world is not dramatic—it
is monotonous; the novelist makes it dramatic by his silences, his suppressions, and his exaggerations. No one, for example, in fiction behaves
quite in the same way as in real life; as on the stage, if an actor unfolds and
reads a letter, the simple action is done with an exaggeration of gesture which

calls attention to the thing and to its importance; so in romance, while nothing should be allowed which does not carry on the story, so everything as it occurs must be accentuated and yet deprived of needless accessory details. The gestures of the characters at an important juncture, their looks, their voices, may all be noted if they help to impress the situation. Even the weather, the wind and the rain, with some writers, have been made to emphasize a mood or a passion of a heroine. To know how to use these aids artistically is to the novelist exactly what to the actor is the right presentation of a letter, the handing of a chair, even the removal of a glove.

A third characteristic of Fiction, which should alone be sufficient to give it a place among the noblest forms of Art, is that, like Poetry, Painting, and Music, it becomes a vehicle, not only for the best thoughts of the writer, but also for those of the reader, so that a novelist may write truthfully and faithfully, but simply, and yet be understood in a far fuller and nobler sense than was present to his own mind. This power is the very highest gift of the poet. He has a vision and sees a thing clearly, yet perhaps afar off; another who reads him is enabled to get the same vision, to see the same thing, yet closer and more distinctly. For a lower intellect thus to lead and instruct a higher is surely a very great gift, and granted only to the highest forms of Art. And this it is which Fiction of the best kind does for its readers. It is, however, only another way of saying that Truth in Fiction produces effects similar to those produced by Truth in every other Art.

So far, then, I have showed that this Art of Fiction is the most ancient of all Arts and the most popular; that its field is the whole of humanity; that it creates and develops that sympathy which is a kind of second sight; that, like all other Arts, its function is to select, to suppress, and to arrange; that it suggests as well as narrates. More might be said—a great deal more—but enough has been said to show that in these, the leading characteristics of any Art, Fiction is on exactly the same level as her sisters. Let me only add that in this Art, as in the others, there is, and will be always, whatever has been done already, something new to discover, something new to express, something new to describe. Surgeons dissect the body, and account for every bone and every nerve, so that the body of one man, considered as a collection of bones and nerves, is so far exactly like the body of another man. But the mind of man cannot be so exhausted: it yields discoveries to every patient student; it is absolutely inexhaustible; it is to everyone a fresh and virgin field: and the most successful investigator leaves regions and tracts for his successor as vast as those he has himself gone over. Perhaps, after all, the greatest Psychologist is not the metaphysician, but the novelist.

We come next to speak of the Laws which govern this Art. I mean those general rules and principles which must necessarily be acquired by every writer of Fiction before he can even hope for success. Rules will not make a man a novelist, any more than a knowledge of grammar makes a man know a language, or a knowledge of musical science makes a man able to play an instrument. Yet the Rules must be learned. And, in speaking of them, one is compelled, so close is the connection between the sister Arts, to use not only the same terms, but also to adopt the same rules, as those laid down by painters for their students. If these Laws appear self-evident, it is a proof that the general principles of the Art are well understood. Considering, however, the vast quantity of bad, inartistic work which is every week laid before the public, one is inclined to think that a statement of these principles may not be without usefulness.

First, and before everything else, there is the Rule that everything in Fiction which is invented and is not the result of personal experience and observation is worthless. In some other Arts, the design may follow any lines which the designer pleases: it may be fanciful, unreal, or grotesque; but in modern Fiction, whose sole end, aim, and purpose is to portray humanity and human character, the design must be in accordance with the customs and general practice of living men and women under any proposed set of circumstances and conditions. That is to say, the characters must be real, and such as might be met with in actual life, or, at least, the natural developments of such people as any of us might meet; their actions must be natural and consistent; the conditions of place, of manners, and of thought must be drawn from personal observation. To take an extreme case: a young lady brought up in a quiet country village should avoid descriptions of garrison life; a writer whose friends and personal experiences belong to what we call the lower middle class should carefully avoid introducing his characters into Society; a South-countryman would hesitate before attempting to reproduce the North-country accent. This is a very simple Rule, but one to which there should be no exception—never to go beyond your own experience.[1] Remember that most of the people who read novels, and know nothing about the art of writing them, recognize before any other quality that of fidelity:

[1] It has been objected to this Rule that, if followed, it would entirely shut out the historical novel. Not at all. The interest of the historical novel, as of any other novel, depends upon the experience and knowledge which the writer has of humanity, men and women being pretty much alike in all ages. It is not the setting that we regard, so much as the acting of the characters. The setting in an historical novel is very often absurd, incorrect, and incongruous; but the human interest, the skill and knowledge of character shown by the writer, may make us forget the errors of the setting. For instance, "Romola" is undoubtedly a great novel, not because it contains a true, and therefore valuable, reproduction of Florentine life in the time of the early Renaissance, for it does not; nor because it gives us the ideas of the age, for it does not; the characters, especially that of the heroine, being fully of nineteenth century ideas: but it is great as a study of character. On the other hand, in the "Cloister and the Hearth," we do really have a description of the time and its ideas, taken bodily, sometimes almost literally, from the pages of the man who most truly represents them—Erasmus. So that here is a rule for the historical novelist—when he must describe, he must borrow. If it be objected, again, that he may do the same thing with contemporary life, I reply that he may, if he please, but he will *most assuredly be found out* through some blunder, omission, or confusion caused by ignorance. No doubt the same blunders are perpetrated by the historical novelist; but these are not so readily found out except by an archæologist. Of course, one who desires to reproduce a time gone by would not go to the poets, the divines, the historians, so much as to the familiar literature, the letters, comedies, tales, essayists, and newspapers. [Besant]

the greatness of a novelist they measure chiefly by the knowledge of the world displayed in his pages; the highest praise they can bestow upon him is that he has drawn the story to the life. It is exactly the same with a picture. If you go to the Academy any day, and listen to the comments of the crowd, which is a very instructive thing to do, and one recommended to young novelists, you will presently become aware that the only thing they look for in a picture is the story which it tells, and therefore the fidelity with which it is presented on the canvas. Most of the other qualities of the picture, and of the novel as well, all that has to do with the technique, escape the general observer.

This being so, the first thing which has to be acquired is the art of description.

.   .   .   .

What is next required is the power of Selection. Can this be taught? I think not, at least I do not know how, unless it is by reading. In every Art, selection requires that kind of special fitness for the Art which is included in the much abused word Genius. In Fiction the power of selection requires a large share of the dramatic sense. Those who already possess this faculty will not go wrong if they bear in mind the simple rule that nothing should be admitted which does not advance the story, illustrate the characters, bring into stronger relief the hidden forces which act upon them, their emotions, their passions, and their intentions. All descriptions which hinder instead of helping the action, all episodes of whatever kind, all conversation which does not either advance the story or illustrate the characters, ought to be rigidly suppressed.

Closely connected with selection is dramatic presentation. Given a situation, it should be the first care of the writer to present it as dramatically, that is to say as forcibly, as possible. The grouping and setting of the picture, the due subordination of description to dialogue, the rapidity of the action, those things which naturally suggest themselves to the practised eye, deserve to be very carefully considered by the beginner. In fact, a novel is like a play: it may be divided into scenes and acts, tableaus and situations, separated by the end of the chapter instead of the drop-scene: the writer is the dramatist, stage-manager, scene-painter, actor, and carpenter, all in one; it is his single business to see that none of the scenes flag or fall flat: he must never for one moment forget to consider how the piece is looking from the front.

The next simple Rule is that the drawing of each figure must be clear in outline, and, even if only sketched, must be sketched without hesitation. This can only be done when the writer himself sees his figures clearly. Characters in fiction do not, it must be understood, spring Minerva-like from the brain. They grow: they grow sometimes slowly, sometimes quickly.

.   .   .   .

As for the methods of conveying a clear understanding of a character, they are many. The first and the easiest is to make it clear by reason of some mannerism or personal peculiarity, some trick of speech or of carriage. This is the worst, as may generally be said of the easiest way. Another easy method is to describe your character at length. This also is a bad, because a tedious, method. If, however, you read a page or two of any good writer, you will discover that he first makes a character intelligible by a few words, and then allows him to reveal himself in action and dialogue.

.   .   .   .

Again, the modern English novel, whatever form it takes, almost always starts with a conscious moral purpose. When it does not, so much are we accustomed to expect it, that one feels as if there has been a debasement of the Art. It is, fortunately, not possible in this country for any man to defile and defame humanity and still be called an artist; the development of modern sympathy, the growing reverence for the individual, the ever-widening love of things beautiful and the appreciation of lives made beautiful by devotion and self-denial, the sense of personal responsibility among the English-speaking races, the deep-seated religion of our people, even in a time of doubt, are all forces which act strongly upon the artist as well as upon his readers, and lend to his work, whether he will or not, a moral purpose so clearly marked that it has become practically a law of English Fiction. We must acknowledge that this is a truly admirable thing, and a great cause for congratulation. At the same time, one may be permitted to think that the preaching novel is the least desirable of any, and to be unfeignedly rejoiced that the old religious novel, written in the interests of High Church or Low Church or any other Church, has gone out of fashion.

Next, just as in Painting and Sculpture, not only are fidelity, truth, and harmony to be observed in Fiction, but also beauty of workmanship. It is almost impossible to estimate too highly the value of careful workmanship, that is, of style. Everyone, without exception, of the great Masters in Fiction, has recognized this truth. You will hardly find a single page in any of them which is not carefully and even elaborately worked up. I think there is no point on which critics of novels should place greater importance than this, because it is one which young novelists are so very liable to ignore. There ought not to be in a novel, any more than in a poem, a single sentence carelessly worded, a single phrase which has not been considered. Consider, if you please, any one of the great scenes in Fiction—how much of the effect is due to the style, the balanced sentences, the very words used by the narrator! This, however, is only one more point of similarity between Fiction and the sister Arts. There is, I know, the danger of attaching too much attention to style at the expense of situation, and so falling a prey to priggish-ness, fashions, and mannerisms of the day. It is certainly a danger; at the same time, it sometimes seems, when one reads the slipshod, careless English which is often thought good enough for story-telling, that it is almost im-possible to overrate the value of style. There is comfort in the thought that no reputation worth having can be made without attending to style, and that there is no style, however rugged, which cannot be made beautiful by attention and pains. "How many times," a writer once asked a girl who brought him her first effort for advice and criticism; "how many times have you re-written this page?" She confessed that she had written it once for all, had never read it afterwards, and had not the least idea that there was such a thing as style. Is it not presumptuous in the highest degree to believe that what one has produced without pains, thought, or trouble will give any pleasure to the reader?

In fact every scene, however unimportant, should be completely and carefully finished. There should be no unfinished places, no sign anywhere of weariness or haste—in fact, no scamping. The writer must so love his work as to dwell tenderly on every page and be literally unable to send forth a single page of it without the finishing touches. We all of us remember that kind of novel in which every scene has the appearance of being hurried and scamped.

To sum up these few preliminary and general laws. The Art of Fiction requires first of all the power of description, truth, and fidelity, observation, selection, clearness of conception and of outline, dramatic grouping, direct-ness of purpose, a profound belief on the part of the story-teller in the reality of his story, and beauty of workmanship. It is, moreover, an Art which requires of those who follow it seriously that they must be unceasingly occupied in studying the ways of mankind, the social laws, the religions, philosophies, tendencies, thoughts, prejudices, superstitions of men and women. They must consider as many of the forces which act upon classes and upon individuals as they can discover; they should be always trying to put themselves into the place of another; they must be as inquisitive and as watchful as a detective, as suspicious as a criminal lawyer, as eager for knowledge as a physicist, and withal fully possessed of that spirit to which nothing appears mean, nothing contemptible, nothing unworthy of study, which belongs to human nature.

I repeat that I submit some of these laws as perhaps self-evident. If that is so, many novels which are daily submitted to the reviewer are written in wilful neglect and disobedience of them. But they are not really self-evident; those who aspire to be artists in Fiction almost invariably begin without any understanding at all of these laws. Hence the lamentable early failures, the waste of good material, and the low level of Art with which both the novel-writer and the novel-reader are too often contented. I am certain that if these laws were better known and more generally studied, a very large proportion of the bad works of which our critics complain would not be produced at all. And I am in great hopes that one effect of the establishment of the newly founded Society of Authors will be to keep young writers of fiction from rushing too hastily into print, to help them to the right understanding of their Art and its principles, and to guide them into true practice of their principles while they are still young, their imaginations strong, and their personal experiences as yet not wasted in foolish failures.

After all these preliminary studies there comes the most important point of all—the story. There is a school which pretends that there is no need for a story: all the stories, they say, have been told already; there is no more room for invention: nobody wants any longer to listen to a story. One hears this kind of talk with the same wonder which one feels when a new monstrous fashion changes the beautiful figure of woman into something grotesque and unnatural. Men say these things gravely to each other, expecially men who have no story to tell: other men listen gravely; in the same way women put on the newest and most preposterous fashions gravely, and look upon each other without either laughing or hiding their faces for shame. It is, indeed, if we think of it, a most strange and wonderful theory, that we should continue to care for Fiction and cease to care for the story. We have all along been training ourselves how to tell the story, and here is this new school which steps in, like the needy knife-grinder, to explain that there is no story left at all to tell. Why, the story is everything.

.   .   .   .

One thing more the Art student has to learn. Let him not only believe his own story before he begins to tell it, but let him remember that in story-telling, as in almsgiving, a cheerful countenance works wonders, and a hearty manner greatly helps the teller and pleases the listener. One would not have the novelist make continual efforts at being comic; but let him not tell his story with eyes full of sadness, a face of woe and a shaking voice.

.   .   .   .

Let me say one word upon the present condition of this most delightful Art in England. Remember that great Masters in every Art are rare. Perhaps one or two appear in a century: we ought not to expect more. It may even happen that those modern writers of our own whom we have agreed to call great Masters will have to take lower rank among posterity, who will have great Masters of their own. I am inclined, however, to think that a few of the nineteenth-century novelists will never be suffered to die, though they may be remembered principally for one book—that Thackeray will be remembered for his "Vanity Fair," Dickens for "David Copperfield," George Meredith for the "Ordeal of Richard Feverel," George Eliot for "Silas Marner," Charles Reade for the "Cloister and the Hearth," and Blackmore for his "Lorna Doone."

.   .   .   .

Ought we not to be full of hope for the future, when such women as Mrs. Oliphant and Mrs. Thackeray Ritchie write for us—when such men as Meredith, Blackmore, Black, Payn, Wilkie Collins, and Hardy are still at their best, and such men as Louis Stevenson, Christie Murray, Clark Russell, and Herman Merivale have just begun?

24

HENRY JAMES

(1843–1916)

By the beginning of the twentieth century the distinction between English and American novelists on the basis of nationality becomes more academic than realistic. The classic proof of this fact is the case of Henry James, usually treated as an American novelist because of his birth in New York City, his education at the Harvard Law School, and his prolific contributions to such American periodicals as the *Atlantic Monthly*, wherein his first important novel, *Roderick Hudson* (1876), was published. Yet James studied also in various European centers, lived in England for the largest part of his life, and became a British citizen one year before his death. If the factual evidence alone did not justify considering him with the British novelists, the influence of his theories and practice on such British writers as Moore, Ford, Joyce, Forster, Greene, and Conrad would; for half a century he was the most influential novelist in England.

James's distinctive theme—the contrast between American and European culture—derives from his own internationalism. He characteristically dramatizes this duality by presenting an American visitor being initiated into European ideals: *Roderick Hudson* (1876), *The American* (1877), *Daisy Miller* (1879), and *The Portrait of a Lady* (1881). After dealing wholly with the American scene in *The Bostonians* (1886) and writing a subtle analysis of English character in *The Tragic Muse* (1890), he returned to contrasting American and European character in his three last great novels: *The Wings of the Dove* (1902), *The Ambassadors* (1903), and *The Golden Bowl* (1904).

Beginning with *The Tragic Muse*, James became devoted to a refined style, marked by precise diction, qualification of meaning, and formal structure. This obsession was a product of his insistence on the status of the novel as art, in contrast to the general tendency of contemporary novelists—with some exceptions, such as Meredith and Conrad—to view it either as entertainment or as a vehicle for morality and reform. The promotion of this attitude—

acquired from the French novelists, Flaubert and Balzac, and from the Russians, Turgenev, Tolstoy, and Dostoevsky—is the one general contribution James made to fiction.

A more specific impact was his later interest in the inner conflicts of his characters. His brother, William James, was a leader in the development of psychology in the United States, and it is no coincidence that Henry James enlarged the possibilities of fiction in this manner. He also condemned the omniscient point of view, wherein authors imposed, explicitly or implicitly, their own interpretations. He advocated the invisible artist and sought to present action in his novels through the consciousness of one character. The resultant complexities of psychological analysis, the use of a detached observer, as well as subtleties of style, made heavy demands on the reader and narrowed his audience to a select group of qualified devotees.

In addition to his novels, James produced more than one hundred short stories, of which "The Turn of the Screw" (1898) is best known; his fiction comprises twenty-six volumes in the "New York Edition" of 1907-9, for which he composed his critical prefaces. At the head of his literary criticism is "The Art of Fiction," first published in *Longman's Magazine* for September, 1884. His basic thesis that "A novel is a living thing, all one and continuous," instead of a combination of various independent parts, as was assumed by writers arguing plot vs. character, was new only in its forceful expression; the principle of organic unity had not been unrecognized. As Fred W. Boege says, comparing the article with that by Besant:

But Besant handles the subject in an easy, flaccid style, with an enthusiasm and tone more suitable for telling his listeners how to finish a piece of furniture than how to write good fiction; whereas James, letting us look over the shoulder of an artist who has sweated and agonized for twenty years, writes like a saint who finds his profoundest realities in the trials and triumphs of an unseen world. It is the play of two very different intelligences on the same material which produced on the one hand a commonplace discussion of a few innocuous ideas and on the other a magnificent manifesto for the novel, still vital.
　　　　　—"Sir Walter Besant: Novelist," *Nineteenth Century Fiction*, XI (1956), 38.

The place of James's critique in novel criticism is summed up by Leon Edel:

I have spoken of James as the greatest of theorists in the art of the novel. The first essay here reproduced ["The Art of Fiction"], together with his letter to the Deerfield Summer School, has become, in the intervening half century, a kind of novelist's manifesto, one of those great pronouncements which seems to offer the last word on the subject. Concerning fictional theory James could talk—and did—without exhausting himself. And in this essay he has embodied the very core of his beliefs.
　　　　　—"Introduction," *The Future of the Novel: Essays on The Art of Fiction*
　　　　　　　　　　　　　　　　　　　　　　　　　　　(New York, 1956), p. x.

In the course of time, developments in fiction motivated James to express his ideas in subsequent essays. "The Future of the Novel" (1899) expressed his continued admiration for the form and his confidence in its future. Finally, in "The New Novel," written two years before he died, "one finds," in the words of Edel:

stated in the complex prose of the "later manner," James's formula for fiction as opposed to that of Tolstoy and the "saturation" school. It was this article which led to the celebrated exchange with H. G. Wells whose fictional methods came under James's criticism. . . . With Henry James, form and matter were inseparable, and he turned away from Wells and Bennett to praise the technique of Joseph Conrad—which was, to a degree, a case of the Master looking at his own image in a disciple's mirror.

Ibid., pp. xiv–xv.

THE ART OF FICTION
(1884)

I should not have affixed so comprehensive a title to these few remarks, necessarily wanting in any completeness upon a subject the full consideration of which would carry us far, did I not seem to discover a pretext for my temerity in the interesting pamphlet lately published under this name by Mr. Walter Besant. Mr. Besant's lecture at the Royal Institution—the original form of his pamphlet—appears to indicate that many persons are interested in the art of fiction, and are not indifferent to such remarks, as those who practise it may attempt to make about it. I am therefore anxious not to lose the benefit of this favourable association, and to edge in a few words under cover of the attention which Mr. Besant is sure to have excited. There is something very encouraging in his having put into form certain of his ideas on the mystery of story-telling.

It is a proof of life and curiosity—curiosity on the part of the brotherhood of novelists as well as on the part of their readers. Only a short time ago it might have been supposed that the English novel was not what the French call *discutable*. It had no air of having a theory, a conviction, a consciousness of itself behind it—of being the expression of an artistic faith, the result of choice and comparison. I do not say it was necessarily the worse for that: it would take much more courage than I possess to intimate that the form of the novel as Dickens and Thackeray (for instance) saw it had any taint of incompleteness. It was, however, *naïf* (if I may help myself out with another French word); and evidently if it be destined to suffer in any way for having lost its *naïveté* it has now an idea of making sure of the corresponding advantages. During the period I have alluded to there was a comfortable, good-humoured feeling abroad that a novel is a novel, as a pudding is a pudding, and that our only business with it could be to swallow it. But within a year or two, for some reason or other, there have been signs of returning animation—the era of discussion would appear to have been to a certain extent opened. Art lives upon discussion, upon experiment, upon curiosity, upon variety of attempt, upon the exchange of views and the comparison of stand-points; and there is a presumption that those times when no one has anything particular to say about it, and has no reason to give for practice or preference, though they may be times of honour, are not times of development—are times, possibly even, a little of dullness. The successful application of any art is a delightful spectacle, but the theory too is interesting; and though there is a great deal of the latter without the former I suspect there has never been a genuine success that has not had a latent core of conviction. Discussion, suggestion, formulation, these things are fertilizing when they are frank and sincere. Mr. Besant has set an excellent example in saying what he thinks, for his part, about the way in which fiction should be written, as well as about the way in which it should be published; for his view of the "art", carried on into an appendix, covers that too. Other labourers in the same field will doubtless take up the argument, they will give it the light of their experience, and the effect will surely be to make our interest in the novel a little more what it had for some time threatened to fail to be—a serious, active, inquiring interest, under protection of which this delightful study may, in moments of confidence, venture to say a little more what it thinks of itself.

It must take itself seriously for the public to take it so. The old superstition about fiction being "wicked" has doubtless died out in England; but the spirit of it lingers in a certain oblique regard directed toward any story which does not more or less admit that it is only a joke. Even the most jocular novel feels in some degree the weight of the prescription that was formerly directed against literary levity: the jocularity does not always succeed in passing for orthodoxy. It is still expected, though perhaps people are ashamed to say it, that a production which is after all only a "make-believe" (for what else is a "story"?) shall be in some degree apologetic—shall renounce the pretension of attempting really to represent life. This, of course, any sensible, wide-awake story declines to do, for it quickly perceives that the tolerance granted to it on such a condition is only an attempt to stifle it disguised in the form of generosity. The old evangelical hostility to the novel, which was as explicit as it was narrow and which regarded it as little less favourable to our immortal part than a stage-play, was in reality far less insulting. The only reason for the existence of a novel is that it does attempt to represent life. When it relinquishes this attempt, the same attempt that we see on the canvas of the painter, it will have arrived at a very strange pass. It is not expected of the picture that it will make itself humble in order to be forgiven; and the analogy between the art of the painter and the art of the novelist is, so far as I am able to see, complete. Their inspiration is the same, their process (allowing for the different quality of the vehicle) is the same, their success is the same. They may learn from each other, they may explain and sustain each other. Their cause is the same, and the honour of one is the honour of another. The Mahometans think a picture an unholy thing, but it is a long time since any Christian did, and it is therefore the more odd that in the Christian mind the traces (dissimulated though they may be) of a suspicion of the sister art should linger to this day. The only effectual way to lay it to rest is to emphasize the analogy to which I just alluded—to insist on the fact that as the picture is reality, so the novel is history. That is the only general description (which does it justice) that we may give of the novel. But history also is allowed to represent life; it is not, any more than painting, expected to apologize. The subject-matter of fiction is stored up likewise in documents and records, and if it will not give itself away, as they say in California, it must speak with assurance, with the tone of the historian. Certain accomplished novelists have a habit of giving themselves away which must often bring tears to the eyes of people who take their fiction seriously. I was lately struck, in reading over many pages of Anthony Trollope, with his want of discretion in this particular. In a digression, a parenthesis or an aside, he concedes to the reader that he and this trusting friend are only "making believe". He admits that the events he narrates have not really happened, and that he can give his narrative any turn the reader may like best. Such a betrayal of a sacred office seem to me, I confess, a terrible crime; it is what I mean by the attitude of apology, and it shocks me every whit as much in Trollope as it would have shocked me in Gibbon or Macaulay. It implies that the novelist is less occupied in looking for the truth (the truth, of course I mean, that he assumes, the premises that we must grant him, whatever they may be) than the historian, and in doing so it deprives him at a stroke of all his standing-room. To represent and illustrate the past, the actions of men, is the task of either writer, and the only difference that I can see is, in proportion as he succeeds, to the honour of the novelist, consisting as it does in his having more difficulty in collecting his evidence, which is so far from being purely literary. It seems to me to give him a great character, the fact that he has at once so much in common with the philosopher and the painter; this double analogy is a magnificent heritage.

It is of all this evidently that Mr. Besant is full when he insists upon the fact that fiction is one of the *fine* arts, deserving in its turn of all the honours and emoluments that have hitherto been reserved for the successful profession of music, poetry, painting, architecture. It is impossible to insist too much on so important a truth, and the place that Mr. Besant demands for the work of the novelist may be represented, a trifle abstractly, by saying that he demands not only that it shall be reputed artistic, but that it shall be reputed very artistic indeed. It is excellent that he should have struck this note, for his doing so indicates that there was need of it, that his proposition may be to many people a novelty. One rubs one's eyes at the thought; but the rest of Mr. Besant's essay confirms the revelation. I suspect in truth that it would be possible to confirm it still further, and that one would not be far wrong in saying that in addition to the people to whom it has never occurred that a novel ought to be artistic, there are a great many others who, if this principle were urged upon them, would be filled with indefinable mistrust. They would find it difficult to explain their repugnance, but it would operate strongly to put them on their guard. "Art", in our Protestant communities, where so many things have got so strangely twisted about, is supposed in certain circles to have some vaguely injurious effect upon those who make it an important consideration, who let it weigh in the balance. It is assumed to be opposed in some mysterious manner to morality, to amusement, to instruction. When it is embodied in the work of the painter (the sculptor is another affair!) you know what it is: it stands there before you, in the honesty of pink and green and a gilt frame; you can see the worst of it at a glance, and you can be on your guard. But when it is introduced into literature it becomes more insidious—there is danger of its hurting you before you know it. Literature should be either instructive or amusing, and there is in many minds an impression that these artistic preoccupations, the search for form, contribute to neither end, interfere indeed with both. They are too frivolous to be edifying, and too serious to be diverting; and they are moreover priggish and paradoxical and superfluous. That, I think, represents the manner in which the latent thought of many people who read novels as an exercise in skipping would explain itself if it were to become articulate. They would argue, of course, that a novel ought to be "good", but they would interpret this term in a fashion of their own, which indeed would vary considerably from one critic to another. One would say that being good means representing virtuous and aspiring characters, placed in prominent positions; another would say that it depends on a "happy ending", on a distribution at the last of prizes, pensions, husbands, wives, babies, millions, appended paragraphs, and cheerful remarks. Another still would say that it means being full of incident and movement, so that we shall wish to jump ahead, to see who was the mysterious stranger, and if the stolen will was ever found, and shall not be distracted from this pleasure by any tiresome analysis or "description". But they would all agree that the "artistic" idea would spoil some of their fun. One would hold it accountable for all the description, another would see it revealed in the absence of sympathy. Its hostility to a happy ending would be evident, and it might even in some cases render any ending at all impossible. The "ending" of a novel is, for many persons, like that of a good dinner, a course of dessert and ices, and the artist in fiction is regarded as a sort of meddlesome doctor who forbids agreeable aftertastes. It is therefore true that this conception of Mr. Besant's of the novel as a superior form encounters not only a negative but a positive indifference. It matters little that as a work of art it should really be as little or as much of its essence to supply happy endings, sympathetic characters, and an objective tone, as if it were a work of mechanics: the association of ideas, however incongruous, might easily be too much for it if an eloquent voice were not sometimes raised to call attention to the fact that it is at once as free and as serious a branch of literature as any other.

Certainly this might sometimes be doubted in presence of the enormous number of works of fiction that appeal to the credulity of our generation, for it might easily seem that there could be no great character in a commodity so quickly and easily produced. It must be admitted that good novels are much compromised by bad ones, and that the field at large suffers discredit from overcrowding. I think, however, that this injury is only superficial, and that the superabundance of written fiction proves nothing against the principle itself. It has been vulgarized, like all other kinds of literature, like everything else to-day, and it has proved more than some kinds accessible to vulgarization. But there is as much difference as there ever was between a good novel and a bad one: the bad is swept with all the daubed canvases and spoiled marble into some unvisited limbo, or infinite rubbish-yard beneath the back-windows of the world, and the good subsists and emits its light and stimulates our desire for perfection. As I shall take the liberty of making but a single criticism of Mr. Besant, whose tone is so full of the love of his art, I may as well have done with it at once. He seems to me to mistake in attempting to say so definitely beforehand what sort of an affair the good novel will be. To indicate the danger of such an error as that has been the purpose of these few pages; to suggest that certain traditions on the subject, applied *a priori*, have already had much to answer for, and that the good health of an art which undertakes so immediately to reproduce life must demand that it be perfectly free. It lives upon exercise, and the very meaning of exercise is freedom. The only obligation to which in advance we may hold a novel, without incurring the accusation of being arbitrary, is that it be interesting. That general responsibility rests upon it, but it is the only one I can think of. The ways in which it is at liberty to accomplish this result (of interesting us) strike me as innumerable, and such as can only suffer from being marked out or fenced in by prescription. They are as various as the temperament of man, and they are successful in proportion as they reveal a particular mind, different from others. A novel is in its broadest definition a personal, a direct impression of life: that, to begin with, constitutes its value, which is greater or less according to the intensity of the impression. But there will be no intensity at all, and therefore no value, unless there is freedom to feel and say. The tracing of a line to be followed, of a tone to be taken, of a form to be filled out is a limitation of that freedom and a suppression of the very thing that we are most curious about. The form, it seems to me, is to be appreciated after the fact: then the author's choice has been made, his standard has been indicated; then we can follow lines and directions and compare tones and resemblances. Then in a word we can enjoy one of the most charming of pleasures, we can estimate quality, we can apply the test of execution. The execution belongs to the author alone; it is what is most personal to him, and we measure him by that. The advantage, the luxury, as well as the torment and responsibility of the novelist, is that there is no limit to what he may attempt as an executant—no limit to his possible experiments, efforts, discoveries, successes. Here it is especially that he works, step by step, like his brother of the brush, of whom we may always say that he has painted his picture in a manner best known to himself. His manner is his secret, not necessarily a jealous one. He cannot disclose it as a general thing if he would; he would be at a loss to teach it to others. I say this with a due recollection of having insisted on the community of method of the artist who paints a picture and the artist who writes a novel. The painter *is* able to teach the rudiments of his practice, and it is possible, from the study of good work (granted the aptitude), both to learn how to paint and to learn how to write. Yet it remains true, without injury to the *rapprochement*, that the literary artist would be obliged to say to his pupil much more than the other, "Ah, well, you must do it as you can!" It is a question of degree, a matter of delicacy. If there are exact sciences, there are also exact arts, and the grammar of painting is so much more definite that it makes the difference.

I ought to add, however, that if Mr. Besant says at the beginning of his essay that the "laws of fiction may be laid down and taught with as much precision and exactness as the laws of harmony, perspective, and pro-portion", he mitigates what might appear to be an extragavance by applying his remark to "general" laws, and by expressing most of these rules in a manner with which it would certainly be unaccommodating to disagree. That the novelist must write from his experience, that his "characters must be real and such as might be met with in actual life": that "a young lady brought up in a quiet country village should avoid descriptions of garrison life", and "a writer whose friends and personal experiences belong to the lower middle-class should carefully avoid introducing his characters into society"; that one should enter one's notes in a common-place book; that one's figures should be clear in outline; that making them clear by some trick of speech or of carriage is a bad method, and "describing them at length" is a worse one; that English Fiction should have a "conscious moral purpose"; that "it is almost impossible to estimate too highly the value of careful workmanship—that is, of style"; that "the most important point of all is the story", that "the story is everything": these are principles with most of which it is surely impossible not to sympathize. That remark about the lower middle-class writer and his knowing his place is perhaps rather chilling; but for the rest I should find it difficult to dissent from any one of these recommendations. At the same time, I should find it difficult positively to assent to them, with the exception, perhaps, of the injunction as to entering one's notes in a common-place book. They scarcely seem to me to have the quality that Mr. Besant attributes to the rules of the novelist—the "precision and exactness" of "the laws of harmony, perspective, and pro-portion". They are suggestive, they are even inspiring, but they are not exact, though they are doubtless as much so as the case admits of: which is a proof of that liberty of interpretation for which I just contended. For the value of these different injunctions—so beautiful and so vague—is wholly in the meaning one attaches to them. The characters, the situation, which strike one as real will be those that touch and interest one most, but the measure of reality is very difficult to fix. The reality of Don Quixote or of Mr.

Micawber is a very delicate shade; it is a reality so coloured by the author's vision that, vivid as it may be, one would hesitate to propose it as a model: one would expose one's self to some very embarrassing questions on the part of a pupil. It goes without saying that you will not write a good novel unless you possess the sense of reality; but it will be difficult to give you a recipe for calling that sense into being. Humanity is immense, and reality has a myriad forms; the most one can affirm is that some of the flowers of fiction have the odour of it, and others have not; as for telling you in advance how your nosegay should be composed, that is another affair. It is equally excellent and inconclusive to say that one must write from experience; to our supposititious aspirant such a declaration might savour of mockery. What kind of experience is intended, and where does it begin and end? Experience is never limited, and it is never complete; it is an immense sensibility, a kind of huge spider-web of the finest silken threads suspended in the chamber of consciousness, and catching every air-borne particle in its tissue. It is the very atmosphere of the mind; and when the mind is imaginative—much more when it happens to be that of a man of genius—it takes to itself the faintest hints of life, it converts the very pulses of the air into revelations. The young lady living in a village has only to be a damsel upon whom nothing is lost to make it quite unfair (as it seems to me) to declare to her that she shall have nothing to say about the military. Greater miracles have been seen than that, imagination assisting, she should speak the truth about some of these gentlemen. I remember an English novelist, a woman of genius, telling me that she was much commended for the impression she had managed to give in one of her tales of the nature and way of life of the French Protestant youth.[1] She had been asked where she learned so much about this recondite being, she had been congratulated on her peculiar opportunities. These opportunities consisted in her having once, in Paris, as she ascended a staircase, passed an open door where, in the household of a *pasteur*, some of the young Protestants were seated at table round a finished meal. The glimpse made a picture; it lasted only a moment, but that moment was experience. She had got her direct personal impression, and she turned out her type. She knew what youth was, and what Protestantism; she also had the advantage of having seen what it was to be French, so that she converted these ideas into a concrete image and produced a reality. Above all, however, she was blessed with the faculty which when you give it an inch takes an ell, and which for the artist is a much greater source of strength than any accident of residence or of place in the social scale. The power to guess the unseen from the seen, to trace the implication of things, to judge the whole piece by the pattern, the condition of feeling life in general so completely that you are well on your way to knowing any particular corner of it—this cluster of gifts may almost be said to constitute experience, and they occur

[1] *The Story of Elizabeth*, which James describes, was written by Anne Thackeray, Lady Ritchie, the daughter of Thackeray.

in country and in town and in the most differing stages of education. If experience consists of impressions, it may be said that impressions *are* experience, just as (have we not seen it?) they are the very air we breathe. Therefore, if I should certainly say to a novice, "Write from experience and experience only", I should feel that this was rather a tantalizing monition if I were not careful immediately to add, "Try to be one of the people on whom nothing is lost!"

I am far from intending by this to minimize the importance of exactness —of truth of detail. One can speak best from one's own taste, and I may therefore venture to say that the air of reality (solidity of specification) seems to me to be the supreme virtue of a novel—the merit on which all its other merits (including that conscious moral purpose of which Mr. Besant speaks) helplessly and submissively depend. If it be not there they are all as nothing, and if these be there, they owe their effect to the success with which the author has produced the illusion of life. The cultivation of this success, the study of this exquisite process form, to my taste, the beginning and the end of the art of the novelist. They are his inspiration, his despair, his reward, his torment, his delight. It is here in very truth that he competes with life; it is here that he competes with his brother the painter in *his* attempt to render the look of things, the look that conveys their meaning, to catch the colour, the relief, the expression, the surface, the substance of the human spectacle. It is in regard to this that Mr. Besant is well inspired when he bids him take notes. He cannot possibly take too many, he cannot possibly take enough. All life solicits him, and to "render" the simplest surface, to produce the most momentary illusion, is a very complicated business. His case would be easier, and the rule would be more exact, if Mr. Besant had been able to tell him what notes to take. But this, I fear, he can never learn in any manual; it is the business of his life. He has to take a great many in order to select a few, he has to work them up as he can, and even the guides and philosophers who might have most to say to him must leave him alone when it comes to the application of precepts, as we leave the painter in communion with his palette. That his characters "must be clear in outline", as Mr. Besant says —he feels that down to his boots; but how he shall make them so is a secret between his good angel and himself. It would be absurdly simple if he could be taught that a great deal of "description" would make them so, or that on the contrary the absence of description and the cultivation of dialogue, or the absence of dialogue and the multiplication of "incident", would rescue him from his difficulties. Nothing, for instance, is more possible than that he be of a turn of mind for which this odd, literal opposition of description and dialogue, incident and description, has little meaning and light. People often talk of these things as if they had a kind of internecine distinctness, instead of melting into each other at every breath, and being intimately associated parts of one general effort of expression. I cannot imagine composition exist-ing in a series of blocks, nor conceive, in any novel worth discussing at all, of a passage of description that is not in its intention narrative, a passage of dialogue that is not in its intention descriptive, a touch of truth of any sort that does not partake of the nature of incident, or an incident that derives its interest from any other source than the general and only source of the success of a work of art—that of being illustrative. A novel is a living thing, all one and continuous, like any other organism, and in proportion as it lives will it be found, I think, that in each of the parts there is something of each of the other parts. The critic who over the close texture of a finished work shall pretend to trace a geography of items will mark some frontiers as artificial, I fear, as any that have been known to history. There is an old-fashioned distinction between the novel of character and the novel of incident which must have cost many a smile to the intending fabulist who was keen about his work. It appears to me as little to the point as the equally celebrated distinction between the novel and the romance—to answer as little to any reality. There are bad novels and good novels, as there are bad pictures and good pictures; but that is the only distinction in which I see any meaning, and I can as little imagine speaking of a novel of character as I can imagine speaking of a picture of character. When one says picture one says of character, when one says novel one says of incident, and the terms may be transposed at will. What is character but the determination of incident? What is incident but the illustration of character? What is either a picture or a novel that is *not* of character? What else do we seek in it and find in it? It is an incident for a woman to stand up with her hand resting on a table and look out at you in a certain way; or if it be not an incident I think it will be hard to say what it is. At the same time it is an expression of character. If you say you don't see it (character in *that—allons donc!*), this is exactly what the artist who has reasons of his own for thinking he *does* see it undertakes to show you. When a young man makes up his mind that he has not faith enough after all to enter the church as he intended, that is an incident, though you may not hurry to the end of the chapter to see whether perhaps he doesn't change once more. I do not say that these are extraordinary or startling incidents. I do not pretend to estimate the degree of interest proceeding from them, for this will depend upon the skill of the painter. It sounds almost puerile to say that some incidents are intrinsically much more important than others, and I need not take this precaution after having professed my sympathy for the major ones in remarking that the only classification of the novel that I can understand is into that which has life and that which has it not.

The novel and the romance, the novel of incident and that of character —these clumsy separations appear to me to have been made by critics and readers for their own convenience, and to help them out of some of their occasional queer predicaments, but to have little reality or interest for the producer, from whose point of view it is of course that we are attempting to consider the art of fiction. The case is the same with another shadowy category which Mr. Besant apparently is disposed to set up—that of the "modern English novel"; unless indeed it be that in this matter he has fallen into an accidental confusion of stand-points. It is not quite clear whether he intends the remarks in which he alludes to it to be didactic or historical. It is as difficult to suppose a person intending to write a modern English as to suppose him writing an ancient English novel: that is a label which begs the question. One writes the novel, one paints the picture, of one's language and of one's time, and calling it modern English will not, alas! make the difficult task any easier. No more, unfortunately, will calling this or that work of one's fellow-artist a romance—unless it be, of course, simply for the pleasant-ness of the thing, as for instance when Hawthorne gave this heading to his story of *Blithedale*. The French, who have brought the theory of fiction to remarkable completeness, have but one name for the novel, and have not attempted smaller things in it, that I can see, for that. I can think of no obligation to which the "romancer" would not be held equally with the novelist; the standard of execution is equally high for each. Of course it is of execution that we are talking—that being the only point of a novel that is open to contention. This is perhaps too often lost sight of, only to produce interminable confusions and cross-purposes. We must grant the artist his subject, his idea, his *donnée*:[2] our criticism is applied only to what he makes of it. Naturally I do not mean that we are bound to like it or find it interesting: in case we do not our course is perfectly simple—to let it alone. We may believe that of a certain idea even the most sincere novelist can make nothing at all, and the event may perfectly justify our belief; but the failure will have been a failure to execute, and it is in the execution that the fatal weakness is recorded. If we pretend to respect the artist at all, we must allow him his freedom of choice, in the face, in particular cases, of innumerable pre-sumptions that the choice will not fructify. Art derives a considerable part of its beneficial exercise from flying in the face of presumptions, and some of the most interesting experiments of which it is capable are hidden in the bosom of common things. Gustave Flaubert has written a story about the devotion of a servant-girl to a parrot, and the production, highly finished as it is, cannot on the whole be called a success.[3] We are perfectly free to find it flat, but I think it might have been interesting; and I, for my part, am extremely glad he should have written it; it is a contribution to our knowledge of what can be done—or what cannot. Ivan Turgénieff has written a tale about a deaf and dumb serf and a lap-dog, and the thing is touching, loving, a little masterpiece.[4] He struck the note of life where Gustave Flaubert missed it—he flew in the face of a presumption and achieved a victory.

Nothing, of course, will ever take the place of the good old fashion of "liking" a work of art or not liking it: the most improved criticism will not

[2] *donnée:* information.
[3] *Un coeur simple.*
[4] *Mumu.*

abolish that primitive, that ultimate test. I mention this to guard myself from the accusation of intimating that the idea, the subject, of a novel or a picture, does not matter. It matters, to my sense, in the highest degree, and if I might put up a prayer it would be that artists should select none but the richest. Some, as I have already hastened to admit, are much more remunerative than others, and it would be a world happily arranged in which persons intending to treat them should be exempt from confusions and mistakes. This fortunate condition will arrive only, I fear, on the same day that critics become purged from error. Meanwhile, I repeat, we do not judge the artist with fairness unless we say to him.

Oh, I grant you your starting-point, because if I did not I should seem to prescribe to you, and heaven forbid I should take that responsibility. If I pretend to tell you what you must not take, you will call upon me to tell you then what you must take; in which case I shall be prettily caught. Moreover, it isn't till I have accepted your data that I can begin to measure you. I have the standard, the pitch; I have no right to tamper with your flute and then criticize your music. Of course I may not care for your idea at all; I may think it silly, or stale, or unclean; in which case I wash my hands of you altogether. I may content myself with believing that you will not have succeeded in being interesting, but I shall, of course, not attempt to demonstrate it, and you will be as indifferent to me as I am to you. I needn't remind you that there are all sorts of tastes: who can know it better? Some people, for excellent reasons, don't like to read about carpenters; others for reason even better, don't like to read about courtesans. Many object to Americans. Others (I believe they are mainly editors and publishers) won't look at Italians. Some readers don't like quiet subjects; others don't like bustling ones. Some enjoy a complete illusion, others the consciousness of large concessions. They choose their novels accordingly, and if they don't care about your idea they won't, *a fortiori*, care about your treatment.

So that it comes back very quickly, as I have said, to the liking: in spite of M. Zola, who reasons less powerfully than he represents, and who will not reconcile himself to this absoluteness of taste, thinking that there are certain things that people ought to like, and that they can be made to like. I am quite at a loss to imagine anything (at any rate in this matter of fiction) that people *ought* to like or to dislike. Selection will be sure to take care of itself, for it has a constant motive behind it. That motive is simply experience. As people feel life, so they will feel the art that is most closely related to it. This closeness of relation is what we should never forget in talking of the effort of the novel. Many people speak of it as a factitious, artificial form, a product of ingenuity, the business of which is to alter and arrange the things that surround us, to translate them into conventional, traditional moulds. This, however, is a view of the matter which carries us but a very short way, condemns the art to an eternal repetition of a few familiar *clichés*, cuts short its development and leads us straight up to a dead wall. Catching the very note and trick, the strange irregular rhythm of life, that is the attempt whose strenuous force keeps Fiction upon her feet. In proportion as in what she offers us we see life *without* rearrangement do we feel that we are touching the truth; in proportion as we see it *with* arrangement do we feel that we are being put off with a substitute, a compromise and convention. It is not uncommon to hear an extraordinary assurance of remark in regard to this matter of rearranging, which is often spoken of as if it were the last word of art. Mr. Besant seems to me in danger of falling into the great error with his rather unguarded talk about "selection". Art is essentially selection, but it is a selection whose main care is to be typical, to be inclusive. For many people art means rose-coloured window-panes, and selection means picking a bouquet for Mrs. Grundy. They will tell you glibly that artistic considerations have nothing to do with the disagreeable, with the ugly; they will rattle off shallow common-places about the province of art and the limits of art till you are moved to some wonder in return as to the province and the limits of ignorance. It appears to me that no one can ever have made a seriously artistic attempt without becoming conscious of an immense increase—a kind of revelation—of freedom. One perceives in that case—by the light of a heavenly ray—that the province of art is all life, all feeling, all observation, all vision. As Mr. Besant so justly intimates, it is all experience. That is a sufficient answer to those who maintain that it must not touch the sad things of life, who stick into its divine unconscious bosom little prohibitory inscriptions on the end of sticks, such as we see in public gardens—"It is forbidden to walk on the grass; it is forbidden to touch the flowers; it is not allowed to introduce dogs or to remain after dark; it is requested to keep to the right". The young aspirant in the line of fiction whom we continue to imagine will do nothing without taste, for in that case his freedom would be of little use to him; but the first advantage of his taste will be to reveal to him the absurdity of the little sticks and tickets. If he have taste, I must add, of course he will have ingenuity, and my disrespectful reference to that quality just now was not meant to imply that it is useless in fiction. But it is only a secondary aid; the first is a capacity for receiving straight impressions.

Mr. Besant has some remarks on the question of "the story" which I shall not attempt to criticize, though they seem to me to contain a singular ambiguity, because I do not think I understand them. I cannot see what is meant by talking as if there were a part of a novel which is the story and part of it which for mystical reasons is not—unless indeed the distinction be made in a sense in which it is difficult to suppose that any one should attempt to convey anything. "The story", if it represents anything, represents the subject, the idea, the *donnée* of the novel; and there is surely no "school"—Mr. Besant speaks of a school—which urges that a novel should be all treatment and no subject. There must assuredly be something to treat; every school is intimately conscious of that. This sense of the story being the idea, the starting-point, of the novel, is the only one that I see in which it can be spoken of as something different from its organic whole; and since in proportion as the work is successful the idea permeates and penetrates it, informs and animates it, so that every word and every punctuation-point contribute directly to the expression, in that proportion do we lose our sense of the story being a blade which may be drawn more or less out of its sheath. The story and the novel, the idea and the form, are the needle and thread, and I never heard of a guild of tailors who recommended the use of the thread without the needle, or the needle without the thread. Mr. Besant is not the only critic who may be observed to have spoken as if there were certain things in life which constitute stories, and certain others which do not. I find the same odd implication in an entertaining article in the *Pall Mall Gazette*, devoted, as it happens, to Mr. Besant's lecture. "The story is the thing!" says this graceful writer, as if with a tone of opposition to some other idea. I should think it was, as every painter who, as the time for "sending in" his picture looms in the distance, finds himself still in quest of a subject—as every belated artist not fixed about his theme will heartily agree. There are some subjects which speak to us and others which do not, but he would be a clever man who should undertake to give a rule—an *index expurgatorius*—by which the story and the no-story should be known apart. It is impossible (to me at least) to imagine any such rule which shall not be altogether arbitrary. The writer in the *Pall Mall* opposes the delightful (as I suppose) novel of *Margot la Balafrée* to certain tales in which "Bostonian 'nymphs' appear to have 'rejected English dukes for psychological reasons'". I am not acquainted with the romance just designated, and can scarcely forgive the *Pall Mall* critic for not mentioning the name of the author,[5] but the title appears to refer to a lady who may have received a scar in some heroic adventure. I am inconsolable at not being acquainted with this episode, but am utterly at a loss to see why it is a story when the rejection (or acceptance) of a duke is not, and why a reason, psychological or other, is not a subject when a cicatrix is. They are all particles of the multitudinous life with which the novel deals, and surely no dogma which pretends to make it lawful to touch the one and unlawful to touch the other will stand for a moment on its feet. It is the special picture that must stand or fall, according as it seem to possess truth or to lack it. Mr. Besant does not, to my sense, light up the subject by intimating that a story must, under penalty of not being a story, consist of "adventures". Why of adventures more than of green spectacles? He mentions a category of impossible things, and among them he places "fiction without adventure". Why without adventure, more than without matrimony, or celibacy, or parturition, or cholera, or hydropathy, or Jansenism? This seems to me to bring the novel back to the hapless little *rôle* of being an artificial, ingenious thing—bring it down from its large, free character of an immense and exquisite correspondence with life. And what *is* adventure, when it comes to that, and by what sign is the listening pupil to recognize it? It is an adventure —an immense one—for me to write this little article; and for a Bostonian nymph to reject an English duke is an adventure only less stirring, I should

[5] The author is James himself; the story is *An International Episode* (1879).

say, than for an English duke to be rejected by a Bostonian nymph. I see dramas within dramas in that, and innumerable points of view. A psychological reason is, to my imagination, an object adorably pictorial; to catch the tint of its complexion—I feel as if that idea might inspire one to Titianesque efforts. There are few things more exciting to me, in short, than a psychological reason, and yet, I protest, the novel seems to me the most magnificent form of art. I have just been reading at the same time, the delightful story of *Treasure Island*, by Mr. Robert Louis Stevenson and, in a manner less consecutive, the last tale from M. Edmond de Goncourt, which is entitled *Chérie*. One of these works treats of murders, mysteries, islands of dreadful renown, hair-breadth escapes, miraculous coincidences and buried doubloons. The other treats of a little French girl who lived in a fine house in Paris, and died of wounded sensibility because no one would marry her. I call *Treasure Island* delightful, because it appears to me to have succeeded wonderfully in what it attempts; and I venture to bestow no epithet upon *Chérie*, which strikes me as having failed deplorably in what it attempts—that is in tracing the development of the moral consciousness of a child. But one of these productions strikes me as exactly as much of a novel as the other, and as having a "story" quite as much. The moral consciousness of a child is as much a part of life as the islands of the Spanish Main, and the one sort of geography seems to me to have those "surprises" of which Mr. Besant speaks quite as much as the other. For myself (since it comes back in the last resort, as I say, to the preference of the individual), the picture of the child's experience has the advantage that I can at successive steps (an immense luxury, near to the "sensual pleasure" of which Mr. Besant's critic in the *Pall Mall* speaks) say Yes or No, as it may be, to what the artist puts before me. I have been a child in fact, but I have been on a quest for a buried treasure only in supposition, and it is a simple accident that with M. de Goncourt I should have for the most part to say No. With George Eliot, when she painted that country with a far other intelligence, I always said Yes.

The most interesting part of Mr. Besant's lecture is unfortunately the briefest passage—his very cursory allusion to the "conscious moral purpose" of the novel. Here again it is not very clear whether he be recording a fact or laying down a principle; it is a great pity that in the latter case he should not have developed his idea. This branch of the subject is of immense importance, and Mr. Besant's few words point to considerations of the widest reach, not to be lightly disposed of. He will have treated the art of fiction but superficially who is not prepared to go every inch of the way that these considerations will carry him. It is for this reason that at the beginning of these remarks I was careful to notify the reader that my reflections on so large a theme have no pretension to be exhaustive. Like Mr. Besant, I have left the question of the morality of the novel till the last, and at the last I find I have used up my space. It is a question surrounded with difficulties, as witness the very first that meets us, in the form of a definite question, on the threshold. Vagueness, in such a discussion, is fatal, and what is the meaning of your morality and your conscious moral purpose? Will you not define your terms and explain how (a novel being a picture) a picture can be either moral or immoral? You wish to paint a moral picture or carve a moral statue: will you not tell us how you would set about it? We are discussing the Art of Fiction; questions of art are questions (in the widest sense) of execution; questions of morality are quite another affair, and will you not let us see how it is that you find it so easy to mix them up? These things are so clear to Mr. Besant that he has deduced from them a law which he sees embodied in English Fiction, and which is "a truly admirable thing and a great cause for congratulation". It is a great cause for congratulation indeed when such thorny problems become as smooth as silk. I may add that in so far as Mr. Besant perceives that in point of fact English Fiction has addressed itself preponderantly to these delicate questions he will appear to many people to have made a vain discovery. They will have been positively struck, on the contrary, with the moral timidity of the usual English novelist; with his (or with her) aversion to face the difficulties with which on every side the treatment of reality bristles. He is apt to be extremely shy (whereas the picture that Mr. Besant draws is a picture of boldness), and the sign of his work, for the most part, is a cautious silence on certain subjects. In the English novel (by which of course I mean the American as well), more than in any other, there is a traditional difference between that which people know and that which they agree to admit that they know, that which they see and that which they speak of, that which they feel to be a part of life and that which they allow to enter into literature. There is the great difference, in short, between what they talk of in conversation and what they talk of in print. The essence of moral energy is to survey the whole field, and I should directly reverse Mr. Besant's remark and say not that the English novel has a purpose, but that it has a diffidence. To what degree a purpose in a work of art is a source of corruption I shall not attempt to inquire; the one that seems to me least dangerous is the purpose of making a perfect work. As for our novel, I may say lastly on this score that as we find it in England to-day it strikes me as addressed in a large degree to "young people", and that this in itself constitutes a presumption that it will be rather shy. There are certain things which it is generally agreed not to discuss, not even to mention, before young people. That is very well, but the absence of discussion is not a symptom of the moral passion. The purpose of the English novel—"a truly admirable thing, and a great cause for congratulation"—strikes me therefore as rather negative.

There is one point at which the moral sense and the artistic sense lie very near together; that is in the light of the very obvious truth that the deepest quality of a work of art will always be the quality of the mind of the producer. In proportion as that intelligence is fine will the novel, the picture, the statue partake of the substance of beauty and truth. To be constituted of such elements is, to my vision, to have purpose enough. No good novel will ever proceed from a superficial mind; that seems to me an axiom which, for the artist in fiction, will cover all needful moral ground: if the youthful aspirant take it to heart it will illuminate for him many of the mysteries of "purpose". There are many other useful things that might be said to him, but I have come to the end of my article, and can only touch them as I pass. The critic in the *Pall Mall Gazette*, whom I have already quoted, draws attention to the danger, in speaking of the art of fiction, of generalizing. The danger that he has in mind is rather, I imagine, that of particularizing, for there are some comprehensive remarks which, in addition to those embodied in Mr. Besant's suggestive lecture, might without fear of misleading him be addressed to the ingenuous student. I should remind him first of the magnificence of the form that is open to him, which offers to sight so few restrictions and such innumerable opportunities. The other arts, in comparison, appear confined and hampered; the various conditions under which they are exercised are so rigid and definite. But the only condition that I can think of attaching to the composition of the novel is, as I have already said, that it be sincere. This freedom is a splendid privilege, and the first lesson of the young novelist is to learn to be worthy of it.

Enjoy it as it deserves [I should say to him]; take possession of it, explore it to its utmost extent, publish it, rejoice in it. All life belongs to you, and do not listen either to those who would shut you up into corners of it and tell you that it is only here and there that art inhabits, or to those who would persuade you that this heavenly messenger wings her way outside of life altogether, breathing a superfine air, and turning away her head from the truth of things. There is no impression of life, no manner of seeing it and feeling it, to which the plan of the novelist may not offer a place; you have only to remember that talents so dissimilar as those of Alexandre Dumas and Jane Austen, Charles Dickens and Gustave Flaubert have worked in this field with equal glory. Do not think too much about optimism and pessimism; try and catch the colour of life itself. In France to-day we see a prodigious effort (that of Emile Zola, to whose solid and serious work no explorer of the capacity of the novel can allude without respect), we see an extraordinary effort vitiated by a spirit of pessimism on a narrow basis. M. Zola is magnificent, but he strikes an English reader as ignorant; he has an air of working in the dark; if he had as much light as energy, his results would be of the highest value. As for the aberrations of a shallow optimism, the ground (of English fiction especially), is strewn with their brittle particles as with broken glass. If you must indulge in conclusions, let them have the taste of a wide knowledge. Remember that your first duty is to be as complete as possible—to make as perfect a work. Be generous and delicate and pursue the prize.

25

ROBERT LOUIS STEVENSON

(1850–1894)

Three months after James's credo of realism in "The Art of Fiction" appeared, Robert Louis Stevenson expressed his formal disagreement and a statement of the aims of romance in "A Humble Remonstrance," published in the same periodical. The emphasis on the Jamesian analytical novel of character had provoked by way of reaction a renaissance of the novel of adventure, and Stevenson became the champion of such romancers as Kipling and Barrie. The two essays stand at the head of the opposing schools of fiction.

Although we now see that Stevenson's challenge of James's position was unsuccessful, his essay "remains a valued nineteenth-century statement by a writer on his art" (Leon Edel, "Introduction," *The Future of the Novel: Essays on the Art of Fiction*, New York, 1956, p. xiv). Its value is emphasized by a modern critic, David Daiches:

. . . our serious modern critics hang on every word which James has to utter about the art of fiction, and nobody has anything to say for Stevenson's remarks on the subject. You will look in vain in any anthology of criticism prepared for college students of literature for Stevenson's essay, "A Humble Remonstrance," which appeared in December 1884 as a reply to James's article, "The Art of Fiction," which came out the previous September and which all our brighter students know about. Yet Stevenson's essay is as penetrating a study as James's; it takes some of James's points and qualifies them and develops them in a way that aroused James's warm admiration. Further, the whole attitude displayed by Stevenson to his art is thoroughly congenial to the modern mind.

—*Stevenson and the Art of Fiction* (New York, 1951), pp. 6–7.

In addition to categorizing novels and giving advice to young writers, Stevenson makes the point that fiction is not to be confused with life. A later essay, "Books Which Have Influenced Me" (1887), defines his attitude:

The most influential books, and the truest in their influence, are works of fiction. They do not pin the reader to a dogma which he must afterwards discover to be inexact; they do not teach him a lesson which he must afterwards unlearn. They repeat, they rearrange, they clarify the lessons of life; they disengage us from ourselves, they constrain us to the acquaintance of others; and they show us—that web of experience, not as we can see it for ourselves, but with a singular change—that monstrous, consuming *ego* of ours being, for the nonce, struck out. To be so, they must be reasonably true to the human comedy; and any work that is so serves the turn of instruction.

Stevenson's own life was a romance, determined in large degree by a chronic, lifelong bronchial affliction which at first led to omnivorous reading to supplement his irregular education and later prompted him to travel extensively in search of health. Having no inclination for the family profession of designing lighthouses, he agreed to study law and was called to the bar in 1875 but never practiced. Finding himself adept in describing his frequent excursions in essays and travel books, he proved himself a versatile writer by producing numerous short stories (some collected as *The New Arabian Nights*, 1882) for the newly enlarged magazine market, a dozen novels, some plays, poems, and essays. When he went to California to marry an American woman he had met in France, he continued his travels until he settled in Samoa, writing constantly in various genres and striving for an effective prose style.

As a novelist Stevenson has had his detractors, who point to his adventure, active heroes, and exotic settings as the traditional ingredients of romance, and observe that in comparison with his other work he wrote few novels. Another view is that his achievement in the short story obscures his work in the novel. It is true that some of his novels are addressed to a juvenile audience and thus limit the number that can be evaluated without reservation. Of these, *Treasure Island* (1883), *The Black Arrow* (1888), and *Kidnapped* (1886) are the best known. *The Master of Ballantrae* (1889) is his first adult novel; in this category may be mentioned the unfinished *Weir of Hermiston* (1896). Certainly we may consider that Stevenson had a large influence on such disciples as Anthony Hope (*The Prisoner of Zenda*, 1894), Henry Rider Haggard (*King Solomon's Mines*, 1885), and Arthur Conan Doyle (*The Lost World*, 1912). Furthermore, the revival of the horror tale was initiated by Stevenson's most famous piece of fiction, *The Strange Case of Dr. Jekyll and Mr. Hyde* (1886).

As a practicing artist, Stevenson was always conscious of his techniques. Atmosphere plays an important part in his fiction. He experimented with point of view and utilized the detached narrator in a manner that closely agrees with James's precepts. In a letter of 1884 to James, who became a friend as well as an antagonist, he comments on the mistaken public belief that striking situations and good dialog result from a study of life, whereas they derive from deliberate artifice. Likewise, in "Some Gentlemen in Fiction" (1888), he destroys a common illusion of laymen that character is a Pygmalion miracle; character is the result of technical artifice, mechanical necessity, and convention. Other critical essays published in various periodicals concern literature in general rather than the novel in particular. He maintains the duty of the author to truth in "The Morality of the Profession of Letters" (1881); he defines realism as method rather than subject in "A Note on Realism" (1883); and he states that the true aim of the creative writer is to satisfy the longings and daydreams of the reader, in "A Gossip on Romance" (1882).

A HUMBLE REMONSTRANCE
(1884)

I

We have recently enjoyed a quite peculiar pleasure: hearing, in some detail, the opinions, about the art they practise, of Mr. Walter Besant and Mr. Henry James; two men certainly of very different calibre: Mr. James so precise of outline, so cunning of fence, so scrupulous of finish, and Mr. Besant so genial, so friendly, with so persuasive and humorous a vein of whim: Mr. James the very type of the deliberate artist, Mr. Besant the impersonation of good nature. That such doctors should differ will excite no great surprise; but one point in which they seem to agree fills me, I confess, with wonder. For they are both content to talk about the "art of fiction"; and Mr. Besant, waxing exceedingly bold, goes on to oppose this so-called "art of fiction" to the "art of poetry." By the art of poetry he can mean nothing but the art of verse, an art of handicraft, and only comparable with the art of prose. For that heat and height of sane emotion which we agree to call by the name of poetry, is but a libertine and vagrant quality; present, at times, in any art, more often absent from them all; too seldom present in the prose novel, too frequently absent from the ode and epic. Fiction is in the same case; it is no substantive art, but an element which enters largely into all the arts but architecture. Homer, Wordsworth, Phidias, Hogarth, and Salvini, all deal in fiction; and yet I do not suppose that either Hogarth or Salvini, to mention but these two, entered in any degree into the scope of Mr. Besant's interesting lecture or Mr. James's charming essay. The art of fiction, then, regarded as a definition, is both too ample and too scanty. Let me suggest another; let me suggest that what both Mr. James and Mr. Besant had in view was neither more nor less than the art of narrative.

But Mr. Besant is anxious to speak solely of "the modern English novel," the stay and breadwinner of Mr. Mudie;[1] and in the author of the most pleasing novel on that roll, *All Sorts and Conditions of Men*, the desire is natural enough. I can conceive then, that he would hasten to propose two additions, and read thus: the art of *fictitious* narrative *in prose*.

Now the fact of the existence of the modern English novel is not to be denied; materially, with its three volumes, leaded type, and gilded lettering,

---

[1] Charles E. Mudie (1818–90), founder of Mudie's Lending Library.

it is easily distinguishable from other forms of literature; but to talk at all fruitfully of any branch of art, it is needful to build our definitions on some more fundamental ground than binding. Why, then, are we to add "in prose"? *The Odyssey* appears to me the best of romances; *The Lady of the Lake* to stand high in the second order; and Chaucer's tales and prologues to contain more of the matter and art of the modern English novel than the whole treasury of Mr. Mudie. Whether a narrative be written in blank verse or the Spenserian stanza, in the long period of Gibbon or the chipped phrase of Charles Reade, the principles of the art of narrative must be equally observed. The choice of a noble and swelling style in prose affects the problem of narration in the same way, if not to the same degree, as the choice of measured verse; for both imply a closer synthesis of events, a higher key of dialogue, and a more picked and stately strain of words. If you are to refuse *Don Juan*, it is hard to see why you should include *Zanoni* or (to bracket works of very different value) *The Scarlet Letter*; and by what discrimination are you to open your doors to *The Pilgrim's Progress* and close them on *The Faery Queen*? To bring things closer home, I will here propound to Mr. Besant a conundrum. A narrative called *Paradise Lost* was written in English verse by one John Milton; what was it then? It was next translated by Chateaubriand into French prose; and what was it then? Lastly, the French translation was, by some inspired compatriot of George Gilfillan (and of mine) turned bodily into an English novel; and, in the name of clearness, what was it then?

But, once more, why should we add "fictitious"? The reason why is obvious. The reason why not, if something more recondite, does not want for weight. The art of narrative, in fact, is the same, whether it is applied to the selection and illustration of a real series of events or of an imaginary series. Boswell's *Life of Johnson* (a work of cunning and inimitable art) owes its success to the same technical manœuvres as (let us say) *Tom Jones*: the clear conception of certain characters of man, the choice and presentation of certain incidents out of a great number that offered, and the invention (yes, invention) and preservation of a certain key in dialogue. In which these things are done with the more art—in which with the greater air of nature—readers will differently judge. Boswell's is, indeed, a very special case, and almost a generic; but it is not only in Boswell, it is in every biography with any salt of life, it is in every history where events and men, rather than ideas, are presented—in Tacitus, in Carlyle, in Michelet, in Macaulay—that the novelist will find many of his own methods most conspicuously and adroitly handled. He will find besides that he, who is free—who has the right to invent or steal a missing incident, who has the right, more precious still, of wholesale omission—is frequently defeated, and, with all his advantages, leaves a less strong impression of reality and passion. Mr. James utters his mind with a becoming fervour on the sanctity of truth to the novelist; on a more careful examination truth will seem a word of very debatable propriety, not only for the labours of the novelist, but for those of the historian. No art—to use the daring phrase of Mr. James—can successfully "compete with life"; and the art that seeks to do so is condemned to perish *montibus aviis.*[2] Life goes before us, infinite in complication; attended by the most various and surprising meteors; appealing at once to the eye, to the ear, to the mind—the seat of wonder, to the touch—so thrillingly delicate, and to the belly—so imperious when starved. It combines and employs in its mani- festation the method and material, not of one art only, but of all the arts. Music is but an arbitrary trifling with a few of life's majestic chords; painting is but a shadow of its pageantry of light and colour; literature does but drily indicate that wealth of incident, of moral obligation, of virtue, vice, action, rapture, and agony, with which it teems. To "compete with life," whose sun we cannot look upon, whose passions and diseases waste and slay us—to compete with the flavour of wine, the beauty of the dawn, the scorching of fire, the bitterness of death and separation—here is, indeed, a projected escalade of heaven; here are, indeed, labours for a Hercules in a dress coat, armed with a pen and a dictionary to depict the passions, armed with a tube of superior flake-white to paint the portrait of the insufferable sun. No art is true in this sense: none can "compete with life": not even history, built indeed of indisputable facts, but these facts robbed of their vivacity and sting; so that even when we read of the sack of a city or the fall of an empire, we are surprised, and justly commend the author's talent, if our pulse be quickened. And mark, for a last *differentia,* that this quickening of the pulse is, in almost every case, purely agreeable; that these phantom reproductions of experience, even at their most acute, convey decided pleasure; while experience itself, in the cockpit of life, can torture and slay.

What, then, is the object, what the method, of an art, and what the source of its power? The whole secret is that no art does "compete with life." Man's one method, whether he reasons or creates, is to half-shut his eyes against the dazzle and confusion of reality. The arts, like arithmetic and geometry, turn away their eyes from the gross, coloured and mobile nature at our feet, and regard instead a certain figmentary abstraction. Geometry will tell us of a circle, a thing never seen in nature; asked about a green circle or an iron circle, it lays its hand upon its mouth. So with the arts. Painting, ruefully comparing sunshine and flake-white, gives up truth of colour, as it had already given up relief and movement; and instead of vying with nature, arranges a scheme of harmonious tints. Literature, above all in its most typical mood, the mood of narrative, similarly flees the direct challenge and pursues instead an independent and creative aim. So far as it imitates at all, it imitates not life but speech: not the facts of human destiny, but the emphasis and the suppressions with which the human actor tells of them. The real art that dealt with life directly was that of the first men who told their stories round the savage camp-fire. Our art is occupied, and bound

[2] *montibus aviis:* in untrodden mountains.—Horace, *Odes* I. 23. 2.

to be occupied, not so much in making stories true as in making them typical; not so much in capturing the lineaments of each fact, as in marshalling all of them towards a common end. For the welter of impressions, all forcible but all discreet, which life presents, it substitutes a certain artificial series of impressions, all indeed most feebly represented, but all aiming at the same effect, all eloquent of the same idea, all chiming together like consonant notes in music or like the graduated tints in a good picture. From all its chapters, from all its pages, from all its sentences, the well-written novel echoes and re-echoes its one creative and controlling thought; to this must every incident and character contribute; the style must have been pitched in unison with this; and if there is anywhere a word that looks another way, the book would be stronger, clearer, and (I had almost said) fuller without it. Life is monstrous, infinite, illogical, abrupt and poignant; a work of art, in comparison, is neat, finite, self-contained, rational, flowing and emasculate. Life imposes by brute energy, like inarticulate thunder; art catches the ear, among the far louder noises of experience, like an air artificially made by a discreet musician. A proposition of geometry does not compete with life; and a proposition of geometry is a fair and luminous parallel for a work of art. Both are reasonable, both untrue to the crude fact; both inhere in nature, neither represents it. The novel, which is a work of art, exists, not by its resemblances to life, which are forced and material, as a shoe must still consist of leather, but by its immeasurable difference from life, which is designed and significant, and is both the method and the meaning of the work.

The life of man is not the subject of novels, but the inexhaustible magazine from which subjects are to be selected; the name of these is legion; and with each new subject—for here again I must differ by the whole width of heaven from Mr. James—the true artist will vary his method and change the point of attack. That which was in one case an excellence, will become a defect in another; what was the making of one book, will in the next be impertinent or dull. First each novel, and then each class of novels, exists by and for itself. I will take, for instance, three main classes, which are fairly distinct: first, the novel of adventure, which appeals to certain almost sensual and quite illogical tendencies in man; second, the novel of character, which appeals to our intellectual appreciation of man's foibles and mingled and inconstant motives; and third, the dramatic novel, which deals with the same stuff as the serious theatre, and appeals to our emotional nature and moral judgment.

And first for the novel of adventure. Mr. James refers, with singular generosity of praise, to a little book about a quest for hidden treasure;[3] but he lets fall, by the way, some rather startling words. In this book he misses what he calls the "immense luxury" of being able to quarrel with his author. The luxury, to most of us, is to lay by our judgment, to be submerged by the tale as by a billow, and only to awake, and begin to distinguish and find fault,

---

[3] Stevenson's own *Treasure Island*.

when the piece is over and the volume laid aside. Still more remarkable is
Mr. James's reason. He cannot criticise the author, as he goes, "because,"
says he, comparing it with another work, "*I have been a child, but I have never
been on a quest for buried treasure.*" Here is, indeed, a wilful paradox; for if he
has never been on a quest for buried treasure, it can be demonstrated that he
has never been a child. There never was a child (unless Master James) but
has hunted gold, and been a pirate, and a military commander, and a bandit
of the mountains; but has fought, and suffered shipwreck and prison, and
imbrued its little hands in gore, and gallantly retrieved the lost battle, and
triumphantly protected innocence and beauty. Elsewhere in his essay
Mr. James has protested with excellent reason against too narrow a conception of experience; for the born artist, he contends, the "faintest hints of
life" are converted into revelations; and it will be found true, I believe, in a
majority of cases, that the artist writes with more gusto and effect of those
things which he has only wished to do, than of those which he has done.
Desire is a wonderful telescope, and Pisgah the best observatory. Now, while
it is true that neither Mr. James nor the author of the work in question has
ever, in the fleshy sense, gone questing after gold, it is probable that both
have ardently desired and fondly imagined the details of such a life in
youthful daydreams; and the author, counting upon that, and well aware
(cunning and low-minded man!) that this class of interest, having been
frequently treated, finds a readily accessible and beaten road to the sympathies of the reader, addressed himself throughout to the building up and
circumstantiation of this boyish dream. Character to the boy is a sealed
book; for him, a pirate is a beard, a pair of wide trousers, and a liberal complement of pistols. The author, for the sake of circumstantiation and because
he was himself more or less grown up, admitted character, within certain
limits, into his design; but only within certain limits. Had the same puppets
figured in a scheme of another sort, they had been drawn to very different
purpose; for in this elementary novel of adventure, the characters need to be
presented with but one class of qualities—the warlike and formidable. So as
they appear insidious in deceit and fatal in the combat, they have served their
end. Danger is the matter with which this class of novel deals; fear, the
passion with which it idly trifles; and the characters are portrayed only so
far as they realise the sense of danger and provoke the sympathy of fear. To
add more traits, to be too clever, to start the hare of moral or intellectual
interest while we are running the fox of material interest, is not to enrich but
to stultify your tale. The stupid reader will only be offended, and the clever
reader lose the scent.

The novel of character has this difference from all others: that it
requires no coherency of plot, and for this reason, as in the case of *Gil Blas*, it
is sometimes called the novel of adventure. It turns on the humours of the
persons represented; these are, to be sure, embodied in incidents, but the
incidents themselves, being tributary, need not march in a progression; and

the characters may be statically shown. As they enter, so they may go out; they must be consistent, but they need not grow. Here Mr. James will recognise the note of much of his own work: he treats, for the most part, the statics of character, studying it at rest or only gently moved; and, with his usual delicate and just artistic instinct, he avoids those stronger passions which would deform the attitudes he loves to study, and change his sitters from the humourists of ordinary life to the brute forces and bare types of more emotional moments. In his recent *Author of Beltraffio*, so just in conception, so nimble and neat in workmanship, strong passion is indeed employed; but observe that it is not displayed. Even in the heroine the working of the passion is suppressed; and the great struggle, the true tragedy, the *scène-à-faire*,[4] passes unseen behind the panels of a locked door. The delectable invention of the young visitor is introduced, consciously or not, to this end: that Mr. James, true to his method, might avoid the scene of passion. I trust no reader will suppose me guilty of undervaluing this little masterpiece. I mean merely that it belongs to one marked class of novel, and that it would have been very differently conceived and treated had it belonged to that other marked class, of which I now proceed to speak.

I take pleasure in calling the dramatic novel by that name, because it enables me to point out by the way a strange and peculiarly English misconception. It is sometimes supposed that the drama consists of incident. It consists of passion, which gives the actor his opportunity; and that passion must progressively increase, or the actor, as the piece proceeded, would be unable to carry the audience from a lower to a higher pitch of interest and emotion. A good serious play must therefore be founded on one of the passionate *cruces* of life, where duty and inclination come nobly to the grapple; and the same is true of what I call, for that reason, the dramatic novel. I will instance a few worthy specimens, all of our own day and language; Meredith's *Rhoda Fleming*, that wonderful and painful book, long out of print,[5] and hunted for at book-stalls like an Aldine; Hardy's *Pair of Blue Eyes*; and two of Charles Reade's, *Griffith Gaunt* and *The Double Marriage*, originally called *White Lies*, and founded (by an accident quaintly favourable to my nomenclature) on a play by Maquet, the partner of the great Dumas. In this kind of novel the closed door of *The Author of Beltraffio* must be broken open; passion must appear upon the scene and utter its last word; passion is the be-all and the end-all, the plot of the solution, the protagonist and the *deus ex machina* in one. The characters may come anyhow upon the stage: we do not care; the point is, that, before they leave it, they shall become transfigured and raised out of themselves by passion. It may be part of the design to draw them with detail; to depict a full-length character, and then behold it melt and change in the furnace of emotion. But there is no obligation of the sort; nice portraiture is not required; and we are content to accept mere abstract

[4] *scène-à-faire*: the big scene.
[5] Now no longer so, thank Heaven! [Stevenson, 1887]

types, so they be strongly and sincerely moved. A novel of this class may be even great, and yet contain no individual figure; it may be great, because it displays the workings of the perturbed heart and the impersonal utterance of passion; and with an artist of the second class it is, indeed, even more likely to be great, when the issue has thus been narrowed and the whole force of the writer's mind directed to passion alone. Cleverness again, which has its fair field in the novel of character, is debarred all entry upon this more solemn theatre. A far-fetched motive, an ingenious evasion of the issue, a witty instead of a passionate turn, offend us like an insincerity. All should be plain, all straightforward to the end. Hence it is that, in *Rhoda Fleming*, Mrs. Lovel raises such resentment in the reader; her motives are too flimsy, her ways are too equivocal, for the weight and strength of her surroundings. Hence the hot indignation of the reader when Balzac, after having begun the *Duchess de Langeais* in terms of strong if somewhat swollen passion, cuts the knot by the derangement of the hero's clock. Such personages and incidents belong to the novel of character; they are out of place in the high society of the passions; when the passions are introduced in art at their full height, we look to see them, not baffled and impotently striving, as in life, but towering above circumstance and acting substitutes for fate.

And here I can imagine Mr. James, with his lucid sense, to intervene. To much of what I have said he would apparently demur; in much he would, somewhat impatiently, acquiesce. It may be true; but it is not what he desired to say or to hear said. He spoke of the finished picture and its worth when done; I, of the brushes, the palette, and the north light. He uttered his views in the tone and for the ear of good society; I, with the emphasis and technicalities of the obtrusive student. But the point, I may reply, is not merely to amuse the public, but to offer helpful advice to the young writer. And the young writer will not so much be helped by genial pictures of what an art may aspire to at its highest, as by a true idea of what it must be on the lowest terms. The best that we can say to him is this: Let him choose a motive, whether of character or passion; carefully construct his plot so that every incident is an illustration of the motive, and every property employed shall bear to it a near relation of congruity or contrast; avoid a sub-plot, unless, as sometimes in Shakespeare, the sub-plot be a reversion or complement of the main intrigue; suffer not his style to flag below the level of the argument: pitch the key of conversation, not with any thought of how men talk in parlours, but with a single eye to the degree of passion he may be called on to express; and allow neither himself in the narrative nor any character in the course of the dialogue, to utter one sentence that is not part and parcel of the business of the story or the discussion of the problem involved. Let him not regret if this shortens his book; it will be better so; for to add irrelevant matter is not to lengthen but to bury. Let him not mind if he miss a thousand qualities, so that he keeps unflaggingly in pursuit of the one he has chosen. Let him not care particularly if he miss the tone of conversation, the pungent material detail of the day's manners, the reproduction of the atmosphere and the environment. These elements are not essential: a novel may be excellent, and yet have none of them; a passion or a character is so much better depicted as it rises clearer from material circumstance. In this age of the particular, let him remember the ages of the abstract, the great books of the past, the brave men that lived before Shakespeare and before Balzac. And as the root of the whole matter, let him bear in mind that his novel is not a transcript of life, to be judged by its exactitude; but a simplification of some side or point of life, to stand or fall by its significant simplicity. For although, in great men, working upon great motives, what we observe and admire is often their complexity, yet underneath appearances the truth remains unchanged: that simplification was their method, and that simplicity is their excellence.

II

Since the above was written[6] another novelist has entered repeatedly the lists of theory: one well worthy of mention, Mr. W. D. Howells; and none ever couched a lance with narrower convictions. His own work and those of his pupils and masters singly occupy his mind; he is the bondslave, the zealot of his school; he dreams of an advance in art like what there is in science; he thinks of past things as radically dead; he thinks a form can be outlived: a strange immersion in his own history; a strange forgetfulness of the history of the race! Meanwhile, by a glance at his own works (could he see them with the eager eyes of his readers) much of this illusion would be dispelled. For while he holds all the poor little orthodoxies of the day—no poorer and no smaller than those of yesterday, or to-morrow, poor and small, indeed, only so far as they are exclusive—the living quality of much that he has done is of a contrary, I had almost said of a heretical, complexion. A man, as I read him, of an originally strong romantic bent—a certain glow of romance still resides in many of his books, and lends them their distinction. As by accident he runs out and revels in the exceptional; and it is then, as often as not, that his reader rejoices—justly, as I contend. For in all this excessive eagerness to be centrally human, is there not one central human thing that Mr. Howells is too often tempted to neglect: I mean himself? A poet, a finished artist, a man in love with the appearances of life, a cunning reader of the mind, he has other passions and aspirations than those he loves to draw. And why should he suppress himself and do such reverence to the Lemuel Barkers? The obvious is not of necessity the normal; fashion rules and deforms; the majority fall tamely into the contemporary shape, and thus attain, in the eyes of the true observer, only a higher power of insignificance; and the danger is lest, in seeking to draw the normal, a man should draw the null, and write the novel of society instead of the romance of man.

[6] Section II was added when the essay was collected in *Memories and Portraits* (1887).

26

GEORGE MOORE

(1852–1933)

Although it is still too early for critical opinion to agree on his importance, George Moore has not generally been accorded major status as a novelist. Yet his contributions to fiction are considerable. In 1870, on the death of his father, an Irish country gentleman and Member of Parliament, Moore used his inheritance to spend several years in France, where he studied art, dabbled in poetry, and became a disciple of Zola and the naturalistic novelists. His first novel, *A Modern Lover* (1883), as well as several others written during the next few years, were strongly influenced by these French authors. His adoption of their technique was a means of freeing English fiction from Victorian prudery.

The vivid realism of *A Mummer's Wife* (1885), the story of a woman who deserted her husband for a strolling player and eventually died of drink, led to its being banned on moral grounds by Mudie's famous circulating library. Moore's response was a threepenny pamphlet, *Literature at Nurse, or Circulating Morals* (1885), attacking the censorship exerted by the circulating libraries as a serious handicap for authors attempting to treat contemporary moral and religious problems. This essay belongs with those notable critiques published in the 1880's by Hardy, Gissing, James, Stevenson, and others, marking not only changing theories and a more serious attitude toward fiction but also the more general use of the essay for the expression of authorial commentary.

Although legal, social, and economic forces had been at work to change the role of women in British society from the reticent, dependent type depicted by Jane Austen to the emancipated, independent, educated woman of George Meredith's novels, the novelistic depiction of her new freedoms needed a champion, and Moore is thought of primarily as a crusader—defending the right of fiction to present truth. By the time his most important novel, *Esther Waters* (1894), appeared, his naturalism had been toned down, and its large sale, stimulated by Gladstone's public approval, overcame the reluctance of

266

the circulating libraries to distribute it. His battle against prudish suppression of truth and moral censorship had been won.

A Mummer's Wife defied convention also by appearing in a single volume. The rebellion against the tyranny of the three-volume format, established by Scott, spread rapidly, and by 1892 it was virtually extinct—thanks primarily to Moore's courage.

Character study became increasingly important in *Evelyn Innes* (1898) and its sequel *Sister Teresa* (1901). So also did form and style—so much so that Moore even rewrote his novels, improving their language and changing their plots and conclusions. It is almost as if he had published his first drafts and, later, his final revisions.

Moving from Ireland to London about 1910, Moore spent some time traveling. He tried his hand—with indifferent success—at drama. Two later works of fiction usually mentioned in studies of the novel are a story of Jesus, *The Brook Kerith* (1916) and a medieval romance, *Héloise and Abélard* (1921).

Of Moore as a critic of the novel, Kenneth Graham has this to say:

His perceptions are at times acute and original, but they are never followed up with much rigour. He is a novelist, responding with sensitivity to the practice of other novelists, and his comments are often better suited to stimulate a fellow-writer than to form part of a full theory of fiction.

—*English Criticism of the Novel 1865–1900* (Oxford, 1965), pp. 119–20.

In addition to his opinions on censorship, Moore makes some interesting observations on structure. *Confessions of a Young Man* (1888), his autobiography, observes:

A sequence of events—it does not matter how simple or how complicated—working up to a logical close, or, shall I say, a close in which there is a sense of rhythm and inevitableness, is always indicative of genius. . . . But in contemporary English fiction I marvel, and I am repeatedly struck by the inability of writers, even of the first class, to make an organic whole of their stories.

A letter of 13 August 1921 to Nancy Cunard, given in her *Memories of George Moore* (London, 1956) contains this passage:

The difficulty of story writing is the even distribution of the theme throughout the chapters. My difficulty is always with the first two or three chapters, most people's with the last, and the explanation of this is that I always write with the end in view, almost gluttonously like a child at the cake during dinner.

Many of Moore's critical articles were collected as *Impressions and Opinions* (1891). In them he discusses such questions as "Whether the writer should intrude his idea on the reader, or leave it latent in the work"; this "is a question of method; and all methods are good." He classifies novelists into "the thought school, and the fact school," defining his statement in *Confessions* that "Art is not nature. Art is nature digested." He argues that "The impersonality of the artist is the vainest of delusions." Techniques of style and character presentation may be learned, he felt, as he himself learned, but for genuine success there must be an instinct for story telling, a serious attitude, and a depth of thought.

FROM "LITERATURE AT NURSE
OR CIRCULATING MORALS"
(1885)

This paper should have been offered to *The Nineteenth Century*, but as, for purely commercial reasons, it would be impossible for any English magazine to print it, I give it to the public in pamphlet form.

In an article contributed to the *Pall Mall Gazette* last December,[1] I called attention to the fact that English writers were subject to the censorship of a tradesman who, although doubtless an excellent citizen and a worthy father, was scarcely competent to decide the delicate and difficult artistic questions that authors in their struggles for new ideals might raise: questions that could and should be judged by time alone. I then proceeded to show how, to retain their power, the proprietors of the large circulating libraries exact that books shall be issued at extragavant prices, and be supplied to them at half the published rate, or even less, thus putting it out of the power of the general public to become purchasers, and effectually frustrating the right of the latter to choose for themselves.

The case, so far as I am individually concerned, stands thus: In 1883, I published a novel called "A Modern Lover." It met with the approval of the entire press; *The Athenæum* and *The Spectator* declared emphatically that it was not immoral; but Mr. Mudie told me that two ladies in the country had written to him to say that they disapproved of the book, and on that account he could not circulate it. I answered, "You are acting in defiance of the opinion of the press—you are taking a high position indeed, and one from which you will probably be overthrown. I, at least, will have done with you; for I shall find a publisher willing to issue my next book at a purchasable price, and so enable me to appeal direct to the public." Mr. Mudie tried to wheedle, attempted to dissuade me from my rash resolution; he advised me to try another novel in three volumes. Fortunately I disregarded his suggestion, and my next book, "A Mummer's Wife," was published at the price of six shillings. The result exceeded my expectations, for the book is now in its fourth edition. The press saw no immoral tendency in it, indeed *The Athenæum* said that it was "remarkably free from the elements of uncleanness." Therefore it is not with a failing but with a firm heart that I return to the

[1] "A New Censorship of Literature," *Pall Mall Gazette*, XL (10 December 1884), in which he demands for the novel seriousness, depth of life, and thought.

fight—a fight which it is my incurable belief must be won if we are again to possess a literature worthy of the name. This view of the question may be regarded by some as quixotic, but I cannot forget that my first article on the subject awakened a polemic that lasted several weeks, giving rise to scores of articles and some hundreds of paragraphs. The *Saturday Review* wrote, "Michel Lévy saved France with cheap publications, who will save England?" Thus encouraged, I yield again to the temptation to speak upon a subject which on such high authority is admitted to be one of national importance. Nor do I write influenced by fear of loss or greed of gain. The "select" circulating libraries can no longer injure me; I am now free to write as I please, and whether they take or refuse my next novel is to me a matter of indifference. But there are others who are not in this position, who are still debutants, and whose artistic aspirations are being crushed beneath the wheels of these implacable Juggernauts. My interest in the question is centred herein, and I should have confined myself to merely denouncing the irresponsible censorship exercised over literature if I did not hear almost daily that when "A Mummer's Wife" is asked for at Mudie's, and the assistants are pressed to say why the book cannot be obtained, they describe it as an immoral publication which the library would not be justified in circulating.

Being thus grossly attacked, it has occurred to me to examine the clothing of some of the dolls passed by our virtuous librarian as being decently attired, and to see for myself if there be not an exciting bit of bosom exhibited here and a naughty view of an ankle shown there; to assure myself, in fact, if all the frocks are modestly set as straight as the title Select Library would lead us to expect.

Perhaps of all moral theories, to do unto others as you would be done unto meets with the most unhesitating approval. Therefore my *confrères*, of whose works I am going to speak, will have nothing to complain of. I shall commence by indicating the main outlines of my story of "A Mummer's Wife," appending the passage that gained it refusal at Mudie's; then I shall tell the stories of three fashionable novels (all of which were, and no doubt still are, in circulation at Mudie's Select Library), appending extracts that will fairly set before the reader the kind of treatment adopted in each case. The public will thus be able to judge between Mr. Mudie and me.

Now as to "A Mummer's Wife." Kate Ede is the wife of an asthmatic draper in Hanley. Attending her husband's sick-bed and selling reels of cotton over the little counter, her monotonous life flows unrelieved by hope, love, or despair. To make a few extra shillings a week the Edes let their front rooms, which are taken by Mr. Dick Lennox, the manager of an opera bouffe company on tour. He makes love to the draper's wife, seduces her, and she elopes with him. She travels about with the actors, and gradually becomes one of them; she walks among the chorus, speaks a few words, says a few verses, and is eventually developed into a heroine of comic opera. The life, therefore, that up to seven-and-twenty knew no excitement, no change of thought or place, now knows neither rest nor peace. Even marriage—for Dick Lennox marries her when Ralph Ede obtains his divorce—is unable to calm the alienation of the brain that so radical a change of life has produced, and after the birth of her baby she takes to drink, sinks lower and lower until death from dropsy and liver complaint in a cheap lodging saves her from becoming one of the street-walkers with whom she is in the habit of associating. That is my story; here is the passage objected to:—

At last she felt him moving like one about to awake, and a moment after she heard him say, "There's Mr. Lennox at the door; he can't get in; he's kicking up an awful row. Do go down and open for him."

"Why don't you go yourself," she answered, starting into a sitting position.

"How am I to go? you don't want me to catch my death at that door?" Ralph replied angrily.

Kate did not answer, but quickly tying a petticoat about her, and wrapping herself in her dressing-gown, she went downstairs. It was quite dark and she had to feel her way along. At last, however, she found and pulled back the latch, but when the white gleam of moonlight entered she retreated timidly behind the door.

"I am sorry," said Dick, trying to see who was the concealed figure, "but I forgot my latch-key."

"It does not matter," said Kate.

"Oh, it is you, dear! I have been trying to get home all day, but couldn't. Why didn't you come down to the theatre?"

"You know that I can't do as I like."

"Well, never mind; don't be cross; give me a kiss."

Kate shrunk back, but Dick took her in his arms. "You were in bed then?" he said, chuckling.

"Yes, but you must let me go."

"I should like never to let you go again."

"But you are leaving to-morrow."

"Not unless you wish me to, dear."

Kate did not stop to consider the impossibility of his fulfilling his promise, and, her heart beating, she went upstairs. On the first landing he stopped her, and laying his hand on her arm, said, "And would you really be very glad if I were to stay with you?"

"Oh, you know I would, Dick!"

They could not see each other. After a long silence she said, "We must not stop talking here. Mrs. Ede sleeps, you know, in the room at the back of the work-room, and she might hear us."

"Then come into the sitting-room," said Dick, taking her hands and drawing her towards him.

"Oh, I cannot!"

"I love you better than anyone in the world."

"No, no; why should you love me?"

Although she could not see his face she felt his breath on her neck. Strong arms were wound about her, she was carried forward, and the door was shut behind her.

Only the faintest gleam of starlight touched the wall next to the window; the darkness slept profoundly on the landing and staircase; and when the silence was again broken, a voice was heard saying, "Oh, you shouldn't have done this! What shall I tell my husband if he asks me where I've been?"

"Say you have been talking to me about my bill, dear. I'll see you in the morning."

[Here Moore summarizes and quotes from three novels in circulation at Mudie's Select Library: *Nadine* by Mrs. Campbell Praed, *A Romance of the Nineteenth Century* by W. H. Mallock, and *Foxglove Manor* by Robert Buchanan. Refering to the libidinous clergyman in the last book, Moore continues.]

. . . but did not one of the thousands of young ladies in the many thousand parsonages you supply with light literature write to tell you that papa was not "the snake of the parish," and your great friend the British Matron, did she never drop you a line on the subject? Tell me, I beseech you.

I say your great friend, my dear Mr. Mudie, because I wish to distinguish between you, for latterly your identities have got so curiously interwoven that it would need a critical insight that few—I may say none—possess, to separate you. Indeed on this subject many different opinions are afloat. Some hold that being the custodian of the national virtue you have by right adopted the now well-known signature as your *nom de plume*, others insist that the lady in question is your better half (by that is it meant the better half of your nature or the worthy lady who bears your name?), others insist that you yourself are the veritable British Matron. How so strange a belief could have obtained credence I cannot think, nor will I undertake to say if it be your personal appearance, or the constant communication you seem to be in with this mysterious female, or the singularly obtrusive way you both have of forcing your moral and religious beliefs upon the public that has led to this vexatious confusion of sex. It is, however, certain that you are popularly believed to be an old woman; and assuming you to be the British Matron I would suggest, should this pamphlet cause you any annoyance, that you write to *The Times* proving that the books I have quoted from are harmless, and differ nowise from your ordinary circulating corals whereon young ladies are supposed to cut their flirtation teeth. The British Matron has the public by the ear, and her evidence on the subject of impure literature will be as greedily listened to as were her views on painting from the nude. But although I am willing to laugh at you, Mr. Mudie, to speak candidly, I hate you; and I love and am proud of my hate of you. It is the best thing about me. I hate you because you dare question the sacred right of the artist to obey the impulses of his temperament; I hate you because you are the great purveyor of the worthless, the false and the commonplace; I hate you because you are a fetter about the ankles of those who would press forward towards the light of truth; I hate you because you feel not the spirit of scientific inquiry that is bearing our age along; I hate you because you pander to the intellectual sloth of to-day; I hate you because you would mould all ideas to fit the narrow limits in which your own turn; I hate you because you impede the free development of our literature. And now that I have told you what I think of you, I will resume my examination of the ware you have in stock.

Without in the least degree attempting to make an exhaustive list of the books which to my surprise this most virtuous literary tradesman consents to circulate, I may venture to call attention to "Puck," by Ouida. This is the history of a courtezan through whose arms, in the course of the narrative, innumerable lovers pass. "Moths," by the same author, tells how a dissolute adventuress sells to her lover the pure white body and soul of her daughter, and how in the end Vera, disgraced and degraded by her ignoble husband, goes off to live with the tenor with whom she fell in love at the beginning of the story. In a book I opened the other day at haphazard, "Phillida," by Florence Marryat, I find a young lady proposing to a young parson to be his mistress. It is true that the feelings that prompt her are not analysed, but does the cause of morals gain I wonder by this slightness of treatment?

It is not for me to put forward any opinion of my own. I have spoken of and quoted only from the works of writers longer and better known to the public than I am. They do not need defence against the Philistine charge of immorality, and it would be ridiculous for me—ostracised as I am by the founder and president of our English Academy, the Select Circulating Library—to accuse them, or even to hint that they have offended against the Mudie code more deeply than myself. I therefore say nothing. I cast no stone. All I seek is to prove how absurd and how futile is the censorship which a mere tradesman assumes to exercise over the literature of the nineteenth century, and how he overrules the decisions of the entire English press.

Were I indeed the only writer who has suffered from this odious tyranny the subject might well be permitted to drop. Many cases might be brought forward, but I will not look further than last month. I am informed on good authority that on being written to repeatedly for a book called "Leicester," Mr. Mudie sent back word to the Athenæum Club that he did not keep naturalistic literature—that he did not consider it "proper." And thus an interesting, if not a very successful, literary experiment is stamped out of sight, and the strange paradox of a tradesman dictating to the bishops of England what is proper and improper for them to read is insolently thrust upon us. However the matter has been brought before the committee of the club, and the advisability of withdrawing the subscription from this too virtuous library is under consideration.

It has been and will be again advanced that it is impossible to force a man to buy goods if he does not choose to do so: but with every privilege comes a duty. Mr. Mudie possesses a monopoly, and he cannot be allowed to use that monopoly to the detriment of all interests but his own. But even if this were not so, it is no less my right to point out to the public, that the character for strength, virility, and purpose, which our literature has always held, the old literary tradition coming down to us through a long line of glorious ancestors, is being gradually obliterated to suit the commercial views of a narrow-minded tradesman. Instead of being allowed to fight, with and amid, the thoughts and aspirations of men, literature is now rocked to an ignoble rest in the motherly arms of the librarian. That of which he approves is fed with gold; that from which he turns the breast dies like a vagrant's child; while in and out of his voluminous skirts run a motley and monstrous progeny, a callow, a whining, a puking brood of bastard bantlings, a race of Aztecs that disgrace the intelligence of the English nation. Into this nursery none can enter except in baby clothes; and the task of discriminating between a divided skirt and a pair of trousers is performed by the librarian. Deftly his fingers lift skirt and under-skirt, and if the examination prove satisfactory the sometimes decently attired dolls are packed in tin-cornered boxes, and scattered through every drawing-room in the kingdom, to be in rocking-chairs fingered and fondled by the "young person" until she longs for some newer fashion in literary frills and furbelows. Mudie is the law we labour after; the suffrage of young women we are supposed to gain: the paradise of the English novelist is in the school-room: he is read there or nowhere. And yet it is certain that never in any age or country have writers been asked to write under such restricted conditions; if the same test by which modern writers are judged were applied to their forefathers, three-fourths of the contents of our libraries would have to be condemned as immoral publications. Now of the value of conventional innocence I don't pretend to judge, but I cannot help thinking that the cultivation of this curiosity is likely to run the nation into literary losses of some magnitude.

It will be said that genius triumphs over circumstances, but I am not sure that this is absolutely the case; and turning to Mr. Mat[t]hew Arnold, I find that he is of the same opinion. He says, . . . "but it must have the atmosphere, it must find itself in the order of ideas, to work freely, and this is not so easy to command. This is why the great creative epochs in literature are so rare . . . because for the creation of a master work of literature two powers must concur, the power of the man and the power of the moment; the creative has for its happy exercise appointed elements, and those elements are not in its own control." I agree with Mr. Mat[t]hew Arnold. Genius is a natural production, just as are chickweed and roses; under certain conditions it matures; under others it dies; and the deplorable dearth of talent among the novelists of to-day is owing to the action of the circulating library, which for the last thirty years has been staying the current of ideas, and quietly opposing the development of fresh thought. The poetry, the history, the biographies written in our time will live because they represent the best ideas of our time; but no novel written within the last ten years will live through a generation, because no writer pretends to deal with the moral and religious feeling of his day; and without that no writer will, no writer ever has been able to, invest his work with sufficient vitality to resist twenty years of criticism. When a book is bought it is read because the reader hopes to find an expression of ideas of the existence of which he is already dimly conscious.

A literature produced to meet such hopes must of necessity be at once national and pregnant with the thought of the epoch in which it is written. Books, on the contrary, that are sent by the librarian to be returned in a few days, are glanced at with indifference, at most with the vapid curiosity with which we examine the landscape of a strange country seen through a railway-carriage window. The bond of sympathy that should exist between reader and writer is broken—a bond as sacred and as intimate as that which unites the tree to the earth—and those who do not live in communion with the thought of their age are enabled to sell their characterless trash; and a writer who is well known can command as large a sale for a bad book as a good one. The struggle for existence, therefore, no longer exists; the librarian rules the roost; he crows, and every chanticleer pitches his note in the same key. He, not the ladies and gentlemen who place their names on the title-pages, is the author of modern English fiction. He models it, fashions it to suit his purpose, and the artistic individualities of his employés count for as little as that of the makers of the pill-boxes in which are sold certain well-known and mildly purgative medicines. And in accordance with his wishes English fiction now consists of either a sentimental misunderstanding, which is happily cleared up in the end, or of singular escapes over the edges of precipices, and miraculous recoveries of one or more of the senses of which the hero was deprived, until the time has come for the author to bring his tale to a close. The novel of observation, of analysis, exists no longer among us. Why? Because the librarian does not feel as safe in circulating a study of life and manners as a tale concerning a lost will.

To analyze, you must have a subject; a religious or sensual passion is as necessary to the realistic novelist as a disease to the physician. The dissection of a healthy subject would not, as a rule, prove interesting, and if the right to probe and comment on humanity's frailties be granted, what becomes of the pretty schoolroom, with its piano tinkling away at the "Maiden's Prayer," and the water-colour drawings representing mill-wheels and Welsh castles? The British mamma is determined that her daughter shall know nothing of life until she is married; at all events, that if she should learn anything, there should be no proof of her knowledge lying about the place a book would be a proof; consequently the English novel is made so that it will fit in with the "Maiden's Prayer" and the water-mill. And as we are a thoroughly practical nation, the work is done thoroughly; root and branch are swept away, and we begin on a fresh basis, just as if Shakespeare and Ben Jonson had never existed. A novelist may say, "I do not wish to enter into those pretty schoolrooms. I agree with you, my book is not fit reading for young girls; but does this prove that I have written an immoral book?" The librarian answers, "I cater for the masses, and the masses are young unmarried women who are supposed to know but one side of life. I cannot therefore take your book." And so it comes to pass that English literature is sacrificed on the altar of Hymen.

But let me not be misunderstood. I would not have it supposed that I am of opinion that literature can be glorified in the Temples of Venus. Were the freedom of speech I ask for to lead to this, we should have done no more than to have substituted one evil for another. There is a middle course, and I think it is this—to write as grown-up men and women talk of life's passions and duties. On one hand there must be no giggling over stories whispered in the corners of rooms; on the other, there must be no mock moral squeamishness about speaking of vice. We must write as our poems, our histories, our biographies are written, and give up once and for ever asking that most silly of all silly questions, "Can my daughter of eighteen read this book?" Let us renounce the effort to reconcile those two irreconcilable things—art and young girls. That these young people should be provided with a literature suited to their age and taste, no artist will deny; all I ask is that some means may be devised by which the novelist will be allowed to describe the moral and religious feeling of his day as he perceives it to exist, and to be forced no longer to write with a view of helping parents and guardians to bring up their charges in all the traditional beliefs.

It is doubtless a terrible thing to advocate the breaking down of the thirty-one and sixpenny safeguards, and to place it in the power of a young girl to buy an immoral book if she chooses to do so; but I am afraid it cannot be helped. Important an element as she undoubtedly is in our sociological system, still we must not lose sight of everything but her; and that the nineteenth century should possess a literature characteristic of its nervous, passionate life, I hold is as desirable, and would be as far-reaching in its effects, as the biggest franchise bill ever planned. But even for the alarmed mother I have a word of consolation. For should her daughter, when our novels are sold for half-a-crown in a paper cover, become possessed of one written by a member of the school to which I have the honour to belong, I will vouch that no unfortunate results are the consequence of the reading. The close analysis of a passion has no attraction for the young girl. When she is seduced through the influence of a novel, it is by a romantic story, the action of which is laid outside the limits of her experience. A pair of lovers—such as Paul and Virginia—separated by cruel fate, whose lives are apparently nothing but a long cry of yearning and fidelity, who seem to live, as it were, independent of the struggle for life, is the book that more often than any other leads to sin; it teaches the reader to look to a false ideal, and gives her—for men have ceased to read novels in England—erroneous and superficial notions of the value of life and love.

All these evils are inherent in the "select" circulating library, but when in addition it sets up a censorship and suppresses works of which it does not approve, it is time to appeal to the public to put an end to such dictatorship, in a very practical way, by withdrawing its support from any library that refuses to supply the books it desires to read.

27

THOMAS HARDY

(1840–1928)

By inclination Thomas Hardy was a poet, by profession he was an architect, by reputation he was a novelist. His father's love of music was undoubtedly reflected in Hardy's lifelong passion for poetry. Unsuccessful at selling his poems to magazines, he turned to fiction, but never abandoned poetry. Several volumes of poems, culminating in *The Dynasts* (1903–8), an epic-drama of the Napoleonic wars, and in an effusion of lyrics during the last years of his life, testify to the intensity of his muse.

As a stylist, Hardy applied to prose fiction what he had learned from poetry, for example, the artistic effect of imperfection: "It is, of course, simply a carrying into prose the knowledge I have acquired in poetry—that inexact rhymes and rhythms now and then are far more pleasing than correct ones" (*The Notebooks*, March, 1875, quoted in Florence E. Hardy, *The Life of Thomas Hardy*, New York, 1962, p. 105).

Hardy's father, a builder by trade, also directed his son into his profession by apprenticing him at sixteen to an ecclesiastical architect. By twenty Hardy was engaged in restoring churches, both in his native Dorsetshire and in London. He continued to write and to read widely, especially in the classics. His work broadened his range of experience and familiarized him more deeply with rural society and its folklore. Gradually, too, influenced at the impressionable age of nineteen by *The Origin of the Species*, a philosophical pessimism supplanted his early orthodoxy; and his belief in the inevitable tragedy of man's struggle against an indifferent "Will" sought for literary expression.

Discouraged by George Meredith, a reader for the publishing firm of Chapman and Hall, who urged the importance of plot, Hardy published *Desperate Remedies* (1871) himself. He recovered most of his investment and sold his next novel, *Under the Greenwood Tree* (1872). The success of *Far from the Madding Crowd* (1874) led him to abandon architecture for fiction writing during the next twenty years. His "Wessex Novels," including *The Return of the Native* (1878), sometimes called his masterpiece, reflect the physical local color of the southwest counties of England; this scene suggests values of a universal and timeless scope. These novels possess a variety denoted by Hardy's own classification into novels of character and environment, novels of ingenuity, and romances and fantasies. Almost all of his more than a dozen novels appeared serially, and he was obliged by conservative editors to modify scenes and expressions in such works as *Tess of the D'Urbervilles* (1891) and *Jude the Obscure* (1895) to avoid offending the delicate sensibilities of readers of periodicals. Even so, severe criticism, especially when offending passages were restored in book publication, combined with a desire to devote himself full time to poetry, led to the termination of his fictional career.

Although the financial returns were a prime incentive, Hardy viewed the novel as a serious form of art through which he could express his intellectual, fatalistic view of the universe. His manuscript revisions were motivated by concern not only for the restrictions of serial publication and for stylistic improvement but were also "the outcome of the novelist's basic preoccupation with such things as timing, point of view and the presentation of character" (Wallace Hildick, "Thomas Hardy," *Word for Word*, London, 1965, p. 111). His prefaces testify to his thoughtful opinions on fiction: e.g. "a novel is an impression, not an argument . . ." (*Tess*). His notebooks contain detached, usually brief, observations:

> The business of the poet and novelist is to show the sorriness underlying the grandest things, and the grandeur underlying the sorriest things.
> —19 April 1885 (quoted *Life*, p. 171).

> The real, if unavowed, purpose of fiction is to give pleasure by gratifying the love of the uncommon in human experience, mental or corporeal. . . . The writer's problem is, how to strike the balance between the uncommon and the ordinary so as on the one hand to give interest, on the other to give reality.
> —July, 1881 (quoted *Life*, p. 150).

> Novel-writing as an art cannot go backward. Having reached the analytic stage it must transcend it by going still further in the same direction. Why not by rendering as visible essences, spectres, etc., the abstract thoughts of the analytic school?
> —4 March 1886 (quoted *Life*, p. 177).

More extended expression of Hardy's theories may be found in several published articles, beginning with his defense of "Dialect in Novels," in *The Athenaeum* for 30 November 1878, and "On the Use of Dialect," in *The Spectator* for 15 October 1881. He protested against the censorship exerted by periodicals and circulating libraries in his "Candour in English Fiction," published in *The New Review* for January, 1890, as one in a series of discussions with Walter Besant and Mrs. E. Lynn Linton. Similarly, a series written with Besant and Paul Bourget for the same periodical included his "The Science of Fiction" in April, 1891. More general in purpose, and giving his considered views on the values of fiction is "The Profitable Reading of Fiction," published in *The Forum* (New York) for March, 1888.

THE PROFITABLE READING OF FICTION
(1888)

When the editor of this review courteously offered me space in his pages to formulate a few general notions upon the subject of novel reading, considered with a view to mental profit, I could not help being struck with the timeliness of the theme; for in these days the demand for novels has risen so high, in proportion to that for other kinds of literature, as to attract the attention of all persons interested in education. But I was by no means persuaded that one whose own writings have largely consisted in books of this class was in a position to say anything on the matter, even if he might be supposed to have anything to say. The field, however, is so wide and varied that there is plenty of room for impersonal points of regard; and I may as well premise that the remarks which follow, where not exclusively suggested by a consideration of the works of dead authors, are mere generalizations from a cursory survey, and no detailed analysis, of those of to-day.

If we speak of deriving good from a story, we usually mean something more than the gain of pleasure during the hours of its perusal. Nevertheless, to get pleasure out of a book is a beneficial and profitable thing, if the pleasure be of a kind which, while doing no moral injury, affords relaxation and relief when the mind is overstrained or sick of itself. The prime remedy in such cases is change of scene, by which, change of the material scene is not necessarily implied. A sudden shifting of the mental perspective into a fictitious world, combined with rest, is well known to be often as efficacious for renovation as a corporeal journey afar.

In such a case the shifting of scene should manifestly be as complete as if the reader had taken the hind seat on a witch's broomstick. The town man finds what he seeks in novels of the country, the countryman in novels of society, the indoor class generally in outdoor novels, the villager in novels of the mansion, the aristocrat in novels of the cottage.

The narrative must be of a somewhat absorbing kind, if not absolutely fascinating. To discover a book or books which shall possess, in addition to the special scenery, the special action required, may be a matter of some difficulty, though not always of such difficulty as to be insuperable; and it may be asserted that after every variety of spiritual fatigue there is to be found refreshment, if not restoration, in some antithetic realm of ideas which lies waiting in the pages of romance.

In reading for such hygienic purposes it is, of course, of the first consequence that the reader be not too critical. In other words, his author should be swallowed whole, like any other alterative pill. He should be believed in slavishly, implicitly. However profusely he may pour out his coincidences, his marvelous juxtapositions, his catastrophes. his conversions of bad people into good people at a stroke, and *vice versa*, let him never be doubted for a moment. When he exhibits people going out of their way and spending their money on purpose to act consistently, or taking a great deal of trouble to move in a curious and roundabout manner when a plain, straight course lies open to them; when he shows that heroes are never faithless in love, and that the unheroic always are so, there should arise a conviction that this is precisely according to personal experience. Let the invalid reverse the attitude of a certain class of critics—now happily becoming less numerous—who only allow themselves to be interested in a novel by the defeat of every attempt to the contrary. The aim should be 'the exercise of a generous imaginativeness, which shall find in a tale not only all that was put there by the author, put he it never so awkwardly, but which shall find there what was never inserted by him, never foreseen, never contemplated. Sometimes these additions which are woven around a work of fiction by the intensitive power of the reader's own imagination are the finest parts of the scenery.

It is not altogether necessary to this tonic purpose that the stories chosen should be "of most disastrous chances, of moving accidents by flood and field."[1] As stated above, the aim should be contrast. Directly the circumstances begin to resemble those of the reader, a personal connection, an interest other than an imaginative one, is set up, which results in an intellectual stir that is not in the present case to be desired. It sets his serious thoughts at work, and he does not want them stimulated just now; he wants to dream.

So much may be said initially upon alleviating the effects of over-work and carking care by a course of imaginative reading. But I will assume that benefit of this sort is not that which is primarily contemplated when we speak of getting good out of novels, but intellectual or moral profit to active and undulled spirits.

It is obvious that choice in this case, though more limited than in the former, is by no means limited to compositions which touch the highest level in the essential constituents of a novel—those without which it would be no novel at all—the plot and the characters. Not only may the book be read for these main features—the presentation, as they may collectively be called—but for the accidents and appendages of narrative; and such are of more kinds than one. Excursions into various philosophies, which vary or delay narrative proper, may have more attraction than the regular course of the enactment; the judicious inquirer may be on the look-out for didactic reflection, such as is found in large lumps in *Rasselas*; he may be a picker-up

---

[1] *Othello*, I, iii, 134–135.

of trifles of useful knowledge, statistics, queer historic fact, such as sometimes occur in the pages of Hugo; he may search for specimens of the manners of good or bad society, such as are to be obtained from the fashionable writers; or he may even wish to brush up his knowledge of quotations from ancient and other authors by studying some chapters of *Pelham* and the disquisitions of Parson Adams in *Joseph Andrews*.

Many of the works which abound in appurtenances of this or a kindred sort are excellent as narrative, excellent as portraiture, even if in spite rather than in consequence of their presence. But they are the exception. Directly we descend from the highest levels we find that the majority are not effectual in their ostensible undertaking, that of giving us a picture of life in action; they exhibit a machinery which often works awkwardly, and at the instigation of unlikely beings. Yet, being packed with thoughts of some solidity, or more probably sprinkled with smart observations on men and society, they may be read with advantage even by the critical, who, for what they bring, can forgive the audible working of the wheels and wires and carpentry, heard behind the performance, as the wires and trackers of a badly constructed organ are heard under its tones.

Novels of the latter class—formerly more numerous than now—are the product of cleverness rather than of intuition; and in taking them up—bearing in mind that profit, and not amusement, is the student's aim—his manifest course is to escape from the personages and their deeds, gathering the author's wit or wisdom nearly as it would have presented itself if he had cast his thoughts in the shape of an essay.

But though we are bound to consider by-motives like these for reading fiction as praiseworthy enough where practicable, they are by their nature of an illegitimate character, more or less, and apart from the ruling interest of the genuine investigator of this department of literature. Such ingredients can be had elsewhere in more convenient parcels. Our true object is a lesson in life, mental enlargement from elements essential to the narratives themselves and from the reflections they engender.

Among the qualities which appertain to representations of life, construed, though not distorted, by the light of imagination—qualities which are seldom shared by views *about* life, however profound—is that of self-proof or obviousness. A representation is less susecptible of error than a disquisition; the teaching, depending as it does upon intuitive conviction, and not upon logical reasoning, is not likely to lend itself to sophistry. If endowed with ordinary intelligence, the reader can discern, in delineative art professing to be natural, any stroke greatly at variance with nature, which, in the form of moral essay *pensée*, or epigram, may be so wrapped up as to escape him.

Good fiction may be defined here as that kind of imaginative writing which lies nearest to the epic, dramatic, or narrative masterpieces of the past. One fact is certain: in fiction there can be no intrinsically new thing at this stage of the world's history. New methods and plans may arise and come into fashion, as we see them do; but the general theme can neither be changed, nor (what is less obvious) can the relative importance of its various particulars be greatly interfered with. The higher passions must ever rank above the inferior—intellectual tendencies above animal, and moral above intellectual whatever the treatment, realistic or ideal. Any system of inversion which should attach more importance to the delineation of man's appetites than to the delineation of his aspirations, affections, or humors, would condemn the old masters of imaginative creation from Æschylus to Shakespeare. Whether we hold the arts which depict mankind to be, in the words of Mr. Matthew Arnold, a criticism of life, or, in those of Mr. Addington Symonds, a revelation of life, the material remains the same, with its sublimities, its beauties, its uglinesses, as the case may be. The finer manifestations must precede in importance the meaner, without such a radical change in human nature as we can hardly conceive as pertaining to an even remote future of decline, and certainly do not recognize now.

In pursuance of his quest for a true exhibition of man, the reader will naturally consider whether he feels himself under the guidance of a mind who sees further into life than he himself has seen; or, at least, who can throw a stronger irradiation over subjects already within his ken than he has been able to do unaided. The new light needs not to be set off by a finish of phraseology or incisive sentences of subtle definition. The treatment may be baldly incidental, without inference or commentary. Many elaborate reflections, for example, have been composed by moralizing chroniclers on the effect of prosperity in blunting men's recollection of those to whom they have sworn friendship when they shared a hard lot in common. But the writer in Genesis who tells his legend of certain friends in such adverse circumstances, one of whom, a chief butler, afterward came to good fortune, and ends the account of this good fortune with the simple words, "Now the chief butler did not remember Joseph, but forgat him,"[2] brings out a dramatic sequence on ground prepared for assent, shows us the general principle in the particular case, and hence writes with a force beyond that of aphorism or argument. It is the force of an appeal to the emotional reason rather than to the logical reason; for by their emotions men are acted upon, and act upon others.

If it be true, as is frequently asserted, that young people nowadays go to novels for their sentiments, their religion, and their morals, the question as to the wisdom or folly of those young people hangs upon their methods of acquisition in each case. A deduction from what these works exemplify by action that bears evidence of being a counterpart of life, has a distinct educational value; but an imitation of what may be called the philosophy of the personages—the doctrines of the actors, as shown in their conversation— may lead to surprising results. They should be informed that a writer whose story is not a tract in disguise has as his main object that of characterizing the

[2] Genesis 40:23.

people of his little world. A philosophy which appears between the inverted commas of a dialogue may, with propriety, be as full of holes as a sieve if the person or persons who advance it gain any reality of humanity thereby.

These considerations only bring us back again to the vital question how to discriminate the best in fiction. Unfortunately the two hundred years or so of the modern novel's development have not left the world so full of fine examples as to make it particularly easy to light upon them when the first obvious list has been run through. The, at first sight, high-piled granary sifts down to a very small measure of genuine corn. The conclusion cannot be resisted, notwithstanding what has been stated to the contrary in so many places, that the scarcity of perfect novels in any language is because the art of writing them is as yet in its youth, if not in its infancy. Narrative art is neither mature in its artistic aspect, nor in its ethical or philosophical aspect; neither in form nor in substance. To me, at least, the difficulties of perfect presentation in both these kinds appear of such magnitude that the utmost which each generation can be expected to do is to add one or two strokes toward the selection and shaping of a possible ultimate perfection.

In this scarcity of excellence in novels as wholes the reader must content himself with excellence in parts; and his estimate of the degree to which any given modern instance approximates to greatness will, of course, depend not only upon the proportion that the finer characteristics bear to the mass, but upon the figure cut by those finer characteristics beside those of the admitted masterpieces as yet. In this process he will go with the professed critic so far as to inquire whether the story forms a regular structure of incident, accompanied by an equally regular development of character—a composition based on faithful imagination, less the transcript than the similitude of material fact. But the appreciative, perspicacious reader will do more than this. He will see what his author is aiming at, and by affording full scope to his own insight, catch the vision which the writer has in his eye, and is endeavoring to project upon the paper, even while it half eludes him.

He will almost invariably discover that, however numerous the writer's excellencies, he is what is called unequal; he has a specialty. This especial gift being discovered, he fixes his regard more particularly thereupon. It is frequently not that feature in an author's work which common repute has given him credit for; more often it is while co-existent with his popular attribute, overshadowed by it lurking like a violet in the shade of the more obvious, possibly more vulgar, talent, but for which it might have received high attention. Behind the broad humor of one popular pen he discerns startling touches of weirdness; amid the colossal fancies of another he sees strokes of the most exquisite tenderness; and the unobtrusive quality may grow to have more charm for him than the palpable one.

It must always be borne in mind, despite the claims of realism, that the best fiction, like the highest artistic expression in other modes, is more true, so to put it, than history or nature can be. In history occur from time to time monstrosities of human action and character explicable by no known law which appertains to sane beings; hitches in the machinery of existence, wherein we have not yet discovered a principle, which the artist is therefore bound to regard as accidents, hinderances to clearness of presentation, and hence, weakeners of the effect, To take an example from sculpture: no real gladiator ever died in such perfect harmony with normal nature as is represented in the well-known Capitoline marble. There was always a jar somewhere, a jot or tittle[3] of something foreign in the real death-scene, which did not essentially appertain to the situation, and tended toward neutralizing its pathos; but this the sculptor omitted, and so consecrated his theme. In drama likewise. Observe the characters of any sterling play. No dozen persons who were capable of being animated by the profound reasons and truths thrown broadcast over *Hamlet* or *Othello*, of feeling the pulse of life so accurately, ever met together in one place in this world to shape an end. And, to come to fiction, nobody ever met an Uncle Toby who was Uncle Toby all round; no historian's Queen Elizabeth was ever so perfectly a woman as the fictitious Elizabeth of *Kenilworth*. What is called the idealization of characters is, in truth, the making of them too real to be possible.

It may seem something of a paradox to assert that the novels which most conduce to moral profit are likely to be among those written without a moral purpose. But the truth of the statement may be realized if we consider that the didactic novel is so generally devoid of *vraisemblance* as to teach nothing but the impossibility of tampering with natural truth to advance dogmatic opinions. Those, on the other hand, which impress the reader with the inevitableness of character and environment in working out destiny, whether that destiny be just or unjust, enviable or cruel, must have a sound effect, if not what is called a good effect, upon a healthy mind.

Of the effects of such sincere presentation on weak minds, when the courses of the characters are not exemplary, and the rewards and punishments ill adjusted to deserts, it is not our duty to consider too closely. A novel which does moral injury to a dozen imbeciles, and has bracing results upon a thousand intellects of normal vigor, can justify its existence; and probably a novel was never written by the purest-minded author for which there could not be found some moral invalid or other whom it was capable of harming.

To distinguish truths which are temporary from truths which are eternal, the accidental from the essential, accuracies as to custom and ceremony from accuracies as to the perennial procedure of humanity, is of vital importance in our attempts to read for something more than amusement. There are certain novels, both among the works of living and the works of deceased writers, which give convincing proof of much exceptional fidelity, and yet they do not rank as great productions; for what they are faithful in is life garniture and not life. You are fully persuaded that the

---

[3] "For verily I say unto you, till heaven and earth pass, one joy or one title shall in no wise pass from the Law, till all be fulfilled" (Matt. 5:18).

personages are clothed precisely as you see them clothed in the street, in the drawing-room, at the assembly. Even the trifling accidents of their costume are rendered by the honest narrator. They use the phrases of the season, present or past, with absolute accuracy as to idiom, expletive, slang. They lift their tea-cups or fan themselves to date. But what of it, after our first sense of its photographic curiousness is past? In aiming at the trivial and the ephemeral they have almost surely missed better things. A living French critic goes even further concerning the novelists of social minutiæ. "They are far removed," says he, "from the great imaginations which create and transform. They renounce free invention; they narrow themselves to scrupulous exactness; they paint clothes and places with endless detail."[4]

But we must not, as inquiring readers, fail to understand that attention to accessories has its virtues when the nature of its regard does not involve blindness to higher things; still more when it conduces to the elucidation of higher things. The writer who describes his type of a jeweled leader of society by saying baldly how much her diamonds cost at So-and-So's, what the largest of them weighed and measured, how it was cut and set, the particular style in which she wore her hair, cannot convey much profit to any class of readers save two—those bent on making a purchase of the like ornaments or of adorning themselves in the same fashion; and, a century hence, those who are studying the costumes and expenditure of the period. But, supposing the subject to be the same, let the writer be one who takes less of a broker's view of his heroine and her adornments; he may be worth listening to, though his simplicity be quite childlike. It is immaterial that our example is in verse:

> Be you not proud of that rich hair
> Which wantons with the love-sick air;
> Whenas that ruby which you wear,
> Sunk from the tip of your soft ear,
> Will last to be a precious stone
> When all your world of beauty's gone.—*Herrick.*[5]

And thus we are led to the conclusion that, in respect of our present object, our concern is less with the subject treated than with its treatment. There have been writers of fiction, as of poetry, who can gather grapes of thorns and figs of thistles.[6]

Closely connected with the humanizing education found in fictitious narrative which reaches to the level of an illuminant of life, is the æsthetic training insensibly given by familiarity with story which, presenting nothing exceptional in other respects, has the merit of being well and artistically constructed. To profit of this kind, from this especial source, very little attention has hitherto been paid, though volumes have been written upon

[4] H. A. Taine, *History of English Literature,* trans. H. Van Laun (New York, 1874), II, 258.

[5] "To Dianeme," ll. 5–10, in *Hesperides.*

[6] "Do men gather grapes of thornes, or figs of thistles?"—Matt. 7:16.

the development of the æsthetic sense by the study of painting and sculpture, and thus adding to the means of enjoyment. Probably few of the general body denominated the reading public consider, in their hurried perusal of novel after novel, that, to a masterpiece in story there appertains a beauty of shape, no less than to a masterpiece in pictorial or plastic art, capable of giving to the trained mind an equal pleasure. To recognize this quality clearly when present, the construction of the plot, or fable, as it used to be called, is to be more particularly observed than either in a reading for sentiments and opinions, or in a reading merely to discover the fates of the chief characters. For however real the persons, however profound, witty, or humorous the observations, as soon as the book comes to be regarded as an exemplification of the art of story-telling, the story naturally takes the first place, and the example is not noteworthy as such unless the telling be artistically carried on.

The distinguishing feature of a well-rounded tale has been defined in various ways, but the general reader need not be burdened with many definitions. Briefly, a story should be an organism. To use the words applied to the epic by Addison, whose artistic feeling in this kind was of the subtlest, "nothing should go before it, be intermixed with it, or follow after it, that is not related to it."[7] Tested by such considerations as these there are obviously many volumes of fiction remarkable, and even great, in their character-drawing, their feeling, their philosophy, which are quite second-rate in their structural quality as narratives. Instances will occur to everyone's mind; but instead of dwelling upon these it is more interesting to name some which most nearly fulfill the conditions. Their fewness is remarkable, and bears out the opinion expressed earlier in this essay, that the art of novel-writing is as yet in its tentative stage only. Among them *Tom Jones* is usually pointed out as a near approach to perfection in this as in some other characteristics; though, speaking for myself, I do not perceive its great superiority in artistic form over some other novels of lower reputation. The *Bride of Lammermoor* is an almost perfect specimen of form, which is the more remarkable in that Scott, as a rule, depends more upon episode, dialogue, and description, for exciting interest, than upon the well-knit interdependence of parts. And the first thirty chapters of *Vanity Fair* may be instanced as well-nigh complete in artistic presentation, along with their other magnificent qualities.

Herein lies Richardson's real if only claim to be placed on a level with Fielding: the artist spirit that he everywhere displays in the structural parts of his work and in the interaction of the personages, notably those of *Clarissa Harlowe*. However cold, even artificial, we may, at times, deem the heroine and her companions in the pages of that excellent tale, however numerous the twitches of unreality in their movements across the scene beside those in the figures animated by Fielding, we feel, nevertheless, that we are under the guidance of a hand which has consummate skill in evolving a graceful, well-balanced set of conjunctures, forming altogether one of those circumstantial

[7] *The Spectator*, No. 267, Saturday, 5 Jan. 1712.

wholes which, when approached by events in real life, cause the observer to pause and reflect, and say, "What a striking history!" We should look generously upon his deficiency in the robuster touches of nature, for it is the deficiency of an author whose artistic sense of form was developed at the expense of his accuracy of observation as regards substance. No person who has a due perception of the constructive art shown in Greek tragic drama can be blind to the constructive art of Richardson.

I have dwelt the more particularly upon this species of excellence, not because I consider it to rank in quality beside truth of feeling and action, but because it is one which so few nonprofessional readers enjoy and appreciate without some kind of preliminary direction. It is usually the latest to be discerned by the novel consumer, and it is often never discerned by him or her at all. Every intelligent reader with a little experience of life can perceive truth to nature in some degree; but a great reduction must be made for those who can trace in narrative the quality which makes the Apollo and the Aphrodite a charm in marble. Thoughtful readers are continually met with who have no intuition that such an attribute can be claimed by fiction, except insofar as it is included in style.

The indefinite word *style* may be made to express almost any characteristic of story-telling other than subject and plot, and it is too commonly viewed as being some independent, extraneous virtue or varnish with which the substance of a narrative is artificially overlaid. Style, as far as the word is meant to express something more than literary finish, can only be treatment, and treatment depends upon the mental attitude of the novelist; thus entering into the very substance of a narrative, as into that of any other kind of literature. A writer who is not a mere imitator looks upon the world with his personal eyes, and in his peculiar moods; thence grows up his style, in the full sense of the term.

> Cui lecta potenter erit res,
> Nec facundia deseret hunc, nec lucidus ordo.[8]

Those who would profit from the study of style should formulate an opinion of what it consists in by the aid of their own educated understanding, their perception of natural fitness, true and high feeling, sincerity, unhampered by considerations of nice collocation and balance of sentences, still less by conventionally accepted examples. They will make the discovery that certain names have, by some accident or other, grown to be regarded as of high, if not of supreme merit in the catalogue of exemplars, which have no essential claims, in this respect, to be rated higher than hundreds of the rank and file of literature who are never mentioned by critic or considered by reader in that connection. An author who has once acquired a reputation

---

[8] Neither eloquence nor method will fail him who chooses a theme judiciously.— Horace, *Ars Poetica* ll. 40–41.

for style may write English down to the depths of slovenliness if he choose, without losing his character as a master; and this probably because, as before observed, the quality of style is so vague and inapprehensible as a distinct ingredient that it may always be supposed to be something else than what the readers perceives to be indifferent.

Considerations as to the rank or station in life from which characters are drawn can have but little value in regulating the choice of novels for literary reasons, and the reader may leave thus much to the mood of the moment. I remember reading a lecture on novels by a young and ingenious, though not very profound, critic, some years ago, in which the theory was propounded that novels which depict life in the upper walks of society must, in the nature of things, be better reading than those which exhibit the ilfe of any lower class, for the reason that the subjects of the former represent a higher stage of development than their less fortunate brethren. At the first blush this was a plausible theory; but when practically tested it is found to be based on such a totally erroneous conception of what a novel is, and where it comes from, as not to be worth a moment's consideration. It proceeds from the assumption that a novel is the thing, and not a view of the thing. It forgets that the characters, however they may differ, express mainly the author, his largeness of heart or otherwise, his culture, his insight, and very little of any other living person, except in such an inferior kind of procedure as might occasionally be applied to dialogue, and would take the narrative out of the category of fiction: *i.e.*, verbatim reporting without selective judgment.

But there is another reason, disconnected entirely from methods of construction, why the physical condition of the characters rules nothing of itself one way or the other. All persons who have thoughtfully compared class with class—and the wider their experience the more pronounced their opinion—are convinced that education has as yet but little broken or modified the waves of human impulse on which deeds and words depend. So that in the portraiture of scenes in any way emotional or dramatic—the highest province of fiction—the peer and the peasant stand on much the same level; the woman who makes the satin train and the woman who wears it. In the lapse of countless ages, no doubt, improved systems of moral education will considerably and appreciably elevate even the involuntary instincts of human nature; but at present culture has only affected the surface of those lives with which it has come in contact, binding down the passions of those predisposed to turmoil as by a silken thread only, which the first ebullition suffices to break. With regard to what may be termed the minor key of action and speech—the unemotional, everyday doings of men—social refinement operates upon character in a way which is oftener than not prejudicial to vigorous portraiture, by making the exteriors of men their screen rather than their index, as with untutored mankind. Contrasts are disguised by the crust of conventionality, picturesqueness obliterated, and a subjective system of description necessitated for the differentiation of character. In the one case the author's word has to be taken as to the nerves and muscles of his figures; in the other they can be seen as in an *écorché*.[9]

The foregoing are a few imperfect indications how, to the best of my judgment, to discriminate fiction which will be the most desirable reading for the average man or woman of leisure, who does not wish the occupation to be wholly barren of results except insofar as it may administer to the pleasure of the hour. But, as with the horse and the stream in the proverb, no outside power can compel or even help a reader to gain good from such reading unless he has some natural eye for the finer qualities in the best productions of this class. It is unfortunately quite possible to read the most elevating works of imagination in our own or any language, and, by fixing the regard on the wrong sides of the subject, to gather not a grain of wisdom from them, nay, sometimes positive harm. What author has not had his experience of such readers?—the mentally and morally warped ones of both sexes, who will, where practicable, so twist plain and obvious meanings as to see in an honest picture of human nature an attack on religion, morals, or institutions. Truly has it been observed that "the eye sees that which it brings with it the means of seeing."[10]

---

[9] *écorché*: a figure depicted without skin, used for the study of the muscles.

[10] H. Thomas Carlyle, *The French Revolution*, Part One, Book I, Chapter II and *Past and Present*, Book IV, Chapter I.

28

SIR THOMAS H.
HALL CAINE

(1853–1931)

All but forgotten today, Hall Caine enjoyed a tremendous popularity in his time and became, in consequence, one of the wealthiest of English novelists. Over one million copies of *The Eternal City* (1901) were sold. Several of his novels were adapted for the stage. His best work romanticizes the picturesque life on the Isle of Man, which was his home for many years: *The Deemster* (1887) and *The Manxman* (1894) reveal his powers as a regionalist. Owing much to the techniques of Wilkie Collins, Caine's sensationalism catered to the contemporary taste for "thrillers." He was knighted in 1918 for service to the Allied propaganda effort during World War I.

Following a period as a schoolmaster on the Isle of Man, Caine became an assistant to a builder and produced some essays on architecture that attracted the notice of John Ruskin. In 1881 Dante G. Rossetti befriended Caine and shared his home with him for the last year of his life; it was at this time that Caine determined to make writing his career. Joining the staff of the *Liverpool Mercury*, he found journalism to be the ideal source of the facts on which he based his fiction. In *My Story* (1908), his autobiography, he writes:

I am now fifty-five years of age, and have had thirty years' experience of the literary life, and if a beginner were to ask me what school I consider best for the novelist, I should answer, without hesitation, the school of journalism.

The imaginative writer needs invention and sympathy, and these are the gifts of Nature; but, whatever the deftness of the workman's hand, he cannot "make bricks without straw," and the life of one man is hardly ever so full of incident as to find material for many books. But the school of journalism is constantly crowding the brain of the student with the incidents of countless lives; and, speaking for myself, I know that in those hours of mingled agony and delight, in which the scheme of a novel is being composed, there come swarming in upon me at every turn of the plot the recollections of my days as a journalist—recollections of this face, or of that voice, of the pathetic figure of the blind mother who had never seen her babe, or of the wistful eyes of the condemned man when he looked at me as he mounted the scaffold. But journalism, to be the best school for the novelist, must be the journalism of the police court, the divorce court, the hospital, and the jail, where human nature is real and stark, if vulgar and low—not the journalism of "society," where humanity is trying its poor best to wear a mask.

Factual data must be modified for fictional purposes. In "The Author to the Reader," prefixed to *The Woman Thou Gavest Me* (1913), Caine states that "as I have in this instance drawn more largely and directly from fact than is usually the practice of the novelist, I have thought it my duty to defeat all possible attempts at personal identification by altering and disguising the more important scenes and characters." Caine did not confuse the function of the novelist with that of the journalist or of the historian. His "Author's Note" appended to *The Christian* (1897) makes this clear:

It will be seen that in writing this book I have sometimes used the diaries, letters, memoirs, sermons, and speeches of recognisable persons, living and dead. Also, it will be seen that I have frequently employed fact for the purposes of fiction. In doing so, I think I am true to the principles of art, and I know I am following the precedent of great writers. But being conscious of the grievous danger of giving personal offence, I would wish to say that I have not intended to paint anybody's portrait, or to describe the life of any known Society or to indicate the management of any particular Institution. To do any of these things would be to wrong the theory of fiction as I understand it, which is not to offer mock history or a substitute for fact, but to present a thought in the form of a story, with as much realism as the requirements of idealism will permit.

To Caine, therefore, the novel was a forum for thought, one that had replaced the stage. Shakespeare would be a novelist, as well as a dramatist, today: "He would find that the only place where we do not utterly fight shy of the greater life problems is the novel" ("The Novelist in Shakespeare," *The Eclectic Magazine*, n.s. LX, September, 1894, 396). At the same time, Caine valued the novel as a means of providing the poor with an escape from the misery of their lot: "The novelists are the magicians wafting them, as on wings, out of their anxieties and sorrows. . . . Some of them are rolling with laughter and some are choking with sobs; but all of them are carried out of themselves and out of their pitiful circumstances. And it is only their poor, pinched bodies that sit there, in their mean and meager garments" ("Hall Caine on the Free Library Movement," *The Independent*, LIV, 6 November 1902, 2633).

"The New Watchwords of Fiction" (*The Contemporary Review*, April, 1890) will be, Caine prophesizes, Romanticism and Idealism—for the next twenty years at least. Representing "the extreme of the idealist position, and the high-water mark of romance theory" (Kenneth Graham, *English Criticism of the Novel 1865–1900*, Oxford, 1965, p. 68), this article defines the province of the novelist in relation to that of the historian, condemns realism, and optimistically hails the new romanticism.

THE NEW WATCHWORDS OF FICTION
(1890)

A little circle of influential writers for the Press are doing their best to persuade the public that "the critical orthodoxies" of the day are opposed to all forms of idealism in literature, that "romanticism" is a "backwater," and that the "stream of tendency" is towards a newer and purer "realism." Now, I feel very strongly that this is utterly untrue, and that somebody should say so with all the emphasis he can command, and thereby warn the public against an error that must be fatal to the making of good literature, the appreciation of good literature, and the moral effects of good literature wherever it gains credence and support. But first let me say what I take these two words "realism" and "idealism" to mean when applied to the literature that we call imaginative. I take realism to mean the doctrine of the importance of the real facts of life, and idealism the doctrine of the superiority of ideal existence over the facts of life. I am not a logician, and may lack skill in stating my definitions, but I think plain people will grasp my plain meaning.

Long ago M. Zola put forth a sort of manifesto in support of the writings of the brothers De Goncourt, and, as nearly as I can remember it, he therein told the world that the school to which they belonged had set out with one clear aim, and one only, that of reproducing actual life. No romance, no poetry, no uncommon incidents, no effects, no situations were to be touched by them. These things had been the machinery of an earlier school of writers, of Dumas and Hugo and Sue. Only the plain, unvarnished, naked, stark fact was to be employed, and with such materials they were going to produce results that should be beyond comparison more potent than any results of romanticism in their influence on man and the world Well, we know what the end of it has been; but I am not going to discuss Zolaism in its effects. Clean-minded people are weary of the talk of it, and I grieve to see that a writer of pure and noble instincts, Thomas Hardy, in his recent protest against the painful narrowness of English fiction, has been betrayed into prescribing a remedy for the evil that is a thousand times worse than the disease. One frequent reply to the plea of the French realist is that in his determination to paint the world as it is he has only painted the world's cesspools. And indeed it is a sufficient answer to say that, though there may be many Madame Bovarys in the world, the Madame Bovarys are not the women whom right-minded people want to know more about, and that though the world holds many harlots, we do not wish to look down into the deep pit that is a harlot's heart. But there is a better rejoinder to the demand of the realist that he should be allowed to paint the world as it is, and that is that he never can—no, not if he were a thousand times a Balzac. And in attempting to do so he is not only missing the real aim of true literature, but running a fearful risk of following a false literature that can never do the world any good.

What I mean is this: the largest view that any one man can take of life "as it is" usually shows him more that is evil than good. The physical eye sees, must see, and always has seen, an enormous preponderance of evil in the world. It is only the eye of imagination, the eye of faith that sees the balance of good and evil struck somewhere and in some way. And if the physical eye in its pride goes abroad to believe only what it can see, it comes home either blurred with tears, as Carlyle's was when he asked himself what God could be doing in the world he had made for man, or shining with ridicule, as Voltaire's was when he protested that there was no God in the rascally world at all. For the former of these there is the salvation of faith always hovering near, but the latter is by much the more likely chance, and for that there is no salvation whatever. It brings cynicism with it, and cynicism is the deadliest enemy that good literature ever had or can have.

Now this is the real pitfall of realism—cynicism. It never has, and never will, lay hold of an imaginative mind, for imagination and cynicism cannot live together, and no man of imagination ever was or will be a cynic. But it possesses, like a passion, another type of mind that none can dare to under-value, a type of mind that is often stronger than the imaginative mind and always more trustworthy on the lesser issues of life. And it is an evil thing in literature, because it leads to nothing. It prompts no man to noble deeds, it restrains no woman from impurity, it degrades the virtues by taking all the unselfishness out of them that is their spiritual part. So when we hear the realist boast that he is painting "life as it is," it will be a sufficient answer to say that he is talking nonsense; but we can add with truth that, if it were possible for him to paint the world as he sees it, the chances are that he would thereby be doing the world much harm.

The true consort of imagination is enthusiasm, the man of imagination has never lived who was not also an enthusiast, and enthusiasm is the only force that has ever done any good in the world since the world began. It is the salt of the earth, the salt without which the earth would rot, and when things rot they stink. We see how surely it has been so with French fiction, which, for twenty years past, has been the least imaginative fiction produced in Europe. It has no salt of enthusiasm in it, and so it rots and stinks. It is cynical, and so it does the world no good. But enthusiasm, living with imagination in the hearts of great men, has again and again set the world aflame, and purified as well as ennobled every nature it has touched, save only the natures that were touched already with fanaticism.

And this enthusiasm, which cannot live at peace with realism, lives and flourishes with idealism. It seems to say, "If we cannot paint the world as it is, we can paint it as it should be," and that is idealism. Don't say the idealist, by my own showing, starts from nowhere. He starts from exactly the same scene as the realist, the scene of daily life, and with the same touch of mother earth, only he realizes that the little bit of life that has come under his physical eye is only a disproportionate fragment of the whole, and the eye of imagination tells him of the rest. If he sees the wicked prosper in this life, he does not content himself with a mere picture of the wicked man's material prosperity, leaving his reader to cry "If this is true, what is God doing?" No; but he shows side by side with the material prosperity a moral degradation so abject and so pitiful, that the reader must rather cry, "Not that, not that at any price!" Thus he shows the man who has failed, as the world goes, that to have succeeded might have been a worse fate, and he reminds the man who has won in life's battle that the man who has lost may yet be his master. Lifting up the down-trodden, encouraging the heavy-laden, "helping, when he meets them, lame dogs over stiles," he does the world some good in his way, and he does it, not by painting life as he sees it, but by virtue of the inward eye that we call Idealism.

Now this idealism has nearly always taken the turn of romanticism when applied to literature. It was so when Schiller, in his youth and wild inexperience, struggled to express himself in *The Robbers*, when Goethe wrote *Faust*, when Coleridge wrote *The Ancient Mariner*, when Scott wrote *Old Mortality* and *The Bride of Lammermoor*. Romance seemed to these writers the natural vehicle for great conceptions. Not that they wanted big situations, startling effects, picturesque accessories, for their own sakes only. These were all good in their way, and no writer of true instincts could have undervalued them. But they were not the prizes for which the authors set out. They had no life of their own apart from the central fire that brought them into existence. It was not the Slough of Despond that produced Christian, but Christian that called for the Slough of Despond. Then, again, Idealism claims Romance as her handmaiden, but she does not require that the handmaiden shall be of surpassing beauty; she may be a very plain-featured body. Romanticism does not live only in the loveliest spots in this world of God, and it does not belong exclusively to the past, as some writers imply. It exists within the four-mile radius at the present hour, and could be found there if only we had a second great idealist like Dickens to go in search of it.

To condemn all forms of romance, as the Zola manifesto tried to do, to banish from fiction all incidents that are out of the common, all effects that are startling and "sensational," all light and colour that are not found in every-day life, is to confound the function of the novelist with that of the historian. To the historian fact is a thing for itself, it is sacred, it dominates all else. To the novelist fact is only of value as a help towards the display of passion; he does not deliberately falsify fact, but fact—mere fact—has no sanctity for him, and he would a thousand times rather outrage all the incidents of history than belie one impulse of the human heart.

The idea at the bottom of the Zola manifesto is a sophism, and a shallow sophism. It seems to say that the novelist, like the historian, has for his chief function that of painting the life of his time, and leaving behind him a record as faithful and yet more intimate. To accept this is to narrow the range of imaginative art, which should have no limits whatever, certainly none of time or healthy human interest. The real function of the novelist has been too frequently propounded, and ought to be too obvious to stand in need of definition. It is that of proposing for solution by means of incident and story a problem of human life. Passion therefore, not fact, lies at the root of the novelist's art. Passion is the central fire from which his fact radiates, and fact is nothing to him except as it comes from that central fire of passion. He looks about him, not for startling situations (though these he would be a fool to despise), but for the great mysteries of life, and then he tries to find light through them. These mysteries are many, and do not belong to an age, but to all time. Two good men love one woman, and one of them goes up to Paradise while the other goes down to Hell. There is a problem of life, a human tragedy occurring constantly. How is it to be solved? What will or should the rejected man do? That is the question the novelist sets himself, and to answer such a question is the novelist's highest and all but his only natural function. But, in answering it, must he limit himself to life as he has seen it? If so, the chances are a thousand to one that he will make the rejected man kill his favoured rival, or else the woman, or both. That is realism, that is painting "life as it is." And is the world likely to be much the better of it?

The idealist goes differently to work. Instead of asking himself what solution to this problem life and the world have shown him, he asks his own heart of what solution human nature at its highest is capable. This leads him to the heroisms which it is so easy for the cynic to deride. And the heroisms, for their better effects, often tempt him to a more inspiring scene and picturesque age than he lives in. He wants all that the human heart can do, and he gets heroism; he wants heroism to look natural, and he gives it a certain aloofness, and that is Romanticism.

It is easy to foresee the kind of objection that may be urged to Idealism as an aim in fiction, and no writer could put it more forcibly than Mr. Russell Lowell did in one of his early letters to the author of *Uncle Tom's Cabin*.

"A moral aim is a fine thing; but, in making a story, an artist is a traitor who does not sacrifice everything to art. Remember the lesson that Christ gave us twice over. First, he preferred the useless Mary to the dishwashing Martha; and nest, when that exemplary moralist and friend of humanity, Judas, objected to the sinful waste of the Magdalen's ointment, the great Teacher would rather it should be wasted in an act of simple beauty than utilised for the benefit of the poor. Cleopatra was an artist when she dissolved her biggest pearl to captivate her Antony-public. May I, a critic by profession, say the whole truth to a woman of genius? Yes? And never be forgiven? I shall try, and try to be forgiven, too. In the first place, pay no regard to the advice of anybody. In the second place, pay a great deal to mine! A Kilkenny-cattish sort of advice? Not at all. My advice is to follow your own instincts, to stick to nature, and to avoid what people commonly call the 'Ideal'; for that, and beauty and pathos and success, all lie in the simply natural. . . . . There are ten thousand people who can write 'ideal' things for one who can see and feel and reproduce nature and character. Ten thousand, did I say? Nay, ten million. What made Shakspere so great? Nothing but eyes and—faith in them. The same is true of Thackeray. I see nowhere more often than in authors the truth that men love their opposites. Dickens insists on being tragic, and makes shipwreck."

Now, forcible and effective, sound and true as this seems at first sight to be, it is, I make bold to say, one of the most misleading bits of criticism ever put forth by a great critic. Surely it would not be hard to dispute every clause of it, but only one of its clauses concerns us at present, and that is the broad statement that "ten million" can write "ideal" things for "one who can see and feel and reproduce nature and character." Exactly the reverse of this is the manifest truth. Indeed, to outstrip Mr. Lowell in his flight of numbers, I will say that there is hardly a living human being who cannot in some measure "see and feel and reproduce nature and character." The merest child can do it, and often does it (such is the strength of the talent for mimicry in man), with amazing swiftness and fidelity. The veriest stable-boy, the simplest village natural, will startle you with his reproductions of the oddities of character, and the novelist who has rendered, however faithfully, however humorously or pathetically, the scene on which his bodily eyes have rested, has achieved no more than the comedian on the stage. But lest this statement of mine should seem to be too daring a negative to the word of so high an authority, let me set Mr. Lowell in contrast with one who can do him no dishonour by a contradiction. "As the actual world," says Bacon, "is inferior to the rational soul, so Fiction gives to Mankind what History denies, and in some measure satisfies the mind with shadows when it cannot enjoy the substance. And as real History gives us not the success of things according to the deserts of vice and virtue, Fiction corrects it, and presents us with the fates and fortunes of persons rewarded and punished according to merit." Obviously Bacon, with all his strong common-sense, was not one of those "who avoid what people commonly call the 'Ideal.'" And Burton, quoting this passage in the Terminal Essay to his monumental "Thousand Nights and a Night," adds, in his virile way: "But I would say still more. History paints, or attempts to paint, life as it is, a mighty maze, with or without a plan: Fiction shows or would show us life as it should be, wisely ordered and laid down on fixed lines. Thus Fiction is not the mere handmaid of History; she has a household of her own and she claims to be the triumph of Art, which, as Goethe remarked, is 'Art because it is not Nature.'" Goethe hits the nail on the head. Merely to "reproduce nature and character" is not Art at all; it is Photography. And for one man capable of that moulding and smelting of nature and character which is rightly called Art, there are whole worlds of men capable of using the "eyes," of which Mr. Lowell makes too much, as a sort of human camera. Of course one cannot be blind to the real force that lies somewhere at the back of this demand for the real to the neglect of the ideal. A bad ideal, an imperfect ideal, a wild and mad ideal, is a trivial and common-place thing, and rather than have such vague imaginative varnishes one asks for the solid facts of life. We know the fascination of fact—any sort of fact, no matter what, any life, however remote or mean—and if it is only real enough to feel it. "Tell us what you know," is our cry again and again when writers seem to be busied with telling us only what they fancy. This craving for the *real* is good and healthy, but it ought by no means to be set (as Mr. Lowell sets it) in opposition to the craving for the ideal. A novelist should know his facts, he should know the life he depicts; yet this knowledge should not be the end of his art, but only its beginning. That should be his equipment to start with, and his art should be adjudged by the good use he puts it to, not by the display he makes of it. Burton could not have expressed more clearly the difference between fiction as Mrs. Beecher Stowe had unconsciously practised it, and as her genial critic would have had her follow it, than by that contrast, drawn from Bacon, of fiction and history: "Fiction is not the mere handmaid of History; she has a household of her own." And I would add for myself as the essence of my creed as a novelist: *Fiction is not nature, it is not character, it is not imagined history; it is fallacy, poetic fallacy, pathetic fallacy, a lie if you like, a beautiful lie, a lie that is at once false and true—false to fact, true to faith.*

Towards such healthy Romanticism as Bacon describes English fiction has long been leaning, and never more so than during the last five-and-twenty years We may see this in the homeliest fact, namely, that craving for what is called poetic justice which makes ninety-nine hundredths of English readers impatient of any close to a story but a happy one The craving is right and natural, though it may be puerile to expect that the threads of all stories should be gathered up to a happy ending. I know that it is usual to attribute to such arbitrary love of what is agreeable the inferiority in which the fiction of this country is said to stand towards the fiction of the rest of Europe. We are asked to say how fiction can live against such conditions of the circulating libraries as degrade a serious art to the level of the nursery tale. The answer is very simple: English fiction has lived against them, and produced meantime the finest examples of its art that the literature of the world has yet seen. Unlike the writers who pronounce so positively on the inferiority of fiction in England, I cannot claim to know from "back to end" the great literatures of Europe; but I will not hesitate to say that not only would the whole body of English fiction bear the palm in a comparison with the whole body of the fiction of any other country, but the fiction of England during the past thirty years (when its degeneracy, according to its critics, has been most marked) has been more than a match for the fiction of the rest of the world. Indeed, I will be so bold as to name six English novels of that period, and ask if any other such bulk of work, great in all the qualities that make fiction eminent—imagination, knowledge of life, passion and power of thought—can be found among the literatures of France, Russia, or America. The six novels are *Daniel Deronda, The Cloister and the Hearth, Lorna Doone, The Woman in White, The Ordeal of Richard Feverel*, and *Far from the Madding Crowd*. All these novels are products of romanticism, and the circumstance that they were written amid the hampering difficulties that are said to beset the feet of fiction is proof enough that where power is not lacking in the artist there is no crying need for licence in the art.

But if liberty is the one thing needful for English fiction, it is not the liberty of the realism of the Third Empire in France, but the liberty of the romanticism of the age of Elizabeth in England; the liberty of all great and healthy passions to go what lengths they will. For many years past the cynicism that has been only too vocal in English criticism has been telling us that it is a poor thing to give way to strong feeling, that strong feeling is the mark of an untaught nature, and that education should help us to control our emotions and conceal them. I am told that this type of superfine cynicism comes from Oxford, but on that point I can offer no opinion. Whatever its source its effects are baneful, for it cuts at the root of the finest quality that imaginative writing can have, the quality of passion. No such plea ever had a hearing in the days when English literature was at its best. It was not a childish weakness to give way to powerful emotions when *Lear* was written. Powerful emotions were sought for their own sakes, and no man was shocked when Cordelia perished in a just cause. Sentiment is different now, and with great passions of the purest kind lying everywhere about us, we who write to please must never touch them, or, touching them, we must never probe them deeply. And this is one of the ways in which the thing called realism is compelled to play its own game backwards.

A doctrine may fairly be judged by the example of its best exponents, and of all the champions of realism the healthiest, I think, is Turgenieff. I do not place Flaubert in that position, because his work seems always to be clouded by the moral shadows that overhung his own life. Neither do I place M. Daudet there, for the reason that the ethical character of his best work is disfigured by what I cannot but consider a wilful determination to find the balance of justice on the wrong side of the world's account. But I place Turgenieff at the head of the realists, because he seems to me to have been an entirely healthy man, who came to an honest conclusion, that poetic justice is false to human life, and that human life is the only model for imaginative art. Well, what of Tourgenieff? We shall never know how much we have lost in him by that accident of exile which brought him under the influence of Flaubert. He does not of set purpose make "the wicked prosper and the virtuous miscarry," still less does he paint the world's cesspools under pretence of painting the world; but he leaves you without hope, without expectation, and in an atmosphere of despair more chilling than the atmosphere of a vault. His novels may be just representations of actual life, but they begin nowhere and end nowhere; and, like the little bits of nature that come under a photographic camera, they are transcripts, not pictures of life. It is not because they end sadly that they outrage poetic justice. It is because they do not in any true sense end at all. *Macbeth* ends sadly, but it ends absolutely, because it ends with justice. *Cato* also ends sadly, but it ends only as the broken column ends, merely because there is no capital to crown it. And, rightly followed, justice is the only end for a work of imaginative art, whatever may be the frequent end of life. Without it what is a work of art? A fragment, a scrap, a passing impression. The incidents of life are only valuable to art in degree as they are subservient to an idea, and an idea is only valuable to man in the degree to which it helps him to see that come what will the world is founded on justice. Torn by the wind a bird's nest falls to the ground, and all the young birds perish. That is a faithful representation of a common incident of life, but a thousand such incidents massed together would not make a work of art. Justice is the one thing that seems to give art a right to exist, and justice—poetic justice, as we call it—is the essence of Romanticism.

And is this Romanticism a "backwater"? Has the stream of literary orthodoxies ceased to flow with it? A little band among the writers of the time are answering, "Yes," but we answer "No"; Romanticism is not a "backwater," can never be a "backwater," and the stream of literary orthodoxies in England is at this moment flowing more strongly with Romanticism than at any time since the death of Scott. It is true that realism has lately had its day in England as well as in France. In France it has been nasty, and in England it has been merely trivial. But the innings of realism is over; it has scored badly or not at all, and is going out disgraced. The reign of mere fact in imaginative literature was very short, it is done, and it is making its exit rapidly, with a sorry retinue of either teacup-and-saucer nonentities or of harlots at its heels. And the old Romanticism that was before it is coming into its own again.

Surely it is impossible to mistake the signs of the times in the affairs of literature. What is going on in Europe? I never meet a Frenchman of real insight but he tells me that Zolaism as a literary force is as nearly as possible dead in France. Its dirty shroud keeps a wraith of it flitting before men's eyes. And what is France going back to? The Idealism of George Sand? The Romanticism of Hugo? Perhaps not, though Hugo is not as far gone in France as some people would have us believe. France is at this moment waiting for a new man, and depend upon it, when he comes, he will be a romanticist. If such are the signs of the literary horizon in France, what are they in the rest of Europe? What in Russia, where Tolstoi has taken all that is good in the Realism of France and engrafted it on to the brave and noble and surpassing idealism of English poetry at the beginning of this century?

What in the Scandinavian countries (the stronghold of the purer and higher Realism), where Björnsen, as I can attest from some personal knowledge of Norway, is a stronger force than Ibsen, himself more than half an idealist? What in America, where the sturdy romance of the soil is pushing from its stool the teacup Realism of the last twenty years, and even the first champions of such Realism, who have said that there is sufficient incident in "the lifting up of a chair," and that "all the stories are told," are themselves turning their backs on their own manifesto, and coming as near to Romanticism as their genius will let them?

On every side, in every art, music, the drama, painting, and even sculpture, the tendency is towards Romance. Not the bare actualities of life "as it is," but the glories of life as it might be; not the domination of fact, but of feeling. I think one might show this yet more plainly by illustrations drawn from the stage of the time. The cry of the stage of to-day is Romance, the cry of fiction is Romance, the cry of music is Romance, and I do not think I belie the facts when I say that the cry of the Science of this hour is also for Romance.

Romance is the cry of the time, and the few cynics of the Press may deride it as much as they like, but Romance is going to be once more the tendency of literature, and the sum and substance of its critical orthodoxy. The world now feels exactly the same want as it has always felt. It wants to be lifted up, to be inspired, to be thrilled, to be shown what brave things human nature is capable of at its best. This must be the task of the new Romanticism, and the new Romanticism can only work through Idealism. It can never be the task of the old realism. The Realists are all unbelievers; unbelievers in God, or unbelievers in man, or both. The Idealist must be a believer; a believer in God, a believer in man, and a believer in the divine justice whereon the world is founded.

So I say that these two are going to be the watchwords of fiction for the next twenty years at least—ROMANTICISM AND IDEALISM.

29

MRS. HUMPHRY WARD

(1851–1920)

Tolstoy regarded Mrs. Humphry Ward as the greatest living English novelist. Her novels were best sellers compared to the public reception given those by her friend Henry James, who despaired of ever teaching her the art of novel writing. Yet no novelist who enjoyed an equal success has ever been so quickly and so completely forgotten. Only her name is memorialized by a settlement for London's poor in Tavistock Square, which philanthropist Passmore Edwards was inspired to found after reading her first successful novel, *Robert Elsmere* (1888).

Born in Tasmania, Mary Augusta Arnold, a niece of Matthew Arnold, was brought to England by her family in 1856 and spent her childhood in the Lake District. At the age of sixteen she moved to Oxford, where, in 1872, she married Thomas Humphry Ward, a fellow and tutor at the University. When her husband took a staff position on *The Times* in 1881, they moved to London. In *A Writer's Recollections* (New York, 1918), Mrs. Ward says: "For the *Times* I wrote a good many long, separate articles before 1884 on 'Spanish Novels,' 'American Novels,' and so forth." She also contributed a dozen critical articles and reviews to *Macmillan's* between 1883 and 1885; among these is "Recent Fiction in England and France" (1884). A large part of her criticism on the British novel takes the form of introductions and prefaces to her novels.

The subject matter of her fiction was, at first, religion. *Robert Elsmere* is a serious spiritual romance, tracing the career of a clergyman whose faith, failing under the impact of science, ultimately finds an opportunity for service in social work. As such, it dramatizes the transition in the later nineteenth century from the conventional theological concerns of the Church to humanitarian activities. *The History of David Grieve* (1892) promotes a "natural religion." In a prefatory letter to this novel she defends the novel of purpose against its detractors and discusses the belief of her reviewers that personal experience should set the limits for a novelist's range. *The Case of Richard Meynell* (1911), another religious novel, provoked a review objecting to the narrative as slight and commonplace. Mrs. Ward's reply, in a subsequently written Introduction, raised a question: "Is not our English novel today—the novel which counts—too much of a continuous strain on writer and reader? Every word, every incident, must have an equal accent, an equal novelty, an equal intensity."

From religion Mrs. Ward turned to politics. An example is *Marcella* (1894), which advocates legislation to improve the lot of the poor. In her Introduction she testifies to the influence of the creative imagination in the composition of *Marcella* and of *The Story of Bessie Costrell* (1895). This recognition of inspiration is the exception in Mrs. Ward's fiction, for she was generally conscious of her methods, writing mechanically and tastefully, with no attempt at technical innovations.

Beginning in 1900, Mrs. Ward published several novels based on historical scandals in high society, thinly disguised in contemporary settings. She thus avoided the difficulties of writing historical fiction, which she discussed in the Introduction to *The Marriage of William Ashe* (1905), the story of Byron's liaison with Lady Caroline Lamb.

THE HISTORY OF DAVID GRIEVE
(1892)

from the Prefatory Letter

London: May 2, 1892.

Dear Mr. Smith,

A few days ago there came into my head the idea of writing you—my friend and publisher—an "open letter" which might serve, if you thought well, as a little preface to the sixth and popular edition of *The History of David Grieve.* . . . .
. . . . . . And first let me return a moment, but in another spirit, to my three latest critics, lest I should inadvertently misrepresent them as they, to my thinking, have sometimes misrepresented *David Grieve.* It is quite true that some of their most formidable dicta "cancel out" with astonishing neatness, and to the stimulus of that sense of humour in which the *Edinburgh* finds David's biographer so deficient. But it is also true that in certain canons and methods of criticism they are very closely agreed; and because it is so, and because the articles are long, simultaneous, and conspicuous, it may be well to take them as representative of much else—I will not say in the mind of the public—but at any rate in the mind of a portion of the press. All three dislike and resent what they call the intrusion of "theology" into a novel, and the two older Quarterlies are especially intolerant of "the novel with a purpose," of any writing within the domain of art which, as the *Quarterly* puts it, aims at "reforming the world." Great stress is also laid—particularly in the *Edinburgh*—on that method of reviewing which consists in putting together all that one may know, or imagine one knows, about the personal history of a writer, and framing one's literary judgement to suit.

Now these points—what is meant by a "novel with a purpose," or by "dragging theology into fiction," and the legitimacy of the "personal" method of reviewing—are worth discussion, and I am not ungrateful to the Quarterlies for having turned my attention to them once more. Let me take the last first, as being the most diverting; for I have a certain love, as I fear my books betray, for a "serious ending." The "personal" method consists apparently in examining whether to your knowledge the author of a given book has ever been personally placed in the precise situations he describes, and judging his work accordingly. It leads to deductions of this kind: "Mr. A.'s pictures of convict life cannot possibly be well done, since Mr. A. —we know it for certain—has never been a convict. As for Mr. B.'s descriptions of immorality and divorce—absurd!—we happen to know that a better husband and father than Mr. B. does not exist. And what does Miss C. mean by talking to us about peasants? Miss C. lives—we have looked it up— in D—— Street, Kentish Town. Now what, we should like to ask, have English, or still more Scotch peasants to do with D—— Street, Kentish Town? As for Mr. F., we know all about his relations, and are not to be taken in; none of them ever attempted what Mr. F. has attempted; the inference is obvious."

The danger of this method is that it is difficult to be informed enough, and that your literary judgements are apt to be kept waiting while you are quarrelling with "Men of the Time" for not supplying you with detail enough to make them. The attractions of the "personal" method of criticism are no doubt great. Sainte-Beuve has a rapturous passage in which he declares that he never understood Chateaubriand till he knew all about Chateaubriand's sisters. Still, by that time Chateaubriand was dead—which in this connexion is something. Information of the personal sort is apt to accumulate after a writer's decease; and criticism, as the *Edinburgh* conceives it, is thereby made easier. During a writer's lifetime I constantly notice that while the critics are spending time and temper over these matters, the public is reading the book,—which is after all more important.

As for the one literary assumption underlying these vagaries,—that a writer must deal with nothing but his or her personal experience,—it is of course a very respectable assumption. All that one has to say is that literature and the public have upset it times without number. It is tolerably obvious that Sir Walter Scott could not have personally observed the society of George II's day, or have lived familiarly in the society of Louis XI; which does not prevent the *Heart of Midlothian* or *Quentin Durward* from being great novels. Another truism, you say. Very well. At any rate the successes of the historical novel prove that the imaginative treatment of life depends upon personal experience as *one* of its great factors, but by no means the only one. Personal experience, at least, of the narrow and technical sort. Every novel that ever touched a reader depends, of course, ultimately upon personal experience—that is to say, upon what the writer *is*, and can put into the framework with which experience or imagination, or research if you like, supplies him. But that is another question.

To return, however, to what are really the "hanging matters," with the Quarterlies, and with other people besides.

"The novel," says a writer in the *New Review*, "will not bear" what the writer of *David Grieve* puts into it; will not bear, that is to say, the introduction of matter drawn from the religious and philosophical field. Naturally the proposition interests me. But it rouses in me a little amused wonder that a critic with so wide a knowledge of literature as Mr. Traill should imagine that the matter can be settled quite so easily. For as one looks back over the history of the novel, nothing seems to be so clear as that it has "borne" everything of whatever kind that a writer who could make himself heard was minded to put into it. In the days of Cervantes the novel, fish-like, swallowed other novels whole, and the adventures of the immortal knight came to a standstill while the fortunes and career of *El Curioso Impertinente* unrolled. In the days of *Julie*, the *cadre* supplied by the loves of Saint-Preux and Madame de Wolmar admitted of the introduction of a vast amount of material which would make the critic of to-day rise in his wrath—discussions of the opera, of the qualities of women of the world, of the existence of God, of the proper management of children and estates, and much else. The discussions happened to be interesting then, and they are interesting historically now. Rousseau wrote as the spirit moved him, choosing out of the variegated spectacle of life what attracted him, and the instant response of his generation—in spite of the sarcasms of Voltaire—showed that he was right. *Wilhelm Meister* wanders, digresses, and preaches as Goethe pleases, but the man who wrote of life and thought in it had lived and thought; and, formless as it is, the book has entered into the training of Europe. Chateaubriand, George Sand, and Victor Hugo have bent the novel to all the purposes of propaganda in turn. Theology, politics, social problems and reforms, they have laid hands on them all, and have but stirred the more vibrations thereby in the life of their time. And which of them, from *Don Quixote* downwards, will you save from this opprobrious category of "novels with a purpose"?—which of them has not tried in its own way and with its own vehemence to "reform the world," whether it be by throwing an effete literature out of window, or by holding up the picture of married virtue and religious faith beside that of illicit love and empty doubt, or by showing forth the wrongs and difficulties of women, or by the passionate attempt to make the world realise the pressure of the pyramid of our civilised society on the poor and the weak at its base?

It is no doubt true, and the fact is one of great psychological interest, that in England the novel has been specially objective, positive, concrete. Our novels since Fielding descend rather from *Gil Blas* and that Spanish picaresque literature, the refuge of a people intellectually starved, which became so popular and found so many imitators in a seventeenth- or eighteenth-century England, than they descend from *Euphues* or *The Countess of Pembroke's Arcadia*. We have always taken more delight in the mere spectacle of life than our neighbours; "ideas" have on the whole, and for good reasons, been more distasteful to us than to France or Germany; and in the novel of our century we have the splendid result of both tendencies, positive and negative. Still there have been considerable exceptions. If one looks back over the fiction of the last fifty years, one comes again and again upon books that have broken bounds so to speak, and that have owed both their motive-power and their success to this desire, which the *Quarterly* finds so terrible and so abominable, of "reforming the world," or, as I should put it, to the expression of "a criticism of life," which may advance, whether in the hearts of the many or the few, thoughts and causes dear to the writers. "Think with me!" "See with me!" "Let me persuade you!" they seem to say, and again and again the world, or rather the world which belonged to the book, has let itself be persuaded, gladly.

Let us, indeed, exchange the idea of "purpose" for the idea "criticism of life," and see how the matter stands. "Poetry," said Mr. Matthew Arnold, "is a criticism of life under the conditions of poetic truth and poetic beauty." For this dictum he has been roughly handled by the school which, in its zeal for certain elements and aspects of art, and under the influence of a narrow conception of criticism, would, if it could, divorce art from criticism and claim for it a divine and irresponsible isolation. But, in my belief at any rate, the task is impossible. Criticism lurks, and will always lurk, in the very holiest and secretest places of art. For the artist there is always the choice between this and that, between good and better, between the congruous and the discordant, between one sequence and another. Every act of literary conception is half-creative, half-critical, and could not be creative without being critical.

Alter two words, then, in Mr. Arnold's definition of poetry, and watch how it applies to the novel. "*A criticism of life under the conditions of imaginative truth and imaginative beauty.*" It is easy to see that the definition so drawn sweeps into its net all the remembered novel-writing of the century. For even Miss Austen—that most detached and impersonal of all the great story-tellers—has her "criticism of life" and makes it felt. With what glee and malice does she hold up to us the absurdities of aristocratic pride in Darcy and in Lady Catherine de Burgh, and how large she writes the lesson of Emma's patronising and meddlesome conceit! As for Scott, Thackeray, Dickens, Charlotte Brontë, compare the "criticism of life" involved in the work of any one of them with that involved in the work of any conspicuous French novelist, of George Sand, or Théophile Gautier, or Octave Feuillet, and the contrasts of nationality will make you realise at once that each of these writers, however objective and positive he may seem, has all the while an ethical and social ideal which he is trying to make prevail. Each delights, as every artist should and does delight, in the mere play of the imaginative gift; but through each and all throbs the wish "to reform the world" in his or her measure. The question is, can you have lasting imaginative work without it?

Well, but—you will perhaps say to me with impatience—this is all trite and familiar enough. What you call "criticism of life" other people call "individuality," and very few dream of denying that the novel or the poem should have individuality—should embody a "criticism of life" up to this point. The question is: How far is the criticism to be carried?

Ah! that is indeed the question, the whole question. All that one can say is there have always been two answers—the answer of those who wish to make of art a protection against life, and the answer of those who attempt to use it as the torch for exploring life. Do not attempt to carry your criticism, say the first, beyond the point of common experience, above all of common agreement. The world is rich enough within these limits; it will give you amply within them the wherewithal to laugh or cry, or wonder; for heaven's sake be content! and join with us in making of fiction and poetry an ark of refuge, a many-coloured shrine for the common perennial passions and emotions and delights of mankind, reared amid the clash of irreconcilable interests, and that surrounding darkness of the Unknown which neither philosophy nor religion, say what you will, can clear away.

A beguiling answer!—and what magicians it has called into its service! It was the creed of Scott and Miss Austen; in words at least of George Eliot; it is implied in the golden art of Mr. Stevenson. We have all felt the charm and the persuasiveness of it; and in certain moods of life there is not a single man or woman that has not wished it, consciously or unconsciously, to prevail.

But there is another answer,—and it is equally legitimate. "Nay, let us have no lines, no exclusions!" it says. "Life divided into sections is life shorn of some of its fulness. There are no hard-and-fast limits in reality; the great speculative motives everywhere play and melt into the great practical motives; each different life implies a different and a various thought-stuff; and there is nothing in art to forbid your dealing—if you can!—with the thought-stuff of the philosopher as freely as with the thought-stuff of the peasant or the maiden. Still less is there any artistic reason why in picturing the individual human existence you should feel yourself bound to cut away from it anything that really *is there*. Either way, let there be no *parti pris*.[1] If *we*, in our zeal to include ideas among the material of imaginative present-ation, make the mistake of supposing that ideas are the whole of life, our work will come to nothing; and if *you*, in your zeal to escape the ideas which torture and divide, or those which present special difficulties to the artist, tend to empty your work of ideas beyond a certain point, it also will come to nothing. Each form of life-reading has its dangers. Success in ours is rarer; permanence less likely; the dangers more obvious than in yours. But the attempt is inevitable, and if we fail, we fail!"

The voices of Rousseau, of George Sand, of Goethe, are in this last answer. And as for me, shrinking under the onslaught of the Quarterlies, may I still be proud to count myself—however feeble, however weak— among that company? I am so made that I cannot picture a human being's development without wanting to know the whole, his religion as well as his business, his thoughts as well as his actions. I cannot try to reflect my time without taking account of forces which are at least as real and living as any other forces, and have at least as much to do with the drama of human existence about me. "The two great forming agencies of the world's history

[1] *parti pris:* sides taken.

have been the religious and the economic," says Professor Marshall. Everyone will agree that in his own way the novelist may handle the "economic." By and by we shall all agree that in his own way he may handle the "religious." For every artist of whatever type there is one inexorable law. Your "criticism of life" must be fashioned under the conditions of imaginative truth and imaginative beauty. If you, being a novelist, make a dull story, not all the religious argument in the world will or should save you. For your business is to make a novel, not a pamphlet, a reflexion of human life, and not merely a record of intellectual conception. But under these conditions everything is open—try what you will—and the response of your fellows, and that only, will decide your success.

Ah! that response—how dear it is to us! Now as I am about to launch this second book into that wider public beyond the circulating libraries to which the ultimate appeal lies, as I launched *Robert Elsmere* four years ago, my mind passes back of these years—over their hopes and emotions and surprises, their delights and their toils. I think of the many thousand persons to whom in that space of time I have become known; of whom in the pauses of work I inevitably think, with alternate yearning and dread. I remember that wave of sympathy which lifted *Robert Elsmere*; I feel it still swelling about me, waiting, I trust, for this new book, to carry it also into prosperous seas. I should be ungrateful indeed were I to show much soreness under criticism, however hostile, however, as I think, unjust. For the world to which they were addressed has sent out kind and welcoming hands to these books of mine; I have in my ears the sound of words that may well stir and quicken and encourage; and in my heart the longing to keep the sympathy gained, and the ambition to deserve it more and more.

Yours always sincerely,

Mary A. Ward

INTRODUCTION

MARCELLA
(1911–12 Edition)

In the summer of 1892 we settled in the Hertfordshire house, which has been, since then, for seventeen years our principal home. All my books since *David Grieve* have been written there, except for occasional flights abroad,

when a more complete isolation than even Stocks can give seemed the only
medicine for a halting story. We left Haslemere in the spring of that year
mainly because the growth of the population all round us, and the rise of
new houses wherever land could be had for building, seemed to foreshadow
a country existence almost as full of social happenings and obligations as
London itself. It became clear, also, that amid the villadom of Surrey,
enchantingly beautiful as the Surrey commons and woods still are, it was
hardly possible to come very close to the traditional life of field and farm, and
I had begun to feel a great wish to come close to it. Till then a townswoman,
living in Oxford or London, and camping for the summer amid the wildness
of the commons between Milford and Peper Harow, I had little practical
knowledge of the familiar routine, the immemorial forces and traditions
which govern rural England. Yet at Hampden in '89, among the remote
woods and lanes of the Chilterns, I had felt strongly the drawing of that life
of the earth and its labours

> "whose dumb wish is not missed
> If birth proceeds, if things subsist";[2]

and as the bricks and mortar of Haslemere increased, and the beautiful hill
we had settled on was soon all built over by others, as much in love as we
with its blue and purple prospect, the restlessness in me began to be shared
by the rest of us. In January, 1892, just about the time of the publication of
David Grieve, an eighteenth-century house in Hertfordshire, close to some
old and dear friends, and standing on a wooded upland near a village where
little or nothing had changed for a hundred years, fell vacant, by the death
of a lady well known and widely loved in the country-side, who had lived
there for sixty years. We came to look at it in January snows, and were
captured by its quiet, its encircling down, its beautiful trees, and its holly
hedges! Here at last was "a harbour and a hold," where reigned tranquillity.
Such at least would have been the impression of any stranger seeing the place
for the first time on that winter day. Yet in truth the fields near Stocks had
just been the scene of a tragedy which was in all men's mouths. In December,
1891, two keepers in the employ of a neighbouring landowner were murdered
by poachers, on the skirts of the big wood which from all time has crowned
the hill above the house. When we made our first visit, two men were in
prison awaiting trial, and they were condemned and executed before we
entered upon our tenancy in the following April. A strong effort was made
after the verdict to get a reprieve, but the Home Secretary stood firm, and
the law took its course.

Naturally such an event had struck deep into the feeling of the village
and the neighbourhood. In the country-houses near, no less than in the cottages, the trial and the agitation for reprieve were eagerly discussed; the
game-laws and game-preserving in general came up for chastisement in the

[2] Matthew Arnold, "Resignation," ll. 193–94.

Radical newspapers, where the murderers were excused as poor men poaching for food, while the Tories, dismissing the hunger excuse with scorn, and declaring that the game was being stolen to sell, like any other tempting commodity, regarded the murder as merely a sordid and brutal example of a sordid and brutal form of crime. When, in the April sunshine, we came to settle at Stocks, and began to roam the beautiful fields around the house, these questionings and debates filled my mind, together with a constant attempt to reconstruct the psychological origins and the local circumstance of the murder. The event in all its bearings—economic, social, political— affected me, as a stranger and observer, more sharply probably than it would have done had I been always country-born and bred. It seemed to focus in itself forces and passions and tendencies at work everywhere in our rural life. The poor battered bodies found on that December morning on the slope under the hill, the hurry of magistrates and police through the quiet lanes, the talk in the cottages, the discussion in the country-houses,—it had all of it, in my eyes, a typical, representative interest. Such a thing could not have happened in France, or Italy, or America,—nowhere, but in England. It suggested itself to me at once as providing a natural centre and core for that leisurely novel of English country life that I had already in mind.

Yet, let it be understood, that when the murder came to be worked out in the novel, scarcely a circumstance of the original event remained. Westall and Hurd had no prototypes in real life. The actual men concerned in the Aldbury murder, and the incidents of the attack on the Pendley gamekeepers were different from anything described in *Marcella*. And I cannot insist too strongly that the book would have had no power and no illusion what- ever, as romance, had it been otherwise. For as with the painter, so with the writer. Until the stuff of what we call real life has been re-created and transformed by the independent, possessive, impetuous forces of imagination, it has no value for the artist, and insofar as it remains "real," i.e., a mere literal copy of something seen or heard, it represents a dead and lifeless element in an artist's work. A commonplace, of course, but one that has to be constantly repeated, especially in connexion with this business of searching one's memory for the hints and suggestions, the crude fact or impression, that set going the story-telling process.

Never, I think, was I conscious of more delight in that process than in the writing of *Marcella*. During the summer of 1892, our first summer at Stocks, an attack of illness kept me on the sofa for many weeks. I was forbidden to move, or to write; and all that was left was to read and rest. And rest was welcome, for there had been many agitations connected with *David Grieve*, and its reception in England and America. August and September passed in this way. Then, with the end of September, health came back, and a hunger to write. The outline of *Marcella* was written first on a half-sheet of paper, and the work began. And probably owing to the long physical rest, it went with great ease and pleasure. Yet except in the writing of *Bessie*

Costrell, I cannot remember being so tyrannously held by the scenes and emotions of any book as by those of *Marcella*. *Helbeck* was written as it were with my whole life and strength. I could, however, get away from it and forget it, but, for weeks, in writing *Marcella*, Hurd's cottage and the winter moonlight on the skirts of the wood were far more real to me than the rooms of Stocks, or the autumn flowers of its old garden, amid which the actual hours were passed. Every writer of tales, in whom there is any share of the special faculty which belongs to the métier, will know what is meant. The psychology of it has hardly been explored. A story, and a good story, can be written without any such experience. Some of the work which, as I look back critically upon it, seems to me of my best—which the public has welcomed most warmly—has been written as it were *intellectually*, following out a logical sequence whether in character or event, under a conviction of necessity and truth, but without any overpowering vision. Imagination indeed placed and dressed the different scenes, conceiving them in a clear succession. But, all through, *one knew how it was done*, and felt that with proper concentration of mind it could be done again. But there are times and crises in imaginative work when this process seems to be quite superseded by another; and afterwards in looking back upon the results a writer will not know how it was done, and will not feel that it could be repeated. Something intervened,—a tranced, absorbed state, in which the action of certain normal faculties seemed suspended in order that others might work with exceptional ease,— like tools that elves had sharpened in the night. I was conscious of this state all through the writing of the scenes before Hurd's execution, and at one or two other points in the book. But I never felt it so strangely, or in a manner apparently so independent of my own will, or of surrounding conditions, as during the writing of *Bessie Costrell*.

30

GEORGE R. GISSING

(1857–1903)

With brilliant potentialities, George Gissing became one of the unhappiest of men, and his novels are characteristically marred by pessimism and bitterness. The scholarly, individualistic idealist who appears as the central figure in much of his work has been labeled "the Gissing man," unhappy in love and ineffective in life. His best-known work, not a novel but a series of autobiographical essays, *The Private Papers of Henry Ryecroft* (1903), portrays these qualities.

Throughout the romantic revival in fiction, realism persisted, and Gissing was a realist:

. . . my characters must speak as they would actually, and I cannot be responsible for what they say.

—Letter to his brother, 23 June 1884.

I have done my best to make the story as realistic as possible. The ending is as unromantic as could be, and several threads are left to hang loose; for even so it is in real life; you cannot gather up and round off each person's story.

—Letter to his brother, 9 August 1885.

Like Moore, Gissing utilized fiction to publicize truth. Like Hardy, he defied convention to present unpleasant truths. Most of all, like Zola, to whom he is closer than is any other British novelist, he pictured details of sordid poverty and sensuality that were calculated to outrage the reader and provoke him to action, for he considered fiction a mouthpiece for social and moral reform. The didactic note in his fiction is rather too obvious.

The earlier novels are characteristically works of social protest utilizing autobiographical material. *Workers in the Dawn* (1880) and *The Unclassed* (1884) depict life in the slums and agitate against conditions that produce poverty. Gissing knew of what he wrote. A student of outstanding promise at Owens College, in Manchester, he was apprehended in a theft undertaken from a misguided zeal of reforming a prostitute by financial help. After a term in prison, he traveled to the United States in 1876, through the charity of friends. His best novel, *New Grub Street* (1891), depicts his precarious existence, wandering about, doing hack writing, taking odd jobs, and living for the most part in poverty and despondency. Returning to London, he married the prostitute and, like the hero of *Workers in the Dawn*, tried in vain to reform her, living in squalor the while. They separated in 1880, but he continued to support her until she died of alcoholism a few years later. Unable to interest a publisher in *Workers in the Dawn*, Gissing published it at his own expense; like all his novels, it had little sale, and he maintained himself in part by private tutoring.

With £100 he had received for *Demos* (1886), a timely exposé of Socialist agitation, he visited Athens and Rome. Returning home, he continued to produce a total of twenty-odd novels. *The Nether World* (1889), sometimes classed among his best, most clearly shows Zola's influence in its extreme sensuality and bestiality; it is his most sordid and pessimistic novel. The inability of his "Gissing man" to survive the moral dilemmas and scenes of poverty in *Born in Exile* (1892) provides an antidote to Mrs. Ward's successful heroes. *The Odd Women* (1893) points up the inadequate career opportunities for the large feminine population in England.

In 1890 Gissing made another unfortunate marriage, which was broken by separation five years later. About this time he turned his attention from slum life to the middle class, as in *In The Year of Jubilee* (1894), an attack on bourgeois vulgarity. His last five years were spent in France, where he formed a liaison with a French girl.

Because he was dependent on his writing for his living, Gissing accepted certain techniques and practices in vogue at the time; in consequence, his novels tend toward the melodramatic and suffer from an excess of characters and from improbable coincidences. His later work benefited from the compactness made possible by the general adoption of the one-volume format.

It is fine to see how the old three volume tradition is being broken through. One volume is becoming commonest of all. It is the new school, due to continental influence. Thackeray and Dickens wrote at enormous length, and with profusion of detail; their plan is to tell everything, and leave nothing to be divined. Far more artistic, I think, is the later method, of merely suggesting; of dealing with episodes, instead of writing biographies. The old novelist is omniscient; I think it is better to tell a story precisely as one does in real life, hinting, surmising, telling in detail what *can* so be told and no more. In fact, it approximates to the dramatic mode of presentment.

—Letter to his brother, August, 1885.

Some good general comparisons and observations on the novel may be found in "Art, Veracity, and Moral Purpose," Chapter Four of Gissing's excellent analysis, *Charles Dickens: A Critical Study* (New York, 1898). So also a recognition of the two general categories of fiction in vogue at the end of the century—the popular entertainment novel and the artistic intellectual novel— is put into the mouth of a character in *New Grub Street*, Jasper Milvain, a professional writer who adapts his talents to exploit the public taste. He expresses scorn for Reardon, the counterpart of Gissing:

But just understand the difference between a man like Reardon and a man like me. He is the old type of unpractical artist; I am the literary man of 1882. He won't make concessions, or rather, he can't make them; he can't supply the market. I—well, you may say that at present I do nothing; but that's a great mistake, I am learning my business. Literature nowadays is a trade. Putting aside men of genius, who may succeed by mere cosmic force, your successful man of letters is your skilful tradesman. He thinks first and foremost of the markets; when one kind of goods begins to go off slackly, he is ready with something new and appetising. He knows perfectly all the possible sources of income. Whatever he has to sell he'll get payment for it from all sorts of various quarters; none of your unpractical selling for a lump sum to a middle-man who will make six distinct profits. Now, look you: if I had been in Reardon's place, I'd have made four hundred at least out of "The Optimist"; I should have gone shrewdly to work with magazines and newspapers and foreign publishers, and—all sorts of people. Reardon can't do that kind of thing, he's behind his age; he sells a manuscript as if he lived in Sam Johnson's Grub Street. But our Grub Street of to-day is quite a different place; it is supplied with telegraphic communication, it knows what literary fare is in demand in every part of the world, its inhabitants are men of business, however seedy.

—Chapter I.

Addressing himself directly to questions of purpose and freedom of the novelist, as well as realism, Gissing expressed his theories in an essay "The Place of Realism in Fiction," written in May and published in the July, 1895, number of *The Humanitarian*. This and another commentary, "Why I Don't Write Plays" (*Pall Mall Gazette*, 10 September 1892), are termed by his biographer, Mabel C. Donnelly, "two important articles which have not received the attention they deserve . . ." (*George Gissing: Grave Comedian*, Cambridge, Mass., 1954).

THE PLACE OF REALISM IN FICTION
(1895)

One could wish to begin with, that the words *realism* and *realist* might never again be used, save in their proper sense by writers on scholastic philosophy. In relation to the work of novelists they never had a satisfactory meaning, and are now become mere slang. Not long ago I read in a London newspaper, concerning some report of a miserable state of things among a certain class of work-folk, that "this realistic description is absolutely truthful," where by *realistic* the writer simply meant painful or revolting, with never a thought of tautology. When a word has been so grievously mauled, it should be allowed to drop from the ranks.

Combative it was, of course, from the first. Realism, Naturalism, and so on, signified an attitude of revolt against insincerity in the art of fiction. Go to, let us picture things as they are. Let us have done with the conventional, that is to say, with mere tricks for pleasing the ignorant and the prejudiced. Let the novelist take himself as seriously as the man of science; be his work to depict with rigid faithfulness the course of life, to expose the secrets of the mind, to show humanity in its eternal combat with fate. No matter how hideous or heart-rending the results; the artist has no responsibility save to his artistic conscience. The only question is, has he wrought truly, in matter and form? The leaders of this revolt emphasized their position by a choice of vulgar, base, or disgusting subjects; whence the popular understanding of the term *realist*. Others devoted themselves to a laborious picturing of the dullest phases of life; inoffensive, but depressing, they invested *realism* with another quite accidental significance. Yet further to complicate and darken the discussion, it is commonly supposed that novelists of this school propound a theory of life; by preference that known as "pessimism." There is but one way out of this imbroglio: to discard altogether the debated terms, and to inquire with regard to any work of fiction, first, whether it is sincere, secondly, whether it is craftsmanlike.

Sincerity I regard as of chief importance. I am speaking of an art, and, therefore, take for granted that the worker has art at his command; but art, in the sense of craftsman's skill, without sincerity of vision will not suffice. This is applicable to both branches of fiction, to romance and to the novel; but with romance we are not here concerned. It seems to me that no novel can possess the slightest value which has not been conceived, fashioned, elaborated, with a view to depicting some portion of human life as candidly and vividly as is in the author's power. Other qualities may abound in the work; some others must needs be present. Tragic power, pathos, humour, sportiveness, tenderness: the novelist may have them one or all; constructive ability and the craft of words he cannot dispense with. But these gifts will not avail him as a novelist, if he lack the spirit of truthfulness,—which, be it added, is quite a different thing from saying that no novel can be of worth if it contain errors of observation, or fall short of the entire presentment of facts.

What do we mean by "reality"? Science concerns itself with facts demonstrable to every formal understanding; the world of science we call "real," having no choice but to accept it as such. In terms of art, reality has another signification. What the artist sees is to him only a part of the actual; its complement is an emotional effect. Thus it comes about that every novelist beholds a world of his own, and the supreme endeavour of his art must be to body forth that world as it exists for him. The novelist works, and must work, subjectively. A demand for objectivity in fiction is worse than meaningless, for apart from the personality of the workman no literary art can exist. The cry arose, of course, in protest against the imperfect method of certain novelists, who came forward in their own pages, and spoke as showmen; but what can be more absurd than to talk about the "objectivity" of such an author as Flaubert, who triumphs by his extraordinary power of presenting life as he, and no other man, beheld it? There is no science of fiction. However energetic and precise the novelist's preparation for his book, all is but dead material until breathed upon by "the shaping spirit of imagination," which is the soul of the individual artist. Process belongs to the workshop; the critic of the completed work has only to decide as to its truth—that is to say, to judge the spirit in which it was conceived, and the technical merit of its execution.

Realism, then, signifies nothing more than artistic sincerity in the portrayal of contemporary life; it merely contrasts with the habit of mind which assumes that a novel is written "to please people," that disagreeable facts must always be kept out of sight, that human nature must be systematically flattered, that the book must have a "plot," that the story should end on a cheerful note, and all the rest of it. Naturally the question arises: What limits does the independent novelist impose upon himself? Does he feel free to select *any* theme, from the sweetest to the most nauseating? Is it enough to declare that he has looked upon this or that aspect of life, has mirrored it in his imagination, and shows it forth candidly, vividly? For my own part, I believe that he must recognize limits in every direction; that he will constantly reject material as unsuitable to the purposes of art; and that many features of life are so completely beyond his province that he cannot dream of representing them. At the same time I joyfully compare the novelist's freedom in England of to-day with his bondage of only ten or twelve years ago. No doubt the new wine of liberty tempts to excess. Moreover, novels nowadays are not always written for the novel's sake, and fiction cries aloud as the mouthpiece of social reform. The great thing is, that public opinion no longer constrains a novelist to be false to himself. The world lies open before him, and it is purely a matter for his private decision whether he will write as the old law dictates or to show life its image as he beholds it.